SCOTTISH POETRY

A CRITICAL SURVEY

SCOTTISH POETRY
A CRITICAL
SURVEY

Edited by
JAMES KINSLEY

CASSELL AND COMPANY LTD
LONDON

CASSELL & CO LTD
37/38 St. Andrew's Hill, Queen Victoria Street,
London, E.C.4

and at

31/34 George IV Bridge, Edinburgh; 210 Queen Street, Melbourne; 26/30
Clarence Street, Sydney; Uhlmann Road, Hawthorne, Brisbane; C.P.O.
3031, Auckland, N.Z.; 1068 Broadview Avenue, Toronto 6; P.O. Box 275,
Cape Town; P.O. Box 1386, Salisbury, S. Rhodesia; Munsoor Building,
Main Street, Colombo 11; Haroon Chambers, South Napier Road, Karachi;
13/14 Ajmeri Gate Extension, New Delhi 1; 15 Graham Road, Ballard Estate,
Bombay 1; 17 Chittaranjan Avenue, Calcutta 13; Avenida 9 de Julho 1138,
São Paulo; Galeria Güemes, Escritorio 518/520 Florida 165, Buenos Aires;
P.O. Box 959, Accra, Gold Coast; 25 rue Henri Barbusse, Paris 5e; Islands
Brygge 5, Copenhagen.

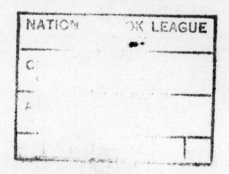

Set in 11 pt Fournier Type
and Printed in Great Britain by
T. & A. Constable Ltd.
Hopetoun Street, Edinburgh
F.355

ACKNOWLEDGEMENTS

GRATEFUL acknowledgement is due to the following authors (or their executors) and publishers for permission to reprint in this volume extracts from poems in which they hold the copyright:

Alexander Anderson: 'The Spirit of the Times' (Simpkin Marshall Ltd.); Marion Angus: 'Alas! Poor Queen', 'The Broken Brig' (Faber & Faber Ltd.); George Bruce: 'Kinnaird Head' (Oliver and Boyd Ltd.); John Davidson: 'To the New Man', 'A Balad of Blank Verse of the Making of a Poet' (John Lane The Bodley Head Ltd.); George S. Fraser: 'In the Far Isles' (Mandeville Publications); W. S. Graham: 'Seven Journeys' (William MacLellan Ltd.); William Jeffrey: 'The Galleys'; Andrew Lang: 'Twilight on Tweed', 'Clevedon Church: In Memoriam H.B.' (Longmans, Green & Co. Ltd.), Preface to 'Hamewith' by Charles Murray (Constable & Co. Ltd.); Hugh MacDiarmid: 'The Watergaw', 'A Drunk Man Looks at the Thistle', and 'To Circumjack Cencrastus' (William Blackwood & Sons Ltd.), 'Cornish Heroic Song for Valda Trevlyn' (William MacLellan Ltd.), 'At Last, at Last' (Methuen & Co. Ltd.); A. D. Mackie: 'Poems in Two Tongues' (The Darien Press Ltd.); Edwin Muir: 'The Labyrinth', 'The Little General' (Jonathan Cape Ltd.); R. Crombie Saunders: 'Tomorrow the Station' (William MacLellan Ltd.); Alexander Scott: 'The Gowk in Lear'; Sydney G. Smith: 'My Moujik Lass' (Oliver and Boyd Ltd.), 'Under the Eildon Tree' (Serif Books Ltd.), 'Ode to Berlioz'; William Soutar: 'Ballad' (Andrew Dakers Ltd.); Rachel Annand Taylor: 'The Magi' (The Richards Press Ltd.); Andrew Young: 'Stay Spring', 'A Prospect of Death' (Jonathan Cape Ltd.).

PREFACE

ASURVEY of Scottish poetry which takes account of modern scholarship, and extends beyond the Union, or Burns, or Scott, to our own time, has long been needed by both the professional student and the literary public. The present book, which will I hope be followed by a similar survey of the Scottish novel and the drama, consists of a series of independently written essays in historical sequence; and (although much has been passed over 'not for want of worth, but of roome') it may perhaps claim to be more nearly sufficient than its predecessors. We have, however, concerned ourselves with the critical assessment of our best poets, rather than with that cultural history and literary cartography which must yet be provided by 'the fortuitous discoveries of many men in devious walks of literature' before a full account of our poetical tradition can be written. If these essays stimulate interest and provoke constructive criticism, we shall have rendered some service to Scottish letters.

The matter of this book makes a significant chapter in the literary history of Britain, and deserves more serious attention than it generally receives—even at points where it is superior to its southern counterpart—in university schools of English. Poets like Henryson, Dunbar and Douglas (who gave Scotland an Indian summer while English poetry lay under frost), the ballad makers, Thomson and Fergusson, Burns (who, in addition to what he did for Scottish poetry, showed the young Wordsworth 'How Verse may build a princely throne On humble truth'), Scott the Last Minstrel, and the best of the moderns, cannot be ignored by anyone seriously professing English literature. Of more than merely Scottish interest, too, are the two-way traffic over the Border, the interplay of two national traditions and two distinct poetical tempers in neighbouring countries, and the fortunes of the Scottish vernacular—under constant pressure both from true 'Sudroun' and from the *lingua inglese in bocca scozzese*, adorning verse sometimes in silk and sometimes in hodden grey, and still in our own day a rich, flexible poetic medium. And the significance of Scottish poetry is not simply insular. As Professor Entwistle delighted to illustrate, 'Scotsmen can meet Europe more easily than Englishmen do . . . and though Scots is only a fraction of English literature, it has exerted something like a parity of influence in Europe. Some of the greatest English writers—e.g. Chaucer, Spenser or Milton—had no European consequence'.

We are here mainly concerned with poetry written in Scots and

English; but an essay on the Latinists has been included, partly to complete the picture of poetic activity in Renaissance Scotland and partly to underline the long Scottish love of things Latin. It was with reluctance that I decided not to include a full survey of Gaelic poetry; for this—involving also an account of the Celtic context—would have increased the cost of the book out of all proportion to demand. But Mr. Young's concluding note illustrates the scope and quality of Gaelic verse, and the part played by Gaelic poets in the modern 'renaissance'.

No apology need be made for the abundance of illustrative quotation from poetry which is so often unfamiliar or difficult of access. Wherever possible, quotations are taken from the earliest or most authoritative texts; the orthography of mediaeval and Renaissance texts has been a little simplified; and words which might cause difficulty have been glossed. The notes provide a substantial amount of information, chiefly bibliographical, for the convenience of students.

Dr. Agnes Mure Mackenzie died while this book was in the press, and her essay did not receive final revision at her hands. She was one of the most versatile and stimulating Scotswomen of her generation, and a lady of great kindliness and personal charm. She spent herself in devotion to her motto, *ut Scotia servetur*; and her death is a loss to Scottish historical studies and to the cultural life of her country.

My greatest debt is to the late Professor W. J. Entwistle, who lent his scholarship and enthusiasm to the planning of this book and was preparing an essay for it at the time of his death. It is a pleasure to acknowledge assistance, criticism and advice generously given to the editor and contributors by Mr. William Beattie and the staff of the National Library of Scotland; Mr. J. N. Bryson; Mr. John Durkan; Mr. W. R. Humphries; Professor Gwyn Jones; Mrs. Helen Kinsley; Mr. Alexander Law; Professor W. L. Renwick; Dr. O. K. Schram; Professor D. Nichol Smith; and Principal Sir Thomas Taylor. To all my collaborators I owe a debt of gratitude for enthusiastic and uncomplaining co-operation in a difficult task.

JAMES KINSLEY

CONTENTS

ix

I

THE MEDIAEVAL MAKARS

JAMES KINSLEY

VERNACULAR poetry flowered late in Scotland. Barbour, the first significant Scottish poet, was Chaucer's elder contemporary; and the mediaeval tradition was virtually at an end when James IV and all his chivalry fell at Flodden in 1513. What has come down to us from the troubled fourteenth and fifteenth centuries, much of it preserved in a few manuscript anthologies, seems to be only the remnant of an extensive literature. There is evidence of an early balladry: Barbour breaks off his account of a feat of arms with

> I will nocht rehers all the maner;
> For quha sa likis, thay may heir
> Young wemen, quhen thay will play,
> Sing it amang thame ilka day.

Sir Thomas Gray of Heton, imprisoned in Edinburgh Castle in 1355, found there Scottish chronicles in prose and verse, including tales of Robert Bruce; and Andrew Wyntoun, half a century later, speaks of 'gret Gestis' commemorating the 'gud dedis and manhad' of Wallace [1]. Barbour himself, despite his solitary eminence, has the assurance and versatility of a poet working in an established tradition. At the end of the fifteenth century Dunbar lamented the deaths of some twenty Scots poets, of whom only a few are now more than names; and the richness and variety of Dunbar's own verse suggest a fertile Scots tradition as well as the impact of Chaucer's genius on a receptive mind. But whatever may have been the range and quality of our lost literature, a substantial body of verse has survived—chronicle and romance, courtly lyric and popular song, *fabliau* and moral tale, panegyric and satire.

Formally, this poetry belongs to a number of common mediaeval genres. Its historical interest and its permanent appeal lie not in any bold departures from the general European tradition, but in the adaptation of stock themes and styles in ways which are congenial to the Scottish temper and appropriate to Scottish life. In England, Chaucer drew heavily on the vast stores of Continental literature; but he so transmuted what he borrowed, and so charged it with his peculiar humour and imagination, that he inaugurated a national tradition. In mediaeval Scotland, other poets brought a narrower but not less dynamic genius to bear on the same common materials, and

1

refashioned them in a distinctively Scots spirit. The poetry of the early 'makars' is the well-head of a long stream of vernacular writing. Barbour chronicled assiduously within the conventions of French romance; but the matter and spirit of his tale are Scots, and the qualities of his language and his narrative style recur in the ballads and in the poetry of Sir Walter Scott. Henryson and Dunbar worked in European modes; but the rhetorical grace and quiet humour of the one, and the formal versatility and tumultuous eloquence of the other, are persistent characteristics of Scottish poetry.

I

Like many another mediaeval poet, John Barbour (*c.* 1320-95) [2] seems to have served his apprenticeship as a translator, and then to have applied the skill he had laboriously learnt to a subject of his own choice. Barbour was almost certainly the author of *The Buik of Alexander*, a verse translation of parts of a French romance

> Of amouris, armis, and of droury,   [*love*
> Of knichtheid and of chevalry.

It is likely that he turned from this exercise in romance-writing to celebrate *The Actes and Life of the most Victorious Conquerour, Robert Bruce King of Scotland*, which he completed in 1376 [3].

In form and style, the *Bruce* is a metrical romance. Barbour's acquaintance with French romance affects his choice and arrangement of historical data and colours his descriptions of men and battles. Nevertheless, he is a serious chronicler and propagandist. If we make allowances for mediaeval notions of historiography, the conspicuous literary element in Barbour's poem does not invalidate his opening prayer:

> Now God gif grace that I may swa
> Tret it, and bring it till ending,
> That I say nocht but suthfast thing.

He is a conscientious historian, anxious to show 'the thing richt as it wes', to 'put in writ a suthfast story' of great national significance lest it pass into oblivion. He ends with a prayer that the descendants of his heroes may 'leid weill the land' in emulation of 'thair nobill elderis gret bounte'. To this grave commemorative and patriotic end, the ornaments of romance are justified; for Barbour subscribes to the orthodox mediaeval doctrine that delightfulness in the 'carping' is a proper adjunct to 'suthfastnes' in the matter of a poem.

The *Bruce* is neither the popular romance of wild adventure and marvel nor the high romance which reflects the refinements of ideal knighthood and the complexities of *amour courtois*. Beneath the garnishings of poetry, it is a record of recent violent historical events.

Its spirit is that of the old *chansons de geste*. The protagonists in Barbour's story, it is true, are painted in conventional chivalric colours; Douglas, for example, is 'wicht and wis', generous, loyal, 'curteis and debonair'. But history seldom finds room for the gentler qualities of the 'verray, parfit gentil knyght', and Bruce and his company belong less to the world of romantic chivalry than to the older, harsher world of French epic and the English *Battle of Maldon*. Their resolve is that of Byrhtwold at Maldon: 'Our courage shall be the harder, our spirit the keener, our valour the greater, as our strength grows less.' They are men

> that war in gret distres,
> And assayit ful gret hardines,
> Er thay micht cum till thair intent. [4]

They have little opportunity to show the 'olde curteisye' of the Arthurian knights. They move, not through the tapestried scenes of court and lady's bower, but, in the eloquent words of a fifteenth-century chronicler, through 'disasters, flights and dangers, hardships and weariness, hunger and thirst, watchings and fasts and cold and nakedness, guile, banishment, imprisonment, slaughter, and destruction of those near and dear' [5]. They are not gentlemen adventurers but desperate defenders of their country's independence against immense odds. Barbour places Douglas with Hector, and Bruce with Tydeus, who fought against forty-nine assailants; and the Scots are the new Maccabees [6]. There is no extravagance in this epic exaltation. The heroes of the *Bruce* show, in all their exploits, the essential virtues of the great warriors of old; and they triumph, not merely through 'strenth corporal', but through 'force spiritual, that is to say, hardy curage . . . the principal foundement of batail' [7].

Although he wrote at a time when poets were overlaying martial chivalry with fanciful *aventure* and the elaborate courtesies of love, Barbour did not abandon history for the sentiment of romance. He would not have joined in his contemporary Sacchetti's complaint that *la cavalleria è morta*. Bruce and his men illustrate, from the recent past, the severely practical and functional virtues of true knighthood. '[Knychthede is] a greit honour, maryit with a greit servitude'—an office instituted to uphold the faith, the 'natural lord', and the 'pepill in thair richtis'; to defend 'puir miserable personis and piteable, and to help the weik agane the stark' [8]. Bruce's qualities are those of the heroic leader of men. His victories are won as much by lively 'slicht' as by physical strength and courage. He acts decisively in a crisis. He shows a warrior's resource in the sudden perils of guerrilla fighting and a general's adroitness in strategy. In his addresses to his troops there is the manly directness and the sagacity of the born commander. Even his gentler qualities are those of a soldier. He is modest in

3

victory and generous in his appraisal of an adversary's worth; and he shows a ready 'curteisye' to 'puir miserable personis'. Through all the violence of the historical campaigns which Barbour reviews with essential veracity, Bruce emerges as a hero worthy of comparison with the noblest warriors of fable and romance.

Despite recent criticism, the traditional view that Barbour's theme is 'fredome' is the most adequate. He is not, like Chaucer, a subtle analyst of human nature; but with the chronicler's concern for accurate reporting he combines a strong interest in the motives and aspirations behind action. Abstract reflection and suggestive explanation abound in the *Bruce*. Beneath the coherent story of a single heroic career lies the deeper unity of an ideal expressed and realized in action. A passionate desire for independence is the mainspring of the whole story. 'We fight', said the barons of Scotland in the Declaration of Arbroath (1320), 'not for glory nor for wealth nor honours: but only and alone we fight for freedom, which no good man surrenders but with his life.' Bruce, says a chronicler, told his knights that

> ni me Scotorum libertas prisca moveret
> haec mala non paterer orbis ob imperium. [9]

Thus Barbour's hero, like Hector and Byrhtnoth the exemplar of the host, exhorts his army before Bannockburn and reminds them that the battle is for

> our livis,
> And for our childer and our wivis,
> And for the fredome of our land.
>
> . . . . .
>
> Ye micht haf livit into thraldome,
> But, for ye yarnit till haf fredome,
> Ye ar assemblit heir with me;
> Tharfor is neidful that ye be
> Worthy and wicht but abaising.   [*without dismay*

The *Bruce* illustrates from history that cult of personal or national honour which lies at the heart of all heroic poetry. Liberty is the *unum necessarium*, the central virtue of an honourable life:

> Fredome all solace to man giffis:
> He levis at ese that frely levis.   [*remains*
> A noble hart may haif nane ese,
> Na ellis nocht that may him plese,
> Gif fredome fail; for fre liking
> Is yarnit our all othir thing. [10]   [*desired above*

Barbour's art subserves his severely practical purpose. His style is freely rhetorical, but never unnecessarily decorative. The *Bruce* is as

4

bare of ornament as the Bayeux Tapestry [11]. Bruce's retreat to the
mountains would have given a romance poet like the author of *Sir
Gawain and the Green Knight* a welcome chance to display his artistry
in description; but Barbour mentions only the effects of wild weather
and the mountain waste on his hero—'hungir, cauld, with schowris
snell'. Where a romance poet would paint in the splendid colours of
an assembly or a feast, Barbour presses on with his story. He discusses
the composition and strength of armies; but even in his elaborate
account of Bannockburn there is little of

> emblazond Shields,
> Impreses quaint, Caparisons and Steeds;
> Bases and tinsel Trappings, gorgious Knights.

He makes his own characteristic apology:

> For suld I tell all thair effer,   [*accoutrements*
> Thair countinans and thair maner,   [*demeanour*
> Though I couth, I suld cummerit be. [12]   [*encumbered*

The people of the *Bruce* may be too desperately intent on savage
business to pause for the leisurely portraiture of romance; but they
express vitality and character in their speech. Bruce meets a country
woman in a lonely place:

> Scho askit him soon quhat he wes,
> And quhyne he com, and quhar he gais.   [*whence*
> 'A travalland man, dame,' said he,
> 'That travalis heir throu the cuntre.'
> Scho said, 'All that travaland ere,
> For saik of ane, ar welcom here.'

She explains, in a spirit which anticipates the humble loyalties of the
Jacobite risings, that 'ane' is Bruce 'richt lord of this cuntre'.

> 'Dame, lufis thou him sa weill?' said he.
> 'Ye, Schir,' scho said, 'sa God me se!'   [*so*
> 'Dame,' said he, 'lo! him heir thee by,
> 'For I am he';—'Sa ye suthly?'   [*say*
> 'Ye, certis, dame.'—'And quhar are gane
> Your men, quhen ye ar thus allane?'
> 'At this time, dame, I have no ma.'   [*more*
> Scho said, 'It may no wis be swa;   [*so*
> I have twa sonnis wicht and hardy,
> Thay sall becum your men in hy.' [13]   [*speedily*

The woman's affectionate reverence is not weakened by her blunt
questions and responses; and the immediate offer of her two sons is the

most complete and effective act of homage she can make to the ill-fortuned king. In such passages, Barbour's very simplicity serves him well. The drama of real life in ravaged Scotland is not obscured by rhetoric.

In his accounts of battle Barbour strikingly anticipates the manner of the Border ballad poets. His pictures have the movement, the violent actuality, and the very rhythm of the ballads:

> Then with a will till him thay yede;   [*went*
> And ane him by the bridill hint;   [*seized*
> But he raucht till him sic a dint,   [*dealt*
> That arme and schuldir flew him fra.

> [He] ruschit in amang thame all;
> The first he met he gart him fall,
> And syne his swerd he swappit out,   [*then*
> And raucht about him mony a rout.   [*blow*

The Archdeacon of Aberdeen has seen something of the active life. He has a nervous responsiveness to the excitements of close combat, felt in the blood, and felt along the heart; and he expresses his unclerkly delight in flashing steel and falling bodies with a concentrated energy unparalleled in Scottish poetry:

> Thay straucht their speris, on athir side,   [*couched*
> And swa rudly gan samyn ride,   [*together*
> That speris all tofruschit war,   [*shattered*
> And fele men dede, and woundit sar;   [*many*
> The blud out at their byrnis brest.   [*mail shirts*
> For the best and the worthiest
> That wilfull war to win honour
> Plungit in the stalwart stour,   [*fierce conflict*
> And rowtis ruid about thaim dang.   [*violent blows*

> [Thay] with axis sic duschis gaff,   [*heavy blows*
> That thay helmis and hedis claff.
> And thair fais richt hardely
> Met thame, and dang on douchtely,   [*struck*
> With wapnis that war stith of steill: [*strong*
> Thar wes the battell strikin weill. [14]   [*fought*

The last line is the enthusiastic outcry of the professional warrior. The shock of battle is described, not in the objective language of the historian, but as it is felt by the participants. Barbour writes in terms of straining muscle, spilt blood and hacked flesh for a fourteenth-century audience to whom such sensations were painfully real.

The *Bruce* is the work of a man with a dry humour and shrewd appreciation of character; an honesty in weighing evidence and judging friend and foe; a thoughtful and fundamental patriotism; and a masculine enjoyment of bloody conflict. Barbour used the techniques of romance critically and imaginatively to perpetuate the fame of a national hero, and contrived to be true to the demands both of history and of art.

The other hero of the War of Independence was celebrated some eighty years later in *The Actis and Deidis of the Illuster and Vailyeand Campioun, Schir William Wallace, Knicht of Ellerslie* [15]. The author of this romance has been traditionally identified with the 'Blinde Hary' mentioned in the Treasurer's Accounts for 1490-2, and with one 'Henricus a nativitate luminibus captus' in John Major's *History*. Henricus, says Major, was an itinerant minstrel who gathered and recited legends of Wallace. That the poet of the *Wallace* was blind from birth is, in view of his graphic powers, very unlikely; either he became blind later in life, or he was not Major's minstrel. He claims as his authority for Wallace's life a Latin history by John Blair, apparently lost; and there were 'gestis' on which he might have drawn. But despite his pretensions, Harry was no historian. The *Wallace* is an imaginative verse novel fabricated from historical data, the fictions of popular legend, and brazen adaptations from the scrupulous work of Barbour. It is probably a final gathering of traditional stories which Harry had elaborated over a lifetime of bardic recitation.

Wallace is a man 'wis, richt worthy, wicht and kind', fired by injustice; a resistance leader watching for opportunities to attack the occupying English soldier and 'cutt his throit or steik him sodanlie'; a 'bonny fechter' avenging wrongs done to his country and his kin:

> It was his lif, and maist part of his fude,
> To se thaim sched the burnand Southron blude.

He has the bravado and resourcefulness of the popular hero, but neither his character nor his persistent endeavour has the tone of high chivalry. He is pledged only to free his subjugated country, 'be cause I am a natif Scottis man'. His ideal of knighthood is reflected in his lament for Sir John Graham:

> My best brothir in warld that evir I had,
> My aefald friend quhen I was hardest stad;   [*truest*
> My hope, my heill, thou wast in maist honour,   [*health*
> My faith, my help, strenthiest in stour.   [*conflict*
> In the was wit, fredom, and hardines;   [*knowledge*
> In the was trewth, manheid, and nobilnes;
> In the was rewll, in the was governans;
> In the was vertu withoutin varians . . .

These are the sturdy virtues of Wallace and Barbour's Bruce. But they embody a less complex and refined ideal than Sir Ector's character of Lancelot, the flower of Arthurian chivalry:

A, Launcelot . . . thou were hede of al Crysten knyghtes! And . . . thou were the curtest knyght that ever bare shelde! And thou were the truest frende to thy lovar that ever bestrade hors, and thou were the trewest lover of a synful man that ever loved woman . . . And thou were the godelyest persone that ever cam emonge prees of knyghtes, and thou was the mekest man and the jentyllest that ever ete in halle emonge ladyes, and thou were the sternest knyght to thy mortal foo that ever put spere in the reeste. [16]

Harry's restricted notion of a knight's accomplishments is best seen in his attitude to love. Wallace has a 'leman' in St. Johnstoun, a Delilah who betrays him; but Harry does not imitate the courtly romancers in describing her charms and wiles. 'Richt unperfyt I am,' he says, 'of Venus play.' Wallace's second and more faithful lady is no 'leman' of courtly love. She virtuously insists on matrimony—'desyr me nocht but intill gudlines'—and despite the views of the chroniclers Harry makes her Wallace's wife. Love is not for him an exalted passion which elicits all that is noblest and bravest in a knight, as it does in Chaucer's *Troilus and Criseyde* or Chrétien's *Yvain*. It is 'folichnes', a destructive fever nearer to the classical *ardor* than to *amour*; it threatens the resolution of a warrior in time of battle. Harry does not dwell on the cruel death of the lady at the hands of the English as a poet of 'gentil herte' like Chaucer would have done. Her fate is only another incentive to Wallace's revenge:

This woman als, that dulfully was dicht,   [*treated*
Out of my mind that dede will nevir bid,
Quhill God me tak fra this fals world so wid.

To the fair queen of England, who comes to entreat him to make peace, this rugged warrior significantly replies:

In speche of luff suttel ye Sotheroun ar;
Ye can us mok. [17]

Harry is familiar with the art of rhetoric. He uses the traditional tricks to good effect in such passages as the epitaph on Graham and his outbursts on Wallace's imprisonment; and some of his books have elaborate descriptive prologues. But his style is generally as economical as Barbour's. He can open a tale in the abrupt, immediately engrossing manner of the ballad poets:

On Gargownno was biggit a small peill,   [*tower and enclosure*
That warnist was with men and vittail weill,   [*garrisoned*
Within a dyk, bathe close, chaumer, and hall;
Captaine tharof to name he hecht Thrilwall.

8

He inherits Barbour's skill in depicting violent action with a few bold strokes:

> Atour the rock the laif ran with gret din.   [*rest*
> Sum hang on craggis, richt dulfully to de,
> Sum lap, sum fell, sum floterit in the se.
> Na Southeron on lif was levit in that hauld,
> And thaim within thay brynt in powdir cauld.   [*burnt*
>
> With ire and will on the hede has him tane,
> Through the bricht helm in sondir bryst the bane.
> Ane othir braithly on the breist he bar;   [*violently*
> His burnist blaid through out the body schar. [18]

But Harry has not caught Barbour's enthusiasm for the clash of steel and the mincing of flesh and brains. He has neither Barbour's eye for detail nor his appreciation of the total movement of a battle; and his diction has less colour and less force.

The virtue of his language is the virtue of common speech. His preliminary account of Wallace's lineage, for example, rambles on like the fireside reminiscence of an old retainer. His lack of sophistication in dialogue enables him to bring his hero to life as an abrupt, practical soldier with his mind always on his job:

> Then Wallace said: 'Madame, your noise lat be.
> To women yet we do but litill ill;
> Na young childer we lik for to spill.   [*destroy*
> I wald haif meit; Haliday, quhat sayis thow?
> For fastand folk to dine gud time war now.'

It gives to some passages in the poem a simple pathos which lies beyond the reach of artifice. In Book VII, Wallace hears from an old servant that his uncle and his kin have been slaughtered. The style of her story is lightly rhetorical; but the language, the sentiment and the scene itself have a melancholy actuality:

> Our men ar slain, that pitee is to se,
> As bestiall houndis hangit our a tre;
> Our trew barrouns be twa and twa past in.
>
> .   .   .   .   .
>
> Out of yon barn, scho said, I saw him born,
> Nakit, laid law on cald erd, me biforn.
> His frosty mouth I kissit in that sted;   [*place*
> Richt now manlik, now bar and brocht to ded.
> And with a claith I covert his licaym;   [*corpse*
> For in his lif he did nevir woman schayme. [19]

Harry's mind seldom probes, as Barbour's does, beyond men and events to the motives behind; he is merely a story-teller. Even as a verse tale, the *Wallace* has not the ordonnance of the *Bruce*. But it is told by a poet skilled in exciting his hearers and moving them to tears; and it has poured into the veins of many besides Burns 'a Scotish prejudice . . . which will boil along there till the flood-gates of life shut in eternal rest' [20].

Romance seems to have been as popular in Scotland as elsewhere; and attempts have been made to claim for Scottish literature a number of Arthurian romances which were either composed or transcribed in a northern dialect. But of the extant poems, only a few are certainly Scots; and qualitatively these add little to 'the matter of Arthur' [21]. The most lively of the Scottish romances is *The Taill of Rauf Coilyear how he harbreit King Charlis* [22]. Charlemagne, lost in a mountain storm, is given shelter by a rough-tongued and ill-mannered charcoal burner. Rauf is later summoned to court, where the emperor discloses his identity and rewards hospitality by making the peasant a knight. Rauf proves his worth in knight-errantry, and the adventure ends in high honour. It has been argued that although the setting of the poem is French, and the theme is common in popular tale and ballad, the poet's description of mountain and storm and his character of a dour, self-assured peasant are distinctively Scots. The chief interest of the *Taill*, however, lies in the treatment of romance conventions.

The poet shows, in his control of the alliterative rhyming stanza and in his descriptions of knights and the court of Charlemagne, that he had a considerable acquaintance with romance style and vocabulary. His account of Rauf's grim battle with the Saracen is clearly a burlesque of the conventional knightly combat; but the *Taill* is not a direct parody of chivalric romance like Chaucer's 'Sir Thopas'. It is a merry popular tale written up in a light moment by a poet with some skill in romance technique, and it inevitably contains an element of parody as well as knockabout farce. Its links with serious romance are many. The king lost in the wilderness, his meeting with a hospitable stranger, the evening meal followed by fireside tales, and the provision of 'ane burly bed . . . closit with curtingis and cumlie clad' for the guest—all these have their analogues in a chivalric romance like *Sir Gawain and the Green Knight*. The essentials of aristocratic hospitality are here, but they are comically inverted by the poet. For the peasant host has strange notions on the reception and entertainment of a guest. Charlemagne stands back to allow Rauf to enter his hut first, but he is rudely thrust forward with the rebuke, 'thou art uncourteis'. When he politely declines to lead Rauf's wife first to table, he receives another reprimand:

'Now is twice,' said the Carl, 'me think thou hes foryet!'
He let gird to the King, withoutin ony mair,   [*blow*
And hit him under the eir with his richt hand.

. . . .

He callit on Gyliane his wife, 'ga, tak him by the hand,
   And gang agane to the buird, quhair ye suld air have gane.
Schir, thou art unskilfull, and that sall I warrand;
   Thou byrd to have nurtour aneuch, and thou hes nane;   [*ought*
Thou hes walkit, I wis, in mony wild land,
   The mair vertue thow suld have, to keip thee fra blame!
Thou suld be curteis of kind, and ane cunnand Courteir.'

      .   .   .   .   .

The king said to him self, 'this is ane evill life,
   Yit was I never in my life thus-gait leird!'   [*taught thus*

This situation is not a serious criticism of courtly behaviour, but
merely the juxtaposition of two strongly contrasted codes of conduct
in a spirit of fun. Despite its triviality, the *Taill* is a brighter and
fresher thing than most of the Scots attempts at high romance; and
it is historically perhaps the earliest of a large number of Middle
Scots poems in which a comic twist is given to a serious genre.

2

    The Scottish romances are the legitimate offspring of French
romance; and the family physiognomy and character descend also,
though with some modification, in the patriotic sagas of Barbour and
Blind Harry. Another and later infusion of foreign blood came from
England. Through Chaucer and others a French poetic tradition,
more delicate and sophisticated than that of the chivalric romance,
passed north into fifteenth-century Scotland. The earliest extant poem
in the French courtly style is *The Kingis Quair*, a narrative love-poem
which is commonly attributed to James I of Scotland (1394-1437). The
Quair [23] is at once a fine example of a highly literary kind of poetry,
and a fresh, personal testament of love. The author justly commends
his work to his 'maisteres dere, Gowere and Chaucere', for he draws
heavily on the stock descriptions, imagery and language of English
courtly verse. But the *Quair* is not pastiche. The poet has learnt from
Chaucer not only to borrow freely but to handle what he borrows
with delicacy and inventiveness. He constructs a garden scene, for
instance, from a number of conventional models, and his birds welcome
May in terms which were familiar from Italy to the North Sea. But
the birds themselves are freshly observed:

    Quhen thay this song had sung a litill thrawe,   [*time*
       Thay stent a quhile, and therewith unaffraid,
    As I beheld and kest myn ene alawe,
       From beugh to beugh thay hippit and thay plaid,
       And freschly in thair birdis kind arraid
    Thair fetheris new, and fret thame in the sonne,   [*preened*
    And thankit luve, that had thair makis wonne.   [*mates*

There is the same accurate perception, and an unusual sensitiveness to colour, in the picture which introduces the traditional catalogue of 'bestis . . . mony divers kynd':

> . . . throu the gravel, bryght as ony gold,
> The cristall water ran so clere and cold,
> That in myn ere maid continualy
> A maner soun, mellit with armony;   [*sound, mingled*
>
> That full of litill fischis by the brym,
> Now here, now there, with bakkis blew as lede,
> Lap and playit, and in a rout can swym   [*leapt*
> So prattily, and dressit tham to sprede
> Thair curall fynnis, as the ruby rede,   [*coral*
> That in the sonne on thair scalis bryght
> As gesserant ay glitterit in my sight.   [*plate-armour*

The lady who walks in the garden and steals the poet's heart is sister to Chaucer's Emily and many another beauty of romance; but conventional diction does not obscure her distinctive loveliness or the sincerity of his adoration:

> And for to walk that fresche Mayes morowe,
> An huke sche had upon her tissew quhite,   [*mantle, dress*
> That gudelier had nought bene sene toforowe,   [*before*
> As I suppos; and girt sche was a lyte;   [*little*
> Thus halfling lous for haste, to swich delyte   [*half loosened*
> It was to see hir youth in gudelihed,
> That for rudenes to speke therof I drede.
>
> In hir was youth, beautee, with humble aport,   [*bearing*
> Bountee, richess, and womanly facture,   [*shape*
> God better wote than my pen can report
> Wisdome, largess, estate, and conning sure   [*skill*
> In every point so guidit hir mesure,   [*proportion*
> In word, in dede, in schap, in contenance,
> That nature might no more hir childe avance.

Some recent critics have said that in the *Quair* the poetry of marriage emerges from the poetry of adultery sanctioned in *amour courtois*. But the reconciliation of courtly love and marriage had been made by poets earlier than the time of James I. The originality of the *Quair* lies rather in the use of allegory and other well-worn devices to celebrate a courtship and marriage which belong, not to the world of fancy, but to real life. The poet who could handle tradition for his own purposes with so much freshness and assurance introduced a new, cultivated strain into Scottish verse.

A less able experiment in a French mode is *The Buke of the Howlat*, written about 1450 for Elizabeth Countess of Moray by Sir Richard Holland, a loyal adherent of the Douglas family [24]. The core of the poem is a parliament of birds; but into this conventional story Holland works some incidental satire and a panegyric on the Douglases. After Chaucer's graceful use of rhyme-royal in *The Parlement of Foules*, Holland's alliterative rhymed stanza seems too heavy and complex for this type of poetry. But in his account of James Douglas's excursion against the Saracens with the heart of Bruce about his neck, he turns the weight of alliterative phrases and the contrast between the long line and the short 'wheel' to fine effect:

> He gart hallow the hairt, and syne cud it hing
> About his hals full hend, and on his awin hart.   [*neck, gracious*
>   Oft wald he kiss it, and cry
>   'O flour of chevalry!
>   Quhy leif I, allace, quhy,
>   And thou deid art?'

> Then in defense of the faith he fure to the ficht,   [*went*
> With knichtis of Christendome to keip his command;
> And quhen the battellis so brym, brathly and blicht   [*fierce, violent*
> War joined thraly in thrang, mony thousand,
> Amang the hethin men the hairt hardely he slang,
>   Said, 'Wend on as thou wont,
>   Throw the battell in bront,   [*thick of the fight*
>   Ay formest in the front
>   Thy fais amang.'

Mediaeval Scots lyric has neither the variety nor the high quality of late Middle English lyric. Dunbar is the only Scot to reach the English level in the poetry of courtly love; and his essays are few. There seems to have been no dearth of artificial love-poetry in the time of Henryson and Dunbar [25]; but one listens long for a clear note of passion to sound through the heavy orchestration of conventional sentiment and rhetoric. The Scots lyrists are most at ease in the dialogue of love, stripped of refinement and subtlety. The *chanson pastourelle*, for instance, in which the wooing of a country maid by a clerk or a gallant is described in a mixture of narrative and conversation, appears to have been popular in Scotland. Our versions run easily into comic characterization and brisk dialogue, and are much livelier than their English counterparts. But too often a wooing poem which opens on a lyrical note deteriorates into graceless obscenity. The Scottish delight in realistic situations and love-talk is given more legitimate scope in rustic tales like 'The Wowing of Jok and Jynny', which are rich in pictures of country manners and are the ancestors of dramatic narrative songs still current.

Genre painting has long been one of the dominant interests of Scots poetry. Two vigorous fifteenth-century accounts of popular conviviality, 'Christis Kirk on the Grene' and 'Peblis to the Play', inaugurate a tradition which reaches down into the nineteenth century [26]. 'Christis Kirk' is the more lyrical of the two. The opening picture of 'damisellis' making holiday is alive with bright colour and gaiety; and the poem dances lightly on in the measure and with the artless clarity of folk-song:

> Of all thir madinis mild as meid
>   Wes nane so gimp as Gillie,   [*neat*
> As ony rose hir rude wes reid,   [*complexion*
>   Hir lyre wes lik the lillie;   [*skin*
> Fou yellow, yellow wes hir heid,
>   And scho of luf so sillie,
> Thoucht all hir kin suld have been deid,
>   Scho wald haf but sweit Willie,
>   allane,
>   At chrystis kirk on the grene. [27]

Despite the appreciation of the human comedy and the interest in manners reflected in lyric verse, there is little evidence in Middle Scots of the Chaucerian delight in a story for its own sake. Of the *fabliau*, a type of narrative verse popular throughout mediaeval Europe, *The Freiris of Berwik* is our only extant example [28]. This poem has been attributed to Dunbar; but it has not his metrical smoothness, and it is too strictly progressive in style. Further, Dunbar shows little interest in the couplet, except as an element in a more complex metrical scheme; and his poems are generally occasional, personal and short. The story of *The Freiris of Berwik* is a common one; but this version surpasses its analogues in structural finish, characterization and sheer zest. The poet has mastered the difficult art of natural verse dialogue, and he knows how to vary the speed of a story and how to manage a hilarious climax. The discovery of the philandering Friar John, conjured from his hiding-place as the fiend Hurlybas, is worthy of Chaucer:

> With that the Freir, that under the troch lay,   [*trough*
> Raxit him sone, bot he wes in a fray,   [*stretched, alarm*
> And up he rais, and wist na bettir wayn,   [*hiding-place*
> Bot of the troch he tumlit our the stane   [*over*
>   . . . . .
> And quhen Freir Robert saw him gangand by,
> Unto the Gudman full lowdly cowd he cry,
> 'Stryk, stryk herdely, for now is tyme to the.'
> With that Symone a felloun flap lait fle,   [*dreadful blow*

14

With his burdoun he hit him on the nek;
He was sa ferce he fell owttour the sek,   [over
And brak his heid upoun ane mustard stane.   [stone mortar
Be this Freir Johine attour the stair is gane
In sic wyis, that mist he hes the trap,
And in ane myr he fell, sic wes his hap,
Wes forty futis of breid undir the stair;
Yet gat he up with clething nothing fair . . .

For vivid comic narrative, this poem has no equal in Scots until 'Tam o' Shanter'.

The humour of the Scottish poets, from Dunbar to our own time, inclines as often to the wildly fantastic as to the quiet and pawky. Dunbar's accredited work contains the best examples of a volatile and bizarre fancy controlled by art; but some anonymous poems of the same period illustrate, with variable literary grace, this characteristic Scottish delight in grotesque comedy. There are tales of the Gyre-Carling, the protean witch of 'auld Betokis bour' who lived on Christian flesh; of King Berdok of Babylon, whose summer residence was a cabbage and who dwelt in winter 'for cauld in till a cokkil schell'; of the king of faery by whom a certain Lichtoun dreamt that he was imprisoned in 'ane lang raip of sand'; and of Lord Fergus Ghaist, a merry creature who steals God's knife, Abraham's whim-wham, and a pair of old shoes from the man in the moon, strangles an ancient chaplain of Pencaitland, and is at last conjured and wedded by a Spanish fly:

And syne marreid the gaist the flie,
And cround him king of Kandelie;
And thay gat thame betwene,
Orpheus king and Elpha quene.   ['elfin' Eurydice

A more considerable jeu d'esprit than any of these is 'The Ballad of Kynd Kittok'. The gay wife Kittok, 'cleir under kell' as a cauldron chain, died (men say) of thirst and went to heaven as 'our Ladyis henwif'; but dissatisfaction with the celestial wine drove her to an alehouse outside the gates, and there, fortified by 'fresche drink', she set up her everlasting rest. 'Kynd Kittok' has been attributed to Dunbar; but it does not show his grip or rhythm. Another and more elaborate fantasy, given with better reason to Dunbar, is 'The Manere of the Crying of ane Playe', the one surviving example of a 'cry' to the May-game. It has the expansive imagination, the peculiar scatological coarseness, the contempt for the Celt, and the strong diction of Dunbar. There is a Rabelaisian breadth, and something of the grand extravagance of Celtic folk-tale, in these pictures of the giants of old:

Ellevin mile wide was his mouth,
His teith wes ten mile squaire.

He wald apone his tais stand,
And tak the sternis doune with his hand,
And set tham in a gold garland,
    Abone his wyfis haire.

. . . Scho fischit all the Spanye seis,
With hir sark lape befor hir theis;   [*tucked up, thighs*
Sevyne dayis saling betwix her kneis
Was estymit and maire.
The hingand brayis on athir side
Scho poltit with hir lymmis wide. . .   [*knocked against*

. . .Or he of eld was yeris thre,
He wald stepe oure the occeane se;
The mone sprang never abone his kne,
    The hevin of him had feire. [29]

3

With Robert Henryson (*fl.* 1480) we enter a new world of
poetry [30]. Scottish verse retained the muscular virtues of the early
poets; but Henryson added new artistic qualities. He extended the
bridgehead of cultivated style established by the author of *The Kingis
Quair*. Some critics have denied that he owed any substantial debt to
the Chaucerian tradition; but he learnt from Chaucer what no Scots
poet of his own day could have taught him—tonal contrasts and the
subtle uses of rhetoric, an appreciation of stanzaic pattern, and above
all the art of mirroring his own personality in his work.

In range of tone and in the richness of its humour, *The Morall
Fabillis of Esope the Phrygian* is Henryson's most considerable
achievement. The *Fabillis* are adaptations of popular beast-tales (not
all Æsop's), with a general literary prologue and with a *moralitas* to
point and adorn each story. Henryson tells us that he made his
translation
    Nocht of my self, for vane presumptioun,
    Bot be requeist and precept of ane Lord,
    Of quhome the Name it neidis not record.

Poets do not usually speak so evasively of their noble patrons; but
the implications of some of the tales make it likely that they were
written to serve the purposes of some powerful politician who had
good reason for remaining anonymous [31]. Henryson is as cautious
as the noble lord. 'The Taill of the Lyon and the Mous', for instance,
contains thinly veiled criticism of the lethargic and harassed James III;
but the responsibility for drawing out the *moralitas* of the story is
diplomatically passed to the ghostly Æsop, who appears to the poet
in a dream. Many of the fables, however, are so general in moral

import that they seem to have been written either as foils to more
pointed parables or simply for the poet's delight. Significantly,
Henryson develops his subtlest and richest animal characters in the
most innocuous tales.

He seeks to blend instruction and delight, drawing 'ane Morall
sweit sentence Oute of the subtell dyte of poetry'. His lack of rhetorical
skill, he says, compels him to write 'in hamelie language and in termes
rude'. This is not simply the false modesty affected by some of
Chaucer's pilgrims. Henryson was an accomplished rhetorician, but
the fables have comparatively little of either 'enamellit' diction or
sustained eloquence. He uses rhetorical devices and weighty language
in incidental argument and in the abstract commentary of the *moralitas*.
Occasionally, too, the ornate style serves a comic purpose. Thus a
resounding overture in the language of astrology introduces a learned
Fox calculating his destiny by 'Astrolab, Quadrant, or Almanak'; and
the hen Pertok laments the abduction of Chantecleir with courtly
grace:

> Yone wes our drowrie, and our dayis darling,   [*love*
> Our nichtingall, and als our Orloge bell,
> Our walkryfe watche, us for to warne and tell   [*sleepless*
> Quhen that Aurora with hir curcheis gray   [*kerchief*
> Put up hir heid betwix the nicht and day.
>
> Quha sall our leman be? quha sall us leid?
> Quhen we ar sad, quha sall unto us sing?
> .   .   .   .   .   .
> Now eftir him, allace, how sall we leif?

But Henryson's fundamental manner in these tales is simple and often
highly colloquial. He talks his way familiarly into a story, without
preliminary flourish:

> Esope, mine Authour, makis mentioun
> Of twa myis, and thay wer Sisteris deir,
> Of quham the eldest dwelt in ane Borous toun,   [*borough*
> The uthir wynnit uponland weill neir.   [*dwelt*

His animals, whether lions or mice, speak in the blunt and 'hamelie'
language of Fife:

> 'Byde' (quod the Lyoun), 'Lymmer, let us se   [*rogue*
> Gif it be suth the selie yow hes said.'   [*ewe*
>
> The Burges Mous prompit forth in pride,   [*bounced*
> And said, 'Sister, is this your daily fude?'
> 'Quhy not,' quod scho, 'is not this meit richt gude?'

'Na, be my saull, I think it bot ane scorne.'
'Madame,' quod scho, 'ye be the mair to blame;
My mother sayd, sister, quhen we wer borne,
That I and ye lay baith within ane wame.' [32]

Such unaffected, realistic speech woven into a metrical pattern was managed only on occasion by Barbour and Blind Harry; but it gives perpetual vitality to all Henryson's animals and holds even *The Testament of Cresseid* down to the Scottish earth. From Chaucer, who mastered this art of poetic talk in a long and not always happy apprenticeship, Henryson learnt it and passed it on. The narrative and dialogue of the *Fabillis* have, to the ear of a Lowland reader, the unmistakable ring of spoken Scots.

It is by a constant impression of matter-of-fact reality that Henryson gets much of his comic effect. In his Prologue, he tries gravely to reinforce the moral significance of the beast-fable by saying that the animals once 'spak and Understude' like men, and that carnal man has an animal nature. But in the *Fabillis* he is prone, like Chaucer, to draw a *comic* parallel between the bestial and the human; and his success lies not so much in his moral applications, which are often too ingenious for modern taste, as in retaining the essential animality of his creatures while he freely develops the joke of making them speak and think like men. In 'The Taill of the Uponlandis Mous and the Burges Mous' he draws a comic contrast between the cheerful country mouse, contented with little and affectionately hospitable, and her self-important, critical town sister. But while these two grow more delightfully human under the poet's pen, assuming the characters of their two-legged counterparts in town and country, they retain their mousy interests and their mousy minds. The Burges Mous takes her sister to her 'worthie Wane' and, with the hospitality of a provost, offers her the freedom of the larder. The menu, however, is a mouse's choice; and

> Ane Lordis fair thus couth thay counterfeit,
> Except ane thing, thay drank the watter cleir
> In steid of wine, bot yit thay maid gude cheir.

Henryson's art lies in holding the human and the animal in balance. Indeed, in this tale the Burges Mous comes off worse because she affects the human too much: the Uponlandis Mous has the sturdy, sceptical independence of a Scots peasant woman confronted with newfangled luxury, but in her home, her diet and her preoccupations she remains a mouse. Despite its apparent simplicity, Henryson's beast characterization is more subtle than that of Chaucer, whose Chaunticlere and Pertelote eat, sleep, love and play as fowls, but display an incongruous interest in the intellectual pursuits and arts of mankind.

18

Henryson's method of playing human and animal traits off against each other is well illustrated in the story of the Wolf, the Fox and the Cadgear (hawker). There appear two canine rogues lusting for mutton and chicken-flesh; but this bestial appetite is wrapped in a comic human *politesse*. The Fox saw the Wolf coming,

> And with ane bek he bad the Wolf gude day.
> 'Welcum to me' (quod he), 'thou Russell gray;'
> Syne loutit doun and tuke him be the hand.
> 'Ryse up, Lowrence, I leif the for to stand.

> 'Quhair hes thou bene this sesoun fra my sicht?
> Thou sall beir office, and my Stewart be,
> For thou can knap doun Caponis on the nicht,   [*strike*
> And, lourand law, thou can gar hennis de.'   [*skulking, make*

The Cadgear leading a pony loaded with herring providentially passes by, singing 'huntis up, up, upon hie' with unconscious irony; and he comes near to being outwitted in his human innocence by the deceitful roguery of two beasts.

Henryson shows an imaginative sympathy with animals and birds which is not common in mediaeval poetry. Chaucer and the poet of *The Kingis Quair* and others describe with delight the colour and movement of the beasts; but Henryson alone has sufficient sympathy with animal nature to make his creatures speak in colloquial Scots and in character. He treats small animals with special tenderness. At the end of a long procession climbing uphill to 'the Parliament of fourfuttit Beistis',

> The marmisset the Mowdewart couth leid,   [*mole*
> Because that Nature denyit had hir sicht.

It is the mouse, however, that is most gently and understandingly portrayed in the *Fabillis*. The story of the Burges Mous and her sister is the finest of the tales in characterization and comedy; but there is a delightful daintiness, and a sense of the anxious timidity of mice, in 'The Taill of the Paddok and the Mous':

> Upon ane time (as Esope culd Report)
> Ane litill Mous come till ane Rever side;
> Scho micht not waid, hir schankis were sa schort,
> Scho culd not swim, scho had na hors to ride:
> Of verray force behovit hir to bide,
> And to and fra beside that Revir deip
> Scho ran, cryand with mony a pietuous peip.

> 'Help over, help over,' this silie Mous can cry,
> 'For Goddis lufe, sum bodie over the brym.'   [*flood*

Henryson's perception of the delicate movement of small creatures links him with Burns and Disney across the centuries. The mice romp gaily round the sleeping lion:

> He lay so still, the Myis wes not affeird,
> Bot to and fro out over him tuke thair trace;   [*track*
> Sum tirlit at the Campis of his beird,   [*whiskers*
> Sum spairit not to claw him on the face;
> Merie and glaid thus dansait thay ane space.

Henryson is chiefly interested in character and action. He shows little concern, in the *Fabillis* and elsewhere, for setting; the barest hints suffice. Yet for all his economy, the sights and sounds of the Lowland countryside come freshly through in some of the tales. The ornate conventional pageant of the seasons in 'The Preiching of the Swallow' passes, with the coming of 'wynter wan', into a harshly realistic picture of the northern landscape which has drawn poetry from Scots in every century:

> Than flouris fair faidit with froist man fall,   [*must*
> And birdis blyith changit thair noitis sweit
> In still murning, neir slane with snaw and sleit.

> Thir dalis deip with dubbis drounit is,   [*pools*
> Baith hill and holt heillit with frostis hair;   [*covered, hoar*
> And bewis bene laifit bair of blis,
> Be wickit windis of the winter wair.   [*?wild*
> All wild beistis than from the bentis bair
> Drawis for dreid unto thair dennis deip,
> Coucheand for cauld in coifis thame to keip.   [*hollows*

Henryson is the first of the Scots poets to merit Allan Ramsay's description of the 'old *Bards*':

> Their *Poetry* is the Product of their own Country ... Their *Images* are native, and their *Landskips* domestick; copied from those Fields and Meadows we every Day behold. The *Morning* rises ... as she does in the *Scottish* Horizon. We are not carried to *Greece* or *Italy* for a Shade, a Stream, or a Breeze [33].

Written in the 'gudelie termis' and 'heigh stile' of the rhetoricians, *The Testament of Cresseid* is the most Chaucerian of Henryson's poems. But the story of Cresseid's infidelity to Troilus, and the example of rhetorical composition, are his only debts here to Chaucer. He has no sooner described how he settled down by the fire on a winter night—a fresh, Scottish variation on the conventional spring-tide prologue—with a drink to cheer his spirits and the book of *Troilus and Criseyde*, than he asks 'quha wait gif all that Chauceir wrait was trew?' and turns for Cresseid's later history to 'ane uthir quair'. *The Testament* is a corrective sequel to Chaucer's *Troilus*. The 'flour of luf in Troy', cast off by Diomede for whom she had forsaken Troilus, and now 'fra lufferis left and all forlane', rebukes the gods for their falseness; she is arraigned before the celestial court, is cursed with leprosy, and dies in wretchedness [34].

Henryson deplores her going 'amang the Greikis . . . sa giglotlike', but declares:

> I sall excuse, als far furth as I may,
> Thy womanheid, thy wisdome and fairnes;
> The quhilk Fortoun hes put to sic distres
> As hir plesit, and nathing throw the gilt
> Of the, throw wickit langage to be spilt.   [*ruined*

These lines echo Chaucer's characteristic charity to his fallen heroine; in *Troilus and Criseyde*, judgment is 'kept in the balance until her end; and that, with the finest tact, is edged off the page' [35]. But although Henryson recognizes the influence of 'fell Fortoun' in Cresseid's history, he is no more a simple fatalist than Chaucer. His poem is the story of Cresseid's crime against love, her punishment and her purgation through suffering. The rejected paramour who once in angry pride cursed the high gods is brought to death accusing none but herself; and Troilus, for all his love, can say in the end only that 'scho was untrew, and wo is me thairfoir'. Chaucer 'wolde excuse hire yet for routhe'; but Henryson spares her nothing. He cannot feel all Chaucer's pity for a heroine of *amour courtois* whose apostasy is due as much to circumstance and the subtleties of her own nature as to simple faithlessness. He is a practised moralist with a strongly legal bent [36]; and he is more persistently logical than Chaucer, less inhibited by an inquisitive and affectionate delight in the weaknesses of fallen humanity. His mind remains disengaged, although his insistence on full justice is tempered and enriched by a sense of the tragedy of human love, in which he sees

> greit variance,
> Quhyles perfyte treuth, and quhyles Inconstance.

The humour of Henryson has its gay and farcical side; but even in the *Fabillis* there are glints of a sardonic personality beneath. The common portrait of the schoolmaster of Dunfermline, a quiet, elderly, 'serious good man', is inadequate. It is easy enough to see the moralizing dominie in Henryson's work; but the hard ironist is also there. A cold smile breaks on the recorder's face when, after Cresseid wakes from her fearful dream of Saturn's judgment and finds that she is indeed stricken with leprosy, her father bids her come to supper 'and sayis your prayers bene to lang sum deill'; and when the leper-folk, divining that she was of noble family, 'with better will thairfoir . . . tuik her in'. The poet is emotionally engrossed in the justice of Cresseid's fate: she is forsaken by that Diomede for whom she had forsaken Troilus, and love is dissipated into lust; she is punished by the destruction of that beauty by which she lived, caressing and caressed, and by which she sinned; Troilus, in whose mind her image lingered, looks down upon her as she sits begging by the roadside, and knows not 'quhat scho was'; and her spirit, which had been 'with fleschlie lust sa maculait' in the 'Court commoun' is bequeathed to chaste Diana 'to walk with hir in waist Woddis and Wellis'. Justice is consummated in art.

Entangled with the moralist's resolute pursuit of justice is an emotional predilection for the grim and repulsive. Henryson shows it in 'The Thre Deid Pollis' [death's heads] 'holkit and how [hollowed out], and wallowit [withered] as the weid', in the description of the frog in 'The Taill of the Paddok and the Mous', and in some of the portraits of the gods who judge Cresseid. But the finest example of the repellent is the account of the leprosy with which she is cursed. There is a terrible appropriateness in this punishment, which was regarded in biblical and mediaeval times as the reward of heinous sin; and Saturn turns her 'play and wantones To greit diseis' in the most violent and incurable form of it [37]:

> Thy Cristall Ene minglit with blude I mak,
> Thy voice sa cleir, unplesand hoir and hace,   [hoarse
> Thy lustie lyre ouirspred with spottis blak,   [complexion
> And lumpis haw appeirand in thy face.   [livid
> Quhair thou cumis, ilk man sal fle the place.
> Thus sall thou go begging fra hous to hous
> With Cop and Clapper like ane Lazarous.

For the best of the mediaeval poets, rhetoric was a subtle instrument for expressing exalted feeling. Henryson has learnt the grave eloquence of Chaucer; and the measured rhythms and splendid simplicity of Cresseid's lament will stand comparison with similar passages in *Troilus and Criseyde* or with Arcite's dying speech in 'The Knightes Tale'. Henryson's declamatory 'Testament' is not so starkly realistic as Villon's 'Les Regrets de la Belle Heaulmière', but it is no less poignant. The elaborate metrical form and the resolution of personal sorrow in moral admonition do not prevent Cresseid's grief and despair from thrilling through Henryson's lines. His art lies in patterning and accentuating an austerely simple diction in stately rhythms:

> My cleir voice, and courtlie carrolling,   [song-dance
> Quhair I was wont with Ladyis for to sing,
> Is rawk as Ruik, full hiddeous hoir and hace,   [hoarse

My plesand port all utheris precelling:
Of lustines I was hald maist conding.   [*delight, worthy*
Now is deformit the Figour of my face. . . .

Nocht is your fairnes but ane faiding flour,
Nocht is your famous laud and hie honour
But wind Inflat in uther mennis eiris.
Your roising reid to rotting sall retour: [*rosy*
Exempill mak of me in your Memour,
Quhilk of sic thingis wofull witnes beiris,
All Welth in Eird, away as Wind it weiris. . . .   [*wastes away*

There is the same simple *gravitas*, and the same passion transcending
its rhetorical fabric, in the complaint in 'Orpheus and Eurydice':

O dulful harp, with mony dully string,   [*sorrowful*
turne all thy mirth and musik in murning,
and seiss of all thy sutell songis sueit;
now weip with me, thy lord and cairfull King,
quhilk lossit hes in erd all his liking;

                .   .   .   .   .

cryand with me, in every steid and streit,   [*place*
'quhair art thou gone, my luve Ewridicess?'

Henryson is as accomplished in less elaborate styles. He strikes a
clear singing note in the moralized ballad of 'The Bludy Serk' and in
'The Garmont of Gud Ladeis'; and the *pastourelle* 'Robene and
Makyne' is perfect of its kind. The theme of this wooing poem is
conventional enough, and has its analogues in French and English
lyric. Robene, a shepherd, is loved by Makyne but will have none of
her. When he does return to her in the rôle of a tardy and contrite
suitor, it is only to be told that

The man that will nocht quhen he may
sall haif nocht quhen he wald.

The sequence of wooing and parting is beautifully ordered; and the
dialogue, although robustly colloquial, never loses the rhythm of
song:

'Robene, I stand in sic a styll;   [*plight*
I sicht, and that full sair.'   [*sigh*
'Makyne, I haif bene heir this quhyle;
At hame God gif I wair.'
'My huny, Robene, talk ane quhill,
Gif thow will do na mair.'
'Makyne, sum uthir man begyle,
For hamewart I will fair.'

For all its formal artistry, 'Robene and Makyne' has the winning simplicity of a Burns song:

'Abyd, abyd, thow fair Makyne,
A word for ony thing;
For all my luve it sal be thyne,
Withowttin depairting.'

'Makyne, the nicht is soft and dry,
The wedder is warme and fair,
And the grene woid richt neir us by
To walk attour all quhair . . .'   [*all about*

Here is a lyrical grace only half explicit in Henryson's more elaborate poems; but, no less than his rhetorical eloquence, it is the fruit of a disciplined training in form and expression.

Henryson is the first considerable Scots poet to draw his inspiration from Chaucer, and yet he is, within the Chaucerian tradition, a highly independent writer. He stands apart from Chaucer in many important respects. He shows a constant moral concern in his work, perhaps even in the lightsome 'Robene and Makyne'. Despite his heavy debts to Chaucer the rhetorician, he continues the native tradition of simple narrative and colloquial dialogue with a new subtlety and subdued grace. To conventional poetic themes he brings a whimsical and sometimes sardonic humour very different from Chaucer's and unmistakably Scots.

Henryson and Dunbar [38], though writing about the same time in neighbouring parts of Scotland and in the same general tradition, make one of the strangest contrasts in our literary history. Henryson read English poetry with critical respect, and his very individuality grows from firm roots in the school of Chaucer; Dunbar, despite his formal recognition of Chaucer's eminence, is startlingly unique. Henryson's interests are those of almost any educated man of his time in Europe; Dunbar's best poetry is the reflection of the manners and culture of a Stuart court. His historical and personal virtues lie in the range of his metrical skill, his inventive manipulation of innumerable poetic kinds, and his command of the now rich resources of the Scottish tongue. French and Latin lyrical measures, English modifications of Continental forms, and the old indigenous alliterative verse are all drawn in to serve his need; and he uses them with an assured versatility. He turns his restless hand to allegory and dream-poem, panegyric, complaint, religious and didactic lyric, debate, comic narrative and satire. His diction ranges from the strong speech of the Edinburgh streets and the obscenities of the boudoirs of Holyrood to the aureate language of official praise.

He is a volatile, chimerical character: now paying compliments to the King, now importunately begging the royal bounty; celebrating public occasions and recording court scandal with equal facility; eloquent in cursing and in prayer; cutting a caper with trim Mistress Musgrave in the Queen's chamber, and at other times bemoaning his headaches or his penury and lamenting the impermanence of earthly delights. He throws into relief the contrasting scenes of court life and the crowds who clustered round a fascinating, versatile and (if we believe Dunbar) injudicious king. A few poems are written in praise of other airts, and one describes the noise and odorous vitality of a Royal Mile that has changed little with the centuries:

> May nane pas throw your principall gaittis
> For stink of haddockis and of scattis,
> For cryis of carlingis and debaittis,   [old women
> For fensum flyttingis of defame . . .   [offensive quarrels

But Dunbar's milieu was the court of Holyrood in its splendour and sordidness; and of the culture and the 'rash fierce blaze of riot' of that court his verse is the most lively memorial.

His moral and religious verse, although the least novel and in some ways the least personal part of his work, has not received the attention it deserves. In serious mood he shows a strong piety and a sombre wisdom grounded in experience. His religious poetry is not illuminative, and to the modern reader some of it is marred by extravagant virtuosity. 'In all poetry which attempts to represent the intercourse between an individual soul and its Maker there is a conflict between the ostensible emotion—adoring love, absorbed in the contemplation of its object, or penitence, overwhelmed by the sense of personal unworthiness—and the artist's actual absorption in the creation of his poem'; in the religious poetry of Dunbar the conflict disappears in verbal ornament and formal artifices. It is a poetry almost devoid of tenderness and imagination. His account of the Passion, for instance, has all his characteristic vividness and force—

> Onto the crose of breid and lenth
> To gar his lymmis langar wax,   [make
> Thay straitit him with all thair strenth,
> Quhill to the rude thay gart him rax . . .   [stretch

> The erde did trimmill, the stanis claif,
> The sone obscurit of his licht;
> The day wox dirk as ony nicht,
> Deid bodiis rais in the cite;
> Goddis deir Sone all thus was dicht,   [treated
> O mankynd, for the luif of the . . .

—but this is passionless rhetoric beside the imaginative pity of Langland's lines:

Consummatum est quod Cryst and comsed for to swowe, [began to swoon
Pitousliche and pale as a prisoun þat deyeth;   [prisoner
Þe lorde of lyf and of liȝte þo leyed his eyen togideres.   [then
Þe daye for drede withdrowe and derke bicam þe sonne,
Þe wal wagged and clef and al þe worlde quaued.   [trembled
Ded men for that dyne come out of depe graues,
And tolde whi þat tempest so longe tyme dured.

It is, however, just Dunbar's power in rhythm and phrase that enables him to celebrate a festival of the Church in splendid exultation:

Done is a battell on the dragon blak,
Our campioun Christ confountet hes his force;
The yettis of hell ar brokin with a crak,
The signe triumphall rasit is of the croce ...

Dungin is the deidly dragon Lucifer,   [beaten
The crewall serpent with the mortall stang;
The auld kene tegir with his teith on char   [open
Quhilk in a wait hes lyne for us so lang,   [lain
Thinking to grip us in his clows strang ...

Few of his reflective poems are mere rhetorical exercises in conventional modes. Behind traditional turns and commonplace sentiments is the intimate, admonitory tone of a man saddened and made wise by the world. He voices, in a style which 'maintains majesty in the midst of plainness', the sage melancholy of the later Middle Ages, their sense of the futility of earthly joy and their quiet acceptance of ultimate loss:

For feir of this all day I drowp:
No gold in kist, nor wine in cowp,
    No ladeis bewtie, nor luiffis blis
    May lat me to remember this,   [hinder
How glaid that evir I dine or sowp. [39]

The finest example in these poems of a common convention adapted to a personal mood is the 'Lament: Quhen he was Sek', a poetical danse macabre. The solemn and reluctant procession of humanity towards the grave was a frequent theme in fifteenth-century mural painting, sculpture and poetry. Whatever examples of the danse macabre Dunbar may have come across on his travels, he probably knew Lydgate's 'Daunce of Death' and the stone carvings in Rosslyn Chapel near Edinburgh, which were completed about 1480 [40]. The 'Lament' opens on a subjective note:

I that in heill wes and gladnes,   [*health*
Am trublit now with gret seiknes,
And feblit with infermite;
Timor mortis conturbat me.

These reflections on disease and death serve as a prologue to the grey
procession of the *morts*:

On to the ded gois all Estatis,
Princis, Prelotis, and Potestatis,
Baith riche and pur of al degre;
Timor mortis conturbat me.

Representatives of human society pass in review—the knight, the
infant, 'the campion in the stour [conflict]' and 'the lady in bour ful of
bewte', the scholars and the poets. All 'playis heir ther pageant, syne
gois to graif'; and so must Dunbar:

Sen he hes all my brether tane,
He will nocht lat me lif alane,
On forse I man his nixt prey be;   [*especially*
Timor mortis conturbat me.

Dunbar drastically reduces the number of type-figures—most versions
of the *danse macabre* have upwards of thirty *morts*; but he keeps to the
traditional scale by cataloguing twenty-four of his own profession.
The column which unrolls from his dejected mind is led by the shadowy
great of the earth; but the ghosts become more familiar and significant
as the poets pass, and the reiterated response from the Office for the
Dead rises into a cry from the poet's heart.

The procession in the 'Lament' illustrates a favourite technique of
Dunbar's. Catalogues are commonplace ornament in mediaeval and
renaissance poetry; but Dunbar's are rarely mere artifice. His imagination is cumulative: and the catalogue is one of his most natural modes
of expression, whether he is reflectively analysing human nature,
compiling black-lists of court hangers-on, or liberating floods of abuse
on his rival Kennedy. In his graver verse, the catalogue adds point and
concrete illustration to abstract thought:

The slidand joy, the glaidnes schort,
The feinyeid luif, the fals confort,
The sweit abayd, the slichtful trane,   [*delay, snare*
For to considder is ane pane.

The sugurit mouthis with mindis thairfra,
The figurit speiche with faceis twa,
The plesand toungis with hartis unplane,
For to considder is ane pane. [41]

27

His catalogues have not always this measured dignity, in which the
bitterness of his mind is softened in rhetorical grace. In the 'Remon-
strance to the King', for instance, the roll of James's court servants
becomes a crescendo of vituperation as the poet gathers in the char-
latans and opportunists who stand in his light:

> on your hienes follows eik   [*also*
> Ane uthir sort, more miserabill,
> Thocht thay be nocht sa profitable:
> Fenyeouris, fleichouris, and flatteraris;   [*fawners*
> Cryaris, craikaris, and clatteraris;   [*boasters*
> Soukaris, groukaris, gledaris, gunnaris;   [*suckers ? ?*
> Monsouris of France, gud clarat-cunnaris.   [*claret-drinkers*

The catalogue is used to greatest effect in this torrential style; the
poet's wrath and verbal resourcefulness expand together to confound
the reader and destroy the victim. Dunbar's most astonishing performance is 'The Flyting of Dunbar and Kennedy'. The *flyting*, for
which James VI justly recommended 'Rouncefallis or Tumbling verse',
was a popular Renaissance exercise. Skelton tried it; Sir David Lindsay
'flyted' James V; and Montgomerie fought in verse with Polwarth. In
so far as it is an abusive dialogue between rival poets, the *flyting* may
be distantly related to the French *tenson*; and is clearly an offshoot of
the ubiquitous mediaeval *débat*. Whatever its ancestry, it appealed to
the contumelious Scot. Centuries later Burns made jottings for a
'literary scolding'; and the habit is not yet dead [42]. But for calculated
volubility Dunbar holds the palm among 'flytaris'. He takes the part
of the true poet against the pretender Kennedy, whose eloquence he
says is only that of Gaeldom, with 'littill feill of fair indite'. He offers
the virtuous disclaimer of the classical satirist—'Flyting to use richt
gritly I eschame': scurrility is the wretched Kennedy's familiar art, but
Dunbar stoops to it only under provocation. Yet he gives a terrible
description of the power of his satiric muse:

> The erd sould trimbill, the firmament sould schaik,
> And all the air in vennaum suddane stink,
> And all the divillis of hell for redour quaik,   [*terror*
> To heir quhat I sould wryt with pen and ink.

Dunbar and Kennedy use different methods of attack. Kennedy takes
a characteristically 'Hielant' line: he defends his noble lineage and
assails Dunbar's, which does not seem to have been without spot. He
defends Gaelic against 'Inglis' (Dunbar's Scots) as the true national
tongue. He is pretentiously allusive, and depends for effect chiefly on
history and on coarse anecdote. Dunbar, on the other hand, uses the
more direct method of vivid caricature. His picture of Kennedy's

outward gracelessness is one of the best pieces of grotesquerie in
Scots poetry:

> ... hiddowis, haw, and holkit is thine ee;   [*livid, hollow*
> Thy cheik bane bair, and blaiknit is thy ble;   [*pale, complexion*
> Thy choip, thy choll, garris men for to leif chest;   [*jowll, chaste*
> Thy gane it garris us think that we mon de: [*face, makes*
> I conjure the, thow hungert heland gaist.

> ... Thy rigbane rattillis, and thy ribbis on raw,
> Thy hanchis hirklis with hukebanis harth and haw,   [*contract, hard*
> Thy laithly limis are lene as ony treis;
> Obey, theif bard, or I sall brek thy gaw,
> Fowll carribald, cry mercy on thy kneis.   [*monster*

The quality of Dunbar's invective is variable; but in such a bizarre
kind of writing, the only requisite is a rolling flood of alliterative abuse.
Nowhere else does he so fully illustrate the richness and power of
colloquial Scots. Saintsbury too hastily dismissed the 'Flyting' as
'alternate torrents of sheer Billingsgate', overlooking the poets'
resourcefulness in language and figure and their sustained rhetorical
power. Dunbar's second appearance is a *coup de théâtre*. He holds the
stage in dramatic monologue: he postures, mimicks and gesticulates;
he rants and whispers; he sniggers and guffaws uproariously; and
swaggers off in a cascade of verbal fireworks.

His versatility in metre and diction is equalled by his skill in adapting
established poetic kinds to serve an occasion or reflect a passing
humour. It is easy to sort his work into conventional categories; but
everywhere a restless, irrepressibly comic temperament is turning old
conventions to original uses. Such a perspicacious humorist as Dunbar
is easily provoked to laughter by a personage or an event; but he contrives to give his merriment a literary colour in parody and adaptation.
In 'The Petition of the Gray Horse, Auld Dunbar', the begging-poem
is given a new, ironical twist. He uses the beast-fable form to record
the reprehensible 'Wowing of the King . . . in Dumfermeling'. The
old device of the poetic testament goes to make the self-revealing and
self-destructive monologue which Burns later perfected in 'Holy
Willie's Prayer':

> I, Maister Andro Kennedy,
>   Curro quando sum vocatus,
> Gottin with sum incuby,
>   Or with sum freir infatuatus;
> In faith I can nought tell redly,
>   Unde aut ubi fui natus,
> Bot in treuth I trow trewly,
>   Quod sum diabolus incarnatus.

The Office for the Dead is parodied with blasphemous ingenuity for a witty epistle in the 'Dirige to the King, Bydand our Lang in Stirling'. In 'The Fenyeit Freir of Tungland' Dunbar, in his daftest mood, uses the dream convention to deride the ill-fated flying experiment of an eccentric charlatan about the court. The metre and the exaggerations of the romance are parodied in 'Of Sir Thomas Norny' to ridicule a Holyrood Braggadocio. Called to celebrate à court tournament of 1508, the 'Emprise du Chevalier Sauvage â la Dame Noire', Dunbar gently mocks the conventional praise of a lady's pink and white beauty:

> Lang heff I made of ladyes quhytt,
> Now of ane blak I will indytt,
> That landet furth of the last schippis;
> Quhou fain wald I descryve perfitt,
> My ladye with the mekle lippis.

The French trick of recording a courtly lovers' dialogue which the poet claims to have overheard *en cachette* is used in 'In Secreit Place' to open a licentious wooing; and the conventional protestations of unrequited love—'How lang will ye with danger* deill? Ye brek my hart, my bony ane'—give way to the giggles, the playful abuse and the baby-talk endearments of a man and a willing maid:

> 'Tehe!' quod scho, and gaif ane gawfe,   [*guffaw*
> 'Be still my tuchan and my calfe   [*calf-skin*
>   .   .   .   .   .
> My belly huddrun, my swete hurle bawsy,   [*glutton*
> My huny gukkis, my slawsy gawsy,
> Your musing waild perse ane harte of stane,
> Tak gud confort, my grit heidit slawsy.'

The *chanson pastourelle* is made fit for Holyrood. In 'The Dance of the Sevin Deidly Synnis' the traditional procession of the Sins is not, as in less volatile poets, an elaborate pictorial allegory, but a wild revel probably inspired by a spectacle at court [43]. The 'Dance' is a lurid carnival of vice. The Sins and their cronies wheel grotesquely through swirling verse; but their obscene and ghastly merriment heightens rather than obscures the diabolical agonies of Hell.

'The Tretis of the tua Mariit Wemen and the Wedo', Dunbar's longest poem, is the fullest illustration of his original treatment of literary conventions. Formally, the 'Tretis' is a debate on love among three ladies celebrating Midsummer Eve in a garden bower. The poet, *en cachette* behind a hedge, overhears their conversation. The Widow

---

* disdain, reluctance in love: a key-word in the vocabulary of *amour courtois*.

assumes the rôle of president of the court, and sets her companions a *demande d'amour*. They take it up in turn, answering pragmatically from their experience in and out of wedlock. On the setting of the debate, and on the participants, Dunbar lavishes all the rich ornament and 'enamellit termis' of sophisticated descriptive poetry: the garden is an earthly paradise, and the ladies are heroines of romance. They are familiar with the diction and ideas of *amour courtois*, practise adultery with art, and profess the virtues of secrecy and 'pitee'. No one, says the Widow generously, will go from me unloved;

> And gif his lust so be lent into my lyre quhit,   [*complexion*
> That he be lost or with me lig, his lif sall nocht danger.   [*lie*

But this is only a jocular echo of courtly sentiment. The Widow's 'honour' is an accessible commodity; she claims noble birth, but she is less a courtly lover than an amateur strumpet. Her use of the rules and language of *amour courtois* is deliberately comic; and when she ends her defence of promiscuity as the exercise of 'pitee', her companions laugh loudly and promise to 'wirk efter hir wordis'. She is a vivacious cousin to the Wife of Bath [44]. Despite their courtly veneer, all three ladies are drawn from Edinburgh town. One confesses she is tied to a 'hur maister', a dashing man-about-town 'brankand and blenkand [swaggering and casting an eye] to the brichtest that in the burgh duellis'. They have a highly coloured vocabulary and a reserve of strong simile which still enliven vernacular conversation in street and closemouth in Scottish towns:

> I have ane wallidrag, ane worme, ane auld   [*sloven*
>   wobat carle,   [*caterpillar*
> A waistit wolroun, na worth bot wordis to clatter;   [*boar*
> Ane bumbart, ane dron bee, ane bag full of flewme   [*drone*
>
> . . . . .
>
> With goreis his tua grym ene are gladderrit all about,   [*filth*
> And gorgeit lyk twa gutaris that war with glar stoppit.   [*muck*

The debate has been described as 'cold obscenity'. But the ladies have a hot vitality both in imagination and in speech. Dunbar draws a satiric contrast between their outward beauty and delicacy, and their inward corruption. Ideal loveliness is revealed as the whited sepulchre of lust, and what seems to be of the bower is seen to belong to the street. Even as they expose themselves, these three bawdy, jesting 'cummaris' cynically pretend, as part of their festive joke, some allegiance to courtly love.

In the 'Tretis' the old alliterative measure is used on two levels. It is possible that Dunbar had Scottish models for the alliterative abuse of the 'Flyting'; it is much more certain that by his day this measure was associated with serious poetry. In the ornate prologue to the 'Tretis' he shows his skill in the sophisticated style. The smooth, rapid run of the verse and the rich phraseology give the listener what he expects in this measure, and seem to set the tone of the poem. Metre, diction and portraiture harmonize. Then the alliterative line, retaining its flexibility but gradually increasing in force, is turned to a new and startling use in the speech of the first lady. The centre of the poem is a contrast between appearance and reality, between the ideal world of courtly poetry and the 'spotted actuality' of the women's minds and habits; and the alliterative line, with its romance associations, is the formal base on which Dunbar develops a tonal contrast between the conventional description and 'enamellit termis' of the prologue, and the coarse sentiment and coarser conversation in the debate which follows [45].

In his poetic vision 'The Goldyn Targe', Dunbar praises Chaucer as the 'rose of rethoris all'. This formal recognition of one of the less significant characteristics of Chaucer, repeated by fifteenth-century poets *ad nauseam*, has been too much emphasized. The aureate style is not obviously a major interest of Dunbar's, though he may have earned his bread by it; and he is not, save in a few points, a disciple of Chaucer. He is an assured and independent inheritor of a European tradition, far removed from Chaucer in temperament. There is nothing in him of Chaucer's love of philosophy, theology and classical letters; and he has not Chaucer's sophisticated courtliness, his tolerance, his oblique humour or his 'high seriousness'. Chaucer, on the other hand, has not the turbulent, masculine fancy of Dunbar, or his intoxication with language. Dunbar is much more, however, than a wild court poet with fire in his belly. He is a keen and humorous observer of a part of the human pageant, a moody but finely reflective moralist, a word-hurler and castigator on the grand scale, and a persistent experimenter in an age when the English poetic tradition had hardened into derivative formalism. The vocabulary of his poems awaits critical analysis; but it is clear at least that he had a sense of the weight and colour of words, and a resourcefulness in marshalling and deploying words, unequalled in his generation or the next. Whether through some inner inadequacy or because of the circumstances of his life at court, he is too often deficient in matter. His intellectual interest is more restricted than Henryson's; he has neither the humour nor the humanity of a Henryson or a Burns. 'The people of Scotland,' Sir Herbert Grierson remarks, 'clannish as they are, have never taken Dunbar to their hearts: "he wants the natural touch".' Yet in linguistic and metrical variety, assurance and exuberant imagination he is the richest of our poets.

II

THE RENAISSANCE POETS
(1) SCOTS AND ENGLISH

AGNES MURE MACKENZIE

TO secure a true perspective on Scottish letters in the century and a half this chapter covers, one must bear in mind three things very often forgotten. In the first place, we have only part of our data, and we cannot take for granted that what survives is necessarily the most important. Alexander Scott, for instance, lives for us only in what George Bannatyne happened to find, or fancy: the two men moved in different social circles, while in small Scotland, as in larger countries, court verse (and Scott's was that) was read aloud, passed from private hand to hand in manuscript, or copied in what our grandmothers knew as albums, which a later generation, who could not read them or disapproved of them, cast out as rubbish. Even print had often little better fortune: the *Gude and Godlie Ballatis*, a best-seller, scarcely survives. Because it was popular, copies wore out, fell to bits, and were thrown away.

The second point, still more often ignored, is this. Even if we had the whole of this chapter's matter, it would still be no more, after all, than a part of the corpus of Scottish letters for its time. There is more of Scotland than lies between Tweed and Forth and east of the Cairngorms; and the Scots and Scoto-English dealt with here had beside it the stately tradition of bardic verse in Gaelic, hardening out of creativeness by 1500 but reviving by the end of the century in the *dolce stil nuovo* of Mary Macleod (*c.* 1615-1707) and the steel-pointed satire of Charles II's Gaelic Laureate, John Macdonald. Indeed, for much of the seventeenth and eighteenth centuries, Gaelic was from the artistic point of view the most important language of the country.

Finally, Scotland was no St. Brandan's Isle, but as much a part of Europe as France or Holland [1]. During this time, as for the last thousand years, Latin was still a live international language, not only as the diplomatic tongue or the lingua franca of European scholars [2], but increasingly and brilliantly as the medium of creative work, where in a crowded European field a Scotsman was acknowledged the great master.

Scots and Scoto-English verse of this time, therefore, is only one among the country's voices. Even at that, it speaks in two different tones, of which only one concerns us here: for alongside the courtly, highly literate and often only too literary verse there runs a voluminous

33

stream of 'folk' literature, of uncommon force and vigour for the most part, and some of it of extraordinary beauty. Nor is there, in practice, any sharp division between the creators of the two different kinds. The courtier Lindsay was vastly popular. Intensely aristocratic Border ballads are genuine 'folk' stuff, and the kinds shift and fuse. The wild tragic pride of 'The Bonnie Earl of Moray' is street-corner political propaganda; and nearly every writer of court verse could turn out vigorous folk verse, and often did, with no more snobbery than is implied in the fact that the courtiers seem to avoid the tragic side. 'Marie Hamilton' comes from the stable-yard or the kitchen, the knaves of *Ane Satyre of The Thrie Estaits* from the Lord Lyon.

I

The later brilliant years of James IV show an interlacement of literary 'kinds'. The vernacular Scots, the new classical stream that was flowing from Italy, the mediaeval whose soul derived from France, blend together in the work of Gavin Douglas [3]—an innovator, with his place in a court which not only read books but volubly discussed them—some, no doubt, because they really cared about them, others because, as in times nearer our own, there was prestige in the proper admirations. Douglas (who had dry humour and a thin skin) hits these last off neatly in *The Palice of Honour*, where the poet is terrified by the approaching clamour of 'a heird of beistis stamping with loud cry', to discover when at last they come in sight that they are merely Minerva's courtiers who, as he very pointedly does not say, are of course all talking loudly and at once. Elsewhere, his almost frantic efforts to anticipate and parry criticism suggest what life meant to a sensitive innovator faced not with the long-range sniping of press-cuttings but with verbal mauling by self-certified experts, who

> Or evir thay rede the werk, biddis burn the buke
> [And] castis thame evir to spy out falt and cruke.

Douglas had his faults for his critics to point out, for his verse, though competent, is thin in the rhythm. His language, however, is another matter: the new perfections of Greek and of classical Latin were already throwing light on the limitations, and potentialities, of vernacular speech, and in all Western Europe were rousing men of letters to a zest in the enrichment of their own. Some, no doubt, were pedants, displaying their height of brow. Others were patriots who (as one might try to enrich his country's mind by founding a college or a chair) sought to create a sharpened tool of thought, and for the average educated man, and even for many without much education, made the varied use and manipulation of words as exciting as we find that of assorted balls. Douglas's elder contemporary Dunbar very

probably sought this enrichment consciously. Douglas himself undoubtedly did so. What Lindsay, his younger contemporary, still calls
'Inglis' had now been for a century the court speech, and had grown
apart from the court speech of England to the point where Douglas
can justly call it 'Scottis'. Being a scholar who loved a clean precision
of language and a man who loved Scotland (his scoundrel nephews
must have been a heartbreak), it was natural that in gaining control of
his medium he should realize more clearly its limitation: 'Besyde
Latyne, our langage is imperfyte.' He will not condemn it: rather, he
works at it, adding words not only from Latin and from French but
from the Northern vernaculars and from English, though claiming
that he writes 'in the langage of Scottis natioun', with apology rather
than pride for his innovations. What he wants, he says in the Prologue
to *Eneados* I, is

to mak it braid and plane,

Kepand na Sudroun, bot our awin langage,
And speikis as I lerit quhen I wes page.
Nor yet sa clene all Sudroun I refuse,
Bot sum word I pronunce as nychtbour dois.
Like as in Latyne bene Grew termes sum,   [*Greek*
So me behuvit quhilum, or than be dum,
Sum bastard Latyne, Frensch or Inglis ois;   [*use*
Quhar scant war Scottis, I had nane othir chois.
    Nocht for our toung is in the selvin scant,   [*self, same*
Bot for that I the fouth of langage want;   [*plenty*
Quhair as the colour, of his properte
To keip the sentence, thairto constrenit me,   [*sense*
Or that to mak my saying schort sum tyme,
Mair compendious, or to liklie my ryme.   [*match*

He was artist enough to blame himself, not his tool, and artist
enough to have something to do with it. Though he had not a great
deal of fictive imagination, and builds contentedly to given plans, he
was keenly sensitive to external impressions of both art and nature. To
be sure, Dunbar had been that, as witness the symphony of colour,
direct light, and reflected light building up to the soar of white in 'The
Goldyn Targe': but for detailed awareness of external nature and a
passionate delight in that awareness, Douglas reached a point few men
in Europe attained before the later eighteenth century. One would, I
rather think, have to seek in China any contemporary parallel to the
marriage of objective precision with subjective reverberance in

The wyld geis claking eik by nichtis tyde
Attour the citie fleand herd I glyde.

One may guess that with these things in mind *The Palice of Honour*
was a deliberate assay-piece. It is the chivalric-religious allegory which,

from the French Lorris in the mid-thirteenth century to the English
Spenser in the late sixteenth, was as much a standard form as our
'whodunit' or stream-of-consciousness novel. There are the dream in a
garden on a May morning; the processional pageants of classical-
allegorical figures—Melchisedek with Cicero in Minerva's train [4];
the inset fantasias of technical terms of music, architecture, astronomy
—the literary equivalent, in fact, of the *chutes d'armes* on the walls of
Palladian building. Its nine-line stanzas with only two rhymes apiece
are deliberately difficult, and they close in the fireworks of a ballade of
honour whose first verse has two internal rhymes to the line, the second
three and the third no less than four.

Yet there is not only a certain genuine feeling in the wish for a morally
more fastidious world. He can laugh at his own orthodox displays [5],
and he has a nice northern inventiveness of nightmare, as the sharp
stab of sound through the roar of Cocytos river, 'In quham the fisch
yelland as elvis schoutit': and again—a very Northern quality—he
can glance from the Humanity Classroom window and watch humanity
at unclassic antics. The mirror of world history shows Scriptures and
Classics on most orthodox lines: but then, as a sort of border of tiny
grotesques,

> I saw Rauf Coilyear with his thrawin brow,
> Craibit John the Reif and auld Colkelbis sow,
> And how the Wren cam out of Ailssay,
> And Peris Plewman that maid his workmen fow,   [*fou, drunk*
> Greit Gowmakmorne and Fin MakCoull, and how
> Thay suld be goddis in Ireland as thay say.
> Thair saw I Maitland upon auld Beird Gray,
> Robene Hude, and Gilbert with the Quhite Hand,
> How Hay of Nauchton flew in Madinland . . .

Just so, in a Northern Swedish seventeenth-century church, I have
seen, tucked into the fine baroque of the pulpit, among carefully
Palladian scrolls and cherubs, a dragon whose mother, several sizes
larger, had sailed as figure-head of a Viking ship. And his eye for the
natural object shows already: his dawn, with the colours clearing out of
the darkness, is more than convention.

King Hart belongs to the same 'kind', but is rather less than half as
long, and not only because it was, probably, never finished—it seems
at least to stop rather than end—but because he is learning *attack*: all
the elaborate dream-frame is discarded, and we have at once

> King Hart into his cumlie castell strang,
> Closit about with craft and meikill ure.   [*good fortune*

It is allegory again, perhaps *à deux clefs*. King Hart, besieged agreeably
by Dame Pleasance, and less so, without defence, by Decrepitus, is

primarily Mansoul, but may have some reference to an actual person: it seems to come rather late to fit Douglas's king. It shows an advance: the octave stanza is better chosen and more firmly handled, and though the castle and siege are stock images, they are not only freshly visualized but seen with a lively sense of dramatic values.

Douglas's 'place in the story' depends, however, not on these two good examples of a well-worn mode, but on what was doubly a piece of pioneer-work—doubly, as one of the earliest in Europe of the great Renaissance translations, and as in its Prologues, which are not translations, the first to take an emotionally charged perception of external nature, in itself and for its own sake, as the subject, not merely the frame and the setting of the *poesis*. In part as an exercise to strengthen the language, in part to bring Virgil to the common reader, he set to work to translate the *Æneid*.

For centuries Virgil had been a name of power, but as—literally— the Wizard of the South and as an authority, among others better, on the history of Troy and of early Rome. In 1490, with Douglas a boy in his teens, Caxton had printed what professes to be an English *Æneid*. It was rather the mediaeval equivalent of our filmed or potted versions of the classics, being based on a French romance, with an infusion of Boccaccio; and exasperation with this travesty was certainly one of Douglas's stimuli. Direct translations, however, were not quite new: there is an Irish-Gaelic one, at least, before the end of the fourteenth century [6], and though Douglas was probably unable to read it, he may well have known the next earliest we have, which a French writer, Octovien de St. Gelais, made in his own tongue about 1500. New French books came easily to the Scottish court, and it may be this one that moved Douglas's kinsman, Henry Lord Sinclair, 'Fader of buikis, protectour to science and lare' (incidentally the captain of the *Great Michael*), to demand of his poet-cousin a similar work [7].

Douglas, worshipping the *Æneid*, 'sa wyslie wrocht, with nevir ane word in vain', was appalled. He felt, too, the limitations of the translator, 'attachit on till a staik', and those of his medium the vernacular: but—and this too is visibly sincere—Virgil would still be Virgil if Douglas failed, and moreover, if not very logically, his success would do something to clear his beloved master of the shocking injury done to his fame by Caxton, with whose 'faltis and crukis' Douglas deals faithfully. So, in the same decasyllabic couplet as St. Gelais, to work he went, and put his heart in the business of giving the poet he loved to his own people: he hopes, in fact, that the book may be used in schools, and that the vernacular, quickened by this rich content and sharpened to match its exquisite precision, may achieve new power. Nor does he do ill: his couplet, a rather definitely closed one, lacks the varied roll of the hexameter, but he was winning a greater control of metre, and was too profoundly conscious as well of the magic to miss conveying something of it, at least. He does best, as one might guess, the most Celtic parts: the Douglases come from the Celtic third of the Lowlands.

> Thay walkand furth, sa derk uneth they wist   [*scarcely*
> Quhidder thay went, amid dim schaddowis thair,
> Quhair evir is nicht, and nevir licht dois repair
> Throwout the waist dongeon of Pluto king,   [*donjon* or *keep*
> Thae voyde boundis and that gowsty ring,   [*kingdom*
> Siclyke, as quha wald throw thik woodis wend
> In obscure licht, quhair mune may nocht be kend. ...

He laid his own roses also about the shrine, giving each book a Prologue. One is a long set-piece on the *remedium amoris*, probably early work, being purely mediaeval and stiffly handled. V begins with a pretty if conventional spring-scene, but goes on to deal with the trials of a translator, swiping once more at Caxton on the way. VI handles the conception of Hell, as described by both philosophers and poets. VIII, IX, X, XI are virtual sermons in verse: the first of these, in an intricate rhymed-alliterative form with bob-and-wheel ends, takes the stock theme of the falsehood of the world, but one wonders— he was in touch with the diplomats—if he had looked from his desk across threatening Europe, where the King his master was nearing the end, in failure, of his long effort to turn the Western Powers from their narrow greeds to face the huge menace towering in the East.

Among these familiar things stand out three new ones, VII, XII and XIII. They are portraits of seasons, winter, spring and summer ... did his under-mind know what that autumn was to bring, that he left out what for his city is loveliest of all? These are enough to give him a place on Parnassus. 'Spring' is the least new: it had been a familiar theme for a thousand years, but this is a Northern May, in her happier mood, and with Douglas's eye, and heart, upon the object. It is not only the mass of delicate detail—'Seir [many] downis smal in dentelion sprang'—but the sense of it as a radiance over all:

> For to behald it was ane gloir to se
> The stabillit windis and the calmye se,
> The soft sesoun, the firmament serene,
> The lown illuminate air and firth amene.   [*graciously pleasant*
>   *wood*

'Illuminate air' (I am writing on just such a day) is the one word for Edinburgh's magic light. The lines are well known, but that last is hard to hackney.

The most original of the three is 'Winter', which was to stand alone in civilized Europe [8] till—again from Scotland—James Thomson followed in 1726. Douglas does not propose to *enjoy* a wet day in winter: but he sees, with intensity that is in itself delight, the slow elaborate pattern built of its detail, the gleam of wet in the faded yellowish landscape, the 'rede wede on the dyk' stirred by the wind against the low drumly clouds, the movement of hailstones 'hoppand on the causay' and of the 'scharp soppis of sleet', and then

> The callour air, penetrative and pure,   [*freshly cold*
> Dasing the blude in every creature

(and that is Edinburgh in a north-easter)

> Made seik warm stovis and bien fyris hote,   [*snug*
> In doubill garmont cled, and wylecote,   [our *cardigan*
> With michty drink, and meitis confortive,
> Aganis the sterne winter for to strive.

'Sterne' is the perfect word there, with its overtone of the other meaning, 'star'.

'Summer' is June, with the sun going down in the north, the bats flying over the mist that fills the hollows, and (Douglas was a realist) the midges. The short luminous dusk goes by, and the afterglow of the sunset becomes the dawn:

> Yondir doun dwynis the evin sky away   [*fades*
> And upspringis the bricht dawing of the day
> Intil ane uthir place, not far in sundir,
> That to behald was plesance and half wondir.

—the Romantic, in the nobler critical sense, glowing out from the architrave of the Classical, as centuries later it would in the greatest of Scott. And under the magic light he does what the Dutch painters (and Scott himself) were to do, sees the movement of the countryside as it wakens, the rousing beasts, the mistress calling the cheery sleepy lasses, the grieve rousing the lads from the chalmer to yoke and go forth to their work in the long bright day.

It was no long day for Gavin Douglas, poet. He finished his *Eneados* on the 22nd July 1513. Before a month was out the army was mustering on the Burgh Muir: in three weeks more the kind book-loving sailor who had set him to work lay by his master, and Douglas's father and brothers, where the Branxton Burn ran red below the rain; and the Provost of St. Giles had closed his inkpot and was heartening his folk to labour day and night at the Flodden Wall. (A week after the news of the battle had reached the city, the Town Council snatched time to make him a free burgess.) The rest was foul politics and death in exile: not until he had been dead thirty years was his *Eneados* printed, and then abroad and without his name to it. It set off Surrey [9], who cribbed it handsomely, and invented in the process English blank verse; but far from its being used in Scottish schools, almost two centuries passed before a Scots printer was to set hand to it, not as gate to the golden universe of the classics, but as an antiquary's tool— or toy.

2

When Lord Sinclair was stirring the Provost of St. Giles to cope with the *Æneid*, a Fife gentleman in his twenties, David Lindsay, Younger of the Mount, was already at court, acting (in blue and yellow taffeta) in a play at Holyroodhouse in 1511 [10]. Not a professional scholar, he was still a man of wide and varied reading, no poet, but a writer who could use verse alike for entertainment and polemic, to such effect that his reputation was not only wide but popular and lasting. His first known poem comes in 1528, when the sixteen-year-old King had broken from his stepfather and set himself, with the precocious ability of his house, to give peace and justice to sorely troubled Scotland.

As with many writers who succeed by their faults as much as by their virtues, Lindsay's early work is a good deal the more attractive. There is something very likeable in 'The Dreme', in which he reminds the lad new come to power of the days when its writer would comfort and amuse a harried bairn whose crown had crashed on to his head at eighteen months old, tucking him up in bed, singing to him—

> The first sillabis that thow didst mute   [*murmur*
> Was 'Pa, Da Lyn.' Upon the lute
> Then played I twenty springis—   [*dance tunes*

and telling him stories of Greek and Roman and biblical heroes, of Merlin and Thomas the Rhymer and the Reid Etin. Now he offers a new tale, opening with the long fashionable dream, this time on the wintry shore on a New Year's Day. (It is New Year for the distracted kingdom, and we must read against the grim fifteen years of misrule and insistent danger that had followed the Golden Age 'before the war'.) Dame Remembrance takes him to Hell, where the 'men of kirk lay bounden into bingis' and the other two Estates are no better off, nor are their wives. They pass on swift Dantean journey through Purgatory, Limbo, the Elements, the Spheres and the Heavenly Court, returning to Earth for a geographical survey, all most ornamentally erudite. Then comes the cake within this elaborate icing. Lindsay asks to see Scotland, and does, with its rich possibilities of wealth in the widest sense, and its grim actualities. Remembrance tells him

> it lakkis na uthir thing
> Bot labour and the pepillis governing, [11]

which lack comes from the 'want of justice, polycie, and peace' in 'sleuthful hirdis': the heads of the State care only for their own profit—

which happened, at the time, to be perfectly true. Against them as witness comes the lean ragged man Jhone Comoun Weill, whose bitter complaint, spoken here with harsh and moving sincerity, laments 'the realm that hes owr young ane King'. Then a ship comes to anchor off the shore, and the guns of her salute to the New Year, and reign, rouse the dreamer, who, waking, advises his young master in a very sound exposition of a king's duties, candid, sensible and with real affection in it for king and kingdom.

It was the first, and the best, of many sermons. Between the 'Dreme' and the Glorious Revolution of 1688, to preach at the sovereign (not to say to nag him) was a sport as popular, in some quarters, as golf: and Lindsay might well have captained the national team. He even preaches in the begging letters that most poets then and long after bestowed on their patrons: when, next year or so, he is asking for a rise, he not only recalls his nursery services and gives a candid picture of the Douglas régime, including Angus's deliberate debauching of his young King and stepson, to keep him quiet: he tells the King that since he is trying to achieve good order, he should cause it too in the 'spiritualitie' . . . and now will he lend his old playmate £1000 till the Bass and the May forgather on Mount Sinai? Failing that, will God at least make his Sovereign oblige with the wherewithal 'of quiet lyf and sober rent'? A similar piece, of the middle thirties, is set in the mouth of 'the Kingis auld hound callit Bagsche', whose nose has been put out by that new pup Bawtie. It is one of the pleasantest of begging letters, for it lacks the self-righteous shrillness that grew on Lindsay, and its dry humour can still turn on himself, blending the canine and human agreeably.

But Bagsche owns that he has 'maid bludie sarkis' in his time. Lindsay, in fact, as he rose into his forties, was setting up as *le Caton de nos jours*, and that is always a dangerous trade for Cato—most of all, perhaps, when his skin is fairly safe. *The Testament and Complaynt of our Soverane Lordis Papyngo* is a polemic piece in the cause of that Reformation for which many both within and without the Old Church were striving. The decoration, at once traditional and topical, is possibly a little overweight. Its bright background is the royal aviary: James had a liking for fantastic birds, keeping not only herons, cranes and peacocks but so many coloured parrots and parroquets that they needed the services of a whole-time warden. The thing opens with a procession of vernacular poets, dead and living, with in its forefront a very handsome tribute to 'Gawane Dowglas, Bischope of Dunkell', and as ghostly a rear-rank of dead fashionables as those in Dunbar's 'Lament: Quhen he wes sek'. He will not compete with such distinguished writers, so falls back on the sad tale of the King's pet parrot, who on her death-perch after an accident has to scold not only the King but also his father, who is saddled surprisingly with the guilt for

Flodden—not for fighting the battle with obsolescent armament, but actually for fighting it at all [12]. The Papyngo bids farewell, with an immortal line, to Edinburgh, 'thow heich triumphant toun', to the other palaces, Stirling, Linlithgow and Falkland with its lovely park but shocking ale in the pubs, and then gets to business by calling three canon lawyers to make her will. They prove to be the Pye, the Gled [kite], and the Raven, and there follows the conventional onslaught on clerical greed, with a careful exception in favour of the new Priory of the Sciennes.

Lindsay's attitude still, however, is less that of the political polemist than of the professionally outspoken person with the tail of an eye upon the muckle pierglass. In the middle thirties the King and his Lord Lyon (perhaps to James's relief) held a formal *flyting*. Lindsay's half survives, and though the shrillness is growing, there is still affection under the invective. Of course, like all prophets since (and before) Isaiah, he had to have a shot at women's fashions. 'Ane Supplicatioun in Contemplatioun of Syde Taillis [voluminous trains]', written between 1537 and 1542, is famous, foul, and (as increases on him) far too long for its point. Quite as heartfelt and possibly rather earlier—the Queen married and died in 1537—is 'The Deploratioun of the Dethe of Quene Magdalene', a duty-piece by the recognized laureate. There is a certain dramatic colour in the panorama of painted scaffolds ready to hold the players, of wine wherewith the fountains should have flowed, of the craftsmen's green coats, the burgesses' crimson and scarlet, the purple, black and brown silk of the Town Council, that the Queen should have passed below her canopy of cloth of gold, 'all turnit into sable', the music to dirges. But 'Da Lin' shows less grief for his master's charming bride of not quite seventeen than does the Lord Lyon for his wasted labour in stage-managing pomps that are not going to come off.

The King died in the end of 1542. Lindsay saw him turn, with that 'litill smyle of lauchtir', to the wall. Thereafter the growing shrillness gains upon him, and the humour is apt to be stock sculduddery and stock invective. 'Kitteis Confessioun', of the 1540s, is a tolerably nasty piece of work. The attack on abuses of the confessional was not unjustified, but the self-righteous dirt is far from endearing. An uglier specimen, to those at least who happen to know the facts, is *The Tragedie of the Umquhyle maist Reuerend Father David . . . Cardinall and Archibyschope of Sanctandrois*, which gloats, at more length than Knox though with better manners, on the murder of that prelate. To the Extreme Left in religion at that time, England was much what Russia is nowadays to their political equivalent. The reader who knows what Henry VIII said of Scotland (a subject on which he was in fact not sane) and what his troops, by their own showing, did there, finds his jaw dropping at the damnation of Beaton for opposing the quisling

Earls of Arran and Angus and as the warmonger who caused the sack and burning of Edinburgh . . . for which Beaton was responsible in the same sense as Sir Winston Churchill for the bombing of London. But the public to whom the *Tragedie* was addressed had not read Henry's official communiqués, far less his careful orders to his troops, and as propaganda the thing is quite brilliantly done, 'carrying' the better for the sound and genuine sense of its conclusion, where the bishops are adjured to keep their oaths and the 'princes' to take as much trouble in choosing them as they would do in choosing a cook or a tailor.

Of the other three late works which have survived, *The Historie of ane nobil and wailyeand squyer William Meldrum vmquhyle Laird of Cleische and Bynnis* (written about 1550) is pleasanter reading. Even there, to be sure, the taste is somewhat doubtful: it is *biographie romancée*, with fairly frank detail, of a man newly dead and a lady who was possibly still alive: but at any rate it is both kindly and lively. His hero is an agreeable young soldier, of a type that for centuries was a standard export—a tall man of his hands, a favourite with the ladies, and the lover of a wealthy young widow, Lady Haldane of Gleneagles, who is reft from him by her recalcitrant kinsmen. The octosyllabic couplet has straightforward vigour, and the thing is a really spirited novel in verse.

Its readability does not carry over (at any rate for the twentieth-century reader) to the more ambitious work of about the same time, *Ane Dialogue betuix Experience and ane Courteour off the Miserabyll Estait of the Warld*, commonly known as the *Monarche*, which Lindsay probably thought his supreme achievement. It is dedicated to the Regent Arran, his half-brother Archbishop Hamilton (the heads of the civil and spiritual powers) and the Estates, and professes to show that the ghastly total war which their friend Henry VIII had loosed upon the country is no more than the just reward for Scotland's sins, which will be much worse if she imports arms from France. There are over six thousand mortal lines of it, mainly octosyllabic couplet with 'exclamatiounis' and other trimmings in assorted stanza. Their main substance, with much parade of information, is a pious summary of world history, from Eden through the Four Monarchies of Babylon and Persia, Greece and Rome, to the fall of the Papal Fifth, and the Last Judgment . . . with a wipe at the old grievance of ladies' trains. Its informativeness, its often really eloquent abuse, made it long popular, even as a school-book: it is, in fact, the close equivalent of *The Outline of History* by the late H. G. Wells, and frankly intended for 'Colyearis, Cairtairis and Cukis, for Iok and Thome' . . . learning-made-easy, with a view of the Heid Yins that adds moral to intellectual self-satisfaction, an infallible recipe for the best-seller.

Dead popular learning is very dead indeed, and to tackle the *Monarche* now needs firm resolution and strong black coffee. This is not true of a very different work whose purpose was not dissimilar in the main, though here Lindsay keeps clear of foreign politics. Though the plan of this book excludes discussion of drama, one cannot in fairness to Lindsay leave out all mention of the great morality-play *Ane Satyre of The Thrie Estaits* (probably first performed in 1540), which is by far his most important work: it seems to have been to the Scottish Reformation what *Le Mariage de Figaro* was to the French Revolution, but its quality does not depend on its political effect on its own time. Those who have seen it staged must of course make allowance for the brilliant cutting of Mr. Robert Kemp [13], which gives it a shapeliness the original lacks: but even in its untidier version on paper, the thing has an actuality and verve beyond any drama in England and most in France until Lindsay had been dead for a generation.

Dead is indeed the operative word for most of Lindsay's contemporary rivals, whom he mentions at the beginning of the 'Papyngo'. James V himself (not included there) wrote verse, but not even royal authorship cheated fortune, unless (which is not at all improbable) the admirable genre-pieces, 'Peblis to the Play' and 'Christis Kirk on the Grene', are indeed his.* But the 'ballatts farses and pleasand playis' of Abbot Inglis of Culross have disappeared, and so have not only the works but all personal record of Galbraith and Kinloch. Kyd has a solitary 'copy of verses'. Stewart, who 'desired' (did it not come off?) 'a staitly style', and Stewart of Lorne (who may have been the Captain of the King's Guard) are rival candidates for a dozen pieces in the Bannatyne or Maitland MSS., varying through a sermon on sin, the customary preaching at the King, and of course love-poems, to a begging letter and a flyting of soutars: one at least of them had a turn for graceful rhythm, though the other was—let us call him, in respect for the dead, conscientious. The Ballantyne of the rather sour reference is probably John Bellenden, no poet but the prose translator, by his sovereign's orders, of Livy and Hector Boece, for the public good. They are drowned as deep in the undertow of Lethe as at least thirteen of Dunbar's sad one-and-twenty: yet these ghosts were well-thought-of writers about a court a little over four hundred years ago.

With the later Lindsay one may place the collection called variously *The Psalms of Dundee*, *The Psalms of Wedderburn*, *Godlie and Spirituall Sangs*, and *Gude and Godlie Ballatis* [14]. In all countries affected by the Reformation (with the odd exception of then very musical England), vernacular song played a great part in spreading and emotionalizing the new movements. This collection, in fact, had a huge success, being reprinted again and again for two generations: then, very probably, its Lutheran background lost favour with both the Episcopalian wing of the Reformation Kirk, which was increasingly

---

* They have also been attributed to James I. See *supra*, Chapter I, note 26.

44

Arminian, and the Presbyterian, which was wholly and very strongly Calvinist.

It appears to have been compiled in the early forties by one or more of three brothers Wedderburn, sons of a Dundee merchant [15]. It is avowedly a devotional work, prefaced by a Kalendar, a Catechism, the Ten Commandments, the Creed and the Lord's Prayer, which was not yet thought 'unfit for the use of Christians' as Papistry. There are metrical versions of these, including a fine straightforward Apostles' Creed, graces, parables and canticles in verse, and a number of hymns. Of these, several are from German and one from Danish, while a Danish and Swedish connection shows throughout. Quality varies, but most have dignity, and all show piety rather than polemic. There follow 'The Psalmes of Dauid and vthir new plesand Ballatis'. The psalms (where English influence shows) are freely handled: indeed, the *Miserere* (Ps. li) runs to twenty stanzas of fourteen lines apiece. They vary from wooden to really dignified, as in the grave rhyme royal of the thirteenth.

Following these, comes the section best known to tradition, a series 'changit out of prophane ballatis in godlie sangis for auoydance of sin and harlatrie'. These are 'echoes' of popular songs, using their tunes and sometimes their refrains. A few of them, like the 'Hey trix' quoted (selectively) by Scott, allow the singer that contemplation of 'harlatrie' combined with self-righteousness which has made so often for popularity. Others are unintentionally comic:

> Johne, cum kis me now,
> Johne, cum kis me now,
> Johne cum kis me by and by,
> And mak no moir adow.
>
> The Lord thy God I am
> That Johne dois the call:
> Johne representis man
> Be grace celestiall,

which is based on a well-known and graceless English *chanson à mal mariée*. Again, an English tune whose original words begin 'Begone, begone, my juggy, my puggy' is turned into the gracious 'Quho is at my window'; and there are others of its level, or higher—

> For lufe of ane, I mak my mone
> Richt secretlie,

'All my hart ay, this is my sang', 'My lufe murnis for me', the fine Magnificat (the book shows none of the later rancour against the Mother of Jesus), 'Doune be yon river I ran', and the lovely 'Go hart', these last two of humble thanks for the Incarnation. The finest, perhaps, is the haunting 'All my lufe, leif me not' [16]. In spite of its patches of a frankly nasty brand of anti-clericalism, the book holds both beauty and genuine religion [17].

There was plenty of other propagandist verse, a lot of it 'pagane' enough, through the century [18]. Most is Protestant and anonymous, or pseudonymous, for a number of pieces are assigned to 'Maddie, Priores of the Caill Mercat'. These broadsheets and tavern songs were the equivalent, for the popular mind, of the film and *Express* type of news-sheet in our day, as the pulpits were of our broadcasting system. The laudations of 'that sweit Josue' Moray, and of Darnley as a miracle not only of beauty, scholarship and accomplishments but of modesty, piety and kingly wisdom, throw some light on the popular charges against the Queen. Writers known by name are Nicol Burn and John Davidson, but the best known is Robert Sempill, probably an ex-sailor, who lived long enough to mourn that blessed martyr the Regent Morton in 1581 and lampoon Archbishop Adamson three years later. He combines swinging verse with a telling sense of phrase and a gift for the snigger, not only in denunciation of Mary, laudation of her late espousèd saint, and panegyrics upon Moray and Morton, but in testimonials to the professional skill of various leading ladies of the pavement.

Very different, though his verse also is mainly topical, and among the most likeable figures of the time, is the man whom his 1830 editor described as 'the tasteful and industrious Collector and pious Preserver of Ancient Scottish Poetry', Sir Richard Maitland of Lethington [19], Nestor of men of letters in Mary's time, and father of her brilliant treacherous Secretary, 'Michael Wylie'. Some forty pieces in the Folio MS. collection and as many (though they largely overlap) in the Quarto are Maitland's own. He did not commence poet until he was sixty, and all are occasional or gnomic pieces, shrewd, witty and graceful. Like Horace, he loves a mid-of-the-road good sense, and like Horace can feel a flaming passion for it as he looks on what confusion has unbuilt in 'Ane auld fre realme as it lang time hes bein'. He could be a Reformer but a loyal Scotsman, fastidious in ethics but no Puritan, a satirist—and a very lively and observant one—without losing either his sanity or his manners. Had he been twenty years younger and with his eyesight, his Queen and country might have been saved much suffering.

He welcomes Mary's return with a call to the kingdom to rejoice as in the good old times with tournaments, while

All burrowis tounis evirilk man yow prayis   [*press*
To mak banefyris, farceis, and clerk playis,
And throw your rewis carrollis dans and sing   [*streets*
And at your croce gar wyn rin sindrie wayis,

46

As wes the custome in our eldaris dayis,
Quhen that they maid triumph for ony thing,
And all your stairis with tapessarie gar hing.
Castellis schut gunnis, schippis and galayis
Blaw up your trumpatis and on your drummis ding.

But he goes below the outward rejoicings to the right mental attitude, and though what he says has no picturesque extremes to catch the mob, its sound kind sense was as wholesome, and rare, in politics then as now. The blind eyes see shrewdly, and with mirth behind them, whether it is the wealthy burgess wives lifting velvet trains to show their striped silk stockings, or the graver follies that would kill gaiety—

    . . . na gysaris all this yeir,   [*masquers*
    Bot kirkmen cled lyk men of weir
    Hald nather Yuill nor Pace   [*Easter*

—and he has small use for those fervent Protestants who think anti-Catholicism the whole of religion:

    Thay think it weill and they the Pape do call   [*if*
    The Antichrist, and mess idolatrie,   [*mass*
    And syne eit flesche upon the Frydayis all,
    That they serve God richt then accordinglie,
    Thoch in all thing thay leif maist wickedlie.

Like Lindsay, he takes upon him to advise a young sovereign whom he sincerely loves, but though he speaks frankly enough, it is always with a tender courtesy, as well as shrewd sense, humour and neat verse. His quality shows in such things as 'Aganis Oppressioun of the Commounis' (by his own party), 'Aganis the Divisiones of the Lordis', and (losing his temper and laughing at himself for doing so) in the pointed invective 'Aganis the Theivis of Liddisdail', which throws a slant of dry light on the Border ballads.

His own and his daughter's collections were probably made by degrees in the minority of James VI, and in one of the last of his own pieces there the old man of nearly ninety gives wise and kind advice to the boy King,

    That he may tak our lang dolour away,
    In his nonage that we have done sustein. [20]

There was plenty of other verse at Mary's brief court, though most as fugitive as the gaiety. Not all of it was Scots, by any means. George Buchanan, counted the chief Latin poet of his day in Europe, was not only reading Livy with the Queen but writing delicate verses to her ladies, in a crystal Latin jewelled with compliment. The English ambassador in his despatches has a casual mention of Italian masques.

Ronsard, still held the foremost French man of letters, had begun his career as a page to Mary's father, adored the daughter, and visited her court as an honoured guest. Queen Mary, like an earlier Scots Dauphine, wrote verse in French, though the famous 'Adieu' and the graceful little lament for King François are now taken from her: Ronsard himself (who was a notable critic as well as poet) protested vigorously at the attempt to saddle her with the bad French of the Casket Sonnets [21], and if we have anything we can fairly call hers, it is the brief Latin hymn 'O Domine Deus', written, with death in sight, on a leaf of her *Horae*.

Like all Stewart courts, Queen Mary's was full of music. The Queen herself (says Brantôme) had a sweet singing voice, and (says Melville) harped 'reasonably for a Queen'. Songs in those days were often poetry, and echoes of what had enough success at court to spread outwards into less exalted circles survive in another manuscript collection, the deservedly famous one of George Bannatyne [22], who in the grim winter of 1568, when the plague lay heavily on Edinburgh, found escape in copying eight hundred folio pages of verse, mainly Scots although a few pieces are English. The compiler was neither poet nor courtier, but he clearly cared for poetry, and read and listened to what was going about. As luck had it, he did more than any man to save something of our shadowy literature: but for his work, Dunbar and Henryson would have little more substance than the 'Papyngo' ghosts, and Alexander Scott would be a name.

The collection, unlike the Asloan, Maitland and Reidpath MSS., was probably intended from the start not merely for Bannatyne's pleasure but for print [23]. The 406 poems are given a formal preface and conclusion, with an index, and are 'dewly devydit', with some flourish of penmanship, into five parts:

> The first concernis Godis gloir and our salvatioun.
> The nixt are morale, grave, and als besyde it,
> Grund on gud consaile. The thrid, I will nocht hyd it,
> Are blyth and glaid, maid for our consolatioun;
> The ferd, of luve and thair richt reformatioun,
> The fyft ar talis and storeis weill descydit.

Some of its ghosts—Mersar, Rule, Brown, Patrick Johnston—are named by Dunbar, and so are outside our time, and some, like Master Alexander Kyd, were probably enough expendable. Arbuthnot, who praises women as the consummation of all the Almighty's work, *may* be the printer of the first Scottish Bible: if he is, he died in 1586. Clapperton has a lively *chanson à mal mariée* in an ancient tradition, John Blyth a drinking-song in an intricate stanza, well handled, Norvall a grave meditation on the text 'He that woll leif most lerne to dy'; and Balnaves can moralize in neat 'cuttit' verse. There is a rather

stock-pattern love-song assigned to Darnley, and a ghostly John Mair
recovers life for a breath in

> Pansing of lufe quhat lyf it leidis,   [*thinking*
> My will express with resoun pleidis,
> And nocht I find to stop thair feidis   [*feuds*
> Plane,
> Bot lufe to reput best remeid is
> Vane

—a pretty song with the '-ane' rhyme throughout for its burden.

Some of the best things are anonymous—the three fine hymns
already mentioned, 'Now glaidith', 'The Sterne is risin' and the superb
'Ierusalem reioss', and some courtly love-songs with the sound of
clarsach or lute in their overtones. The stuff is conventional—or
universal? The form is individual and enchanting, in 'Quhen Flora had
ourfret the firth' (on the theme 'I luve bot I dar nocht assay') or 'Baith
gud and fair and womanlie', or 'Fairweill my Hart':

> How sall I do, quhen I mon yow forgo?   [*must*
> How sall I sing, how sall I glaid than be?
> How sall I leif? I luve yow and na mo.
> Quhat sall I do? How sall I confort me?
> How sall I than thir bittir painis dre,   [*endure*
> Quhair now I haif als mekill as I may
> Of cairis cauld in syching everie day?

Loveliest, perhaps, with alternate stressed and muted internal rhymes
(and a text too clearly 'mankit and mutilat') is 'Quhat art thow, Lufe?'
with its realist but generous conclusion:

> Quhat art thow, Lufe, for till allow
> Hes brocht me now into this pain and wo,
> Or yit avow hes gart me trow,   [*made*
> And reft my dow and daliaunce me fro?   [*dove*
> Fy on the Lord of Lufe, set me so heich abufe,
> And als, but rest or rufe, hes gart me go. [24]   [*without*

It is with this group that we must class the loveliest and most
individual work of Alexander Scott [25]. Good Dr. Cranstoun shakes
a solemn head at his lack of high seriousness, and refuses him 'passion'.
I should say myself that though he is never solemn, his love-songs are
as passionate as Burns's (though of course the passion need be no more
lasting) and he can feel with considerable force the unhappier features
of Scottish life in his time. His dates are uncertain, but his May-piece
speaks of pilgrimages to Our Lady's shrine at Musselburgh, and also
mentions pageants of Robin Hood: and by the time Queen Mary
returned in 1561 both these had been made capital offences—though
when it was proposed to hang an Edinburgh shoemaker for playing

Robin Hood in despite of law, there was a noble riot in the High Street, with the gallows smashed, the Tolbooth door 'dang up with foir-hammeris' and the Provost and Bailies treed in a lawyer's office and forced to claim help from an unsympathetic Constable of the Castle.

Scott's 'New Yeir Gift to the Quene Mary quhen scho come first Hame' sounds as if he were by that time middle-aged. It is likeable—the familiar sermon to the sovereign, but in the key of Maitland, not of Lindsay. It is sensible advice too, frank, courteous and gracefully put: the delicate shifts of pause and epithet in the opening stanza suggest an illuminated initial. Scott, like Maitland, was a Reformer, but a sane one, demanding penalties for 'wickit pastouris', but without illusions about the scandalmongering and 'covetise' that already mark too many of their successors, or those who famish the 'puir folk . . . with thir fassiounis new', or argue on things they know nothing whatever about—

> For limmar laddis and litle lassis, lo,   [rascally
> Will argue baith with bischop, priest, and freir.

The thing is full of the aching recurrent desire that marks the end of a long minority in a country bedevilled with wars both red and white, civil and for , in a hideous tangle: for God's sake, let there be stable laws at last, and a sovereign to see that all men do their duty—and let the Court be gay with jousts and dancing, 'Aganis thy Grace get ane gud man this yeir.'

There is a hint of the jousts in his own burlesque, 'The Justing and Debait up at the Drum', in which Will and Sim, in the manner of their betters, arrange to meet each other in a combat which, after vast preparation, deep potation and much piling of suspense, does not come off. The familiar matter is carried by the sheer devilment of the verse—octosyllabic octave with a bob-and-wheel refrain where the mock-solemn stanza explodes in a joyous howl like a dancer's *hooch*.

Superlative verse-craft, in fact, is Scott's chief glory. It redeems his conventional satire upon women, and it is the *fingering* of the rhythm that gives both wit and passion (he can combine them) to such things as the longing of

> Quha is perfyte
> To put in wryte
> The inwart murning and mischance,
> Or to indyte
> The greit delyte
> Of lustie lufis observance,
> Bot he that may certain
> Patiently suffer pain
> To win his soverain,
> In recompance.

The man who tripled that penultimate rhyme before the wave comes
home again was no prentice. And he could use that very stanza with a
quite different emotional colour, as witness 'In June the jem' with its
twinkling anti-climax:

> Pleiss scho to rew,
> I sall persew
> With subject servyce every sesoun:
> Be scho untrew,
> Fairweill, adew,
> For as scho changis I sall cheiss ane.
> Bot gif scho steidfast stand
> And be not variand,
> I am at hir command . . .
> Conform to resoun.

One or two are well known from anthologies, and deserve it—the
'Lament of the Master of Erskine', 'Oppressit hart, endure', and the
double rondel

> Lufe is ane fervent fyre
> Kendillit without desyre:
> Schort plesour, lang displesour,
> Repentance is the hyre.
> Ane pure tressour without mesour,
> Lufe is ane fervent fyre.

The remembrance endured a while, apparently. 'How suld my febill
body fure' appears, without author's name, but with its music, in the
Aberdeen *Cantus* after the Restoration: and ghost as he is, Scott is
luckier than most of his fellows [26].

3

Mary's court had been literate, in a casual fashion, rather than
literary. (Bothwell's delicate fastidious handwriting, in the new Italian
mode, is an interesting comment on tradition.) Her son, in spite of an
insistent concern with rather acutely practical politics, that might be
also fatal at any moment, loved scholarship as much as his son loved
painting. He was a real and considerable scholar, who cared for not
only learning as such but letters, and was anxious that his subjects
should love them also. Even before he broke from virtual prison in
1583, when he was seventeen, he was gathering about him a 'Castalian
Band' who, resuming Douglas's work of seventy years back, sought
to do for Scots what the Pléiade had done for French in the
fifties and sixties [27]. Scotland, perhaps from her own polyglot habit
(she spoke six, perhaps seven, tongues in the twelfth century) and

perhaps too from the rich range of sounds in both Scots and Gaelic, had always bred men 'delicately linguished'. They could not all, like Mark Alexander Boyd, sit dictating to three secretaries at once in as many languages, or like Fowler write macaronics in six at a time, but many were fully bi-lingual or even tri-lingual: and now it became and remained a pervasive fashion to be as well read in the moderns as in the classics [28]. There was some exchange of literary visits and much international literary correspondence, for which the King himself set the example. An Englishman remarks that Philip Sidney was as widely mourned in Edinburgh as in London, and Sidney himself, in one of his last letters, bids the Master of Gray 'hold me in the gracious remembrance of your King, whom indeed I love' [29].

Not only reading was the mode, but writing: not only royal secretaries or the Master of the King's Music, but the Lord Chancellor, the Master of the Mint, a distinguished physician, the O.C. Artillery to the Elector Palatine [30], and a gentleman doing Fifth Column work for England could all oblige with neat if not highly original verbal bouquets if a friend died or married, arrived on a visit, built a new summer-house, or published a book: and the women seem to have played the game as well. Of course, as usual, we have only a chance collection of survivals: of all the considerable body of verse that was certainly turned out by the Castalians, there was none printed in the author's lifetime, so far as we know, but two volumes of the King's, Hudson's *Judith*, undertaken by royal command, and Montgomerie's famous *The Cherrie and the Slae*—this last so much cut that one guesses at piracy. They were read aloud after supper over the wine, sung by the fire or by the garden fountain, or handed about as ribboned *épîtres galantes*. And again there is no guarantee that what survives is the best of what was written.

Not its best poet, but an active and helpful Preses of the Band, was the young King himself, who very early shows an intelligent interest not only in literature but in its technique. Letters had sheltered him in that dreadful youth, and given him, too, an outlet of self-expression the boy must have needed to the verge of madness. Calderwood has a piece in his collection marked 'The Kings verses when he was Fyfteene year old':

> Since thought is free, think what thou will,
> O troubled heart, to ease thy pain:
> Thought unrevealed can do no ill,
> But words passed out comes not again.
> With patience then see thou attend   [wait
> And hope to vanquish in the end. [31]

He was barely eighteen when he published *Essayes of a Prentise in the Divine Art of Poesie*: but already he took a serious interest in versecraft, for the book includes an interesting and intelligent study of technique, the 'Revlis and Cautelis to be obseruit and eschewit in Scottis Poesie'. It *may* have been suggested by the Englishman Gascoigne's *Notes of Instruction*, its only known British predecessor, published, in 1575, when James was nine: but unless one takes it as an axiom that every book must derive from another book (how voluminous an author must Adam have been!) it is a little difficult to be certain. Since James and Gascoigne are describing similar objects, they naturally make some similar observations: but they work not only in a different order but with a rather different approach, and though neither is longer than, say, an article in a monthly review, James has considerably more to say. He deals with rhyme and 'flowing' (we should say rhythm), with a sensitive ear for the changing weight of accents, the shift of caesuras. Taking for granted, as a man of his time, that lyric verse is meant to be actual song, he makes the music of it its 'verie twiche stane' and demands that close relation between the two which was to be the glory of Robert Burns. On the relationship of sound and meaning, on figures, and on writing stock-pattern stuff, he talks sense as a rule, though he has his time's shyness of long words in verse . . . and there can be no rules, says he, for the fundamental, 'inuentioun', which is not to be had 'except it come of Nature'. There are notes, too, on actual stanza-forms and on 'kinds', with observations on choice of verse and language [32]. In noting the *Sonet*, 'for compendious pray-sing', he takes the peculiar artistic point of the form, 'quhair sindrie sentences and change of purposis are requyrit'. Though Scots early used the Italian octave-and-sestet, James's specimen here is the quatrains-and-couplet type, with the rhymes interlaced in the manner known to us as Spenserian: it is an early and favourite form in Scotland. James admits, too, besides the standard forms, 'all kyndis of cuttit and brokin verse . . . quhairof new formes are daylie inuentit'. In fact, in its historical position, and with no allowance for the writer's age, the thing is a rather remarkable piece of work.

James at eighteen, or indeed at any age, was a better critic and patron than a poet (we are not to forget his work for the Authorised Version of the Bible). The sonnets that accompany the 'Revlis' are schoolboy stuff, though there is a hint of the Stewart love for salt water that makes one glad the boy had his bit sea-adventure. There is a translation of Du Bartas's *Uranie* [33], in a closed couplet that is oddly eighteenth century in feeling—a phenomenon that henceforth often recurs: it is rather better than the original, but that does not say it has very notable merit. And there is a rather touching 'Metaphoricall Invention of a Tragedie called Phoenix', based on the bitter wreck of the boy's devotion to his dazzling cousin Lennox who had died, banished from him, in 1583.

The *Poeticall Exercises* includes more Du Bartas and an energetic

53

description of Lepanto, apparently written when the King was sixteen: it is no more than an adequate chapbook ballad, with a boyish gusto in the detail of the fighting contradicting traditions of James's dislike of cold steel. Under the gusto there is already an historic sense that can see the battle as victory over a major peril to Europe. There is a chuckle in the note on the godly, who could see only that the King was praising 'a forraigne Papist bastard': he will not recant what he has said of Don John, but as concession to his pious subjects he transfers it to the mouths of Venetian ladies . . . and adds an angelic chorus to the effect that if God so helps those whose worship of Him is mixed with their own inventions, what will He not do for the true believer?

Later work appears in the Bodleian MS. It varies from compliment (as to the Swedish astronomer Tycho Brahe) to rather touching love-poems to the Queen: but perhaps James's best is the sonorous prefatory sonnet, with an unorthodox but effective rhyme-scheme, for the *Basilikon Doron*, the essay on king-craft written for his small son Henry.

To our day as much as to his own, however, the 'maister poet' of the Castalian Band is James's 'belouit Sandirs', Alexander Montgomerie, whom Robert Steven, one of the ghosts in the wings, about 1590 calls the King's 'poyet laureat' [34]. His reputation was to endure for long, but has suffered in our time for a double reason. An editor, having identified as Constable's some pieces in the Drummond MS., assumed them to be verbatim plagiary, when clearly what happened is that Montgomerie, in the manner of the time, had copied them for his own pleasure, perhaps during Constable's visit to Edinburgh. Again, he is said to have plagiarized an English anthology, *A Gorgeous Gallery of Gallant Inventions* (1578). Now Montgomerie had been writing at least ten years earlier, since George Bannatyne includes some work of his, and if we accept the principle of *difficilior lectio*, the plagiary seems to be the other way round.

Far his most famous and most popular poem has been damned too (like *Hamlet* in the well-known story) for being 'too full of quotations'. The longish *Cherrie and the Slae*, in fact, shows a turn for the aphorism to which the Scots tongue is so admirably suited [35]: and Montgomerie's wide popularity made scraps of it pass into the common language, as tags of the Bible and Shakespeare have done. The 'kind' of the poem is at first sight mediaeval: the poet debates whether to try for the cherry on the cliff or content himself with the accessible sloe, and goes on 'considdering the swiddering' for one hundred and fourteen long and complex stanzas, Courage, Dread, Danger, Hope and Experience taking their turn—and making the Victorian critics flap it aside as allegory. In fact, they are less personages, even allegorical ones, than moods of the mind, and the reader who can recall the 1920s recognizes (with a chuckle or with alarm) that the thing is what we call stream-of-consciousness. It is quickened by the elaborate dance of the verse, the gnomic phrasing that made it so quotable, and the charm of feeling for natural beauty, especially for that of reflected light—the colour of the cherries glowing in water, the dancing reflex of the water on their scarlet. But the reader who has not been broken in his youth to Miss Dorothy Richardson and her followers may find it long before he reaches the point where 'The fruite for ripnes fell', to conclude the discussion.

As a contrast, there is a share in a famous flyting with Hume of Polwarth: the tulzie went on apparently for some time, in the manner of a *Scotsman* correspondence, only much more so. The combatants accuse each other of everything from sheep-stealing (which was not, like cattle-lifting, a gentleman's sport) to being unable to write verse when sober. It is no more polite than Lindsay in similar vein, though funnier, and it uses a number of exuberant verse-forms. On the other side are translations of the Psalms—a fashionable ploy, then and much later—into elaborate 'cuttit and brokin' stanza. They are poor enough, and to a modern reader Montgomerie's most attractive work is in his seventy sonnets and still more in his sixty pieces of assorted, generally lyric, verse. These vary in quality, but the best are charming. Most show metrical skill and a vast and precise command of vocabulary, and many are clearly meant to be sung, not read, to the accompaniment of lute or clarsach. The sonnets (some in the true Italian form, though he likes the ring of a concluding couplet) are often graceful, and some sound like genuine passion, as the well-known 'Sa sweit a kis yestrene fra thee I reft'. Those addressed to Margaret Douglas or Euphame Wemyss may be mere splashes of court holy-water, but the dancing drops glitter very bonnily, even when he adapts the spray of them from another sonnet to another lady.

Other pieces are more or less the equivalent of, say, Burns's epistles in verse: but the best of Montgomerie is undoubtedly the songs, like 'To the, Echo, and thou to me agane', a slight thing but music, with a second voice answering, and for its close 'Quhair is our joy? O Echo, tell agane. . . . Gane!' 'The Well of Love' has a floating rhythm and an aureate diction that might be Dunbar's; and the music sounds again in the rippling 'I rather far be fast nor frie' of 'The Commendatioun of Love', in the graceful 'Solsequium', or in 'Sen Fortun is my fo' (perhaps suggested by one of Hudson's English airs though not written to it [36]). In 'Adew, O dasie of delyt' Montgomerie uses the *Cherrie* stanza agreeably, and perhaps to more suitable ends. His best-known piece now, and certainly one of his most delightful, is 'Hey now the day dawis': the triple dance of rhyme gives the great summer-palace of Linlithgow waking beside the water to a bright morning.

Far less well known, though he too could write charming things, is John Stewart of Baldinnes, a younger son of that Lord Innermeath who held the Redcastle lands for a red rose yearly. His manuscript [37] puts in its forefront his version of the *Orlando Furioso*. As an abridged version it is reasonably competent: purely as verse it is often something more. Its decasyllabic quatrains, the rhymes interlaced, not seldom reach a dreamy plangent music. One of the very few things we know about him is that he wrote after the King had drawn up his 'Revlis and Cautelis', and he also seems to have been keenly interested in the technical side of versecraft. His other work includes a longish moral poem, 'Ane Schersing out of Trew felicitie', and sixty-six assorted pieces, religious, occasional and amatory—anything from verses to go to the King with a New Year's gift of a little gold laurel tree to a parting bouquet for a group of ladies who are crossing the Queen's Ferry on a May morning, or prettinesses on a summer-house or a fountain—

> Heir in this place thow may refreschement find
> Both be the well, the shadow, and the wind.

The matter is set by fashion, the manner and metre often very pleasant, with at times something like the poised and wheeling gull-wing quality of Alexander Scott. He experiments freely, in anything from rhymed alliterative verse with a bob to an intricate rhyme-scheme with lines of an iambic foot apiece. Characteristic enough is 'To his Darrest Friend':

> . . . My luifing hart dois weill agrie
> With yow to bie,   Quhair evir I go.
> In weill and wo,   It conforts me,
> The freindschip frie   Betuix us tuo,
> But fleing fro.   Thair is na mo   [*without*
> Quhom I luif so   With firm effect.
> As ye direct,   Gif I say no,
> Even as your fo   Than me reject.

The nearest approach to a professional writer among the Castalians is the shady if less shadowy William Fowler [38]. He was well read in Latin, English, French and Italian, and his own list of his works shows a literary G.P. who would tackle anything from a metrical psalm to a manual for secretaries (with model letters), an *Art of Memorye*, an *Art of Maskarades*, or translations of one Franchart upon Bothwell, of Machiavelli, and—in verse—of the *Trionfi* of Petrarch, this last published in 1587 and dedicated to the wife of Lord Chancellor Maitland. It was possibly this which caught the eye of the King, for though (in a century when, as for the next, Scots and French, by law, were mutually nationalized) most men at court would be familiar with French, Italian was a less common accomplishment. Most of these have been lost, but there survives a fair amount of the usual court mixture, from compliment to Lady Erroll or 'Lady Arbell' (Arabella Stewart) to doggerel sympathy with a friend's hangover, or macaronics in anything up to six tongues at once. Probably his best is in the sequence of seventy-five sonnets oddly called *The Tarantula of Love*, and in another shorter one to 'Bellisa'. He uses both the Italian form and the interlaced quatrain. The matter is conventional enough, as when Bellisa crosses the Queen's Ferry escorted by more heathen deities than the General Assembly would have approved, but he can give his verse a graceful fall, as in the sestet of the funeral sonnet upon Mrs. Cockburn:

> To thee, chaste Dame, the Heavins dois serve for grave.
> Thy funeralles my Muse, with heavy tone
> Shall celebrate, and sound in all men's ears.
> This doth thy vertue and thine honour crave,
> Though careless thou, however this be done,
> Quho sits in Heaven and smyles to see my tears.

Some of the Bellisa sonnets have an unexpected note of Orkney storm: but Fowler is no Douglas, and the storm is seen from the delicate *tourelles* of the Earl's palace, whose gracious walls still brood over Kirkwall town. Ovid at Tomi?—though if Earl Patrick's household resembled his house, it was a tolerably luxurious Tomi.

The Castalians, too, have their ghosts; and with them, though his court life was passed for the most part, apparently, in France, is Mark Alexander Boyd (1563-1601). There is some good Latin verse of his extant—he figures prominently in the Amsterdam *Delitiae Poetarum Scotorum*—some Greek, and a prose treatise in French: in Scots a single powerful and lovely sonnet, 'Fra bank to bank, fra wood to wood I rin', that is too widely known to need quotation.

4

Court verse survived for a time the Union of Crowns, and we shall need to return to it later on. The stream of literary verse, however, which for the last century had—in Scots at least—found its main sources in or about the court, was dividing again, and from now until into the reign of James's son there is a double current—a Cavalier, which is mainly but not wholly of the court, and an extra-courtly group, Presbyterian in sympathy. Best known of these last, and deservedly remembered, if by one poem from a fair bulk of work, is Alexander Hume [39]. He rather disapproved of his own poetic impulse, complaining that 'in the houses of greate men and at the assemblies of yong gentilmen and yong damosels the chiefe pastime is to sing prophane sonnets and vaine ballatis of loue, or to rehearse some fabulos faits of Palmerine, Amadis, or other such-like raueries'. Which, and for several pages, is very shocking: so he will provide stuff that shall enable them to be at the same time fashionable and godly. He does his best, though a certain human liking for fun breaks in, as when celebrating the defeat of the Armada he calls for national rejoicing in a fascinating detail of decorations (including setting out all the family plate) as background to 'cumlie comedies, pleasant playes, and morall tragedies': he would not have called for such flippancies four years later, in the brief ascendancy of Andrew Melville! The piece has interest besides its manners-painting, for its closely stopped couplet, with severely marked elisions, is an early and conspicuous example of that foreshadowing of the eighteenth century which is strong in so much Scots verse of the late sixteenth and early seventeenth. At least once he attains a real and gracious beauty, in the pageant of the famous 'Day Estivall', the slowly wheeling course of a summer day, where Douglas's mantle has fallen upon his shoulders. It is full of individual felicities of observation, but they blend one into the next like its changing light: even its naïveties, its pleasure in cool ale and well-dressed salads, add to the lovable quality of the whole.

Zachary Boyd [40], a scholar and a Covenanter, had considerable status in his party, a traditional 'name', and a share in the Metrical Psalms. Though far from dull, the flowers of his *Garden of Zion*, a collection of metrical tales from the Old Testament, are rather remote in tone from King James's Bible: a favourable specimen is this brief but ingenious life of Judge Ibsan:

> After Jephte, IBSAN of Bethlehem
> Was judge: this man had three-score of children.
> At last he died, as in Scripture appeares
> When he Israel had judged seven years.
>
> *The Use*
> Happie is he who dies with a good name,
> Though volumes be not written of his fame.

Several men on the Covenant side, like Boyd himself and that admirable journalist Robert Baillie, were fine scholars, and a number wrote excellent and racy prose: but in verse their major figure is Sir William Mure of Rowallan, Montgomerie's nephew [41]. In his youth he emulated his famous uncle, loving music and writing love-songs and *vers de société*, with a classical narrative 'Dido and Æneas': they seldom quite come off, though there are moments, as in the pretty

> Must I unpittied still remain,
> But regaird   [*without*
> Or reward,
> Nothing caird,
> Bot by my suetest slain?

By his thirties, however, he was abandoning such worldliness, and thereafter his work is either religious or political, honest enough, and often with more real passion in it than his songs, for he had the sad experience of many men, supporting the Covenant Party in opposition, and scunnered by its tyranny in power. His religious work shows again in its technique the forward look. *The Trve Crvcifixe*, a long statement of Christian doctrine, is in a sharp closed couplet. He is best in the sonnet, but as with so many Scots writers since his time, one feels that he could have done better if he had worked, if he had not been taigled by a subconscious feeling that creative writing was something one should not take quite seriously [42].

Both Boyd and Mure, however, left their mark if not their names upon the popular mind by their contribution to the Metrical Psalms. An assembly of English Presbyterian divines, called and closely controlled by the English Parliament [43], had met at Westminster in 1643, and by 1648 had produced a *Directory of Public Worship*, a *Confession of Faith* and the *Larger* and *Shorter Catechisms*, which, sent up to the General Assembly and accepted by that body as they stood, are still major standards of all Presbyterian Churches. The Westminster men also took in hand a psalter, at first accepting the metrical version composed by Francis Rous, Provost of Eton. Alternatives, however, were put forward, and there was a notably violent collieshangie, with Lords, Commons and divines loudly at odds. Rous was revised, with Zachary Boyd intervening, and the result sent up to Edinburgh.

It is possible that someone had suggested that it was perhaps a little inconsistent to rouse opposition to the Scottish Prayerbook of Wedderburn and Maxwell by denouncing it as merely an English import, and then to accept without question or alteration a whole series of forms indubitably English: at all events, the Assembly now raised objections, and eventually appointed a Committee (including a mathematician of repute) to carry out a further elaborate revision. The proceedings are too complex to give here, but their result was the 1650 Psalter, now in use in all Scottish Presbyterian Churches. The Assembly themselves were still, for whatever reason, to call it Rous's, but actually little of him was left. In a detailed examination, the late W. P. Rorison traced only 878 lines of his remaining in its 8620, while there are 754 of Zachary Boyd, 516 of King James (whom they had repudiated with contumely) and only 49 of Mure, who by tradition shares the main credit with Rous [44]. The results can hardly stand as literature beside the Authorised Version, let alone Coverdale: but they are endeared by long familiar use and association with many most noble tunes from at least four countries.

Not all writers outside the court set were Covenanters. After the flitting of the court, in fact, the Episcopalian and Royalist Aberdeen became and (till the Covenant persecution of the forties) remained the main cultural centre of Scotland, producing one of the chief Latin poets of his time in Europe, and the group of outstanding scholars known as the Aberdeen Doctors. Most, however, looked to a European audience, and their medium was more commonly Latin than Scots, though the 'remains' of John Lundie, Professor of Humanity at King's in the peaceful first decade of Charles I's stormy reign and a Latin dramatist, show the professoriate scribbling verse to each other in the vernacular as in learned tongues. But Scots, or by this time rather Scoto-English, is the language of the two Alexander Gardynes, one an advocate, the other in the philosophy chair at King's. Either may have produced *A Garden of Grave and Godlie Flowers* (1609), a charming piece of Edinburgh printing but the work of a highly mortuary muse, though there are congratulations to King James 'on his deliverie from the Sulphurious Treason in the Parliament House'. The famous *Theatre of the Scotish Kings* (1612-25, companioned by a lost *Theatre of Scotish Worthies*) is more Scots in language in spite of its later date: it consists of portraits in verse, often well-turned, and is notable for its sympathy with Mary. With them we may mention the fairly voluminous work of Alexander Craig [45], 'Scoto-Britane', a Banff man with sufficient reputation to be invited south to help with the masques for the royal visit of 1618. His medley of modes has some historical interest: the *Pilgrime* reverts to the fifteenth-century alliterative-metrical stanza, and beside it is the poulter's verse of the English sixteenth, and sonnets *à la mode* to ladies with pretty classical pseudonyms.

5

The major stream, however, is still from the court, where there was still a keen interest in letters, with at least four men keeping up the Castalian tradition. James's new subjects in general did not want him, though he was to win a good deal of affection in time. Men of letters, however, greeted him with joy. Elizabeth, though a well-read and even scholarly woman, had never been a patroness of letters: James was to prove an appreciated patron to Shakespeare, Bacon, Chapman, Daniel, Beaumont and John Donne, as well as to the London Scot Ben Jonson, while his courtiers inclined to follow the royal example. The two eldest of the four Scots were both the King's juniors only by a year, and had probably been of the original Band. These are Sir David Murray of Gorthy and Lord Stirling. Gorthy's [46] work is Scoto-English, but in spite of its London printer's orthography, with a good deal of emphasis upon the 'Scoto'. *Sophonisba*, in fact, may have been made in the Castalian days: it is a long classical narrative in rhyme-royal, in the mode of the literary (not the popular) Senecans. *Coelia*, a shortish sonnet-sequence, has some rather graceful things, like the seventh—'Pale sad Aurora, leave thy showres to raine'.

There is more both of and to Sir William Alexander of Menstrie, later Earl of Stirling and Viscount Canada [47], incidentally but quite copiously a poet. The 'first fancies of the author's youth' as a Castalian were the fashionable sonnet-sequence *Aurora*—a set of one hundred and five, interspersed with lyric, in which last his sonorous muse is not too happy. The sonnets themselves can be graceful enough, however: for example, No. xxxiii:

> O if thou knew'st how thou thyself dost harme,
> And dost prejudge thy blisse, and spoile my rest,
> Then thou would'st melt the ice out of thy brest,
> And thy relenting heart would kindly warme.
> O if thy pride did not our joyes controule,
> What world of loving wonders should'st thou see,
> For if I saw thee once transform'd in me,
> Then in thy bosome I would poure my soule,
> Then all thy thoughts should in my visage shine,
> And if that ought mischanc'd thou should'st not mone
> Nor beare the burthen of thy griefs alone:
> No, I would have my share in what were thine,
> > And whil'st we thus should make our sorrowes one,
> > This happie harmonie would make them none.

What made the young Milton (and probably Dryden) read him and Addison praise him two generations later, was less *Aurora*, however, than the *Monarchick Tragedies*. The powerful influence of Seneca had entered the European drama in general very largely through Buchanan's Latin *Jephthes* (1554), which laid the foundation of the French classical drama. It was very strong, too, in the great English movement that began in 1561 with *Gorboduc*—like the French work on austerely classical lines, though its English followers show a greater interest in Seneca's ghosts and murders and vengeances. The Scot Alexander prefers to follow Buchanan and Jodelle. *The Monarchick Tragedies*, however—*Croesus*, *Darius*, *Alexander* and *Julius Caesar*—are closet drama in a consecutive series, portraying the successive falling monarchies of the Prophet Daniel, with perhaps something too of the still popular *Monarche* of Lindsay. They are thoughtful things, the thought Alexander's own in the sense that he honestly thought it, but familiar: and it is the thought, on rule and its implications, that matters to a seventeenth-century Stockmar. They do not attempt to create personalities, and the drama is not seen in terms of action, but lies in the development of the ideas by means of a grave, often nobly sounded, quatrain, interspersed with stichomythic dialogue and with choruses in 'cuttit and brokin' verse. Alexander, however, was apparently a type of the thin-skinned Scot who is easily terrorized by a lifted eyebrow: in revision the language grows more anglicized, the sonority less, the movement stiffer and the rhyme more metallic.

Sir Robert Aytoun [48] took life and letters more easily, though he

SCOTTISH POETRY

wrote in four tongues, Greek, Latin and French as well as Scoto-English. Ben Jonson, who feared nor flattered any flesh and was a terror to his brother poets, made it his boast that Aytoun was his friend: and indeed he was namely for wit, charm and grace. His best verse has a casual elegance, salted with irony, very French in temper, as in 'I loved thee once, I'll love no more' or 'I do confess thou'rt smooth and fair', both in his graver mood, and clearly songs; or the wicked twinkle of

> There is no worldly pleasure here below
> Which by experience doth not folly prove;
> But among all the follies that I know
> The sweetest folly in the world is love.
>
> But not that passion which by fools' consent
> Above the reason bears imperious sway,
> Making their lifetime a perpetual Lent,
> As if a man were born to fast and pray.
>
> . . . Yet have I been a lover by report:
> Yea, I have died for love, as others do.
> But praised be God, it was in such a sort
> That I revived within an hour or two.

Robert Ker, Earl of Ancrum (1578-1654), was born too late to have been a Castalian, but he seems to have kept up the tradition of the literary courtier—too much so, in fact, in not condescending to print, for all his work to survive is a copy, in the Drummond MSS., of one fine sonnet in praise of a life of quiet. Patrick Hannay may be placed beside this group, though his earliest known work was not printed till 1619, and he was soldier and civil servant rather than courtier [49]. *A Happy Husband* is a companion piece to the very popular *Wife* of the English Overbury. *Philomela, or the Nightingale*, based on Ovid, suggests an earlier date: it has one hundred and ten stanzas resembling those of *The Cherrie and the Slae*, and a tune for singing. Apart from what must have been formidable lung-power, Hannay's most notable quality is the strong eighteenth-century anticipation (again) in *Sheretine and Mariana*, a romance from Austro-Hungarian history (though in sixains, not couplet)*, and along with that the light on the social habit of the age shown by the dedication of *Songs and Sonnets* to an exceedingly tough professional soldier, Sir Andrew Gray, who was also, it

---

* *Sheretine and Mariana*, with its passion and melodrama, seems to be the only Scots contribution—and a slight one—to the seventeenth-century vogue of verse romance represented in England by Bosworth, Kynaston, Chalkhill, Chamberlayne and others. It is peculiar, however, in being written in the first person as by the heroine, a favourite device of the early writers of prose fiction.—*Editor.*

seems, a poet in his spare time. Hannay's work, as with many amateurs, would have gained if he had taken the time to make it shorter. Braced by the sonnet, he can be graceful, however.

> As doth Solsequium, lover of the light,
> Experienced Nature in this latter age,
> Willing her masterpiece should then be wrought,
> Such my fair Coelia set on earth's large stage,
> As all the Gods in emulation brought,
> For they did think, if Nature only might
> Brag of her work, she should insult o'er them,
> Wherefore they agree'd to have an equal right,
> That they of her perfection part might claim.
> Pallas gave wisdom, Juno stateliness,
> And the mild Morning gave her modesty,
> The Graces, carriage, Venus loveliness,
> And chaste Diana choicest chastity:
> Thus Heaven and Earth their powers did combine
> To make her perfect. Kind Love, make her mine.

One Patrick Gordon (who may have been the later lively historian of *Britenes Distemper*, and in that case was a son of the Laird of Ruthven), was publishing Latin poems of mourning for Prince Henry and congratulations to his sister on her marriage, in London in 1614. Next year he had two books published at Dort—*The Famous Historie of Penardo and Laissa . . . done into Heroick Verse*, and *The Famous Valiant Historie of . . . Robert surnamed the Bruce* [50]. This is generous-hearted, patriotic stuff, and its octaves have echoes of Spenser and Ariosto: but Bannockburn was a greater thing than his models could teach him to handle, and it proved too much for the muse of Patrick Gordon.

All this last group belonged almost as much to Charles's reign as his father's, and their centre was as much London as Edinburgh. But two of the most notable 'courtly' figures remained, apart from travel, and in one case war and exile, in their own country. Much the lesser man but the more important poet of these was William Drummond of Hawthornden [51]. He was born with a background of both court and letters, for his father was one of the King's Gentlemen Ushers, and his mother was a sister of William Fowler. What Milton's nephew (who was to be his posthumous editor) describes as his 'polite and verdant genius' belongs to the same type as Milton's own, or Gray's. They are not in the same class, or even the same kind, but they all have the same mode of vision: perception of life is mediated for them by a wide and familiar knowledge of literature. This does not mean that they perceive untruly. Nor is such a vision of necessity insincere or artificial: to see life through art is quite as natural and can rouse quite as genuine an emotion as to see it through natural science or economics. It is apt to make the poet a little withdrawn, casting a crystal coolness over his colour, and it *can* make him frigid: but possibly its chief danger is the temptation it sets before editors to blind readers with clouds of parallels and sources. The scholarly editor who is himself no poet may conceivably miss two points of some importance—that if borrowings are wide and rich enough, their synthesis may be highly original, and that (to take an instance from Drummond himself) the poet may take a mere *précieuseté* of the egregious Pontus de Tyard, and turn it into genuine poetry.

Drummond was well read in half a dozen languages, adding Spanish to the usual French and Italian [52]. His outlook is conservative on the whole. He loved Ronsard, but had small use for Malherbe: his classic is that of Mansart, Inigo Jones or William Bruce, not that of Gabriel or Athenian Stuart. Historically, one can see in him a belated Castalian. He shows the Castalian pleasure in the handling of words and rhythms for their own sake. His best work, where he uses his exquisite technique to express something that has been deeply felt, may take images from Italian, French or Spanish, but in the total effect has a grave cool Northern quality of its own. His congenial forms are the sonnet, in which he is a master, and the short madrigal. The latter are sometimes mere toys, even ribald occasionals, but the best have a delicate sculptured quality:

> Like the Idalian Queene,
> Her Hair about her Eyne,
> With Necke and Brests ripe Apples to be seene,
> At first Glance of the Morne,
> In Cyprus Gardens gathering those faire Flowrs
> Which of her Bloud were borne,
> I saw, but fainting saw, my Paramours.
>
> The Graces naked danc'd about the Place,
> The Winds and Trees amaz'd
> With silence on Her gaz'd,
> The Flowrs did smile, like those upon her Face,
> And as their Aspine Stalkes those Fingers band
> (That Shee might read my Case)
> A Hyacinth I wisht mee in her Hand.

Of the sonnets, the greatest is the well-known, and magnificent, 'John Baptist', with its foreshadowing of Milton. Less known are the noble 'Content and Resolute' (*Flowres of Sion*, xxiv); or, in a mood more usual with him:

> I know that all beneath the *Moone* decayes,
> And what by Mortals in this World is brought,
> In *Times* great periods shall returne to nought,
> That fairest States have fatal Nights and Dayes:

64

> I know how all the *Muses* heavenly Layes,
> With Toyle of Spright that are so dearely bought,
> As idle sounds, of few or none are sought,
> And that nought lighter is than airie Praise.
> I know frail *Beautie* like the purple Flowre
> To which one Morne oft Birth and Death affords,
> That Love a Jarring is of Mindes Accords,
> Where *Sense* and *Will* invassal *Reasons* power.
> Know what I list, this all cannot mee move
> But that (ô me!) I both must write and love.

'An Hymne of the Fairest Fair', on 'the Nature, Attributes, and Works of God', may have been suggested by Ronsard, though the suggestion is much amplified, and technically it is forward-looking, in a stopped couplet whose clear, noble movement is beautifully fingered. There is something of the same quality in 'The Shadow of the Iudgement', an unfinished Doomsday-piece, baroque in imagery but not in form.

The recluse of Hawthornden was highly reputed, and an official request for a speech of greeting to James VI in 1618 brought that delightful piece of work, *Forth Feasting*. Its fervour may startle the modern reader a little, though in fact by the conventions of the time its bouquets are no more hypocritical than I when I assure Dear Mrs. Smith I am Hers very truly at the end of a letter designed to get out of dining with the woman because I cannot stand her at any price. And there was in fact some cause for a certain warmth. James at seventeen had taken over a Scotland which for years had been a mere welter of civil war: now it could look back to twenty-odd years of peace, and forward too to almost another twenty before his son cowped the carefully balanced creel. Drummond brought to the business some of his best writing, and the thing is done in a beautiful swift couplet, with a lovely evocative handling of proper names. Its success brought a similar request in 1633 to handle the elaborate pageantries of Charles I's coronation entry to the capital, and here again the verse has much grace and charm.

One feels less assurance, however, as if Drummond foresaw what was to happen before five years had gone. He loved balance and sanity in more than verse: an Episcopalian, and a sincerely devout one, he could get on with the moderate Presbyterians: but he loathed the increasing dominance of the extremists responsible for the second Covenant. His late fierce satire, *A Character of the Anti-Covenanter or Malignant*, crashes into the delicate texture of his work, making a man of the Cant or Warriston school describe a Royalist in such a fashion that he reveals himself. Its blistering satire is merely a development, however, of the broad comedy that can emerge from his moonlight. It is not quite certain, but probable enough (though we cannot date it), that he did write the macaronic *Polemo-middinia* [53], a mock-heroic tale of a Fife village feud, in a rich amalgam of Latin and (very) broad Scots:

Nymphae quae colitis highissima monta Fifaea,
Seu vos Pittenwema tenent, seu Crelia crofta,
Sive Anstraea domus, ubi nat haddocus in undis,
Codlineusque ingens, et fleucca et sketta pererrant   [*flounder*
Per costam, et scopulis lobster monyfootus in udis
Creepat, et in mediis ludit whitenius undis,
Et vos skipperii . . .
Whistlantesque simul fechtam memorate bloodaeam,
Fechtam terribilem, quam marvellaverit omnis
Banda Deum et Nympharum Cockelshelleatarum
Maia ubi sheepifeda atque ubi solgoosifera Bassa
Suellant in pelago . . .

Drummond's serious work is the link between two ages. The early links him to the Castalians; the later, especially that in the couplet, takes up and goes beyond those hints in theirs which look forward to the age of Gallicized classic, to Corneille and Racine, to Dryden, Pope and, as the wheel came slowly round, to Gray. But the harvest of those seeds did not spring in Scots letters: though the spirit that formed them quickened before very long, it was not in writing but in stone and lime [54]. The courtly tradition in verse, the accomplishment of the soldier-courtier-scholar, died the year after Drummond, on a dark May day at Edinburgh Cross, when Montrose swung there in three fathoms of a rope. And though his life was charged, and his death more, with the very essence of great poetry, what survives of his verse is no more than a handful of casual odds and ends—in effect, little more than the fantastic blend of personal passion and political in 'My dear and only love', with its one perfect quatrain that was for him no brag—

He either fears his Fate too much
Or his Deserts are small
That puts it not unto the Touch,
To win or lose it all—

and two brief fierce epigrams, one on his own coming death, one on his master's, written, says a contemporary, 'with the point of his sword' . . . and if that is not fact (which it certainly is not) it is a figure that expresses truth [55].

More memory than we are apt to think may have carried on across the dismal decade that divides Montrose's death from the Restoration, at any rate in the Royalist and Episcopalian North-East [56]. The pleasant collection of *Cantus, Songs, and Fancies*, composed 'for the

Musick Schoole of Aberdene' in 1662, credits that city with for its Town Council 'a harmonious heavenly concert of as many musicians as magistrates' [57], and gives their children some pretty things to sing that show the courtly tradition still remembered. The songs come from as far back as Alexander Scott, with three, perhaps four, of Montgomerie's, and various agreeable anonyms, not known elsewhere but certainly Scots, though some English songs are included. Not all are courtly: one must mention, for love of the deathless Rittmeister, the obvious original of his favourite ditty,

> When cannons are roaring and bullets are flying,
> He that would honour win must not fear dying;

and there is what looks like (though in Scotland of course it need not be) a folkpiece, 'The gowans are gay, my jo', and a strange lovely carol, 'Jesus to us, to God a Son', done Scots fashion in the Johannine terms of light. The courtly tradition—one would say a latish example—shows in the charming 'In a garden so green' and that other, lovely in parts, though it needs cutting:

> Where art thou, hope, that promised me relief?
> Come, hear thy doom pronounced by disdain.
> Alas, sweet hope,
> Where is thy scope,
> Or where shalt thou remain?
> Since hope is gone, and cannot me remeid,
> In bondage thus I must bide Fortune's feid,
> I must bide Fortune's feid.

And so was it also for the Lowland Muse, whose crown, for a long generation, passed to Gaelic.

III

THE RENAISSANCE POETS

(2) LATIN

JAMES W. L. ADAMS

I

ONE of the consequences of the Renaissance was a tremendous enthusiasm for Latin verse composition, since the discovery, or renewed study, of ancient Latin authors led to attempts to imitate them in language and theme. The accentual Latin poetry of the Middle Ages, hymns such as Abelard's 'O quanta, qualia', drinking-songs such as the famous 'Mihi est propositum', the love-songs of the 'Archpoet' and the Benedictbeuern Manuscript were now rejected, and replaced by Ovidian elegiacs, Virgilian eclogues, Horatian odes and Lucretian didactic. The movement started in Italy, and some of the greatest exponents of this new *imitatio veterum* were Italians. 'Ability to write Latin verse', said Guarino of Verona (1374-1460), 'is one of the essential marks of an educated person'. With the spread of Renaissance ideals in education and culture there went the writing of Latin verses. The movement reached Scotland about the year 1500 [1].

The output throughout Western Europe was enormous. In the early years of the seventeenth century Janus Gruter, a Dutchman whose mother was English, produced a series of *Delitiae*, anthologies of the Latin verse of various countries. In the French collection (three volumes, containing about 100,000 lines in all) 108 poets are represented; the 'Belgian' (Dutch) collection has 129 names, the Italian has 203 and the German 211. In 1637 a Scottish *Delitiae* on Gruter's model appeared at Amsterdam, edited by Sir John Scot of Scotstarvet and Arthur Johnston. It omits Buchanan, the greatest of them all, but it contains thirty-seven names. *Musa Latina Aberdonensis*, which confines itself to poets from the North-east, adds about as many names again; probably over a hundred Scots had their verses published at one time or another, and there are others whose work has never been printed.

These 'neo-Latin' poets attract little attention nowadays. Very few scholars in Britain or on the Continent work in this field, though in America there would seem to be slightly more interest, not only among classical scholars but among students of English and other modern literatures. There are various reasons for this neglect. Latin is a difficult language, and few reach the stage of being able to read it fluently enough, without a translation, to appreciate it as literature.

68

Most people who do have this ability are professional classical scholars, who are naturally more interested in the ancient Romans themselves, and in their literature as a witness to ancient civilization in general, than in the productions of people who were writing in an idiom artificially resuscitated after a thousand years. Nor can it be denied that much of what was written, what Mark Pattison called 'the ocean of mediocre Latin verse which the sixteenth century bequeathed to us', deserves neglect. A great deal of it consists of dull odes written in flattery of forgotten potentates, frigid didactic poems embellished with a stucco of classical mythology, and invectives whose interest was necessarily ephemeral. Few of the neo-Latins had much originality. Their professed task was to imitate the ancients; and this blight of imitation had infected the ancients themselves. The all-pervading influence of rhetoric in education during the Roman imperial period resulted in an emphasis on form rather than matter. We are aware of this pernicious influence as early as Virgil; by the time of Ausonius and Sidonius Apollinaris it had completely spoiled Latin literature: and the Renaissance poets took up the work where Ausonius had left off. The modern reader should therefore be warned before starting upon the neo-Latins. He must not expect striking originality. He must not expect sublimity, passion or lyric fervour. The absence of such lyrical feeling even in classical Latin is noted, for example, by E. E. Sikes in his book on Roman poetry. Mr. John Sparrow has well illustrated the weakness of modern Latin verse in writing of Milton, 'who when he wrote in Latin ceased to be a poet and became an imitator'. Mr. Sparrow has produced two delightful little collections of *Poems in Latin* (incidentally, containing no Scottish contributions except by the modern J. W. Mackail). His aim was to choose authors who wrote poetry, not verse. And Professor H. W. Garrod doubts if much more that is truly poetry could be gathered. 'If Mr. Sparrow ran to a third booklet, verily I believe he would run out of poetry into verse. He would run into that kind of accomplishment which I think not worth while in this after-the-war world; a world dying for want of poetry' [2].

Practically all neo-Latin writers give the impression that their work is a pastiche; and the more Latin one knows the more frequent are the classical tags and reminiscences which one discovers, those 'fragments of antiquity with which Latin poetry ought always to be inlaid' [3]. Often, no doubt, the writers were even imitating imitations; they had got the phrases from Vida, Fracastoro, Pontanus, rather than from Virgil or Ovid. But this artificiality in language inevitably makes a modern reader wonder whether the feelings expressed are likewise artificial or conventional. 'He that courts his mistress with Roman imagery', said Dr. Johnson, 'deserves to lose her; for she may with good reason suspect his sincerity.'

The classical scholar is often repelled from the neo-Latins for one more reason—their metrical shortcomings. Far too many of them yield a crop of false quantities which make modern students of metre wince. It is said, for instance, that the great Porson was once persuaded to read Buchanan, of whom he had never heard, but threw him away after reading a page or two because he discovered a false quantity [4]. Some of these false quantities are probably due to the inferior texts then in use; some may have been caused by the influence of spoken Latin; but the blemish remains.

The quality of neo-Latin verse is often not high: but some of the best exponents of the art were Scots, and the number of Scots who attempted it during the sixteenth and seventeenth centuries is, relatively to other countries, astonishingly large. The best English writers, Gray, Vincent Bourne, John Jortin, Landor, belong to the period after 1700, when Latin verse composition was fostered at the great public schools and practised as an elegant pastime by gentlemen. From 1500 to 1650 the Scots far outnumber the English. Johnson admitted that 'the Latin poetry of the *Delitiae Poetarum Scotorum* would have done honour to any nation: at least until the publication of May's Supplement [to Lucan, 1640] the English had very little to oppose' [5]. And Macaulay in the first chapter of his *History* also pays tribute to the 'indisputable superiority in mental cultivation' of the Scots, who 'wrote Latin verse with more than the delicacy of Vida'. The Scots of the period were conscious of their skill: in 1614 John Barclay published his *Icon Animorum*, the fourth part of his *Satyricon*, in which he outlines the talents of the various European nations. Of the Scots, he says, 'animi illis in quaecumque studia inclinant mirifico successu inclyti, ut nullis maior patientia castrorum, vel audacia pugnae, et Musae nunquam delicatius habeant quam cum inciderunt in Scotos' [6]. The Scots had long been less insular than the English. Even in the days of the school-men the number of Scottish scholars is striking; and then came the famous wandering scholars of the Renaissance. 'Scots are everywhere', said one of them, John Leech, writing early in the seventeenth century:

> Scotus ubique latet, nusquam vestigia figit;
> Perque soli longas it, pelagique vias.

Many of them were doubtless, like Ninian Winzet, 'nocht acquyntit with your Southeroun'; and at a time when their native tongue was being little exploited for literary purposes, when the Latin which they used daily in the classroom gave access to an international audience and promise of immortality, they naturally chose that vehicle for their verse. The comparative dearth of poets in the vernacular at this time should therefore be offset by the writings of the scholars, although it cannot be denied that their choice impoverished their native literature, even as their European domicile must often have deprived their native country of cultural and political leaders.

The Scots neo-Latinists can be divided fairly conveniently into three groups, which coincide with the periods of ascendancy of three forms of the Christian religion:—(1) The period before Buchanan, ending about 1560. The writers, for example 'John Ireland' (Johannes de Irlandia), James Foulis, Roderick Maclean, are still Roman Catholics, and the spirit of their work is still partly mediaeval, although the influence of the Renaissance can be seen in their choice of metres. (2) The Presbyterian period, dominated by Buchanan, from 1560 to 1615 (the date of the complete Edinburgh edition of his works). Buchanan's prestige clearly stimulated younger poets, such as Andrew Melville, Thomas Maitland, John Johnston, Mark Alexander Boyd, Sir Thomas Craig the lawyer, and Patrick Adamson, who later went over to the Episcopalian side. (3) The Episcopalian period. The leading figures of the earlier generation had now been removed by death or exile. Their successors were Sir Robert Aytoun, John Leech, Andrew Aidie, John Barclay, David Hume of Godscroft and (greatest of them all) Arthur Johnston. Many of the poets of this period were encouraged by Drummond of Hawthornden, who did not himself compose in Latin, and by his brother-in-law, Scot of Scotstarvet; and their achievement culminated in the publication of the *Delitiae* in 1637. Finally, in the years following the Restoration, Scots neo-Latin poetry had a not unworthy swansong in the works of Ninian Paterson and Archibald Pitcairne.

From the Middle Ages little has been preserved. Worthy of mention, however, are the lines of unknown date on the death of Wallace, beginning:—

> Invida Mors tristi Gulielmum funere Vallam,
> Quae cuncta tollit, sustulit. [7]

It is indeed, as Irving says, 'highly improbable that this ode was composed at so remote a period', but it is probably quite early, and it is not without significance that patriotism should supply the theme. The three Latin hymns of John Ireland sent by him to James III from Paris show, as their editor says, 'taste and metrical accuracy, if a rather conventional imagination' [8]. In 1510, at Paris, appeared the first Latin verse published by a Scotsman, the *Calamitose pestis elega deploratio et alia quedam carmina*, by James Foulis of Colinton, later an eminent lawyer in the reign of James V [9]. The early period is of importance rather for its formative influence than for the actual merit of the work produced. The Renaissance, with its emphasis on *imitatio veterum*, seems indeed to have penetrated the Arts curriculum in Scotland before it succeeded in displacing the schoolmen in the 'higher' studies of philosophy and theology. Even acknowledged scholastics like John Mayor could compose, and the importance of educationists such as

Cuthbert Simson, Boece and John Vaus in this connexion has yet to be evaluated [10]. By the reign of James V there are several Latin poets connected with the court. Here the young Buchanan composed the *Somnium* (a free rendering of 'How Dunbar was desyrit to be ane Fryer'), and the *Franciscanus*, which were later to bring him into trouble with the Inquisition, and here Ronsard received instruction in poetry from 'un gentil-homme Escossois, nommé le Seigneur Paul, tresbon poëte Latin' [11]. The mediaeval note is still predominant in the two books of odes in Horatian metres published in 1549 by Roderick Maclean (*d.* 1553), the last pre-Reformation Bishop of the Isles. They celebrate, in quite skilful verse, the legends and miracles connected with St. Columba and his disciples (*De Intuitu Prophetico d. Columbae* and *De Virtutibus et Miraculis d. Columbae*). To this period, too, belongs 'Florence Wilson' (Florentius Volusenus, *c.* 1504-1551), 'the earliest of the wandering Scots who achieved fame in Latin poetry' [12]. His poems, of which four are printed in the *Delitiae*, are undistinguished, and he is more justly remembered for his philosophical prose work *De Animi Tranquillitate* (Lyons, 1543, and frequently reprinted). Wilson's death at Vienne, while he was returning to Scotland, was commemorated by Buchanan, who knew him, in an epitaph classical in its touching brevity:

> Hic Musis, Volusene, iaces carissime, ripam
> Ad Rhodani, terra quam procul a patria!
> Hoc meruit virtus tua, tellus quae foret altrix
> Virtutum, ut cineres conderet illa tuos.*

2

The second period is dominated by the greatest of all Scots Latin poets, George Buchanan (1506-82) [13]. A brief autobiography in Latin gives us the main outlines of his career, which can be filled in here and there from other sources. Born near Killearn, he studied at Paris and St. Andrews, taught in Paris, Bordeaux and Coimbra, was tutor to various eminent people including James VI, and after his return to Scotland about 1561 played a considerable part in the turbulent politics and religious disputes of the period. His Latin history of Scotland and his tract on political theory, *De Iure Regni apud Scotos*, would by themselves be a sufficient claim to a permanent place in literature, but it was first and foremost as a Latin poet that his contemporaries and succeeding generations sang his praises. This they did in no half-hearted fashion. Much admired by Ascham and Sir Philip Sidney, he

---

* 'Here, Wilson, beloved of the Muses, thou liest by the banks of the Rhône, far indeed from thy native land. This thy virtue deserved, that the land which fosters virtues should hold thine ashes.'

was hailed by the younger Scaliger, himself the most influential scholar of the period, as 'unus in tota Europa omnes post se relinquens in Latina poesi', and H. Stephanus considered him to be 'poetarum nostri saeculi facile princeps'. Two centuries after his death Dr. Johnson could still speak of him as 'the only man of genius his country ever produced' (a dictum which, in the mouth of a contemporary of Hume, can only make Scotsmen smile), and as one 'whose name has as fair a claim to immortality as can be conferred by modern Latinity'. Johnson, who was well read in the neo-Latinists and no bad judge of their productions, elsewhere remarks that Buchanan 'used fewer centos than any modern poet' [14]. This fact, noticed also by Professor Bradner and Dr. Naiden, makes Buchanan's work more attractive to a modern reader. Although, like all Renaissance poets, he has his share of what Mark Pattison called 'the felicities of imitative diction which relieve the monotony of the modern Latinists' set themes', the general impression given is of a man so thoroughly steeped in the language that he was its master, not its servant, and could use it as a vehicle to express his own personality. The influence of many classical writers is of course obvious (reminiscences of Claudian are particularly noticeable), but, on the whole, in language and style, he was 'nullius addictus iurare in verba magistri'.

Buchanan's work is so varied—satire, drama, elegy, pastoral, epigram, ode, didactic and translation—that it is difficult in small space to deal adequately with it. Among his earliest writings are the *Somnium* (in elegiacs) and *Franciscanus* (in hexameters) already mentioned, satirical pieces attacking the hypocrisy and corruption of the Franciscans, which were composed with the approval of James V. The *Franciscanus* is too long for modern taste (over 900 lines), and recalls the lengthy mediaeval diatribe rather than the shorter satires of Horace and Juvenal. But the rhetoric is well sustained, and Buchanan seasons his trenchant invective with a humour which one may be pardoned for calling typically Scots. Scots too, we feel, despite precedents in the Latin satirists, is the frequent coarseness. The result is a work which contrives to remind the modern reader at once of Juvenal and of Burns. Satire in more palatable doses is also found in the elegiac and iambic poems against loose women. The ladies in question were in all probability imaginary, and Buchanan was simply following a fashion established by Catullus and Horace and taken up with enthusiasm by the Renaissance poets.

The three books of 'epigrams' are much more pleasing. The word is used in its classical sense (as, for example, by Martial), to include epitaphs and laudatory poems as well as satire. Many of the epitaphs have a classical terseness. The lines on Florence Wilson have already been quoted. Another fine example is the poem on André de Gouvéa, the man whom Montaigne called 'sans comparaison le plus grand principal de France' (*Essais*, I. xxv), and who had invited Buchanan to his staff, first at Bordeaux and then at Coimbra:

> Alite non fausta genti dum rursus Iberae
> Restituis Musas, hic, Goveane, iaces.
> Cura tui Musis fuerit si mutua, nulla
> Incolet Elysium clarior umbra nemus.*

The conciseness and point of the satiric epigrams are well illustrated in the two familiar couplets:

> Frustra ego te laudo, frustra me, Zoile, laedis:
> Nemo mihi credit, Zoile, nemo tibi,†

and:

> Sylvius hic situs est, gratis qui nil dedit unquam:
> Mortuus et, gratis quod legis ista, dolet.‡

As a last example, the lines on Neaera, his fictitious love, may be quoted:

> Illa mihi semper praesenti dura Neaera,
> Me, quoties absum, semper abesse dolet.
> Non desiderio nostri, non moeret amore,
> Sed se non nostro posse dolore frui.§

Two of Buchanan's finest complimentary poems are connected with Mary, Queen of Scots, of whom he, like so many of his countrymen, had the highest hopes. One is the dedication of his translation of the Psalms, beginning

> Nympha, Caledoniae quae nunc feliciter orae
> Missa per innumeros sceptra tueris avos,
> Quae sortem antevenis meritis, virtutibus annos,
> Sexum animis, morum nobilitate genus,||

---

* 'Under an unlucky star, Gouvéa, didst thou bring back the Muses to the Iberian people: for here thou liest. If the Muses have as much care for thee as thou hadst for them, no shade in the Elysian grove shall have greater glory.'

† 'In vain do I honour thee, Zoilus, in vain dost thou dishonour me. None believeth me, or thee.'

‡ 'Here lies Sylvius, who never gave anything for nothing. Even when dead, he grieves that there is no charge for reading this.'

§ 'Neaera is ever hard when I am with her, yet ever she grieves when I am absent. It is not for yearning, or love of me that she pines, but because she cannot enjoy my torture.'

|| 'Nymph who now with heaven's favour holdest the sceptre of the Caledonian land, the sceptre handed down through countless generations, whose deserts surpass thy lot, whose virtues thy years, whose courage thy sex, and nobility thy lofty race.'

and ending with the graceful compliment that his version owes its
preservation solely to the favour that it had found in her sight. The
other is the Epithalamium on Mary's marriage to the Dauphin (*Sylvae*,
iv), justly famous for the magnificent passage describing the Scotland
and the Scots whom Mary brings as dowry—'Accipe dotales Mavortia
pectora Scotos' [15]—the Scotland which had provided France with
allies in her hours of victory and defeat:

> sine milite Scoto
> Nulla umquam Francis fulsit victoria castris,
> Nulla umquam Hectoridas sine Scoto sanguine clades
> Saevior oppressit. [16]

In his poems on public affairs Buchanan sometimes challenged
comparison with Horace by his use of the Alcaic metre for political or
moral themes. Examples are the ode on the capture of Calais by the
French in 1558 (triumphal, of course, for England was still the 'auld
enemy'), and the earlier ode on the allegorical love of his patron, the
Maréchal de Brissac, for Arete (the personification of moral worth).
The concluding stanzas will give some idea of the tone, the celebration
of virtue which recalls Horace (*Odes* III. ii. 17 ff.) and, as Bradner says,
anticipates Milton:

> O diva, custos pacis amabilis,
> Bellique formidabilis arbitra,
> Quae iura fatorum superba
> Non metuis, dominasque Parcas!

> Fac ne maligni iniuria temporis
> Tot vestri amoris pignora deleat,
> Aut obruat caecae sepulta
> Sub tenebris taciturnitatis.*

To the same class of political poem, though in a different metre, may
be assigned the Genethliacon on the future James VI. Its hexameters
recall Virgil's fourth Eclogue, which also celebrated the birth of a
child who was to see the world reborn to a happier age. But Buchanan
was by this time (1566) having doubts about the ability of the Stewarts
to reign unaided, and he took the opportunity to preach a sermon on
the ideal king. The concept is Stoic, and can be traced back to the
Hellenistic age, but Buchanan's treatment gives a foretaste of his *De
Iure Regni*. Nothing, we are told, can surpass a 'moderate' king, but
God himself will punish the tyrant. James will have an empire wider

---

* 'Goddess, guardian of winsome peace, and arbitress of dread war, who
fearest not the haughty decrees of destiny and all-powerful Fates! Grant that
the assaults of envious time destroy not these pledges of your mutual love,
or bury them unsung in the darkness of the tomb.'

than Alexander's if he can rule himself as well as his subjects—'Si poterit rex esse sui, rex esse suorum.' It is tempting to speculate how much of James's doctrine of Divine Right was a reaction against his tutor [17]. Less successful as a philosophical poem than the odes to de Brissac and James is the lament written in 1564 on the death of Calvin. Again there is the praise of virtue, but Buchanan does not take advantage of his opportunity to set forth Calvin's theology, and turns aside to attack Roman Catholics. Despite these attacks, one wonders if he was yet (or ever) a very enthusiastic reformer: his sentiments were orthodox enough only six years earlier when he celebrated the capture of Calais.

The famous ode on the 'Calendae Maiae', much admired by Wordsworth despite its false quantity, offers a convenient transition from the official to the personal side of Buchanan's poetry. Here is perhaps the finest example of his power to put new wine in old bottles, to blend the pagan joy in spring—the joy expressed, for example, in the *Pervigilium Veneris*—with Christian hope of immortality. The second half of the poem will show how the themes are connected:

> Talis beatis incubat insulis
> Felicis aurae perpetuus tepor,
>   Et nesciis campis senectae
>   Difficilis, querulique morbi.
>
> Talis silentum per tacitum nemus
> Levi susurrat murmure spiritus,
>   Lethenque iuxta obliviosam
>   Funereas agitat cupressos.
>
> Forsan supremis cum Deus ignibus
> Piabit orbem, laetaque saecula
>   Mundo reducet, talis aura
>   Aethereos animos fovebit.
>
> Salve fugacis gloria saeculi,
> Salve secunda digna dies nota,
>   Salve vetustae vitae imago,
>   Et specimen venientis aevi.*

* 'Even such the never-failing warmth of the kindly breeze that broods over the isles of the blest, over the plains that know not crabbed age or carping disease. Even such the breath that whispers with gentle murmur through the silent groves of the shades, and lightly sways the mournful cypresses beside forgetful Lethe. Perchance when God cleanses the world with the last fires, and brings back the age of joy to the earth, such will be the air that warms ethereal spirits. Hail, glory of the fleeting years, hail day well worthy of joyful mark, hail image of the spring-time of the world, foretaste of life that is to be.'

The collection of *Sylvae*, which contains the Epithalamium on Mary and Francis and the Genethliacon of James, also provides two fine examples of Buchanan's method of adapting the classical pastoral; these are the lament for an absent friend Ptolomaeus Luxius Tastaeus and the 'Desiderium Lutetiae'. In the latter, the conventional 'bucolic masquerade' of the amatory pastoral is used to express his longing, from Portugal, for 'Amaryllis'—apparently an allegorical way of referring to Paris [18]. The atmosphere is reminiscent of 'Lycidas', with which the 'Desiderium' is compared by Bradner, and the emotion portrayed, although not as deep as Milton's, seems genuine enough. But the main attraction of the poem is probably its delightfully neat versification. The poet addresses the winds, that are able to blow across the sea and visit his lady:

> O quoties Euro, levibus cum raderet alis
> Aequora, dicebam 'Felix Amaryllide visa
> Dic mihi num meminit nostri? num mutua sentit
> Vulnera? num veteris vivunt vestigia flammae?'*

Two Portuguese damsels try to supplant Amaryllis, but in vain:

> Et prius aequoribus pisces et montibus umbrae,
> Et volucres deerunt silvis, et murmura ventis,
> Quam mihi discedent formosae Amaryllidos ignes:
> Illa meum rudibus succendit pectora flammis,
> Finiet illa meos moriens morientis amores.†

If 'Amaryllis' does stand for Paris, the iambic poem 'Adventus in Galliam' offers a pleasant pendant to the 'Desiderium'. The cheerful, tripping metre is well chosen to express the poet's joy at his return to his beloved France:

> Ieiuna miserae tesqua Lusitaniae,
> Glebaeque, tantum fertiles penuriae,
> Valete longum. At tu beata Gallia
> Salve bonarum blanda nutrix artium,

---

* 'How often have I said to the East wind, when with light wings it skimmed the sea, "Happy thou that hast seen Amaryllis, tell me, doth she remember me? Are her wounds of love equal to mine? Do traces of the ancient passion still remain?" '

† 'And sooner shall the seas lose their fishes, the mountains their shadows, the woods their birds, and the winds their murmurs, than my love for the fair Amaryllis depart from me: she it was who first kindled the flame in my heart; she it will be who in death brings to an end the love in my dying breast.'

Caelo salubri, fertili frugum solo,
Umbrosa colles pampini molli coma,
Pecorosa saltus, rigua valles fontibus,
Prati virentis picta campos floribus,
Velifera longis amnium decursibus.*

Buchanan had not always had such a high opinion of all things French. An early poem, 'On the sad lot of Latin teachers in Paris', draws a vivid picture of the hardships of a sixteenth-century don—long hours, little pay, unresponsive pupils: the teacher carries his whip in one hand and his Virgil in the other:

Dextera crudeli in pueros armata flagello est:
Laeva tenet magni forte Maronis opus.

While he was a teacher at Bordeaux he translated the *Medea* and *Alcestis* of Euripides into Latin, and wrote two original plays for the boys to perform, on the stories of Jephtha and John the Baptist. The *Baptistes* was once thought to allude to the Scottish court, James V being Herod, Patrick Hamilton perhaps the Baptist, Beaton Malchus, and so on. But during his trial before the Inquisition Buchanan said that he meant to represent, 'quantum materiae similitudo patiebatur', the accusation and death of Sir Thomas More, and we need not doubt his word. Then Herod will be Henry VIII, and Herodias, presumably, Anne Boleyn. The plays are probably the least attractive of all Buchanan's writings. For one thing, many of the rules of Latin dramatic prosody were not discovered until long after his time, and there are inevitably metrical faults. Moreover, his model was Seneca (although the prologues are Terentian), and Seneca, despite his great influence at the Renaissance, was never 'good theatre'. There are the usual monologues and rhetorical declamations; there are classical allusions that are ludicrously out of place, and anachronisms such as the reference to Vesuvius as a volcano in *Baptistes* (296). Jephtha's daughter, who is called Iphis, is strongly reminiscent of Iphigeneia and Polyxena in Euripides. Buchanan had no gift as a dramatist. His only other attempt at writing for the stage was after his return to Scotland, when he composed Latin masques for the court of Mary. From one of them we have a fine ode 'In castitatem', which, as Bradner says, 'must have seemed sufficiently out of place'.

---

* 'A long farewell, ye hungry deserts of wretched Portugal, ye fields fertile only in penury. But thou, blessed Gaul, all hail, kindly nurse of civilization, with thy healthy air, soil fruitful in corn, hills shaded by the vine's soft foliage, glades rich in cattle, well-watered vales, green meadow-flats painted with flowers, the long courses of thy rivers with their countless ships.'

The union of classical metrical form and non-classical material is also seen in the famous version of the Psalms which Buchanan composed during his captivity in Portugal. One cannot but admire his great metrical facility (he uses about thirty different metres, mostly lyrical), yet, despite their tremendous popularity at the time and long afterwards, for they were still in use as a school-book in Scotland in the nineteenth century, his versions seem nowadays rather absurd hybrids, and can hardly be considered more than a lengthy *tour de force*. It should be remembered, however, that the taste of his age differed from ours, and, of the many versions produced by Latinists, Buchanan's was generally regarded as supreme. Over seventy editions have appeared. The first three verses of Psalm cxxxvii, on which he is thought to have bestowed especial pains, may serve as an example of how he expands his Vulgate original:

1. Dum procul a patria maesti Babylonis in oris,
    Fluminis ad liquidas forte sedemus aquas,
   Illa animum subiit species miseranda Sionis,
    Et numquam patrii tecta videnda soli.
   Flevimus, et gemitus luctantia verba repressit,
    Inque sinus liquidae decidit imber aquae.
2. Muta super virides pendebant nablia ramos,
    Et salices tacitas sustinuere lyras.
3. Ecce ferox dominus, Solymae populator opimae,
    Exigit in mediis carmina laeta malis:
   Qui patriam exsilio nobis mutavit acerbo,
    Nos iubet ad patrios verba referre modos,
   Quale canebamus, steterat dum celsa Sionis
    Regia, finitimis invidiosa locis.*

There remains the didactic poem in five books, *De Sphaera*, a treatise on astronomy begun for the benefit of de Brissac's son, and never completed, although Buchanan worked upon it after his return to Scotland. None of his works has evoked more varied judgments

---

* 'While haply far from our native country we sat sadly in the land of Babylon, by the liquid waters of a river, the sad vision of Sion came into our mind, and the abodes of our native soil that we must never see. We wept, and a groan choked our struggling words, and a rain of liquid water fell upon our bosoms.

'Our harps hung silent upon the green boughs, and the willows supported our voiceless lyres.

'Behold the fierce lord, spoiler of the wealth of Jesusalem, demands songs of joy in the midst of our woes: he who drove us from our native land in bitter exile orders us to sing the words of our country's songs, even as we sang while the lofty palace of Sion stood, the envy of surrounding peoples.'

from critics, but Hallam's opinion that it is the best of them all [19]
receives strong support from its recent editor, Dr. Naiden. Buchanan
holds, against Copernicus, that the earth is at rest in the centre of the
universe, and, against Tycho Brahe, that nothing can change in the
region above the moon (this despite evidence to the contrary such as
Tycho Brahe's *nova stella*). But for his material he rejects the mediaeval
prose treatise of Sacrobosco (himself, according to some, a Scot!)
which had held the field before the Renaissance, and draws directly
upon classical authors, especially the Greek astronomers Ptolemy and
Cleomedes, but also Pliny, Hyginus and Stobaeus. Despite his dis-
agreement with Tycho Brahe, Buchanan was apparently well informed
on contemporary astronomical work, and he devotes considerable
attention to current controversies, such as the habitability of the tropics,
on which subject the opinion of Posidonius had recently been confirmed by sailors, and the claims of astrology, which Buchanan
rejected, herein again differing from Tycho Brahe. Although, like
almost all didactic poems, the *Sphaera* has its dull stretches, the
idealism and faith which have already been noticed in the ode to de
Brissac and the 'Calendae Maiae' are here developed on an ampler
canvas, and Buchanan can be trusted to do his best, like his great model
Lucretius, 'quasi Musaeo dulci contingere melle'. Although Virgil,
Ovid, Manilius and other Latin poets as well as Lucretius are imitated,
he again contrives to impose himself on his language, so that the poem
does not give the impression of a cento. Some of the finest passages are
in the fifth book—the invective against astrologers, for example, and
the mythological episode inserted by way of traditional embellishment,
the story of Endymion, beloved of Diana, who reveals to him the
secret of why the moon is eclipsed. But perhaps the noblest lines of all
are those at the beginning of book V, where the poet, following Pliny,
and expanding a well-known passage in Ovid's *Fasti* (i, 297 ff.),
praises scientists and astronomers who for no selfish motive have
penetrated the secrets of nature:

> Macti animi heroes saeclis melioribus orti,
> Qui primi ingenii nixi pernicibus alis,
> Perque leves vecti stellas totque orbibus orbes
> Implicitos, magni intrastis penetralia caeli,
> Ausi ingens facinus, penitus penitusque repostas
> Naturae in latebris causas ratione sagaci
> Detexistis, et in caeca caligine mersi
> Certa ostendistis terris vestigia veri.
> Non caeca ambitio vobis, non blanda voluptas,
> Non vigiles curae, non lucri pallida tabes,
> Sublimes fregere animos, quin invia rerum
> Sensibus humanis mentis penetraret acumen,

Eque deum arcanis adytis per saecula longa
Astrorum erueret cassas interprete leges.*

Perhaps Buchanan was fortunate in the time of his appearance. The great age of the Italian Latinists was past, and his most gifted Continental contemporaries were turning more to scholarship than to original composition, while in England, with its richer vernacular, it was the generation of the Elizabethan translators. Wright and Sinclair [20] describe his personality as 'ill-tempered, pedantic and abusive', but one feels that they are taking the satirical pieces too seriously, and it would be just as easy to extract from his references to de Tève and Tastaeus, and from his correspondence, the picture of a kindly and devoted friend. Although he excelled in the hexameter, one must admire his versatility and all-round skill. Despite the poems on loose women (he even wrote a defence of a bawd to a Councillor of the Parlement of Bordeaux, but that, too, is a *jeu d'esprit*) his work as a whole breathes a lofty idealism which reminds us of Spenser and Milton rather than of the Renaissance Italians. His posthumous fame was tremendous; in all, seventeen editions of the *Poemata Omnia* were produced, the last in 1725. It was indeed ironical that the man whom Scaliger considered the 'supremum culmen' of poetry should be remembered by popular Scots tradition as a kind of rustic buffoon, almost the 'Jamie Fleeman' of James VI.

Andrew Melville (1545-1622), Buchanan's associate in religious policy, had at one time a considerable reputation as a Latin poet, being 'sometimes ranked second to Buchanan' [21]. Although he is in fact a mediocre poet, he holds a central position among the Scots Latinists of his generation, for at one time or another he was connected with Patrick Adamson, John Johnston, Hercules Rollock, Adam King and Sir Thomas Craig, and when in exile in his later years at Sedan he had Arthur Johnston as a colleague. (They can hardly have been congenial.) During his early residence in Geneva he composed a hexameter poem on the Creation and other Biblical paraphrases, including the Song of

---

* The following is Dr. Naiden's translation: 'O mighty souls, heroes born in happier time, you who were the first, relying on the swift wings of genius and borne through the light stars and through so many circles inside of circles, to penetrate the shrines of the vast sky—a tremendous deed to dare, yet you discovered the deeply, deeply hidden secrets of nature with sagacious reason, and showed undeniably the path of truth, at that time sunk in impenetrable darkness. Not by blinding ambition, nor by pleasurable delights of the flesh, nor by annoyances that keep men awake, nor by the pallid sickliness of profit-seeking was your sublime spirit broken; instead the acumen of the mind penetrated the pathless secrets of creation, inaccessible to the human senses, without the mind, and from the arcane shrines of the Gods in the course of long centuries it uncovered the laws of the stars, which had lacked expounders.'

Moses in Deuteronomy xxxii. (Basel, 1573). On his return to Scotland he became, after the death of Buchanan, a kind of unofficial Latin laureate to James VI, celebrating various events down to the Gunpowder Plot. Such poems, as Bradner says, must have been inspired by patriotism rather than personal regard for 'God's sillie vassal'. During the same period he began an epic, 'Gathelus', on the origin and history of the Scottish race. Only some one hundred and fifty lines are preserved, but they are enough to show that Melville had no gift in this direction [22]. He was also in the habit of writing satires and epigrams against his enemies, mostly Episcopalians, and a collection of these, *Musae*, appeared in 1620. Because of the Presbyterian sentiments expressed in one of his epigrams he was imprisoned for nearly four years in the Tower, and he spent the later years of his life in exile. In choosing Melville's contributions to the *Delitiae* the editors naturally omitted the poems directed against Episcopacy. His attack on the English universities is worth remembering, if only for its delightful title—'Antitamicamicategoria'. He also wrote several epitaphs, of which that on John Wallas is perhaps the best. Professor Bradner rightly praises its conclusion—'a conclusion worthy of Buchanan':

> Nunc stat cuique dies sua, est
> Aevi summa fugax irrevocabilis.
> Vixit sat sibi, sat diu
> Exul, quem patrius duxit amor domum.*

Some of his paraphrases have a pleasing simplicity and directness of translation, and compare well with Buchanan's more ornate renderings. Thus he translates 'I am distressed for thee . . .':

> Te propter ingens me, Ionathan, premit
> Mi frater, angor; dulcis amor tui
> Mi lucis instar: vicit in me
> Femineos tuus ardor ignes.†

Melville's great opponent in ecclesiastical policy, Patrick Adamson, was a better poet. Their lives ran parallel in many ways. Both had been graduates of St. Andrews and travelled abroad, both were apparently sincerely religious men, although they differed on the question of church government. At one period Adamson stood high in royal favour (he was made Archbishop of St. Andrews in 1576), but in later years he

---

* 'Each has his appointed day; fleeting is the sum of our years, that none can recall. Long enough has been his life, long enough his exile, whom his Father's love has called homeward.'

† 'Because of thee great grief cometh upon me, Jonathan my brother; thy sweet love was like a light unto me; thy love for me surpassed the passion of women.'

quarrelled with James, who had once deigned to write a sonnet in his honour, and when, in 1592, he was dying in poverty, it was Melville, not James, who helped him. His works include *De Papistarum Superstitiosis Ineptiis* (Edinburgh, 1564), a paraphrase of Job, and a Genethliacon (one of the many) on James VI. A collection was published after his death (*Poemata Sacra*, London, 1619). One of his best poems, an address to his departing soul, reminds the reader of Hadrian's 'Animula, vagula, blandula' and, if it is not 'as much superior as Christianity is superior to paganism' [23], its sincere tone of resignation and Christian hope is indeed impressive. It begins:

> O anima! assiduis vitae iactata procellis,
> Exilii pertaesa gravis, nunc lubrica tempus
> Regna tibi, et mundi invisas contemnere sordes:
> Quippe parens rerum caeco te corpore clemens
> Evocat, et verbi crucifixi gratia caeli
> Pandit iter, patrioque beatam limine sistet

and ends:

> Alme Deus! Deus alme! et non effabile numen!
> Ad te unum et trinum moribundo pectore anhelo.*

The influence of Buchanan is also seen in John and Thomas Maitland, sons of Sir Richard Maitland (himself a poet, though better known and esteemed as the man who preserved so much of Scottish vernacular poetry [24]), and brothers of Secretary Lethington. John, later Lord Thirlestane, Chancellor of Scotland, wrote epigrams, of which some thirty figure in the *Delitiae*. Perhaps the best is that commemorating the 'wonderful year', 1588:

> Papa Dei, petit orbis Iber, Dux Guisius Orci
> Regna; annus mirus, si potientur, erit.†

Another sonnet of James VI commemorated Maitland's death in 1595. Thomas, the interlocutor in Buchanan's *De Iure Regni*, who died in 1572 at the age of twenty-two, was a better poet, although he hardly had time to reach maturity. In his 'Sylvae', reminiscences of Buchanan

---

* 'My soul, tossed by the never-ending storms of life, weary of thy grievous exile, now cometh the time for thee to despise the unsure kingdoms, the hateful defilement of this world: the Father of all things in His mercy calleth thee forth from thy blind body, and the grace of the Word that was crucified openeth the way to Heaven, and will bring thee in glory to thy Father's threshold. . . . Merciful God, God of mercy, ineffable power! For Thee, the Three in One, my heart panteth in my dying breast.'

† 'The Pope seeks the kingdom of God, the Spaniard the kingdom of the earth, the Duke of Guise the kingdom of hell. It will be a wonderful year if they all reach their goal.'

are evident, but in his elegies and epigrams the influence of Ovid and Catullus can be detected. Bradner has pointed out that he is the first of the Scots poets to show this influence, which he probably derived from his stay abroad and from the knowledge of contemporary European Latinists which he there acquired. He, too, produced epigrams; that on 'Gilla' recalls several of a similar strain in Martial:

> Gilla, tibi nostris magis est pretiosa puellis
> Forma, illis gratis contigit, empta tua est.*

As befitted the pupil of Buchanan, James VI himself wrote Latin verse. The sentiments expressed are undistinguished, but the lines flow smoothly enough. A hexastich which formed part of the royal contribution to the collection published by the University of Cambridge to commemorate the death of Sir Philip Sidney (1587) may be of interest:

> Vidit ut exanimam tristis Cytheraea Philippum
> Flevit, et hunc Martem credidit esse suum.
> Eripuit digitis gemmas, colloque monile,
> Marti iterum numquam ceu placitura foret.
> Mortuus humana qui lusit imagine divam,
> Quid faceret iam si viveret ille? rogo.†

The most famous of all the wandering Scots of this period was James Crichton, 'the Admirable' [25]. His exploits, as recorded for instance by Sir Thomas Urquhart, are indeed admirable enough, but allowance must be made for Urquhart's powers of romancing, and the few poems that are preserved fall sadly short of Crichton's reputation. They include an Asclepiad piece to Aldus Manutius, the great Venetian printer, which is full of Horatian tags, and one in hexameters on Venice, stereotyped and frigid. Crichton's namesake, George (1555?-1611), was a much superior poet, and a good scholar, being both a jurist and professor of Greek in the Collège de France [26]. The *Delitiae* contains several of his epigrams and complimentary poems, but his work has never been collected into one volume. The influence of Ovid is evident in the *Heroides* and *Hymni* of Mark Alexander Boyd (1563-1601) [27]. The title *Hymni* is misleading, the poems being concerned with various plants and flowers, and sundry myths connected with them. The ver-

---

* 'Gilla, your beauty is dearer than the beauty of our girls. They got theirs for nothing—yours is bought.'

† 'When sad Venus saw Philip lying dead she wept, and thought he was her own dear Mars. She tore the rings from her fingers, the necklace from her throat, as if she would never more give pleasure to Mars. When in death he could deceive a goddess by his human form, what would he do were he still alive? I ask.' (See *supra*, Chapter II, note 29.)

sification is competent but uninspired. Hercules Rollock (1550-99) is represented in the *Delitiae* by an Epithalamium on the marriage of James VI to Anne of Denmark [28], a collection of 'Sylvae' (which include an address to Queen Elizabeth and a lament on the unsettled state of Scotland), and some epigrams, poems that scan backwards as well as forwards, and similar Ausonian trifles. Although his own work lacks inspiration, Rollock seems to have had wide literary connexions: he was Rector of the High School of Edinburgh, and brother of Robert Rollock, who became the first Principal of Edinburgh University. Another member of the learned circle at Edinburgh in the later years of the century was Sir Thomas Craig, the feudal lawyer [29]. Craig wrote poems of the usual type on various state occasions such as the birth of James in 1566 and his departure to England in 1603. As befitted a lawyer, he seems to have been impressed with the political possibilities of the Union of the Crowns. It was now Britannia who ruled the waves, he says: 'Illa tibi undarum regina Britannia servit.'

David Kinloch (1559-1617), who was in his later years a doctor in Dundee, wrote two hexameter poems, each of some 1200 lines, on anatomy and human reproduction [30]. It was not unusual to expound scientific subjects in verse, and the Italian Fracastoro's poem *Syphilis, sive De Morbo Gallico* (1530), was renowned.* Kinloch's work is competent, and sometimes shows poetic feeling, but it hardly lends itself to quotation, since he avoided the mythological and moralizing digressions which were often inserted to embellish such themes. Adam King (1560?-1620), a contemporary of Kinloch at St. Andrews University, was professor of philosophy and mathematics at Paris, but returned to Edinburgh in later life. He was the author of one of the many panegyrics to James in 1603, and of various hexameter poems on the life and resurrection of Christ which show metrical skill and religious feeling. He also completed the fourth and fifth books of Buchanan's *Sphaera*. Thomas Seget of Seaton (1570-1627) [31] was a student at Leyden under the great scholar Justus Lipsius. The *Delitiae* contains his *Meletemata Hypogeia*, short rhetorical pieces on ancient Greek and Roman characters which are reminiscent of the stock declamatory theses used by ancient rhetoricians. The themes are hackneyed, but are often vigorously developed. No. xvi, in which Cleopatra apostrophizes Octavian, is short enough to be quoted in full:

> Tune mihi regum matri, tot regibus ortae,
> Tune mihi, dominam nuper quam Roma timebat,
> Tu mihi Caesareum expertae Antonique cubile,
> Degener usque adeo pectus, Romane, putasti,

---

* A version 'English'd by Mr. Tate' was published as late as 1693 in Dryden's miscellany *Examen Poeticum*.

Vitae ut amore tui paterer caput esse triumphi?
Romanos non sola animos tua Roma ministrat.
Digna exempla viris et molli oriunda Canopo
Praebebit mulier: sit quamvis maxima, Caesar,
Nil tua par nostrae referet victoria morti.*

John Johnston, professor of theology at St. Andrews from 1593 until his death in 1611, wrote religious poems, mostly paraphrases of passages of the Bible, and various sets of historical epigrams (following a style begun by Ausonius and revived by Renaissance poets) on the kings of Scotland from Fergus I (330 B.C.) to James VI, Scottish secular heroes from Wallace to the Admirable Crichton, Old Testament figures, the kings of Israel and Judah, and the towns of Scotland. Catalogues of this kind are hardly calculated to inspire great poetry, but Johnston was probably wise in choosing a form that suited his talents. The lines on Alexander III may serve as an example. It will be seen that they hardly bear comparison with 'Quhen Alysandyr oure Kyng wes dede':

Connubio Anglorum stabili nova foedera pacis
    Conciliat, subeunt bella repente nova.
Omnia Norvegus late loca milite complet
    Quem magno intrepidus robore fundit, agit.
Mutua dehinc pacis sociantur foedera: leges,
    Iuraque dat populis munera grata suis.
Res hominum ah fragiles! illum de rupe reclivi
    Praecipitem insani vis fera raptat equi.
Usque adeo certi nihil est mortalibus aevi.
    Et subeunt miseris mille repente neces.†

Johnston was presumably using as his source the histories of Boece and Buchanan, with their magnificently undocumented detail for the early

---

* 'Didst thou think, Roman, that I, mother of kings and daughter of a royal line, I, whom but recently Rome feared as its mistress, who shared the couch of Caesar and of Antony, would be so craven of heart that through love of life I would consent to be the chief ornament of thy triumph? It is not only thy Rome that can breed Roman courage. A woman shall prove that even soft Canopus can furnish an example for men; however great thy triumph, Caesar, it will have nothing that can match my death.'

† 'By a firm marriage with the English he obtained a new treaty of peace, but suddenly wars break out anew. The Norwegian fills the land far and wide with his soldiers, but him he utterly routs with a mighty army. Then a treaty of peace is signed; he gives laws and ordinances to his people, welcome gifts. Alas for the fragile life of man! The fierce might of a frightened horse casts him headlong from a steep cliff: so unsure is all the mortal lot of man. Suddenly a thousand deaths come upon the unhappy land.'

period. What he omits is often as interesting as what he puts in: the lines on Canmore contain no mention of Margaret, and in dealing with William the Lion he patriotically leaves out any reference to ignominious relations with the English.

David Hume (1560?-1630) of Godscroft, or 'Theagrius' as he calls himself, the historian of the house of Douglas, provides a link with the succeeding period; a protégé of Buchanan in his youth, as he tells us, he published his poems after the Union of the Crowns (an event which he celebrated both in prose and verse), and in his imitation of Ovid he is the precursor of the Ovidians of the following generation. He wrote epigrams, love elegies, allegorical eclogues, a thanksgiving for the discovery of the Gunpowder Plot, and a long religious poem in hexameters, *Aselcanus*. Bradner suggests that the earlier Ovidian strain (the passion seems very conventional and literary) may have been abandoned for religious poetry through the influence of Hume's friends, Melville and John Johnston. Hume was another who had considerable technical skill but little inspiration. A few lines from his complimentary epigram on Queen Elizabeth will show that in flattery the Latinists could hold their own with writers in the vernacular. The parallel with James VI's poem (divinity deceived by human excellence) will be noted.

> Nuper belligeros Mavors cum viseret Anglos,
>   Vidit te, et Venerem credidit esse suam.
> Ibat in amplexus, iamque oscula nota ferebat:
>   At tibi virgineus venit in ora pudor.
> Sensit, et 'ergo', inquit, 'flavis prognata Britannis
>   De Venere ambiguum me facit esse mea?*

3

The period of Episcopalian supremacy produced an unprecedented number of Latin poets, the majority being students of one or other of the Colleges at Aberdeen. When James VI returned to Scotland in 1617, floods of welcoming verses were forthcoming, some of which are preserved in the St. Andrews and Edinburgh University volumes, published in 1617, and the collection edited by John Adamson (later Principal of Edinburgh) which appeared in 1618. Nor was it only the academic classes who were thus engaged. When the King came to Perth, several merchants and tradesmen submitted poems of welcome.

---

* 'Recently, when Mars was visiting the warlike English, he saw you and thought you his own Venus. He was coming to embrace you, and was already offering you his wonted kisses, but a maidenly blush coloured your cheeks. He saw his mistake, and said, "Can the daughter of the fair-haired Britons, then, make me doubt which is my own Venus?" '

The verses composed by one of them, Henry Anderson, on this and a previous royal visit (1580) are in the *Delitiae*.

Creditable pastorals in the Virgilian manner were written by Andrew Aidie, an Aberdonian who became professor of philosophy at Danzig, whence he returned in 1614 to become Principal of Marischal College. John Barclay (1582-1621) was born in France of Scottish parents, his father being William Barclay the civilian, Buchanan's opponent in political theory, and the man whom Locke designated 'the great champion of absolute monarchy' [32]. The son was the author of two Latin prose works which were famous in their day, the *Euphormio*, an imitation of Petronius, and the *Argenis*, a romance which Coleridge greatly admired. In the latter he inserted several songs, in which he experimented in combining Latin lyric metres. Professor Bradner regards these innovations favourably, but some classical scholars might frown on such 'contaminations'. Barclay also wrote complimentary addresses in hexameters to James VI and other potentates, pastorals, topical poems (including one in hendecasyllables on a cockfight), and satirical attacks on two women, in the traditional fashion.

William Dempster is one of the most interesting of all the wandering Scots scholars [33]. He was a professor in about a dozen European universities, for he was apparently of a very quarrelsome disposition and never stayed long in one place. He was philologist, civilian and historian, and claimed he could dictate Greek or Latin verse as quickly as a good writer could take down the words. It is perhaps worth remarking that, of all the writers mentioned in this chapter, Dempster has probably the best claim to fame as a scholar in the technical sense. His poems in the *Delitiae* include an Epithalamium, the usual panegyric on James, and a curious piece on the common fly, collecting with great erudition references to flies in sacred and profane authors, and moralizing on the nature and characteristics of the insect. For example:

> Musca malas vitae fraudes, et toxica nescit:
> Atque illi idcirco non ulla animalia bellum
> Intentant. Volucres agitant sua proelia, motus
> Seditioque feras exercet, et humida ponti
> Incola lethales studiis discordibus iras
> Committit: solum est antiquae musca quietis
> Exemplar, sola hoste caret, vivitque beate.*

---

* 'The fly knows not crafty stratagems to kill its prey, nor poison: therefore no animals make war on her. The birds have their own battles, the wild beasts are troubled by strife and quarrels, the damp denizen of the sea joins in fierce and deadly warfare through the warring passions of his heart. The fly alone is the pattern of the peace of old, she alone has no enemy, and lives a life of blessedness.'

The same style of what might be called mock-didactic is seen in the long poem on 'Eggs' written by David Echlin, physician to Henrietta Maria. It begins

> Ova cano. Vati precor adsis ova canenti
> Mnemosyne: teretesque globos, niveumque colorem,
> Et liquidas alborum undas, croceosque vitellos,
> Nectareumque cibum.

He goes on to speak of all that the egg symbolizes, ending with Him who

> Materiemque dedit, vicibus redeuntibus, ova
> Mittere solenni ritu Paschalia.

Then he stops abruptly—

> Nam si
> Temporis in primis tantum consumitur ovis
> Quando erit in mensa ut gustemus mala secunda?*

Sir John Scot of Scotstarvet (1585-1670), a Lord of Session, wrote Latin verse himself; but he is much more important for his influence as patron and as editor of the *Delitiae*, for which he had begun collecting material as early as 1619 and which was produced at his expense in 1637 [34]. It is difficult to determine to what extent Arthur Johnston collaborated. Bradner considers it more likely that Scot was helped by his brother-in-law, Drummond, who in 1627 gave to the University of Edinburgh an important collection of books and manuscripts which had clearly provided material. With Scot may be mentioned another Latinist known in a wider sphere, Sir Robert Aytoun, who wrote agreeable elegiacs to his friends and on state occasions, and an Ovidian epistle, 'Caro Carina'. It is of historical interest, since it deals with the famous Somerset case which led to the downfall of the Howards and the advancement of Villiers.

Arthur Johnston is among Scots Latinists second only to Buchanan [35]. Except for a hexameter poem on the burning of the house of Frendraught, his version of Psalm cxix (in which, to show that he could do it, each of the twenty-two parts is in a different metre), and a few religious paraphrases, Johnston confined himself to the elegiac couplet, which he used with such mastery that he was with reason called the Scottish Ovid. His Latin does indeed resemble Ovid's

---

* 'I sing of eggs: be present, I pray, Mother of the Muses, to help the bard who sings of eggs, their smooth round shells and snowy hue, the liquid waves of the whites, and the saffron yolks, a food fit for the gods . . . gave us cause, as the seasons revolve, to roll Easter eggs in yearly celebration . . . For if so much time is taken over the eggs in the hors d'œuvre, when shall we come to the apples in the dessert?'

in its easy flow, and it is so simple and straightforward that it makes very pleasant reading. But it is only the metre and style that are borrowed. Johnston is not a poet of love, and his urbanity, an urbanity that is more characteristic of the eighteenth century than of his own troubled times, is his own. He rarely aimed at the sublime. 'The verse of Johnston that may still rank as literature', says Robb, 'is good talk, in metre, and satisfies the old definition of poetry—πάντα μέτρον ἔχοντα λόγον. Sometimes it even satisfies the narrower modern conception.' His best poems nearly all deal with Aberdeenshire and its people. He had lived long enough abroad to sigh, like any good Donside man, for 'the back o' Benachie', his 'Gariochaeos tractus', but not long enough to be, like Buchanan, half a foreigner. At least his poetry is more concerned than Buchanan's was with Scotland, and particularly with his own North-east, which its people consider the heart of Scotland. A fine example is the poem on the scene of his boyhood, 'De loco suo natali', which Geddes calls 'perhaps the most graceful, as it is the best known, of his works':

> Aemula Thessalicis en hic Ionstonia Tempe,
>   Hospes, hyperboreo fusa sub axe vides.
> Mille per ambages nitidis argenteus undis
>   Hic trepidat laetos Urius inter agros.
> Explicat hic seras ingens Bennachius umbras
>   Nox ubi libratur lance diesque pari.
> Gemmifer est amnis, radiat mons ipse lapillis,
>   Quis nihil Eous purius orbis habet.
> Hic pandit natura sinum, nativaque surgens
>   Purpura felicem sub pede ditat humum.
> Aera per liquidum volucres, in flumine pisces,
>   Adspicis in pratis luxuriare pecus.
> Hic seges est, hic poma rubent, onerantur aristis
>   Arva, suas aegre sustinet arbor opes.
>   .   .   .   .   .
> Haec mihi terra parens: gens has Ionstonia lymphas,
>   Arvaque per centum missa tuetur avos.
> Clara Maroneis evasit Mantua cunis,*
>   Me mea natalis nobilitabit humus.*

---

* 'Here, stranger, you see, stretched under the northern sky, the vale of the Johnstons, rival of Thessalian Tempe. Here the silvery Urie with its sparkling waters hurries in myriad windings through the smiling farm-land. Here mighty Benachie unfolds his last shadows, when day and night swing equal in the balance. The river has its gems, the mountain, too, sparkles with stones as pure as any that the East can show. Here nature unfolds her bosom, and nature's purple springing up bedecks the ground underfoot. You can see the birds sport in the clear air, the fish in the stream, the cattle

Johnston's early poems include a defence of Buchanan's reputation against a Scottish doctor, Eglishem, and two appeals on behalf of the Rhineland Palatinate and Bohemia in the dangers that threatened them on the outbreak of what was to be the Thirty Years' War. He had a double interest in the cause of the Elector Palatine, as a compatriot of his wife and as a student at Heidelberg. The Ovidian epistle is here used allegorically, and in later life Johnston wrote several other poems in the same rather baffling form. Geddes has disentangled some of the themes, but they have little interest for a modern reader. Johnston's best verse was written after his return to Scotland. The hexameters on the Frendraught affair, when two chiefs of the house of Gordon were burned to death in very suspicious circumstances, are considered by Bradner to be his greatest poem, and 'one of the finest pieces of verse on a tragic subject to be found in modern Latin', but Johnston's compatriots will probably prefer some of his more homely themes. One of the most amusing of these is the defence of an Aberdeen midwife, imprisoned by the magistrates for some lapse of her unbridled tongue. In writing it he no doubt had in mind Buchanan's 'Lena', but his subject is less unsavoury. It ends with the imaginary epitaph on the 'howdie':

> Quae iacet hic, vetulae meruit fors lingua perire,
> Dextera non meruit tam pretiosa mori.*

The justly famous 'Fisher's Apology' deserves to be quoted in full, and little idea of its sustained vigour and vivid descriptive power can be given by excerpts [36]. The main theme is a plea, directed against some interfering Presbyterian minister, for freedom to fish on Sunday, a plea which must have sounded scandalously flippant, if not sacrilegious, to the Puritans. The enthusiastic description of the details of salmon-fishing is worthy of Johnston's successor, Walton. It is amusing to find him using the excuse for not going to the Kirk that comes so readily to the Scottish paterfamilias—that his wife and children can 'put up a prayer for him':

> Templa frequentantes pro me cum coniuge nati
> Tura propinarunt plurima, plura dabunt.

---

in the pastures. Here are crops, here apples redden, the cornland is weighed down with its grain, the trees can scarcely bear their wealth. . . . This is my native land: the Johnstons have held sway over these waters and fields for a hundred generations. Mantua became famous by being the birthplace of Virgil: but to me my native soil will bring renown.' (He was one of the Johnstons of that ilk.)

* 'Here lies an old wife whose tongue perhaps deserved to die, but whose hands were too precious to be killed.'

It is also, as Robb says, perhaps a little surprising, when we remember Johnston's later fame as a translator of the Psalms. Finally comes the appeal to the pocket—fishing is the staple trade of Aberdeen: and wine comes in exchange, for who would drink the harsh 'peat-reek'?—'Quis bibat ingratos, quos praebet Scotia, fumos?'

Johnston is at his best in his epistles to friends—pleading with Gordon of Craig in Auchindoir, stuck in the heather of the Cabrach ('Cabriis affixus ericis'), to leave his rustic solitude, dedicating a set of poems to Robert Baron and telling him how hard a farmer has to work, or congratulating Scot of Scotstarvet on the *Delitiae*. The last contains a justification for writing Latin verse, sensible in that it does not pitch its claims too high:

> Aureus est priscis nitor, et nativa venustas,
> Et sacra maiestas, Romuleusque vigor.
> Vatibus in nostris horum simulacra placebunt,
> Saepe fit exemplo pluris imago suo.*

Most charming of all is the address to his old friend David Wedderburn, himself one of the leading Latin poets of the age. Johnston muses on the changes brought by time: in poetry, he led the way, and Wedderburn followed, but, as so often before, the pupil has surpassed his master. He recalls boyhood days spent together—'We twa hae paidl'd in the burn' ('Saepe petebamus vicinos collibus amnes'). Wedderburn was more fortunate to stay at home, while he wandered afar—'But seas between us braid hae roar'd' ('Quas ego non terras, quae non vagus aequora pressi?'). 'And there's a hand, my trusty fiere!':

> Dum mihi te sisto, dum, quos simul egimus annos,
> Mente puto, mutor, nec mihi sum quod eram.†

Johnston's epigrams are not as a rule satirical, and should be classed with the epistles, of which they are in effect shorter examples. Some of his epitaphs are very fine, for example that on James Seton of Pitmedden:

> Quem tegit hic caespes, fastu Setonus honores,
> Divitias luxu posse carere docet.‡

---

* 'The poets of old have their golden radiance, their native charm, heavenly majesty, and true Roman strength. Their images in our bards will give pleasure. Often the reflection is enhanced by the nature of its original.'

† 'When I have you near me, when I think of the years we spent together, I am changed, and lose my former sadness.' (The parallel with Burns is well drawn by Robb. But how much more evocative is the Lallans!)

‡ 'Seton who sleeps beneath this turf proves that there can be honours without pride and wealth without extravagance.'

And on Denneter, an unknown Belgian:

> Hoc Denneterius, natorum munere, busto
> Conditur, amplexus coniugis ossa suae.
> Quam sacer hic locus est! Tumulo spectantur in isto
> Natorum pietas coniugiique fides.*

Less pleasing to modern taste are the distichs on Scottish nobles and bishops. Johnston had more of the courtier in him than had the great Presbyterians, Melville and Buchanan. On the other hand his royalist and High Church sympathies produced in his lines on the towns of Scotland, 'Encomia Urbium', a tribute to Scotland's romantic past and the ecclesiastical glories of the Middle Ages which the Presbyterians could never have written. The poem on St. Andrews will show how well Johnston, the Aberdonian, expresses the emotion felt by generations of St. Andrews students:

> Urbs sacra, nuper eras toti venerabilis orbi,
> Nec fuit in toto sanctior orbe locus.
>
> . . . . .
>
> Vestibus aequabant templorum marmora mystae,
> Cunctaque divini plena nitoris erant.
> Ordinis hic sacri princeps, spectabilis auro,
> Iura dabat patribus Scotia quotquot habet.
> Priscus honor periit, traxerunt templa ruinam,
> Nec superest mystis qui fuit ante nitor:
> Sacra tamen Musis urbs es, Phoebique ministris,
> Nec maior meritis est honor ille tuis.†

Then he describes the sea, and the fresh morning light so well known to St. Andreans, and the links:

> Proximus est campus, studiis hic fessa inventus
> Se recreat, vires sumit et inde novas.

Yet, curiously enough, it is not at St. Andrews but at Montrose that he talks of golf: 'Vel volucres curvo pellere fuste pilas.'

---

* 'Here lies Denneter, beside his dear wife, in a tomb erected by his children. How holy is the spot, that bears witness to children's affection and wedded love.'

† 'Sacred city, in former days thou wast venerated by the whole world, nor was there a holier place in all the world. . . . The priests in their vestments equalled the splendour of the shrines, and the whole scene shone with a divine radiance. Here the chief of the sacred order, resplendent in gold, gave laws to all the Senators of Scotland. The old honour hath gone; the shrines have fallen in ruin, and the former glory of the priests is departed. Yet art thou a city sacred to the Muses, and to the servants of Phoebus, nor is that honour greater than thy deserts.'

Encouraged by Laud as a rival to the Presbyterian Buchanan, Johnston too produced a version of the Psalms (the favourite Sunday reading, it will be remembered, of the Baron of Bradwardine), and there was in the eighteenth century a lively controversy as to which was superior. Johnston is generally more concise and closer to the original, as will be seen from his rendering of the passage of which Buchanan's version has already been given:

1. Urbe procul Solymae, fusi Babilonis ad undas,
   Flevimus, et lacrumae fluminis instar erant.
   Sacra Sion toties animo totiesque recursans
   Materiem lacrumis praebuit usque novis.
2. Desuetas saliceta lyras et muta ferebant
   Nablia, servili non temeranda manu.
3. Qui patria exegit, patriam qui subruit hostis
   Pendula captivos sumere plectra iubet.
   Imperat et laetos mediis in fletibus hymnos,
   Quosque Sion cecinit nunc taciturna modos.*

Johnston was 'felix opportunitate mortis'. He had written a poem on the Covenant, pleading with his countrymen to ask pardon from Charles. Politically he was out of touch with the most vigorous and patriotic element in the Scotland of his day; but his gloomy contemporaries could well have done with a greater share of his urbane humanity.

David Wedderburn (1580-1646) [37] was Rector of Aberdeen Grammar School for forty years. His Latin grammar held the field in Scotland until ousted by Ruddiman's, and he edited Persius (published at Amsterdam by his brother in 1664). He composed three books of epigrams, competent enough but rather pedestrian, and numerous complimentary pieces, for he was the official poet of the magistrates of Aberdeen. But his best work, as is fitting, is that inspired by his friendship for Johnston (a reply to the epistle quoted above), and a small collection of epitaphs on Johnston's death. Wedderburn was, despite Johnston's generous tribute, no match for his friend in Latin composition, as he himself readily admits; but his epistle in answer to Johnston's is worthy of the occasion and the two poems should be

---

* 'Far from the city of Jerusalem, as we lay by the waters of Babylon, we wept, and our tears were like a river. Again and again the thought of holy Sion came to our mind, and ever called forth fresh tears. The willow-trees held our lyres, now unplayed, and our silent harps, for we could not touch them with the hands of slaves. The enemy who drove us from our country, who destroyed it, orders the captives to take their hanging harps. He orders glad hymns in the midst of our weeping, and the songs that Sion, now silent, used to sing.'

read together. Wedderburn's theme is similar, the days 'when the sun shone brighter far'.

> Has ego cerno nives, cerno, Ionstone, querorque,
>   Et nivis, heu, lacrumae more liquentis eunt.
> Dumque retro specto melioris tempora vitae,
>   Quaeque ferunt anni gaudia prima rudes,
> Deficio, quaerensque tuis solamina curis
>   Implicor, an sileam nescius, anne loquar.
> Heu! ubi, quae nobis quondam florentibus annis
>   Otia, veris ubi blandior aura novi?
> Vivida nunc ubi vis animi? quam serior aetas
>   Usque tibi reparat, deterit usque mihi.*

He grudges the years when they were parted, but rejoices in Johnston's merited fame, and will do his best to console him; but he, as ever, must lead the way:

> Siquid ego interea moduler, tu praecine, Phoebus
>   Unus semper eras tu mihi, semper eris.†

The most versatile of the Aberdonians was John Leech ('Leochaeus') [38]. Leech tried practically every style of composition except the epic—erotic (including 'Anacreontica' and love elegies), epigrams and four books of eclogues (bucolic, piscatory, marine—which reflect the contemporary interest in discovery—and vinitory). His confession that he had led a dissolute life—'Iacche parens et amarae mella Cytheres'—seems true, and his poetic ambition (he admits that he is 'gloriae avidissimus') would appear to have outstripped his capabilities. Professor Bradner, however, considers him 'in many ways the most interesting of the Scottish Latinists after Buchanan', and criticizes Sir John Scot and W. K. Leask for giving so few of his works in the *Delitiae* and *Musa Latina Aberdonensis*. Scot may have been influenced by political and personal considerations which we can guess at, if not prove, but it is also possible that Leech's technical failings may have weighed with both editors, for his scansion and syntax are often odd. One of Leech's friends was George Chalmers ('Camerarius') [39], author of a *Sylva Leochaeo suo* dedicated to Leech (Paris, 1620), and a collection of *Emblemata amatoria* (Venice, 1627),

---

* 'I see these snowy locks, I see them, Johnston, and lament; and my tears run like melting snow. When I look back at our prime, and the earliest joys of unspoiled youth, my spirits fail me; I seek to console thy cares, but waver, knowing not whether to speak or be silent. Alas! where are the pleasures we enjoyed in the days of our vigour, where the kindlier airs of spring? Where now that keenness of mind, which later years ever renew in thee, but ever decrease in me?'

† 'Meanwhile, if I sing aught, do thou lead me, thou alone wast ever my inspirer, and ever will be.'

short pieces dealing with various conventional aspects of love and illustrated by appropriate engravings. Chalmers had the necessary delicacy of touch to handle this rather trifling subject-matter, and his emblems are pleasant to read. The collection included some longer Ovidian amatory epistles. Emblems were also composed by Robert Farley, who graduated M.A. at Edinburgh in 1624. In addition, he wrote epigrams, a poem describing a watch ('Horologium automatum') and 'Naulogia', which deals with navigation from Noah to Drake. Alexander Ross (1591-1654), another minor poet of the period, was a native of Aberdeen who became chaplain to Charles I, friend of Evelyn, and a celebrated controversialist.* He was the author of a long narrative poem on biblical history, *Rerum Iudaicarum Memorabilia*, and a Virgilian cento, *Virgilius Evangelizans*. Urquhart, in his usual exuberant fashion, calls him 'a most indeared minion of the Muses', but later generations probably remembered him best for his appearance in *Hudibras* (I. ii. 1-2):

> There was an ancient sage philosopher
> Who had read Alexander Ross over.

It seems to have been generally felt that Scottish Latinity needed an epic to establish it as a literature, and Ross was not the only writer who tried to supply the want. In 1633 Patrick Panter, professor of theology at St. Andrews, published a fragment of an epic on Wallace, *Valliados libri tres, opus inchoatum*; and Hugo Wallace, an Edinburgh schoolmaster, wrote six books on the same subject, which were published in 1705 but probably written long before that date. The short epic in four books published in 1633 by Andrew Ramsay, professor of divinity at Edinburgh, and reprinted in the *Delitiae* is much superior to these efforts. The circle of Scot and Drummond had wanted Leech to write a religious epic, and Ramsay's subject was Paradise Lost and Regained. The Renaissance epic is probably the least congenial of all neo-Latin genres to modern readers, for in it the vices of imitation and of mechanical reproduction of classical formulae are only too easily perceived. By its very nature, too, it must be μέγα βιβλίον, and here at least most would agree with Callimachus as to the corollary. If it is judged within its class, Ramsay's work is praiseworthy, and it at least deserves more than 'condescending references to Milton's acquaintance with it' [40]. A few lines from the Serpent's speech to Eve will serve as a token:

> Libatis his ore epulis vos regia caeli
> Accipiet divos, vos nulla arcana latebunt,

---

* For Ross's animadversions (a word he was fond of) on Raleigh's *History*, Sir Thomas Browne, and Hobbes's *Leviathan*, see John Bowle, *Hobbes and his Critics*, 1951, and Douglas Bush, *English Literature in the Earlier Seventeenth Century*, 1945.—*Editor.*

Quae sunt, quae fuerant, quae post ventura patescent.
Nec magis ex usu quicquam, aut incundius usquam
Quam secreta deum, quamque orgia mystica scire,
Et mundi penetrare sinus, atque ire per omnem
Naturam, et rerum caecos aperire recessus.*

The canon of Scots Latinists virtually closed with the appearance of the *Delitiae* in 1637 [41], but two poets who wrote after the Restoration deserve mention. Ninian Paterson (1636?-88), minister at Liberton, published in 1678 eight books of epigrams on various subjects, including three books on religious and one on classical themes. Archibald Pitcairne wrote odes and epigrams which were published in *Selecta Poemata* (1727) along with work by other poets [42]. By this time, poems were composed in Latin not because they had a greater chance of immortality in that medium (a view which was still possible in Milton's day), but rather as an elegant pastime, and Pitcairne is comparable with the great English Latinists of the eighteenth century rather than with Buchanan or even Arthur Johnston. His poems are sometimes difficult because of obscure references to his friends or to historical events, but at his best he can write with elegance and vigour, and his political vehemence (he was a strong Jacobite) is a welcome contrast to the classical insipidity of many of his predecessors. His best poem is probably the lament for Claverhouse, which was translated by Dryden:

Ultime Scotorum, potuit quo sospite solo
    Libertas patriae salva fuisse tuae:
Te moriente, novos accepit Scotia cives,
    Accepitque novos, te moriente, deos.
Illa tibi superesse negat, tu non potes illi:
    Ergo Caledoniae nomen inane vale:
Tuque vale gentis priscae fortissime ductor,
    Ultime Scotorum, atque ultime Grame, vale.†

---

* 'When your mouths have tasted this fruit the palace of heaven will admit you as very gods, from you no secrets will be concealed, of all things that are, and have been, and will hereafter be revealed. Nor is anything more useful, more delightful, than to know the secrets of heaven, and its mystic rites, to reach the inmost parts of the world, to fare through all nature, and lay bare its hidden depths. '

† 'Last of the Scots, thy life alone could have maintained the freedom of thy native land: with thy death Scotland hath new citizens, and new gods. Freedom proclaimeth that she cannot survive thee, nor canst thou survive her. Therefore farewell, Scotland, now an empty name. And thou, farewell, mightiest leader of an ancient race, last of the Scots, and last of the Grahams, farewell.' (Dryden's fine paraphrase was printed as 'Epitaphium in Vice-Comitem Dundee. English'd by Mr. Dryden' in *Poems on Affairs of State*, 1704, and in *Poetical Miscellanies: The Fifth Part*, 1704.)

Pitcairne's epigram provides a not unfitting note on which to close this survey. With him too, we may say, the writing of Latin poetry came to an end in Scotland—ἀπέσβετο καὶ λάλον ὕδωρ.

Until the Union of the Parliaments, Scotsmen were more concerned with the problems of religion and politics than with Latin versification, and when in the eighteenth century they returned to literature the conditions which had favoured Latin composition had passed away. Only the medical students now went abroad, while at home the Scottish schools did not, like Eton and Westminster, lay stress on verse composition. And Latin had lost for ever its status as an international language, the vehicle of diplomacy and of *litterae humaniores*.

Mr. John Sparrow speaks of 'the characteristically modern, or English, lineaments' which can be detected in the poets of his collection, and a glance at such a typically English poem as John Jortin's 'Epitaphium Felis' or Dillingham's lines on the Oundle church bells, will show what he means [43]. Murarasu, in his book on the French Latinists of the sixteenth century, similarly finds that 'les néo-Latins donnèrent à leurs poésies l'âme de l'époque, l'âme française avec son enthousiasme, son esprit royaliste, son patriotisme et son souci du problème religieux'. Is there any distinctively Scottish note in the writers surveyed here? There is the interest in religion which one would expect from Scotsmen of this period. Perhaps it is not too much to claim also that in a series which began with a lament for Wallace and ended with a lament for Claverhouse, and which included in its course Buchanan's lines on Mary's dowry, John Johnston's historical epigrams and Arthur Johnston's 'Encomia Urbium', the strongest common element is patriotism.

IV

THE BALLADS

SIR JAMES FERGUSSON

T HE ballads were written down only late in their history, and for a public quite different from their original audience. As the Ettrick Shepherd's mother told Walter Scott, 'they were made for singing an' no for reading'. A literary work, on the other hand, is written down at its inception, fixed, and—subject to the vagaries of editors and printers—final. Ballads grew and developed, changing their shape and order and often breeding offspring. The author of a literary work is usually known, or if unknown may be postulated a single artist. A ballad has no known author and may have had several authors, even many, since every singer who repeated a ballad not quite as he heard it, changing words or lines and adding or dropping verses, tended to contribute something to its growth.

Ballads become literature not when they first achieve print in a broadsheet or chapbook, but when they are collected and critically considered by an editor. The systematic collection of ballads became a branch of serious letters in the eighteenth century and flourished as such for a hundred years and more [1]. The literary critic must begin at and from the point where collectors and editors have, in Mrs. Hogg's phrase, 'broken the charm', where the butterfly has been caught and pinned to the board, the fleeting pattern of its bright colours fixed for ever. There cannot be certainty, and there is often doubt, whether the specimen under the glass is the best, or which of several comparable specimens is the most authentic. Doubt breeds argument; and the first argument to be faced is that of the ballad's origin and the identity of the author or authors.

There are three possible theories about the ballad's origin. You may believe, as Percy and the eighteenth-century collectors believed, in some rustic genius, some Homer of the hills, who either simplified and popularized the ancient metrical romances which had been actual literary creations or else turned the colloquial tales of his time into a metrical form. He possessed (it was supposed) such mastery of proportion and such an instinctive feeling for the pithy and memorable word or phrase that his rough verses, taking the wings of some familiar and haunting tune, passed freely among his neighbours and contemporaries and survived in the memories and on the lips of their descendants. Or you may believe, with the German critics of the Romantic period, in the probability of a communal authorship, and hold that a tale in verse could be generated in the family circle around the hearth, in the group casually met in the tavern, or among the crowd summoned to the wapinschaw. Or, more reasonably, you may believe that the truth probably lies somewhere between these two points.

The late W. Macneile Dixon convincingly suggested [2] that a ballad began with an original chorus, to which successive improvisers added variations, and of which the first development was by the repetition of the most popular phrases until something like an accepted version was in currency. Then came the minstrel, 'an active meddler or artist', who with some creative talent of his own lengthened and improved the version he found, so that his new version gained a wider circulation and displaced its simpler or cruder rivals. The importance of the minstrel is that he is not one of the people contributing on equal terms with others to a common purpose. To him the people are a passive audience, and the work he makes his own.

But the minstrel owned no copyright. Another minstrel, in the same era or a later one, might take his ballad, improve it or spoil it, adapt it for a new audience and give it a more topical or more familiar setting. Of different versions, the wandering minstrel would choose for repetition, in whole or in part, not necessarily the best but that which appealed to him as the best, or the most appropriate. That was what Scott, the Last Minstrel, did; and because he himself was soaked in the tradition of the ballads and intimate with those who still sang them, his versions ring true. If any version of a ballad may be called more authentic than another—which is disputable—Scott's versions have a right to that title; and in discussing the ballads it is chiefly, though not entirely, from the text of his *Minstrelsy of the Scottish Border* that I shall cite examples.

I

In the ballads we have a body of stories in verse, framed, with few exceptions, in the simplest of metres, and generally, although meant for singing, without refrains. A few, such as 'Fine Flowers in the Valley', 'The Twa Sisters' and 'The Carle of Kellyburnbraes', have a refrain which may have been interpolated by the narrator's audience, and which evokes the setting in which the true ballad was performed, to an attentive circle of listeners whose sympathy with the minstrel's story, thus expressed, heightened its emotional effect and drew singer and listeners into the closest intimacy. From others a refrain may have been lost. Or the occasional effect of a refrain may have been given by a stanza repeated episodically which the audience would take up in unison as they recognized its recurrence: for example, the king's successive rejections of Johnie Armstrang's pleas for his life:

> Away, away, thou traitor strang!
> Out o' my sight soon may'st thou be!

> I granted nevir a traitor's life,
> And now I'll not begin wi' thee.

But in most of the ballads the story runs its course without interruption and almost always without introduction, often revealing its theme in the very first line, either in plain statement: 'There was a knight and a lady bright'; or in a challenging question: 'O have ye na heard o' the fause Sakelde?'

Occasionally, however, there is a more self-conscious opening, like that of the romances — 'Listeth lordes of good entent' — as though designed to silence persistent chatter in the corners of the room and call attention to the minstrel's voice:

> Sum speikis of lords, sum speikis of lairds,
> And sic lyke men of hie degree;
> Of a gentleman I sing a sang . . .

But whether the opening words are abrupt or leisurely, one thing is evident. The true ballads—from which I would exclude some pieces commonly printed among ballads, such as 'The Twa Corbies' (which is dramatic dialogue without action) and 'A Lyke-Wake Dirge' (which is incantation)—are always stories. They fall into four fairly well defined groups, though the place of a few lies in a debatable land between them; but all these are only groups of different kinds of stories. The ballad is always narrative.

First, there are ballads based on historical events, whether national or local. They seem to have flourished approximately from the beginning of the fifteenth century to the end of the seventeenth; but ballads were probably current much earlier than James I's time. Barbour's rugged couplets not infrequently suggest the swing of the common ballad stanza, for example:

> [He] ruschit in amang thame all;
> The first he met he gart him fall,   [*made*
> And syne his swerd he swappit out,   [*then*
> And raucht about him mony a rout. [3]   [*blow*

He may even have echoed or borrowed from popular ballads of his day. But 'Otterbourne' is perhaps the earliest survivor left to us, though the form in which Scott printed it is, it must be remembered, a version which had undergone four hundred years of modifying transmission, and we cannot tell how many contemporaries or predecessors it may have had which died out during that period. The sixteenth century, at any rate, seems to have been the most fertile age, and the complete absence of any reference in the ballads to ministers of the Reformed Church contributes to the probability that most of them date from before the Reformation. The episodes which provided the stuff of the 'riding ballads' became rare after the settling of comparative peace on the Borders after 1603. Before that date Scottish history is lamentably rich in tragic episodes which even in the plainest prose read like synopses of ballads.

It is more than probable that the ballad-makers told and retold such events as the street battle of 1520 between the Douglases and the Hamiltons called 'Cleanse the Causeway' [4]; or the mysterious struggle within the chambers of Gowrie House of which the sequel was the disgrace and extinction of the noble family of Ruthven [5]; or the desperate charge of the doomed young laird of Bargany—five men against thirty—in the twilight and the snow against the Earl of Cassillis's ambuscade outside Maybole [6]. There is the very tang of the ballads in all these ancient tragedies, as, to take one more instance, there is in the chronicler's account of the cruel death of Jonet Douglas, widow of the sixth Lord Glamis and wife of Campbell of Skipnish, on a trumped-up charge of treason in 1537:

> She was burnt upon the Castle Hill with great commiseration of the people, in regard of her noble bloud, of her husband, being in the prime of her years, of a singular beauty, and suffering all, though a woman, with a man-like courage; all men conceiving that it was not this fact [her accusation] but the hatred the King carried to her brothers. [7]

As concrete examples of ballads based on actual events we have such pieces as 'Otterbourne', 'Kinmont Willie', 'The Laird o' Logie', 'The Fire of Frendraught', 'The Baron of Brackley' and 'The Bonnie House of Airlie'. These ballads are not history, and it would be dangerous indeed to cite them or details from them as historical evidence. The minstrel's capacity for twisting facts and telescoping events for the sake of dramatic effect is vividly exhibited in 'The Battle of Bothwell-bridge', where unrelated events six years apart and falling in two different reigns are thus combined:

> Then wicked Claverhouse turn'd about,
>   I wot an angry man was he;
> And he has lifted up his hat,
>   And cry'd, 'God bless his Majesty!'

> Then he's awa to London town,
>   Ay e'en as fast as he can drie;
> Fause witnesses he has wi' him ta'en,
>   An' ta'en Monmouth's head from his body.

But the ballads represent the popular version of what took place, compounded of who knows what ingredients: the first-hand account from the survivor of a battle who yet did not see the whole of it, the gossip of a city or a countryside, the popular reputation, prejudicing judgment, of this great lord or that proud lady, and the instinct of the minstrel and his audience for what was dramatically proper. It is easy to tell that 'Jamie Telfer' was the work of someone who had no sympathy with the Elliots, and 'The Bonnie House of Airlie' of someone bent on blackening the name of Argyll; and we have only to set 'Chevy Chase' beside 'Otterbourne' to see how differently the same battle was viewed by minstrels on different sides of the Tweed.

But few indeed have survived of what must have been a large corpus of this kind of ballad. In an age when so small and local an episode (even though it did have repercussions as far away as London) as the rescue of Kinmont Willie, 'William Armstrang of Morton, als callit Will of Kynmonth' [8], could inspire a ballad, it is not to be doubted that other ballads sprang from the disasters of Pinkie, Inverkeithing or Dunbar, from the murders of Riccio or the Regent Moray, or the executions of Montrose and Argyll. There is evidence that at least one long ballad once existed on the battle of Flodden Field, for 'The Laird of Muirhead' is obviously a fragment of it. Two or three ballads, not of the first rank, belong to the wars of the Covenant, in which, contrary to the romantic modern view of those stern times, Claverhouse is 'the wicked Claverhouse' and Montrose is 'our cruel enemy'. And the dramatic doom of any lord or laird whose doings in life had been the talk of his own countryside must often have given birth to a ballad perhaps never more than locally known. The old quatrain

> Edinburgh castle, town and tour,
> God grant thou sink for sinne,
> And that even for the black dinoure
> Erle Douglas gat therein

sounds like the opening verse—or perhaps the closing one—of a lost ballad on that dark episode, with exactly the attitude towards the distant and sinister capital to be expected from the dead Earl's people in Douglasdale or Galloway. And the 'sang of triumphe' grimly quoted by John Knox as having been sung by 'the Papists, bothe in Scotland and France' on the fall of the castle of St. Andrews was probably the refrain of a ballad:

> Preastis, content you now, preastis, content you now;
> For Normond and his cumpany hes filled the galayis fow. [9]

The famous list of songs in *The Complaynt of Scotlande* (published *c.* 1550) contains a few titles that sound like historical ballads, besides two which are easily recognizable as 'Chevy Chase' and 'Otterbourne'. The two lines there quoted

> God sen the Duc hed byddin in France,
> And De la Bauté hed nevyr cum hame,

which sound like a fragment of a ballad, can be related with some certainty to the notorious murder of De la Bauté, otherwise D'Arcy, in 1517, while 'the Duc'—the Regent Albany—*was* in France. Such are the fragments that suggest what once existed.

From ballads with a basis of history, it is an easy step to those which may or may not be founded on fact but are at all events tales of entirely realistic action or adventure: roughly cheerful for the most part, with the hero triumphing over his enemies, but occasionally of a tragic cast, and always placed firmly in the setting of a familiar countryside. Of this type, though not exclusively comprising it, are all the 'riding ballads' of the Border. 'Kinmont Willie' may perhaps be classed with them, though, as already observed, it is popular history; 'Jamie Telfer' is a borderline case also. But 'Dick o' the Cow', 'Hobie Noble', 'Jock o' the Side', 'Archie of Ca'field', 'The Sang o' the Outlaw Murray', and others such as 'Bonny Baby Livingston' not set in the Border country, sound like fiction, giving the impression of being constructed to a popular pattern—the 'thrillers' of their day. There are also the fantastic- ally comic tales like 'Jock o' Noth' and 'The Carle of Kellyburnbraes' and 'Get Up and Bar the Door'—equivalent to light novels. In all these there is invention, pure story-telling, with a deliberately contrived climax and generally an orthodox 'happy ending'.

But there is a higher and more genuinely poetic invention in the third class and the fourth, and it is in them that the ballad reaches its supreme form as literature. In the first of these two there is romance, in the genuine sense of that much debased and overworked word. It may be applied to an almost realistic and not impossible tale, as in 'The Douglas Tragedy', 'Marie Hamilton', 'Young Waters' and 'Clerk Saunders' for sadness, or 'Glenlogie', 'The Lochmaben Harper' and 'The Broom of the Cowdenknowes' for merriment. Often it colours the story with strange gleams and shadows from another world, the world of fairy-tale. The homely sounding names of Carterhaugh or Usher's Well, the broad sunlight of daily life and work, soon yield place to 'the mirk and midnight hour' 'when the fairy folk will ride', when dead lovers wail in the windy darkness outside the closed shutters and when, in the flickering light of the dying fire, the carline wife's three lost sons come quietly home with their hats of the Paradisal birk. It is a swift ride, if not a short one, from the sunshine on Huntly Bank to the dark underworld where

> They saw neither sun nor moon,
> But they heard the roaring of the sea.

Always the remote world of fairyland, to reach which whole lands or oceans must be traversed on fairy steed or fairy ship, is suggested by the most delicately expressive touches, a voice in the darkness, a strain of ghostly music, the appearance of the magic colour of green: no more is needed. This is in strong contrast to the grotesque details piled upon each other in a sophisticated literary fantasy like 'Lichtoun's Dreme'. We have only to compare the sombre horror of

> It was mirk mirk night, and there was nae stern light,
> And they waded through red blude to the knee,
> For a' the blude that's shed on earth
> Rins through the springs o' that countrie

with

> We war weill ware of Enoch and Eli
> Sittand on Yule even in ane fresche grene schaw,
> Roastand strawberries at ane fire of snaw.

The third class of ballads merges into the fourth and last, which is pure folk-tale, not to be claimed, like the previous examples, as something almost wholly our own, but the Scottish variant of a type of story found in many lands and in many languages. This group includes many of the best of our ballads: 'Tam Lin', 'The Daemon Lover', 'The Twa Sisters', 'Johnnie Faa', 'The Gay Goss-Hawk', 'Lord Thomas and Fair Annie', 'Cospatrick', 'Kempion', 'Lord Randal', 'May Colvin' and 'The Laithly Worm'. 'Johnnie Faa', decorated with the name of a gipsy tribe well known in Scotland and of an Earl of Cassillis, is an excellent example of the minstrel's professional trick of adding colour and conviction to a well-worn tale by localising its figures. 'It is observable that ballads are very frequently adapted to the meridian of the place where they are found' [10]. But there is no need here—though the attempt has been absurdly made, and is renewed to this day in the more unreliable of local guide-books—to look for an historical basis to this ballad: the song of the high-born lady who left her castle to wander with the raggle-taggle gipsies is common to all Europe. Similarly 'The Gay Goss-Hawk', localized in the Border hills, is a Scottish echo of the folk-tale behind *Romeo and Juliet*, but with a climax in happiness instead of in tragedy; and 'Sir Hugh le Blond' is a fragment of Arthurian romance, from a source far to the south of Arbattle and Fordoun. In these ballads it is not the story and seldom the characters but, as in the other classes already described, the setting, the construction and the language that we claim for our own.

2

The character of the ballads may be best drawn by discussing these three aspects; and first, the setting. The minstrel uses, in the main, two kinds of topographical colour. There is the well-known name that gives conviction to his story by anchoring it to a locality which all know or can visualize. The King sits 'in Dunfermline toun'—or Edinburgh or Stirling; or the scene is laid at 'my Lord Cassillis' yett'

or the castle of Doune, Airlie or Fyvie; or the hero battles his way into,
or out of, 'Dumfries port', or 'merry Carlisle', or Newcastle, or London
itself. In the historical or 'riding ballads' of the Border, this air of
reality is sharpened by particularly minute reference to roads, fords,
passes, hilltops, towers and other landmarks, and the occurrence of
such names emphasizes that these ballads are local, not national,
literature. It was to an audience that could at once see the scene in its
mind that the minstrel told how

> The King was coming thro' Caddon Ford
> And full five thousand men was he;
> They saw the derke Forest them before,
> They thought it awsome for to see.

But sometimes whole groups of names seem to be introduced for their
sheer music, as in 'Otterbourne':

> And he has burn'd the dales of Tyne,
> And part of Bambrough shire,
> And three good towers on Roxburgh fells,
> He left them all on fire;

or, as in 'The Raid of the Reidswire', to please as many as possible in
the audience:

> Then Tividale came on wi' speid;
> The Sheriff brought the Douglas down,
> Wi' Cranstane, Gladstain, good at need,
> Baith Rewle water, and Hawick town;

or, as in 'Jamie Telfer', blending the map and the melody together,
with an effect that brings into the verse the tramp of hoofs, the creak
of leather, and the ring of metal on stone:

> Warn Wat o' Harden and his sons,
> Wi' them will Borthwick Water ride,
> Warn Gaudilands, and Allanhaugh,
> And Gilmanscleugh, and Commonside.

> Ride by the gate at Priesthaughswire,
> And warn the Currors o' the Lee;
> As ye come down the Hermitage Slack,
> Warn doughty Willie o' Gorrinberry.

It is the Border ballads that are the richest in these homely yet stirring
names, as Burns recognized when he wrote

> Yarrow an' Tweed, to mony a tune,
> Owre Scotland rings;

and Yarrow, Ettrick or Liddesdale often 'rings' in the opening verse,
a name brandished like a flag.

Besides this characteristic use of familiar place-names there is that of others which have a natural and convincing sound but are not to be pinned down in any gazetteer. Where is Erlinton, and where Usher's Well? On the other hand, there may be a score of places called Cowden-knowes or the Broomfield Hill: they are both everywhere and nowhere, in the world of both fact and fancy. Finally, there are one or two names which are real in a sense but stand for the unreal. They were far beyond the journeyings of the minstrel's listeners, known only from travellers' tales; and they are used, as Chaucer and Milton used the fantastic names of Asiatic cities or kingdoms, to suggest not the familiar but the remote. They are like 'the spell of far Arabia', to steal away sense and judgment.

> I will show you how the lilies grow
> On the banks of Italy

is the last wily promise of the Daemon Lover. Even Sir Patrick Spens's voyage to 'Noroway o'er the faem' does not suggest a visit to a Christian kingdom as much as to an outlying province of 'fair Elfland'. And one version of 'The Lawlands of Holland' carries us to a landscape much more distant than the port of Veere:

> New Holland is a barren place: in it there grows nae grain,
> Nor any habitation wherein for to remain,
> But the sugar canes are plenty, and the wine draps frae the tree.
> But the Lawlands o' Holland hae twin'd my love and me.

The London ravaged by Jock o' Noth was a city of legend; and 'beyond the Isle of Skye' was indeed a region of nightmare to a Tweeddale or Clydesdale audience.

Most of the stories, however, are set firmly in the surroundings of home; and details of buildings, furniture, clothes, ornaments and arms are as native as the weather itself. References to the weather, indeed, carry to the modern reader the instant conviction of something that the centuries have in no way changed. Everyone can see, after any autumn spate, the river flowing 'frae bank to brim' such as Buccleuch and his men breasted with the rescued Kinmont Willie; everyone has, at one time or another, shivered in 'the gryming of a new-fa'n snaw' in the cheerless hour before the dawn of 'a cauld day and a snell'; and it is still 'about the Lammas tide', in the bright hot days between the heavy August rains, that 'the muir-men win their hay'. The vividness of these strokes of description should bring home to us that the very same familiarity must once have attached to innumerable small touches that mirror the daily life of four hundred years ago in the laird's tower, the palaces of Falkland and Linlithgow, the burgh or the 'landward toun': archaic to us but commonplaces to their first hearers.

There is, to begin with, the high hall with the great fireplace, the rush-strewn floor, and the long tables 'with white bread and with brown', where the lords, back from the hunt or the tournament, sit at their wine, having dined on 'kinnen and capon . . . and venison in great plentie'—lords who wear golden rings as a matter of course, and 'targats' in their hats, and scarlet cloaks and 'cork-heel'd shoon'. The ladies 'wi' their goud kaims in their hair' look 'frae their loft windows' or sit in their bowers with their white fingers busy at their embroidery, or come tripping down the stair to gang to the kirk, or to play at the ball with their skirts kilted to the knee. It may even be a royal hall, where the King himself sits with a wily lord or an eldern knight at his elbow. Either way, there is a slight air of staginess about it, for this is not a setting familiar to the minstrel at first hand.

Then there is the tower, the more modest but still dignified house with which the minstrel was familiar enough, being a welcome visitor there to speed the long ill-lit winter evening. There is the high peel* surrounding it, the close within the wall containing the deep draw-well and perhaps a small garden also, the tirling-pin at the door, the stout yett of interlaced iron bars, the narrow shot-window through which a message may be whispered or a token passed, the hall in which the laird and his men all dine together, reflecting restlessly that 'Liddesdale has layen lang in' or with satisfaction that their own beasts are safe within the peel. The spear, the twa-handed sword, the jack and the knapscap hang ready on the wall; and the auld wife, 'a wee bit o' the Captain's kin', mutters to herself in her snug corner 'ayont the fire'.

Or again there is the moorland farm, with the cows cosy under the same roof with the family, the rough infield enclosed with a fail-dyke or turf fence, the peat-house and the ewe-bught. The carline wife at Usher's Well, even though 'a wealthy wife was she', expected her sons to sleep three in a bed; and the sons of poor men like Dick o' the Cow probably slept on the earthen floor on a pile of heather or bracken. It was only in desperation that raiders thought such homes worth the trouble of pillaging.

The humble economy of small dwellings like these is reflected in innumerable recorded testaments of the sixteenth and seventeenth centuries. Many a man was gathered to his fathers, leaving, like Jamie Telfer, 'a waefu' wife and bairnies three', and, like Dick o' the Cow, three kye—with perhaps two oxen which had dragged his plough, a

* The word 'peel', popularly misused to mean a stone tower, means in fact the enclosure round it, such as that at the Dodhead which the Captain of Bewcastle's men 'clam' before they 'ramshackled the house'. It was 'originally and strictly a palisade or stockade' (W. Mackay Mackenzie, *The Mediaeval Castle in Scotland*, 1927, p. 19), but came to mean the tower and enclosure together. Compare the lines quoted from Blind Harry's *Wallace*, *supra*, p. 8: 'On Gargownno was biggit a small peill', etc.

mare, a 'staig' or pony, twenty sheep, and half a dozen bolls of oats in his barnyard. His other worldly assets would be no more than perhaps two or three hundred merks owed to him by various neighbours to whom he had sold a beast or two or had lent small sums, and—the final phrase occurs with scarcely varying regularity—'the utencillis and domicillis with the abuilzementis of the defunctis bodie, estimat to tuentie pundis'.

Such were the homes of the men who rode with Wat of Harden or Johnie Armstrang; and in the crabbed and faded writing of the commissariot records a phrase or two sometimes varies the conventional forms of some man's latter will to illustrate the feudal relationship which bound the laird and his men together with reciprocal duties of protection and service. There is, for example, the breath of a ballad, or of the world of the ballads, in the latter will of a Carrick man who died in 1589, which included the clause: 'Item I leif to my maister the laird of Barganie xl *l.* money to be gude to my wyff and bairnis and that he sie na man wrang thame' [11]. Just such a bequest and such a charge might Jock o' the Side have left to the laird of Mangerton.

Of the burghs, on the other hand, we hear little in the ballads, except as scenes of imprisonment or escape. Yet there is the very clatter of a mediaeval street in the memory of the bonnie Earl of Moray 'sounding through the toun', or in the captive Hobie Noble's doomed journey through Carlisle:

> They hae tane him up the Ricker-gate.
> The wives they cast their windows wide;
> And ilka wife to anither can say,
> 'That's the man loos'd Jock o' the Side.'

And a vivid glimpse of a typical market-day bargain appears in 'Dick o' the Cow':

> I'll gie thee ten punds for the gude horse,
> Weel tauld on thy cloak lap they shall be,

though that is not so plainly descriptive, so utterly everyday as the parenthesis earlier in the same tale—an excessively humdrum verse which moreover impels me to believe that some ballads at least were recited, not sung; for it is hard to imagine the following fitted to any tune:

> It was then the use of Pudding-burn house,
> And the house of Mangerton, all hail,
> Them that cam na at the first ca',
> Gat nae mair till the neist meal.

The scenes, then, of the ballads, when not laid in the romantic setting of palace or castle or in the world of pure fancy, are utterly faithful to the life their audience knew. They reproduce a known and familiar background as truly as Jan Steen or David Teniers represents that of a merchant's house or a village inn. The touch of the artist, in the story as in the picture, lies not only in the drawing and the colour but in the arrangement of these homely materials.

But the minstrel as artist seldom shows at his best in the 'riding ballads'. His masterpieces are 'Sir Patrick Spens', 'Otterbourne', 'Kinmont Willie', 'Johnie Armstrang', 'The Bonnie Earl of Moray' and 'Edom o' Gordon' among the more or less historical ballads; 'The Broomfield Hill', 'Clerk Saunders', 'The Douglas Tragedy', 'Marie Hamilton' and 'Edward, Edward' among the tales of romance; and 'Thomas the Rhymer', 'Tam Lin', 'The Daemon Lover', 'The Twa Sisters', 'The Gay Goss-Hawk' and 'Young Benjie' among those which lie on the borders of Elfland. It is in these pieces that the talent for construction and climax, whether studied or unconscious, is most apparent; and since by 'the minstrel' I mean a type and not an individual, it follows that in those generations of the sixteenth and early seventeenth centuries that produced the best of the ballads there must have existed remarkably widely the instinct for those strokes which distinguish the ballads and make them one of Scotland's principal contributions to European literature. These characteristics I would distinguish as direct movement of the story to its catastrophe, economical statement, a telling choice of episode and memorably succinct dialogue. The story does not move laboriously on from point to point, as in the mediaeval romances, but—in the best of the ballads—by a swift succession of scenes, almost in the manner of a film, between which much is left to the imagination of an audience obviously accustomed to exercise that faculty. The minstrel assumes not so much that the audience knows the story as that it is trained to appreciate both the significance of each episode and the transition to the next.

The ballad, in fact, shows the qualities not only of the narrative artist but of the dramatist. Not till the eighteenth century did Scotland begin to produce novelists; not till our own day did she produce dramatists—notwithstanding such intermittent phenomena as *Ane Satyre of the Thrie Estaits* and *The Gentle Shepherd* and *Douglas*. But in the age when she was most distinctly a coherent and self-conscious nation she did, from some group of anonymous and blindly collaborating artists, evolve 'Sir Patrick Spens' and 'The Bonnie Earl of Moray' and 'Bonnie George Campbell' and 'Tam Lin' and the rest of the minstrel's masterpieces. In these there are all the elements of drama, and in them the strong dramatic sense of the Scottish countryman, which found no vent by way of the stage, was expressed with memorable force and with an effect that still speaks to generation after generation.

One can only speculate whether this sense of drama was innate or imitative. To some extent, of course, it is innate in every human society. But in Scotland it may have been strengthened by derivation from more than one source. No single tradition can alone explain any development in a nation of such mixed origins that its mediaeval sovereigns addressed their charters to subjects specified as 'Francis et Anglis et Scotis et Galwensibus' [12]. To the Scottish fashion of ballad-making Celtic folk-lore probably contributed much, though not its terseness of statement. Something too may have been caught up from the French romances

> De Karlemaine e de Rollant
> E d'Oliver e des vassals
> Ki morurent en Renchevals.

Something again may have descended from the Norse sagas: for example, the dialogue of the allied kings in the *Heimskringla* as they wait to intercept Olaf Tryggvason's great ship the 'Long Serpent' is framed and phrased exactly like a ballad; so is many a scene in the saga of *Burnt Njal*. One part too of the ballad's ancestry I am myself inclined to look for in the Old Testament. It is noteworthy that the great age of ballad-making coincides with the spreading of the Scriptures in the English tongue, and there is some affinity of form to be traced between, for instance, Gideon's pursuit after Zeba and Zalmunna and the Scotts' after the Captain of Bewcastle, or between the last verses of the Song of Deborah and those of 'Sir Patrick Spens' or 'The Bonnie Earl of Moray', in each of which women wait hopefully for the heroes who will never come home. It need not be doubted that the Book of Judges was favourite reading with the generation that bred the Scottish regiments of Gustavus Adolphus and the Army of the Covenant. But to guess at such possible influences is not to depreciate the peculiar genius of the ballad-makers for achieving a maximum of effect with a minimum of words, whether in narrative or dialogue, in strong contrast with, for instance, the prolixity of the Robin Hood cycle of English ballads. At its best, this intensity recalls the supreme moments of contemporary English drama.

There is, first, the ability to plunge the listener or the reader into the moving current of the story with the same suddenness as distinguishes the opening scene of *Hamlet*, where 'in fifteen broken lines (or eleven, if we choose to count), we have conveyed to us . . . the place, the freezing cold, the night, the very hour of the night, and withal a kind of creeping expectancy' [13]. With just the same sense of urgency and of fate waiting in the darkness begins 'The Douglas Tragedy':

> 'Rise up, rise up, now, Lord Douglas,' she says,
> 'And put on your armour so bright;
> Let it never be said that a daughter of thine
> Was married to a lord under night.'

There are expressed the midnight hour, the sudden awakening, the
quality of hero and heroine, intrigue, pride, anger and impending
combat—and all in four lines.

Then there is the single stanza, or the single phrase, which in the
starkest and simplest words detonates the climax of the action, sketches
the whole background to it or rapidly paints a contrasting scene. No
dramatist has ever said more in fewer words than the minstrels who
hit upon

> About the middle of the night
> She heard the bridles ring

or

> Oh! lang will his lady
> Look o'er the Castle Doune
> Ere she see the Earl of Moray
> Come sounding through the toun

or

> And mony a horse ran masterless
> And mony a comely cheek was pale

or

> But toom cam his saddle   *[empty*
> All bludie to see;
> Hame cam his gude horse,
> But never cam he.

But the parallel of the minstrel's occasional achievement with the
dramatist's is better seen in dialogue. The minstrel could sometimes
pack as much into four lines of speech as any dramatist: the chill of
doom:

> But I hae dream'd a dreary dream
> Beyond the Isle of Skye.
> I saw a dead man win a fight,
> And I think that man was I;

or a stinging defiance:

> To seik het water beneith cauld ice,
> Surely it is a greit folie—
> I have asked grace at a graceless face,
> But there is nane for my men and me;

or the passion of regret:

> Oh, little did my mother think,
> The day she cradled me,
> What lands I was to travel through,
> What death I was to dee;

or the touch of pity drowned in vindictiveness:

> It were great pity for gude Lord John,
> But none for Rothiemay;

or the summons to action, in words which vividly portray the desperate effort for which they call:

> Gae, fetch a web o' the silken claith,
> Another o' the twine,   [canvas
> And wap them into our ship's side   [bind
> And let na the sea come in—

—words that gain in their effect from being the very last we hear spoken on board the doomed ship, as though a curtain had fallen.

All these are essentially dramatic speeches, and their character is perhaps best underlined by contrasting one more example with a famous line actually written for the stage:

> Busk and boun, my merry men a',   [make ready
> For ill dooms I do guess.
> I canna look in that bonnie face
> As it lies on the grass

conveys the same feeling of belated remorse and of a dawning horror as 'Cover her face: mine eyes dazzle: she died young'.

3

I have said already that the highest achievements of the ballad-makers, whether deliberately contrived or reached by a natural instinct, are, unless set in the world of fairy-tale, compounded of familiar figures moving in a familiar setting. The third outstanding characteristic of the ballads is that not only these episodes but the language in which they are narrated is almost invariably that of the everyday world. The ballads rise to poetry without the verbal conventions of poetry, and there are very few words or phrases in them which could be classed as poetic diction. The exceptions are examples only of stock epithets, many of them carried on or recollected from the romances: the *gallant knight*, the *lady bright*, the *milk-white* or *berry-brown steed*, the *bonnie ship*, the *gude red gowd* and the *wan water*. Many, like other *clichés*, are worn too smooth to shine—though I confess that 'the wan water' has charmed and haunted me ever since my mother taught me as a child the ballad of 'Johnnie Faa', and epithets of colour keep their freshness and vividness for the reason that they occur but rarely. There are also stock phrases like 'As fast as he could drie' or 'As fast as she can hie', as easy for the minstrel to lift from one ballad to another as for the chanteyman to fill in his tale of verses with 'O wake her, O shake her!'

These labour-saving devices apart, the minstrel gains his effects with phrases of workaday speech. They strike home partly because they are subordinate to the movement of the story, the story's machinery rather than its decoration—and the ballad is story above all—and partly because they come straight from the familiar world of toil and struggle, loving and quarrelling, business and pleasure, and from the natural landscape spread before every man's eyes.

Ballad language—phrases and rhythms which might fit appropriately into a verse of a ballad—occurs frequently in sober record, in statutes, and even in legal documents of the sixteenth century and much later. Any formal accusation of a wrongdoer may contain phrases like 'art and part', 'in sober and quiet manner', 'in feir of weir' or 'under cloud and silence of night', which are the merest *clichés* of the Court of Justiciary records. The Register of the Privy Council has page upon page of what is admittedly not ballad verse but is surely ballad prose. One of its editors, Professor David Masson, observed after a prolonged soaking in his subject that 'only intimate acquaintance with the Register of the Council as it stands in manuscript could make one sufficiently aware of the extremely graphic character, the rich old Scottish relish, the excellent faculty of rough descriptive wording, to be found in many of the summaries of facts leading to the decisions' [14]. But it is not even necessary to turn to the passages of narrative of which the Register is so prolific to savour the quality of the daily language of the ballad age. Here is one example of straightforward official prose in the year 1581, the proclamation for a general levy

> to command and charge all and sindre his Hienes liegis . . . betuix sextie and sextene yeris of aige, and utheris fensable personis, duelland alsweill in burgh as to land, within regalitie as rialtie, that thay and ilkane of thame, weill bodin in feir of weir, with fourty dayes victuallis and provisioun efter their cuming, and with palyeonis and cariage to ly on the feildis, addres thameselffis to meit oure Soverane Lord and his lieutennent to be appointit to that effect at sic place or placis as salbe certefeit be the nixt proclamatioun, on sex dayis warning, to pas furthwart as thay salbe commandit to the effect abonewrittin, under the pane of tynsale of lyff, landis, and guidis. [15]

Such was the summons which went forth when a king ordered in real life:

> 'Gar warn me Perthshire and Angus baith,
> Fife up and downe, and Louthians three';

and the regular term 'bodin in feir of weir' may be explained and expanded by the citation of an Act of Parliament of 1540, couched likewise in prose that seems to echo the ballads:

It is statute and ordanit that all our Soverane Lordis liegis haif wapnis and harnes as eftir followis: In the first, that every nobill man sic as erle, lord, knycht and baroune, and every grett landit man haifand ane hundreth pund of yerlie rent, be anarmit in quhite harnes, lycht or hevy as thai pleiss, and wapnit efferand to his honoure.

The Act proceeds to specify the arms that must be borne by others 'of lawer rent and degre', by 'gentillmen unlandit' and yeomen respectively: the jacks, the gorgets, the 'splintis'—that is to say the 'splent on spauld' (armour on shoulder) of Kinmont Willie's rescuers —the gloves of plate or of mail, and the steel bonnets, concluding:

And that na maner of wapnis be admittit in wapinschawingis bot speris, pikis stark and lang of vi ellis of lenth, leicht axis, halbortis, handbowis and arrowis, corsbowis, culveringis, tua handit swordis, and every man to be anarmit as said is. [16]

Such was the equipment of Johnie Armstrang, Watty wi' the Wudspurs, or Dickie of Dryhope, and equally of the five thousand men the King would lead through Caddon Ford when the 'lymmaris' of the Border had to be repressed by force.

Other examples of ballad language in everyday life may be cited from many sources. Here, for example, is the description of a swash-buckling burgess of Dumfries in 1601, John Neilsoun by name, who, it was alleged,

proudlie and contempnandlie resortit up and doun the streitis of the said burgh, bodin and furneist with a lang hacquebute and ane pair of pistolettis, braging and mannassing all sic personis as preist to find fault or querrell him,

and at length discharged his hackbut and wounded a fellow-citizen [17]. Here is a death-bed scene of 1551, soberly recorded by a notary public:

Ane honorable and ane nobill knicht, Sir Andro Ker of the Hirsel, son and apperand air to Mark Ker of Littleden, came to the said Mark Ker his father, lyand on his deidbed, and speirit how he did; and he answerit and said, 'I do as God will, bot ye haif biddin lang fra me'; and the said Sir Andro said, 'My lord Governor wad nocht thole me to come fra him. Bot what will ye haif me doand? Tell me, and it sall be done.' [18]

And here is a glimpse, in 1694, of a pair of lovers in the springtime of their love, before the man proved faithless and the girl was left shamed and alone. A neighbour described how

he saw John Craufuird and Ann Kennedie comeing doun to Donnan Steps heartie and merry together, she haveing her hand upon his shoulder, about eleven hours in the forenoon, and that he never saw any ill appearance betuixt her and him. [19]

Many of the ballad stories, or episodes therein, are concerned not with warfare, nor love, nor witchcraft, but with the land and its produce which were the basis of all living. Jamie Telfer's poignant lament when he finds himself ruined—

> My hounds may a' rin masterless,
> My hawks may fly frae tree to tree,
> My lord may grip my vassal lands,
> For there again maun I never be!

—voices the dread of the typical little landowner whose position in life hangs on the fulfilment of his feudal obligations. If he cannot implement the *reddendo* clause in his charter, his superior may revoke it. The Outlaw Murray, on the other hand, finds himself in the happy position of one promised a Crown charter of *novodamus* with seal and precept of sasine all in order, on making formal resignation of his lands to his superior, who undertakes, in the handsomest manner,

> Now name thy landis where'er they lie,
> And here I render them to thee;

and moreoever—this tale being indubitably popular fiction—the King promises him a sheriffdom into the bargain. The whole theme of 'The Sang of the Outlaw Murray' is the transformation of an irregular tenure into a legal one. These are glimpses of the established system of feudal land-holding, of the business of lawyers and clerks and notaries that lay, ordered and ordinary, at the back of the bustling episodes on which the riding ballads were based. Yet the verse from 'Jamie Telfer', visualizing such vivid, realistic details as strayed hounds, lost hawks, and forfeited holding, evokes a picture of heartrending desolation and loss.

As the themes of the ballads are sometimes such everyday matters, so the dialogue in them often carries the rhythm of everyday speech. The homely orders of the Wife of Usher's Well—

> Blow up the fire, my maidens!
> Bring water from the well!

—eleven words such as any housewife might use—bring human warmth and activity into the eerie return of the three dead sons; and again, the lovely lament for the murdered Earl of Moray is so simple that it might be a direct transcription of the pitying whispers at the street-corners of Falkland or Dunfermline:

> He was a braw gallant,
> And he play'd at the ba',
> And the bonny Earl of Moray
> Was the flower amang them a'.

The encounter of Buccleuch's men with the false Sakelde in 'Kinmont Willie', although so subtly phrased and stressed that we hear in it the set, steady rhythm of the marching feet, is merely an interchange of common, earthy words such as might have been actually spoken in the real story behind the ballad:

> 'Where are ye gaun, ye mason lads,
>   Wi' a' your ladders, lang and hie?'
> 'We gang to herry a corbie's nest,   [*rob, crow's*
>   That wons not far frae Woodhouselee.'   [*lives*

Sometimes there is a lyrical touch in reference to nature. It is true that

> There's the hart, and hynd, and dae, and rae,
>   And of a' wild beastis grete plentie

is a mere catalogue; but there is almost artifice, as there is certainly music, in

> Nae bird flies faster through the wood
> Than she fled through the broom

and

> The flower that springs in May morning
> Was not sae sweet as she.

What sometimes sounds like a mannered phrase may once again turn out to be a snatch of common speech. Johnie Armstrang's boast that he once slew the King of England's nephew 'and on his breist bane brak a trie' echoes a phrase from real life, the defiance of the humorous warrior Patrick Rippett when the Earl of Cassillis's men waylaid Bargany:

> They being all ready to meitt . . . thay beganne to flytt; and Patrick Rippett cryit, 'Laird of Benand! Laird of Benand! Laird of Benand! This is I, Patrick Rippett, that tuik thy hagbut! Cum doun heir in the houm, and brek ane trie, for thy luiffis saik' [20].

So, as the ballads thus reflect real life, real life sometimes gives the impression of reflecting the ballads. Reported speech from authentic history is full of phrases which might have come straight out of ballads—or gone straight into them. Bargany's last words before the fight just mentioned—'Gude sirs, we are ower few!'—might be a line of a ballad. So too might be the fatal self-revelation of King James III a few minutes before his assassination—'I was your King this day at morn'—or the last words of Cardinal David Beaton—'Fy, fy, all is gane!'—or the Master of Glamis's stern comment on the humiliation of the boy king James VI—'It is no matter of his tears, better that bairns should weep than bearded men' [21].

These illustrations seem to lead to one of two conclusions, both questionable: either that the ballads, apart from those which are folk-tale and fairy-story, are not romantic but soberly realistic; or else that real life, in the reigns of James V and VI, was one long romance. The latter can be dismissed at once. Any doubter may be referred to such authentic records of the time as a typical notary's protocol book or the minutes of a burgh court, bailie court or baron court, the one concerned almost entirely with transactions in landed property and the careful transmission of rights in it from the outgoing owner to the new one, the others settling cases, seldom of armed assault or the abduction of lovely ladies, generally of small debts, quarrels between neighbours, petty thefts, trespass or delayed payment of rents. The ballads, on the other hand, are not mere versified reports. They represent a highly stylized version of even such authentically exciting episodes as Kinmont Willie's rescue or the bonnie Earl of Moray's death. They express an attitude to history, a retrospective rearrangement of episode, character, motive and emphasis into a dramatic pattern satisfying to the instinctive dramatic sense of the Scots.

This attitude is a characteristic of a people which views its whole national history in the light of legend, which has always preferred the impulsive character to the earnest one, and reveres those personages who shook their country's structure rather than those who soberly laboured to build it up, once such figures have receded from the light of to-day into the deceptive mists of the day before yesterday: Queen Mary, not the Regent Moray; Montrose, not Argyll; Claverhouse, not Stair; Prince Charles Edward, not Duncan Forbes. The speech and settings alone of the ballads are of the common world. Their form and shape, the clash and climax of their action, represent the human drama not as it is seen but as it is dreamed.

V

THE SCOTTISH AUGUSTANS

A. M. OLIVER

I

THE eighteenth-century Scots who wrote English verse, but little or no verse in Scots, are described conveniently by the title of this chapter—conveniently, but inaccurately. In the sense in which Horace or Pope was Augustan, in poise, clear self-knowledge and serene self-esteem, in mastery of technique and consummate propriety of expression, in a word, in classical perfection, there are no Scottish Augustans. Nor are there many English. The eighteenth-century critics were the first to note the unsatisfactory character of eighteenth-century poetry:

> But not to one in this benighted age
> Is that diviner inspiration giv'n,
> That burns in Shakespeare's or in Milton's page,
> The pomp and prodigality of heav'n.

Johnson voices Gray's lament more temperately, but no less decisively: 'There was no poetry, nothing that towered above the common mark' [1]. The nineteenth century, reacting violently, disliked its predecessor without much discrimination. The more dispassionate and painstaking studies of our own time modify the familiar picture, here and there, in detail, but leave it essentially unchanged. One emerges from an open-minded reading of Chalmers [2] or Anderson with a confirmed impression of immense copiousness and limited inspiration —'Though few can write, yet fewer can refrain'. Trivial themes were handled without urgency. Turning a copy of verses was a social accomplishment, and if the verses had a recognizable origin in Latin poetry, so much the better. Classical authority sanctioned the 'kinds' —epic, didactic, pastoral—which were cultivated side by side with the more congenial and adaptable satire and epistle. The authority of the classics was supported by the immense weight and prestige of Pope. Beside his splendid achievement the efforts of the 'rebels'—Lady Winchilsea, Akenside, even Collins—are slight and fragmentary. Devitalized and mechanical classicism, abortive and spurious romanticism—to how much verse of the period do these discouraging terms apply! They apply to verse by both Scots and English; but the Scots had, in addition, disadvantages peculiar to themselves.

Augustan poetry is central and metropolitan. The Scottish writers of the eighteenth century, drawn along that 'noblest prospect' [3] by the centripetal force of London, were drawn too late; they had spent their formative and impressionable years far from the circumference of wit. Their origins lay in another country, and this marks their verse both for good and bad.

Geography, common sense and expediency triumphed, in the Union of 1707, over history and sentiment. Sentiment had been more accurately reflected in the Act of Security and the Alien Act, passed, by Scotland and by England respectively, not three years before they became, in law but not in love, a United Kingdom. Swift greeted the Act of Union with contempt:

> Blest revolution! which creates
> Divided hearts, united states!
> See how the double nation lies;
> Like a rich coat with skirts of frize.

Poverty was indeed the chief Scottish motive for union, and Thomson, in so frequently celebrating British wealth and commerce, is sensibly enjoying the mess of pottage for which a birthright had been paid. The Scots had little else with which to pay. Their blend of poverty with pride had long been disliked by the English, but Skelton, in attacking it [4], had the advantage of detesting an enemy. The eighteenth-century Englishman, beholding it on nearer view, was not less repelled. Poverty had prevented travel and intercourse in the early, impressionable years. It had not, as would have been the case in England, prevented formal education. Had it done so, the Scots might have stayed at home, or filtered quietly south to fulfil humble and unassuming rôles in the rigidly stratified society of eighteenth-century England. In fact, the Scots who crossed the Border tended to be able men of sound education and narrow culture and experience, whose blend of pride and poverty, self-assurance and self-distrust, was unfamiliar and disconcerting. They were regarded as foreigners, and, in their mutual support and admiration, their haunting of the 'Breetish' coffee-house [5], as foreigners they acted. The London Scottish displayed a team spirit which was natural but tactless. Their speech was not English, but it was close enough to it to irritate rather than to endear.

They felt their identity, and unluckily they showed it. The feeling of separateness was intensified by regret. Arbuthnot's [6] *A Sermon preach'd to the people at the Mercat-Cross of Edinburgh; on the subject of the Union* is cool and rational. It explains succinctly to the Scots what solid advantages they will reap, what illusory shadows they sacrifice. Arbuthnot himself is consistently pleased. His family history, his success and popularity, his happy and adaptable nature ensured this. But throughout the century there is audible an undertone of sadness. It is more than an undertone in John Ramsay's final words on

Dundas of Arniston. 'He left it to younger men to bow to the Dagon of English taste. Though Scotland had lost its rank among the nations, he could say, as the Trojan did of his country after the fall, "Fuimus Troes, fuit Ilium et ingens gloria Teucrorum." ' The least sentimental were moved, at times, to mourn the end of an auld sang [7]. Smollett [8] refers unemotionally in his prose [9] to North Britain, but, when *facit indignatio versum*, he names his verse *The Tears of Scotland*. 'Butcher' Cumberland on the one hand, Bute and his placemen on the other, helped to increase the strain of which Churchill's satire and Johnson's *obiter dicta* are merely the most amusing and celebrated evidences. Of course, there were personal friendships; no one was more charming to individual Scots than Johnson was. But one can love a sinner while not ceasing to hate the sin. Before Walter Scott made of the national marriage of convenience a friendly, tolerant and civilized companion-ship, a century of uneasy adjustment and hearty dislike was to elapse.

This was an unfavourable atmosphere for poetry, especially for Augustan poetry, which is so largely a social growth, depending on and addressed to an audience of equals. The Scot, writing in this atmosphere, was further handicapped by writing in a language which was not his mother-tongue. To say so is easy; fully to realize the fact, and its implications, is not so easy. To the educated Scot of the early and mid-century, who used the dialect in all his familiar relationships, who lectured in and listened to Latin on formal occasions, English was not even a second but actually a third language. It was deliberately learned, chiefly by study of the *Tatler*, the *Spectator* and the *Guardian*. 'Those admirable papers prepared the minds of our countrymen for the study of the best English authors, without a competent knowledge of which no man was accounted a polite scholar'. Ramsay goes on to say that to render the dialect 'polished and correct would have been a Herculean labour, not likely to procure them much renown. Nothing, therefore, remained but to write classical English, which, though exceedingly difficult to men who spoke their mother-tongue without disguise, was greatly facilitated by the enthusiastic ardour with which they studied the best English authors' [10]. The distinction drawn between classical English and the mother-tongue is vital to an under-standing of the Scottish Augustans. They acquired English as Words-worth acquired Greek and Latin. His view of the process, and its results, is relevant and illuminating:

> In fine,
> I was a better judge of thoughts than words,
> Misled in estimating words, not only
> By common inexperience of youth,
> But by the trade in classic niceties,
> The dangerous craft of culling term and phrase

From languages that want the living voice
To carry meaning to the natural heart;
To tell us what is passion, what is truth,
What reason, what simplicity and sense. [11]

Their prose models were excellent, and the Scots learned to write good English prose. 'The Scotch write English wonderfully well,' Johnson commented in sending thanks to Dr. Blair for his sermons. One need look no further than Burns's letters (not, of course, his stilted and pretentious letters to Clarinda) for proof of this. But it was the result of constant vigilance. 'In all their essays at composition, it behoved them to avoid everything that could be called a Scotticism or solecism.' Intelligence, care and enthusiasm did much, but they could not defeat nature. Lord Mansfield told Alexander Carlyle that when he read Hume and Robertson 'he did not think he was reading English' [12].

One cannot doubt that the effort to attain an English prose style was right and necessary. The 'literature of knowledge' must be expressed with as little obstruction as possible, as much lucidity. The eighteenth-century Scots were responding, as the English had done in the sixties of the seventeenth century—and for much the same reasons —to 'the imperious need of a fit prose'. But constant watchfulness, nervous fear of the instinctive and spontaneous phrase, uneasy unfamiliarity and reference to the dictionary (Boswell even consults it in writing his love letters! [13]) make an atmosphere unpropitious to poetry. The living word of 'race' and character is struck out in favour of the safe one. The temptation to write about it and about is overwhelming: many words will surely include the right one. Sometimes they do so, but the result is usually tiresome and distracting overpainting. The writing of familiar verse is impossible in an unfamiliar tongue, and the Scots poets give us little corresponding to the easy, natural verse of Swift or Prior. Burns in his verse epistles, even Beattie in 'To Mr. Alexander Ross', show how admirably they could do it in dialect. Their native fun and humour, so characteristic of their *native* verse, is paralysed by the strain of writing English. 'These English Songs gravel me to death.—I have not that command of the language that I have of my native tongue' [14]. Burns does not merely state the problem; he illustrates the strangling effect in his passages of English verse—'A Winter Night' might have been specially written to display the contrast between the quick and the dead. What is bad in Burns is worse in Beattie, Smollett, Wilkie—all his many compatriots so incomparably less gifted with poetic power. To neglect the mother-tongue is to attain frigidity, or rhetoric,* or dull tameness. The

---

* Compare, for example, the laments for Culloden by Smollett (*The Tears of Scotland*) and by Burns (*The Lovely Lass o' Inverness*).

appropriate criterion of the Scottish Augustan verse is not, perhaps, the English verse of contemporary Englishmen, but their *poemata*.

In a study on this scale it would be pointless to resurrect what is dead, and what indeed never had genuine life, whether it be conventional inanity, like the mechanical lyrics which so strangely contrast, in Smollett's novels, with the vital prose of their context, or whether it be the painful effort of misdirected zeal, like Wilkie's classical epic on the siege of Thebes. Nothing would be easier or more entertaining —at least for the writer—than to poke fun at Wilkie's *Epigoniad* [15]— and nothing could be more useless. It is bad, and everyone has always thought so, except for the Dundas clique who seized it as a stick to beat John Home, and for David Hume, who largely confines himself to retelling the story more clearly than Wilkie does, and whose description of it as 'a performance which may, perhaps, be regarded as one of the ornaments of our language' is remarkable for its judicious qualifying word [16]. The writer devoid of poetic gift, who nevertheless wrote verse for exercise or amusement, offers only the interest of curiosity—and this will be sufficient notice of Boswell's verse output, such as 'The Cub, at Newmarket: a Tale', the undergraduate wit of his metrical effusions to Andrew Erskine, or his nightly five couplets in Holland [17]. But the Scottish Augustans include not merely poetasters. Some were poets, and this preliminary view of the common predicament may help towards an understanding of the imperfect and unsatisfactory nature of much of their work.

2

Most of the defects and virtues of these Scottish poets are apparent in Thomson [18]. His 'outset', to borrow one of Ramsay's favourite terms, was typical—a son of the manse, a manse set in the austere and beautiful Border countryside, he found

> Caledonia stern and wild,
> Meet nurse for a poetic child.

He was fifteen before he left Southdean for Edinburgh University, to study classics and theology, and almost twenty-five before he left Scotland for London. In Edinburgh he had belonged to a club for the study of English. In London he was helped by friendly Scots. The pattern of education, poverty, courage, ambition, emigration and success is familiar, although Macpherson and Beattie visit England after achieving success, and Blair, Wilkie and Blacklock [19] remain in Scotland. But, in intention and aspiration at least,

> Frae the cottar to the laird
> We a' rin South. [20]

Thomson met with immediate recognition (there were four editions of *Winter* in 1726) and a widespread popularity which lasted throughout the century and beyond. This popularity sprang from his tactful blending of the familiar with the strange. The themes which Wordsworth was to present in their own right are served by Thomson as dressings rather than as main dishes. His autobiographical references, for example, are rare and brief. We read of his cheerful morn of youth by the banks of Jed [21], and wish he had told us more. It is possible to feel that Wordsworth has told us more than we desire or deserve. The contemporary reader who opened *The Seasons* found nothing to startle or repel. He found a descriptive and meditative poem which acknowledged its debt to the *Georgics* and to 'Pomona's bard' [22] (and was indeed written, like Philips's *Cider*, in blank verse, which, being '*English* Heroic Verse without Rime', was clearly appropriate where the ultimate model was in hexameters). He found, too, something not unlike *Coopers Hill, Claremont* and *Windsor Forest*, majestically defined by Johnson as '*local poetry*,' of which the fundamental subject is some particular landscape, to be poetically described, with the addition of such embellishments as may be supplied by historical retrospection, or incidental meditation' [23]. Thomson's 'particular landscapes' are many, his survey is global rather than local, but the rest of the definition beautifully covers *The Seasons*. The 'embellishments' are added with a hand so ungrudging that the poem becomes a miscellany—and the eighteenth century loved miscellanies.

The groundwork is of course natural description, and in the context of Wordsworth's undisputed dictum that 'excepting the nocturnal Reverie of Lady Winchilsea, and a passage or two in the "Windsor Forest" of Pope, the poetry of the period intervening between the publication of the "Paradise Lost" and the "Seasons" does not contain a single new image of external nature' [24], one may realize the novelty and attraction of the poem. The familiar—the revolution of the year, the effects of the changing seasons on every form of life—is presented with fidelity. The truth of Thomson's descriptions is a critical truism. His memory was stored with closely observed images; his familiar scenes are full of life and movement. Imagination supplements these with others which are sometimes, as in the incident of Sir Hugh Willoughby's ship icebound in the Arctic seas (*Winter*, ll. 925-35), powerfully rendered.

This incident is a very favourable specimen of another ingredient of Thomson's mixture, the inserted tales. Like the narrative papers which diversified the contemporary periodical essay, these gratified the universal love of a story. Thomson's tales, diffuse and sentimental, are in the sharpest contrast with Pope's. The story of Sir Balaam [25] is *merum sal*; only the reader who knows the Book of Job will fully realize its point and power, and the implication of its climax, 'sad Sir

Balaam curses God'. Thomson's stories can be read with relaxed attention, and their point—such as it is—is obvious. Easy and undemanding reading, they gave mild and widespread pleasure for a time. They appeared in anthologies. The story of Palemon and Lavinia, for example (*Autumn*, ll. 177-310), was one of Goldsmith's *Beauties of English Poesy*, though Goldsmith claims little responsibility for this: 'It is rather given here for being much esteemed by the public, than the editor.' Wordsworth attributes much of Thomson's popularity to these tales. 'In any well-used copy of the "Seasons" the book generally opens of itself with the rhapsody on love, or with one of the stories (perhaps "Damon and Musidora").' If the celebrated copy found in the inn at Linton thus opened of itself, there may have been some irony in Coleridge's exclamation, '*That* is true fame!' [26]

The sugary flavour of the tales is offset by the more solid fare of Thomson's learning. His interest in Newtonian physics is deep and genuine, he *knows* how natural appearances are created, and he loves to instruct his reader. 'The swain' wonders at the bright enchantment of the rainbow, but Thomson knows its woof, its texture:

> Here, awful Newton, the dissolving clouds
> Form, fronting on the sun, thy showery prism;
> And to the sage-instructed eye unfold
> The various twine of light, by thee disclosed
> From the white mingling maze.

Thomson had already treated the subject in *A Poem, Sacred to the Memory of Sir Isaac Newton*, where thirty lines of accurate description of the composition of the rainbow reach a climax in 'How just, how beauteous, the *refractive law*.' The catalogue of spring flowers contains a botanical note:

> From family diffused
> To family, as flies the father-dust,
> The varied colours run.

To the cause of instruction Thomson sacrifices much—too much. With

> Sudden the fields
> Put on their winter-robe of purest white

he had evoked a visual image of the swift transformation wrought by snow; it was the simple, the inspired stroke of an artist. But it gave no information about the function of snow, so the image was blurred in favour of 'The cherished fields'. In the description of the hunted hare he spoils a passage of simple and vivid writing by one didactic touch:

> The fallow ground laid open to the sun
> Concoctive. [27]

The poet had fixed our attention on the plight of the hare; we can only resent the interference of the scientist.

Thomson is a preacher as well as a teacher:

> These, as they change, Almighty Father! these
> Are but the varied God. The rolling year
> Is full of Thee.

His religious feeling is related rather to the dignity and gentlemanliness of Addison than to the emotionalism of Isaac Watts. But Thomson is impressed not only by the spacious firmament on high. He notes

> where gloomily retired
> The villain spider lives, cunning and fierce,
> Mixture abhorred!

He watches the sleeping dogs, and guesses their dreams.

> Nor shall the muse disdain
> To let the little noisy summer-race
> Live in her lay and flutter through her song;
> Not mean though simple.

He accepts them all with affection and appreciation, and is quite unstirred by them to 'thoughts that do often lie too deep for tears'. *His* train of thought is easy enough to follow:

> Behold, fond man!
> See here thy pictured life: pass some few years,
> Thy flowering Spring, thy Summer's ardent strength,
> Thy sober Autumn fading into age,—
> And pale concluding Winter comes at last
> And shuts the scene. [28]

Such thinking is neither original nor profound. It has the qualities which Johnson noted in Gray's *Elegy*, and it helps to explain Thomson's popularity. Beside the awful universality of 'Man that is born of a woman', and the piercing, immediate particularity of 'It is Margaret you mourn for' [29], Thomson's moralizing is conventional and trite. It is politely in keeping with a general poem addressed to the general reader, dedicated to a patron and nicely blended to suit all tastes.

In his choice of theme for his first considerable poem Thomson draws on Scottish tradition. Henryson's description of winter in 'The Preiching of the Swallow', the opening of his *Testament of Cresseid* and Douglas's Prologues are unforgettable in their intensity. They point forward to Burns,

> While winds frae aff Ben Lomond blaw,
> And bar the doors wi' driving snaw,
> And hing us owre the ingle; [30]

and Thomson, though he has (alas!) denied himself their unfettered expression of elemental feeling, yet writes as one having authority. Winter in Scotland can still be harsh and paralysing; in the eighteenth century 'in the more remote parts of the country, for five or six months in the year, social intercourse was almost impossible'. Smollett comments that 'there is no such convenience as a waggon in this country'— because there was scarcely a road fit to bear wheeled traffic [31]. The effect of winter's rigour was to isolate its victims in small, self-contained groups, thrown each upon itself for mutual comfort and support. The sorrows of each member were shared, in sympathy, by all. Thomson's picture of the shepherd lost in the snow, of his family awaiting him in vain, is based on knowledge and is full of feeling, as are his studies of the sufferings inflicted by winter upon birds and animals. Within the isolated groups an intense social intercourse flourished, all the more precious for the misery without. Beside the brilliance and hilarity of 'The Farmer's Ingle', 'The Jolly Beggars' and 'Tam o' Shanter', Thomson's description of village night-life in winter [32] is decorous, yet it suggests what that life meant to the people, and how rich it must have been in inspiration to the young poet, with its jests and games, its traditional music and dancing, and the 'goblin story' arousing superstitious horror. There is vitality here, in contrast to the preachifying and abstract passage, immediately following, on the city's night life. Thomson's studies of peasant life, slight as they are in bulk, and given neither local habitation nor name, initiate a tradition which includes Gray, Goldsmith and Cowper, and culminates in Wordsworth. With the peasants he associates the supernatural, obviously too crude an element to be presented directly in the Age of Reason. It is a *shepherd* of the Hebrid Isles who sees the miraculous vision [33].

Winter brought an intensified and concentrated social life. Further, it threw each man upon his own resources. Thomson's response to the fierce and isolating season recalls Henryson's:

> I mend the fyre, and beikit me about,
> Than tuik ane drink my spreitis to comfort,
> And armit me weill fra the cauld thairout:
> To cut the winter nicht and mak it schort,
> I tuik ane Quair, and left all uther sport.

> Be my retreat
> .   .   .   .   .
> A rural, sheltered, solitary scene,
> Where ruddy fire and beaming tapers join
> To cheer the gloom. There studious let me sit,
> And hold high converse with the mighty dead. [34]

The contrast between them is more significant than the superficial resemblance. Henryson writes in the confidence and power of a native tradition; his 'Quair', moreover, is the mainspring and inspiration of his poem. But Thomson's 'high converse with the mighty dead' is but an excuse for a catalogue of Greek and Roman worthies, a hundred lines long, in the manner of *Liberty*. It is as creditable to the author's reading and general knowledge as it is otiose and irrelevant to his poem.

Summer, *Spring* and *Autumn* resulted from the success of *Winter*, which is unique in its Scottish character and in the fact that Thomson wrote it with no thought of making up a set. The others are sequels, assembled, if not constructed, after the manner of the prototype. *Summer*, for example, includes an excursion to the tropics, as *Winter* has one to the far North. The poem suffers from its length; matter which in a single 'season' might have passed as relevant is instantly seen to be padding. How far from organic much of it is is clear from Thomson's transferring sections from one 'season' to another. *Winter* is a fair specimen of *The Seasons*, in the variety of its content, its accurate natural description, humanitarian exhortation, anecdotal spicings, classical references, contemporary ideas, moralizing reflections and piety. There is something for everyone, and Thomson fed the appetite he created. For *Winter* may finally be taken as representative in the fact that Thomson revised it unceasingly. The first edition (1726) contained 405 lines; in the first complete edition of *The Seasons* (1730), *Winter* had 781 lines, and in Thomson's final edition (1746) it had 1069. The figures are striking, but only a first-hand comparison of the many editions can give any idea of the nature and extent of Thomson's rewriting. *The Seasons* was a different poem at different times, as Wordsworth found to his satisfaction when he maintained that 'the true characteristics of Thomson's genius as an imaginative poet' were by no means those which were earliest or most widely recognized.

Thomson's fundamental weakness, both in content and in style, is his inability to discriminate. A true Augustan, he is alive to the poet's responsibility to teach, to exhort, to be actively a man of his time. Thus he loads his Muse with luggage so heavy and so awkward that movement is difficult and soaring impossible. *The Castle of Indolence*, which relates the destruction of sensuous pleasure by respectable industry, is a convenient symbol of his whole poetic output. The reader swallows—or skips—the didactic passages of *The Seasons* for the sake of the descriptive; but *Liberty* is a purely didactic poem with narrative illustrations. In the tradition of Addison's *A Letter from Italy*, the first three parts provide a condensed classical education, a synopsis of the history and culture of Greece, with a sermon on the reasons for its decay and fall, an approving précis of early Roman history with moralizings on Patience, Hope, Moderation and Independence. The history of Britain, with its extremely unfavourable view of the Stuarts and its adulation of William III—'Than hero more, the patriot of mankind!' [35]—makes the reader feel that it was lucky for Thomson that Johnson so early desisted from his perusal of *Liberty*.

Part V is a summary and restatement of Thomson's purpose, a lecture on the excellence of the British constitution:

> Then was the full, the perfect plan disclos'd
> Of Britain's matchless constitution, mixt
> Of mutual checking and supporting powers,
> King, lords and commons.

Only luxury can hurt it:

> Britons! be firm!—nor let corruption sly
> Twine round your heart indissoluble chains!

For luxury, 'Rapacious, cruel, mean, Mother of vice', caused the fall of Rome and its 'softer shackles' destroyed Venice [36]. Like the preacher on sin, Thomson is 'agin' luxury. It is the peroration of *Britannia*,

> Oh, let not then waste Luxury impair
> That manly soul of toil,

and the burden (in every sense) of *Liberty*, whom he invokes at the close of Part I:

> While I, to nobler than poetic fame
> Aspiring, thy commands to Britons bear.

This is an explicit admission that Thomson has served two masters, and has preferred one of them to poetry. Poetry has taken its revenge.

Thomson's patriotic zeal for industry and commerce, which fills such vast tracts of his work, has one permanent memorial. Britons may no longer read his injunction to venerate the plough, or gratify them-selves with the thought that the Knight of Arts and Industry chose their island as his favourite spot, in which, having approved the soil, the climate and the genius of the land, he 'Bade social commerce raise renownèd marts', and to which he then called the drooping muses [37]. But more than two centuries after the publication of *Alfred, a Masque* they can still sing 'Rule, Britannia' with a vigour and feeling before which 'criticism is suspended' [38].

Thomson has always been the poet of *The Seasons*. This is un-fortunate, for, despite the abiding worth of some parts of that monumental miscellany, *The Castle of Indolence* is finer and more sustained poetry. Thomson wrote it at leisure over the last years of his life, when he was no longer a writer on his probation; he wrote it when he was relatively at ease with English, and in any case his model is Spenser's 'no language'. Here he has spared himself the effort of striving after a grand style in an idiom partly contemporary and partly Miltonic. The first canto reads like Spenser himself, or like Keats:

> The rooms with costly tapestry were hung,
> Where was inwoven many a gentle tale,
> Such as of old the rural poets sung
> Or of Arcadian or Sicilian vale.

Sometimes he anticipates one of Coleridge's lovelier effects:

> He ceased. But still their trembling ears retained
> The deep vibrations of his 'witching song. [39]

Some vibrations of *The Castle of Indolence*, with its bickering streams and woods in summer moonlight, may be audible in *The Ancient Mariner*.

The Seasons tends to exhaustiveness. It would be a captious reader who complained that some aspect of any season, dear and familiar to him, had been ignored in Thomson's survey. In *Spring*, the list of 'the tuneful nations' includes ten different kinds of bird in sixteen lines. Thomson has indeed been 'prodigal of harmony'. In *The Castle of Indolence* he mentions only two bird-songs among the natural sounds which bring sleep:

> And now and then sweet Philomel would wail,
> Or stockdoves 'plain amid the forest deep,
> That drowsy rustled to the sighing gale.

He has learned to select. He is no longer straining every nerve, and his poem in consequence has free and spontaneous life. The memories of boyhood—

> What transport to retrace our boyish plays,
> Our easy bliss, when each thing joy supplied,—
> The woods, the mountains, and the warbling maze
> Of the wild brooks! [40]

—and the personal references to his friends [41], emphasize the poem's informality. With infectious gaiety he celebrates that indolence which was his natural bent and of which he officially disapproved. In the first canto he neither teaches nor preaches. He is as far removed from his didactic and edifying self as is the shepherd of the Hebrid Isles in the astonishing thirtieth stanza which moved Joseph Warton to rapture [42] and can surely never be read without emotion. He is on holiday, but holidays must end. He pulls himself together and re-assumes the familiar rôle of moralist and sage. The Knight of Arts and

Industry triumphs, the colour and light are extinguished, the enchantment disappears, 'Then all at once in air dissolves the wondrous show'.

Eighteenth-century verse as a whole suffers from the habit of deliberately clothing thought with style. The clothes are often ill-chosen and ill-fitting, despite Pope's warning that they are 'more decent, as more suitable' [43]. Thomson is an outstanding example, and from the first his readers have drawn a clear distinction between what he says and how he says it. Somervile considered his faults mere spots in the sun, but advised their removal:

> Read Philips much, consider Milton more;
> But from their dross extract the purer ore.
> To coin new words, or to restore the old,
> In southern bards is dangerous and bold;
> But rarely, very rarely, will succeed,
> When minted on the other side of Tweed.
> Let perspicuity o'er all preside—
> Soon shalt thou be the nation's joy and pride. [44]

Joseph Warton called him 'a favourite author, and who would have been a first-rate poet, if his style had been equal to his conceptions'. Coleridge judged that 'Thomson was a great poet, rather than a good one; his style was as meretricious as his thoughts were natural', and Wordsworth that 'notwithstanding his high powers, he writes a vicious style' [45].

This formidable chorus, from which but a few voices have been selected, had been opened by the Professor of Divinity at Edinburgh who rebuked Thomson for the 'poetically splendid' [46] language he used in explaining a psalm. He seems to have been incapable of effective self-criticism. His fault was not carelessness—far from it. He did not need Somervile's hint—

> Why should thy Muse, born so divinely fair,
> Want the reforming toilet's daily care?

—or, rather, he misapplied it, and added cosmetics where an astringent or a sponge would have met the case. His rhythms are monotonous. Even the notorious 'O Sophonisba! Sophonisba, O!' is paralleled by 'No, fair illusions! artful phantoms, no!' Too often he repeats the effect of

> See where the winding vale its lavish stores,
> Irriguous, spreads!

and

> 'Mid the bright group Sincerity his front,
> Diffusive, rear'd. [47]

These phrases illustrate his fondness for the Latin polysyllable, especially for opening the line, and for adjectives ending in *-ive* (effusive, amusive, afflictive, conjunctive) and *-ous* (sequacious, auriferous, umbrageous, ovarious). Thomson's respect for Latin—and for Milton—leads to some frigidity and obscurity in his English. If 'in cheerful error let us tread the maze', or 'the latent Damon', give nothing more than a moment's regretful amusement, 'inspect sage' has to be deliberately translated to 'wise insight'. 'Ceres void of pain' (crops produced without trouble) evokes memories of one of the tenderest passages of human feeling in *Paradise Lost*:

> .... Which cost *Ceres* all that pain
> To seek her through the world ....

The grief of the bereaved mother is real to Milton, and Ceres is a living and suffering creature. She is real and alive, too, the triumphant embodiment of natural vitality, in Pope: 'laughing Ceres re-assume the land'. Thomson's phrase is mechanical, dead and literary.

He overloads his line with epithet—'Her full-assembled youth innumerous swarm'd'—and with compound words:

> Foul ministers, dark-working by the force
> Of secret-sapping gold. [48]

There is too much rhetorical question, exclamation, exhortation and apostrophe: too much for the reader's patience, or to need illustration. Occasionally, and with an unintended comic effect, Thomson answers his rhetorical questions:

> —was there no father, robbed
> Of blooming youth to prop his withered age?
> No son . . . no friend, forlorn?
>
> . . . . . .
>
> No:—Sad o'er all profound dejection sat.

He closes *Liberty V* with a long series of *Lo! See! Behold! Hark!* as the prospect of future times unrolls before him. His poetic diction— 'plumy people', 'finny race', 'glossy kind'—is notorious. But even into such conventionalities as these he can sometimes infuse feeling, as when he describes the sheep driven into the pool as 'the soft fearful people', or when, writing of the silkworm, he provides a kind of crossword-puzzle clue:

> And let the little insect-artist form,
> On higher life intent, its silken tomb.

This highly characteristic blend of periphrasis, accurate description and tenderness of heart is present also in his injunction to the fisherman to throw back into the stream 'the speckled infant' [49]. The faults of

Thomson's style—verbosity, declamation, the piling-up of epithet, insensitivity and monotony—are cruelly and conveniently obvious in his 'Paraphrase on the latter part of the sixth chapter of St. Matthew':

> Say, does not life its nourishment exceed?
> And the fair body its investing weed?
> Behold! and look away your low despair—
> See the light tenants of the barren air:
>
> .   .   .   .   .
>
> Observe the rising lily's snowy grace,
> Observe the various vegetable race . . . .

Even his variation on the theme in *The Castle of Indolence* (i. 73-90, where 'the merry minstrels of the morn' have a vitality denied 'the light tenants of the barren air') is long-winded and clumsy beside the simplicity of the original.

But Thomson is capable of felicities; he notes the redbreast's 'slender feet', and the 'many-twinkling leaves of aspen'. His wallflower is deservedly famous, and there is an equal precision in

> auriculas, enrich'd
> With shining meal o'er all their velvet leaves.

He is notably successful in rendering the sound and movement of water. The sea in all its moods resounds in his poetry, from 'The murmuring main was heard, and scarcely heard, to flow' to

> Where the Northern Ocean in vast whirls
> Boils round the naked melancholy isles
> Of farthest Thule, and the Atlantic surge
> Pours in among the stormy Hebrides. [50]

The closing phrase, with its echo of 'Lycidas', suggests the poet to whom Thomson is indebted for some of his finest effects—including his splendid use of place-names—as well as some of his worst. Under the impact of grief he writes the language of the heart. His significantly named 'Verses. Occasion'd by the Death of Mr. Aikman, a particular friend of the Author's' may stand with Johnson's 'On the Death of Mr. Robert Levet' as an unaffected, deeply felt expression of sorrow:

> As those we love decay, we die in part,
> String after string is sever'd from the heart;
> Till loosen'd life, at last, but breathing clay,
> Without one pang is glad to fall away.
> Unhappy he, who latest feels the blow,
> Whose eyes have wept o'er every friend laid low,
> Drag'd ling'ring on from partial death to death,
> Till, dying, all he can resign is breath.

Among the earliest of the Scottish Augustans, Thomson is incomparably the most important. He showed his compatriots that success could be won, and how it could be won. His boldness in using blank verse and the Spenserian stanza encouraged others. His themes were taken up by other writers, and it would be difficult to name any notable Scottish contribution to eighteenth-century English poetry which does not owe its hint to Thomson. True, he writes few genuine epistles, but there is little that is noteworthy in those of Armstrong, Mickle, Blacklock or Beattie; he writes no formal verse translations, though here and there he embeds a passage of translation in his own work. His rendering in *Liberty* [51] of the close of the great Regulus ode is diffuse and weak, but what translation in an uninflected tongue could match that original? Thomson writes very little satire, but what he does (for example, the lines in *The Castle of Indolence* on earthly vanity [52]) is well done, which is more than can be said for Mallet's 'Of Verbal Criticism', Falconer's 'The Demagogue', Smollett's *Advice and Reproof*, Blacklock's 'Advice to the Ladies' or Beattie's wretched attack on Churchill's memory. The vein which Thomson opened in the treatment of Scottish scenes and the supernatural was to be exploited with increasing confidence by his successors. Of more immediate effect was his lead in didactic verse.

3

Arbuthnot, more than thirty years older than Thomson, may have composed ΓΝΩΘΙ ΣΕΑΥΤΟΝ, *Know Yourself*, before Thomson could write at all; 'wrote several years before', it was published in 1734. It is convenient to group it with Scottish didactic verse, but it is more philosophical than instructive, related to *De Rerum Natura* rather than to the *Georgics*. The author is concerned with the hybrid and enigmatical nature of man, part animal and part divine. His poem is valuable, not so much for its literary quality as for the light it throws on the serious interests of Arbuthnot, and on his character. He was one of the most attractive figures of the age, witty, kind and unassuming. Swift found in him 'every quality and virtue that can make a man amiable or useful', and the news of his death 'struck [him] to the heart' [53]. Pope's Epistle is but the most celebrated of the tributes paid him by the discerning, such as Berkeley, Gay and Chesterfield. But no member of the Scriblerus Club was safe from attack, and though James Moore Smyth's *One Epistle to Mr. A. Pope, occasion'd by Two Epistles, lately published* (1730) is merely entertaining in its abuse of Arbuthnot as a quack, and a 'puzzling, plodding, prating, pedant Scot', there is some justification for his couplet on

The grating scribbler! whose untuned Essays
Mix the Scotch Thistle with the English Bays.

Arbuthnot, unlike Thomson, paid little attention to style. He is strenuously occupied with the subject of *Know Yourself*, and where the printed text varies from his original manuscript it is for the purpose of expressing his thought with greater clarity and precision. There are incidental stylistic improvements: for example, in his account of metabolism 'The Fabrick changd; the Tenant still remains' becomes 'The mansion changed, the tenant still remains', where the kinship of the words from an identical root (*maneo*) sharpens the antithesis of the thought. More characteristic of the poem as a whole is his rewriting of the passage on the Bible:

> Stupendous is thy power; O light divine
> The sons of darkness tremble at each Line.
> Black doubt, & Hell-Born error shun thy Ray
> As tardy sprights are startled at the day.
> Thow cleard the secret of my high descent,
> Thow told me what those Motly tokens meant.

This appeared in the printed version as:

> Thus the benighted traveller that strays
> Through doubtful paths, enjoys the morning rays;
> The nightly mist, and thick descending dew,
> Parting, unfold the fields, and vaulted blue.
> 'O truth divine! enlightened by thy ray,
> I grope and guess no more, but see my way;
> Thou clear'dst the secret of my high descent,
> And told me what those mystic tokens meant.'

The reader may regret the elimination of the sprights, while admitting their merely decorative character. The image of the benighted traveller clarifies the thought, and directly recalls *Religio Laici*, which the poem so closely resembles in its honest attempt to measure a problem of vital significance, and to reach a solution. Like Dryden too, Arbuthnot might have said:

> Thus have I made my own Opinions clear:
> Yet neither Praise expect, nor Censure fear:
> And this unpolish'd, rugged Verse, I chose;
> As fittest for Discourse, and nearest Prose.

Johnson's comment on lines by Richard Bentley the elder is wholly applicable to Arbuthnot's poem: 'they are the forcible verses of a man of a strong mind, but not accustomed to write verse; for there is some uncouthness in the expression' [54].

There is uncouthness of expression in Armstrong [55] too, despite his more extensive practice in verse. (We cannot guess, of course, how many of Arbuthnot's papers, handed to his children for kite-making,

may have been poetical compositions.) Both men, like Grainger and
Smollett, were doctors of medicine. The first of Dr. Theobald's two
Odes, 'Ad ingenuum Virum, tum medicis, tum poeticis, facultatibus
praestantem, Johannem Armstrong, M.D.', opens with a neatly turned
variant of the common compliment on a twofold kinship with Apollo:

> Artisque Coae O et Citharae sciens,
> Utroque mirè dexter Apolline! [56]

The Art of Preserving Health is admirable in its seriousness, its
effective organization and the power of much of its writing. Armstrong
was conscious of the intractability of his material. He invokes Hygeia's
help to steer him 'Thro' paths the Muses never trod before', because

> 'Tis hard, in such a strife of rules, to choose
> The best, and those of most extensive use;
> Harder in clear and animated song
> Dry philosophic precepts to convey.

In the subject of diet he sees

> A barren waste, where not a garland grows
> To bind the Muse's brow.

Forced to make his own garlands, he weaves them of classical mythology, of passages on flowers and sunlight and music, of resounding
rhetoric on the inevitability of old age and the transience of all things.
Like Thomson, he uses place-words with rich effect:

> the Babylonian spires are sunk;
> Achaia, Rome and Egypt moulder down.

Like him, and indeed like most of these Scottish Augustans, he is moved
by Scots place-names to tender autobiographical writing; his lines on
the 'romantic groves' and 'fairy banks' of Liddel where he bathed and
fished 'when life was new' [57] stand with Smollett's 'To Leven-Water'
as evidence of feeling unaffected by distance, absence or time.

With Armstrong, vocation and avocation are one. His verse is
penetrated by his professional zeal. *A Day*—an epistle to Wilkes—is
full of advice on matters of health, and the four stanzas which end
Canto I in *The Castle of Indolence* were contributed by him. The
portrait of Armstrong (I. lx) in this poem is that of a shy and silent
man, and Alexander Carlyle, who noted his 'sarcastical vein', tells us
that he 'was naturally glumpy'. Clearly he had nothing of Arbuthnot's
happy charm; but he shared his power and honesty. His contemporaries
admired him—except for Churchill, who found in him 'the vain
stiffness of a *letter'd* Scot'. Hume thought he received less fame than
he deserved; Lord Monboddo judged his diction more splendid than
that of Milton's *Paradise Lost*; Boswell found it 'impossible to trans-

late into French his force of style, a force remarkable even in English' [58]. These men have a common factor which may render their praise a little suspect, and Hume's kindly feeling for a fellow-Scot was celebrated. Graham notes that, 'with him blind Blacklock, mildest of poetasters, was a Pindar; Wilkie, dullest of versifiers and most grotesque of mortals, was a Homer; Home was a Shakespeare "without his barbarisms" '. But Goldsmith was unbiased. Though he finds Thomson 'in general, a verbose and affected poet', he gives discriminating praise to Armstrong's occasional verbal felicities. John Nichols, in a friendly and discursive note on the poet, predicts of *The Art of Preserving Health* that it will transmit Armstrong's name to posterity as one of the first English writers [59].

Falconer's *The Shipwreck* [60] transcends its didactic 'kind' through its tragic theme and the passionate sincerity of its handling. The writer, in boyhood 'condemned reluctant to the faithless sea', knew his subject intimately. Alexander Chalmers quotes an expert's opinion that *The Shipwreck* 'is of inestimable value to this country, since it contains within itself the rudiments of navigation: if not sufficient to form a complete seaman, it may certainly be considered as the grammar of his professional science' [61]. Falconer would have rejoiced in this tribute. He took his seamanship with intense seriousness. Each of the three editions published in his lifetime carries a detailed diagram of a ship; he added explanatory notes on his many technical terms; not only action, but time and place are exactly indicated. He would, he says in the Advertisement to the second edition, have referred his readers to dictionaries, but 'he could by no means recommend their explanations, without forfeiting his claim to the character assumed in the Title-Page, of which he is much more tenacious than of his reputation as a poet'. The character is that of 'a sailor', and Falconer guards it jealously. He does not tamper with fact, though he may vary its expression. His accuracy and reliability are shown, for example, in the details of the fate of the crew. A single couplet is changed from

> As o'er the surf, the bending main-mast hung,
> The shrouds still grasping, thirty Seamen clung

to

> As o'er the surf the bending main-mast hung,
> Still on the rigging thirty seamen clung

and finally to:

> As o'er the surge the stooping main-mast hung,
> Still on the rigging thirty seamen clung. [62]

These two 'characters', of seaman and poet, Falconer deliberately cultivates and cherishes. The revisions of the poem show him taking

increasing trouble to make his facts crystal clear; he removes no
technical terms, but he expands and elucidates his explanations.
Anything less than the truth and the whole truth would insult the
'dreadful grandeur of [his] theme'. The reader, to whom such terms are
not unfamiliar through experience or reading ('Here a sheer hulk lies
poor Tom Bowling'!) accepts with fortitude their excessive use. It is
otherwise with Falconer's second 'character'. His attempts to embellish
the poem are, like much of Thomson's revision, the unhappy result
of not letting well alone. The second edition is almost twice as long as
the first; the third is yet longer. The characters at first are distinguished
by their function alone; they are brave men, bearing each his share of
responsibility, facing danger and death. But 'the master' of the first
draft becomes 'Albert'; romantic love and friendship motives are added;
Falconer adds a comparison of the master's grief to that of Priam at
the fall of Troy. The first draft ends with a concise and simple narrative;
this is expanded in the second edition by the introduction of a lengthy
dying speech and an apostrophe; matter which filled sixteen lines is
spun out to fill over a hundred and fifty. 'The design and power (or
influence) of poetry' is a subject of much importance, but Falconer has
seriously underestimated the power of his own narrative in supposing
any reader would welcome a digression on poetry—or on anything
else—at the opening of Canto III. The arrival of the Muses from the
shores of light to tame the savages of old (third edition) is of even less
immediacy to the story than the contrast (in itself pathetic) between
Homer and himself with which Falconer opens the canto in his second
draft. He could not, and he did not, improve on the original edition:

> Now from the side the cumbrous ruins clear,
> The falling prow at last begins to veer.

Alterations in language show a similar straining after elegance. In the
first draft the second paragraph of Canto I ends:

> The fate, in lively sorrow, to deplore,
> Of wand'rers shipwreck'd on a leeward shore.

To this is added, in the second edition:

> And, while my lines the nautic theme display,
> Dissolve in sympathy the weeping lay!

The 'melting' numbers (l. 22) become 'sadly-social' in the second
draft.

Falconer's additions and 'improvements' emphasize the literary
quality which is prevalent in eighteenth-century writing, and in no
writing more than that of the Scots. But his poem is rooted in
experience. Its epigraph is literally true of the writer:

—quaeque ipse miserrima vidi,
Et quorum pars magna fui.

At least one added literary touch of intensely personal appeal is the quotation inserted in the third edition: 'A shipboy on the high and giddy mast' [63]. He must have been an extraordinary shipboy. But admiration for his struggles after self-education, to which his poem freely bears witness, is mingled with regret that these struggles led him so far afield. The finest of all stories of wrecks in that classic sea is not in Pope's *Homer*; it lay to his hand in the Acts of the Apostles. In spite of all his well-meant efforts to improve his poem, Falconer's shipwreck is not unworthy to be named beside St. Paul's.

The first poem of James Grainger [64], 'Solitude. An Ode', proclaimed his belief: 'The height of virtue is to serve mankind'. This he did in the practice of his profession, in his prose *Essay on the more common West India Diseases* (1764), where he urges planters to treat their slaves with humanity, for 'they must answer before the Almighty for their conduct toward their Negroes', and this he conscientiously attempted to do in *The Sugar-Cane: A Poem* (1764), supplementing instruction in verse with copious footnotes in prose. He makes some effort, in Thomson's manner, to embellish his work: he inserts the tale of Junio and Theana; he digresses on Commerce; he touchingly refers to Shenstone, 'my too, too distant friend', and to his childhood:

O might the Muse
Tread, flush'd with health, the Grampian hills again!

Grainger adapts, without improving, lines from Shakespeare, Milton and Gray, and varies his verse, doubtless in honour of 'lofty Maro', with many a pathetic half-line; he does what he can, but his decorations are so ill-matched with his subject and its technical terms that the result reads like merciless parody:

Six times the changeful Moon must blunt her horns,
And fill with borrowed light her silvery urn;
Ere thy tops, trusted to the mountain-land,
Commence their jointing; but four moons suffice
To bring to puberty the low-land cane. [65]

This blend of scientific accuracy with elegant expression reminds the reader of Blackmore's *Creation* and of *The Loves of the Triangles*; but *that* poem was meant to be funny.

Grainger's passion for the whole truth is his undoing. Somervile admitted rabies into *The Chace*, but 'Of lesser ills [his] Muse declines to sing'. Not so Grainger's; she can sing of composts, dung-heaps, yaws, 'nor soil her heavenly plumes'. The cocoa-bean too

In future times, the enraptur'd Muse may sing:
If public favour crown her present lay. [66]

The condition was not fulfilled. Boswell's amusing account of Grainger's reading aloud of *The Sugar-Cane*, and his report of Johnson's remark, 'What could he make of a sugar-cane?' One might as well write the "Parsley-bed, a Poem"; or "The Cabbage-garden, a Poem",' suggest that his contemporaries, despite their love of the man (and Percy thought him 'one of the most generous, friendly and benevolent men [he] ever knew' [67]) felt that his Muse should rest. She had achieved the *reductio ad absurdum* of didactic poetry.

Robert Blair's [68] *The Grave* is secure of immortality through the drawings of Blake. It went through many editions; its blank verse was turned into rhyme by Henry Lemoine (1790); it was frequently reprinted with Young's *Night Thoughts* or Gray's *Elegy*, and figures in the sombre collection printed by Thomas Tegg in 1823, of 'The Grave. By R. Blair. Death. By Beilby Porteus, D.D. The Day of Judgment. By Robert Glynn, M.D. The Last Day. By E. Young, D.D. Deity. By Samuel Boyse.' Blair's theme and tone are so grim that it is no surprise to find Alexander Carlyle avoiding the manse of Athelstaneford, since its occupant 'was so austere and void of urbanity as to make him quite disagreeable to young people' [69]. *The Grave* bears obvious marks of Jacobean drama, but with all its apparatus of mattock, worm and skull, its morality is a mere expansion of Thomson's 'Behold, fond man!' Slight as it is, it conveniently illustrates some of the most striking characteristics of the Scottish Augustans: their respect for what preceded 'the reform of our numbers'; their love of preaching and teaching; their sense of responsibility (Blair describes his poem in a letter to Dr. Doddridge as 'written, I hope, in a way not unbecoming my profession as a minister of the gospel'); their nervous anxiety to please London (in the same letter Blair refers to the arts he has used, sometimes against his inclination, 'to make such a piece go down with a licentious age, which cares for none of those things' [70]). It is characteristic of them, too, in its unevenness of style, and the flashes of poetry which illumine the most unpromising theme:

> Thus, at the shut of ev'n, the weary bird
> Leaves the wide air, and in some lonely brake
> Cow'rs down.

Finally, it associates wild natural conditions with the supernatural. *The Grave* is full of ghosts: twice they are used in similes; they are reported by fame to perform their mystic rounds, to rise grisly at the sound of the wind and the screaming owl, to shriek from the tomb and ring the church bell—even to forewarn men of their death. The schoolboy in the moonlit churchyard

> hears, or thinks he hears,
> The sound of something purring at his heels;
> Full fast he flies, and dares not look behind him.

Half-a-century later Blair's terrifying image was to receive perfect expression at the hands of Coleridge [71].

4

Their treatment of the supernatural is the most fruitful and the most individual contribution made by these Scots to English literature. Addison, speaking for the Age of Reason, had dismissed it with polite contempt: 'Our Forefathers looked upon Nature with more Reverence and Horrour, before the World was enlightened by Learning and Philosophy, and loved to astonish themselves with the Apprehensions of Witchcraft, Prodigies, Charms, and Enchantments.' But in Scotland the forces of learning and philosophy had to contend, not only with the talk

> In rangles round, before the ingle's lowe,
> Fra guid-dame's mouth

but with the authority of the popular *Satan's Invisible World Discovered ... proving ... that there are Devils, Spirits, Witches and Apparitions*. The evidence of the power and prevalence of superstition in eighteenth-century Scotland is so rich that quotation is almost unnecessary. Alexander Carlyle tells a touching little story of his having settled with a dear friend

> that whoever should die first, should appear to the other, and tell him the secrets of the invisible world. I walked every evening for hours in the fields and links of Prestonpans, in hopes of meeting my friend; but he never appeared. This disappointment, together with the knowledge I had acquired at the Logic class, cured me of many prejudices about ghosts and hobgoblins and witches, of which till that time I stood not a little in awe.

Relatively few had Carlyle's advantages of proof by experiment and attendance at the Logic class. Burns's letter to Dr. Moore shows, not only the range and variety of Scottish superstitions and their effect on a poetic imagination, but also their lasting influence even on a sceptic. The passage is of supreme importance for the full understanding of any eighteenth-century writer who spent his boyhood in Scotland. Burns writes of

> tales and songs concerning devils, ghosts, fairies, brownies, witches, warlocks, spunkies, kelpies, elf-candles, dead-lights, wraiths, apparitions, cantraips, giants, inchanted towers, dragons and other trumpery.—This cultivated the latent seeds of Poesy; but had so strong an effect on my imagination, that to this hour, in my nocturnal rambles, I sometimes keep a sharp look-out in suspicious places; and though nobody can be more

sceptical in these matters than I, yet it often takes an effort of Philosophy to shake off these idle terrors. [72]

In the earlier years of the century the Scots poets' dealings with the supernatural were sparing and discreet, and their reception was cool. Arbuthnot removed the 'sprights' when he printed *Know Yourself*, but Chesterfield still found that 'his good understanding could not get the better of some prejudices of his education and country. For he was convinced that he had twice had the second sight, which in Scotch signifies a degree of nocturnal inspiration, but in English only a dream' [73]. Thomson was careful to assign supernatural experience to uneducated peasants [74]. David Mallet [75], a very minor Thomson, is in this respect a little more daring. His claim to 'William and Margaret' stands no longer, but *The Excursion* is his own, with its picture of Night, who

> calls her train
> Of visionary fears; the shrouded ghost,
> The dream distressful, and th'incumbent hag,
> That rise to Fancy's eye in horrid forms,
> While Reason slumbering lies.

His description of the 'place of tombs' is a foretaste of Blair:

> All is dread silence here, and undisturb'd,
> Save what the wind sighs, and the wailing owl
> Screams solitary to the mournful Moon,
> Glimmering her western ray through yonder isle,
> Where the sad spirit walks with shadowy foot
> His wonted round, or lingers o'er his grave.

Moving in imagination, like Thomson, to the far North, Mallet finds a land of fears where

> night by night, beneath the starless dusk,
> The secret hag and sorcerer unblest
> Their sabbath hold, and potent spells compose,
> Spoils of the violated grave. [76]

Armstrong, like Thomson, associates superstition with the peasant. His youthful imitation of Shakespeare 'helped to amuse the solitude of a winter passed in a wild romantic country; and, what is rather particular, was just finished when Mr. Thomson's celebrated poem upon the same subject appeared'. His 'hinds' by the winter fire talk

> Of prodigies, and things of dreadful utterance,
> That set them all agape, rouse up their hair,
> And make the ideot drops start from their eyes;
> Of churchyards belching flames at dead of night,

Of walking statues, ghosts unaffable,
Haunting the dark waste tower or airless dungeon;
Then of the elves that deftly trip the green,
Drinking the summer's moonlight from the flowers;
And all the toys that phantasy pranks up
T'amuse her fools withal. [77]

The talk of these unlettered folk, reported no matter how apologetically, kept the subject before the educated, and, as the century advanced, poets grew bolder. Mickle [78] has ghosts and spectres, wailing or 'ungrav'd', gliding not only on Eskdale Braes but (in simile) in the Siege of Marseilles and ('as the hoary villagers relate') on Almada Hill. His ballad, 'The Sorceress', is lavish in supernatural trappings:

And thrice the witch her magic wand
    Wav'd o'er the skeleton;
And slowly, at her dread command,
    Up rose the arm of bone.

In his 'Dissertation on the Lusiad' he defines the marvellous as 'the very soul of poesy'. Logan's 'Ode written in Spring', in characteristic rocking-horse metre, depicts the lonely milkmaid who

sees the Fairies with their queen,
Trip hand-in-hand the circled green,
And hears them raise at times, unseen,
    The ear-enchanting lay. [79]

Poets grew bolder, and critics, such as Hurd and Warton, grew warmer. Gray, writing to Stonehewer (29 June 1760) about the 'nature and noble wild imagination' of *Ossian*, and the wind that sounds like the voice of a spirit, remarks that 'Thomson had an ear sometimes: he was not deaf to this; and has described it gloriously, but given it another different turn, and of more horror. I cannot repeat the lines: it is in his *Winter*.' The lines Gray had in mind are probably (191-4):

Then too, they say, through all the burdened air
Long groans are heard, shrill sounds, and distant sighs,
That, uttered by the demon of the night,
Warn the devoted wretch of woe and death.

This enthusiasm set Beattie researching 'to gratify [Gray's] curiosity and love of superstition', and Beattie sympathetically traces the Highland superstitions to the silence and solitude of a wild country. 'Nor is it wonderful, that persons of lively imagination, immured in deep solitude, and surrounded with the stupendous scenery of clouds, precipices, and torrents, should dream, even when they think themselves awake, of those few striking ideas with which their lonely lives are diversified' [80]. For evidence that wild scenery and the associated supernatural were especially identified with Scotland, one need look no further than Langhorne's *Genius and Valour* or Collins's *Ode on the Popular Superstitions of the Highlands*.

Interest in the legendary and marvellous, and its appropriate scenery, was fed and raised to fever-pitch by Macpherson's *Ossian* [81]. Shenstone both explains and illustrates its effect: 'The public has seen all that art can do, and they want the more striking efforts of wild, original, enthusiastic genius. . . . Here is, indeed, pure original genius! The very quintessence of poetry' [82]. We may allow it to be the quintessence of opportunism. Macpherson's way had been prepared by Jerome Stone, schoolmaster of Dunkeld, who published a translation of Gaelic poetry, 'Albin and the Daughter of Mey', in the *Scots Magazine* (January 1756). This, says Ramsay, 'though a pretty wild tale, yet being in *verse*, it attracted little notice, being classed with magazine poetry' [83]. Macpherson's measured prose, suggested to him by John Home, is certainly not verse; and he avoided Stone's fate by the independent, though anonymous, publication of his *Fragments* in 1760. Success enlarged his plans and his ambition. Unchecked by the doubts of the judicious and sceptical, the fame and influence of *Ossian* grew and spread till, as Arnold says, all Europe felt the power of its melancholy.

Thoughtful contemporaries were perplexed by the problem of originality or forgery. Johnson's comment is, on the whole, confirmed by later scholarship: 'He has found names, and stories, and phrases, nay passages in old songs, and with them has blended his own compositions, and so made what he gives to the world as the translation of an ancient poem.' Macpherson himself neatly posed their dilemma: 'Those who have doubted my veracity have paid a compliment to my genius.' His 'genius' is still our concern; his originals may be 'a nonexisting non-existence' [84], but that need not discourage the study of Macpherson's printed pages.

The pages themselves provide their own discouragement. The didactic poets, however dull, do at least teach, and there are worse ways of spending time than in learning from an enthusiastic professional who knows his subject, even if his subject is elephantiasis or a compostheap; the absence of humour which permitted so much instruction to be imparted in verse, so earnestly and so ingeniously, is in itself funny. But there is neither instruction nor amusement in *Ossian*—there is wind. Vague scenes of mist and shadow, moonlight and whirling leaves, bearded thistles, floating beards, white-bosomed females, moss, single trees, shielded warriors, harps, caves, tombs, meteors, rainbows, eagles and above all and everywhere ghosts, dissolve into each other with the ease but without the purpose of Shelley's Cloud. Everything is blurred and indistinct. The many epithets ending in -*y* point to and emphasize this vagueness: *beamy*, *streamy*, *foamy*, *wavy*, *woody*. Epithets are piled

on one another so that phrases like 'the wan cold moon', or 'the breeze
—that flies dark-shadowy over the grass', which have, in themselves,
both feeling and charm, are smothered in their context. Rhetorical
questions abound: 'Whence is the stream of years? Whither do they
roll along?' Biblical phrase and image there is in plenty: 'The mighty
have fallen in battle', 'We decay like the grass of the hill; our strength
returns no more', 'Let none tell it in Selma, nor in Morven's woody
land. Fingal will be sad, and the sons of the desert mourn.'

It is impossible to feel any interest in the story. Macpherson's
heroines, disguised as men, follow their lovers to battle, as Cassandra
follows Diomede in *The Epigoniad*; thus oddly are the least prosaic
prose and the most prosaic verse of the century connected. Everyone,
white-bosomed, grey-bearded or ghost, talks alike, in a mournful
recitative. A favourable specimen of a recurring theme is: 'Happy are
they who fell in their youth, in the midst of their renown. They have
not beheld the tombs of their friends, or failed to bend the bow of their
strength.' Beside Thomson's lines on Aikman, painfully wrung from
him by a real grief, this is exposed for the fluent, facile and ready-made
thing that it is. To this fragment of talk we may add some lines of
narrative. Selection is easy, for though Macpherson's cakes are of
different sizes and have different names they are all baked from the
same mixture. Early in Book II of *Fingal* we find:

> As the dark shades of autumn fly over the hills of grass, so gloomy,
> dark, successive came the chiefs of Lochlin's echoing woods. Tall as the
> stag of Morven, moved stately before them the king. His shining shield
> is on his side, like a flame on the heath at night, when the world is silent
> and dark, and the traveller sees some ghost sporting in the beam! Dimly
> gleam the hills around, and shew indistinctly their oaks! A blast from the
> troubled ocean removed the settled mist. The sons of Erin appear, like
> a ridge of rocks on the coast; when mariners, on shores unknown, are
> trembling at veering winds!

Dr. Hugh Blair, in that *Critical Dissertation on the Poems of Ossian*
in which, after comparing him to his advantage with Homer, Virgil
and the romances of chivalry, he assigns him 'a place among those
whose works are to last for ages', warns the reader 'that the beauties of
Ossian's writings cannot be felt by those who have given them only a
single or hasty perusal'. The present writer's perusals have been two,
and as patient as possible. They have ended, like the Marriage Service,
in amazement. Never, one feels, has so much excitement been roused,
in so many, by such fustian.

5

The seventies of the eighteenth century, unlike the decades immediately preceding and following, produced so little that historians of

literature have been thankful to mention Beattie's *The Minstrel; or, the Progress of Genius* [85]. (Mickle's translation of *The Lusiad* is a much more creditable performance.) *The Minstrel* had its day. Cowper, poor as he was, felt that he 'must afford to purchase at least the poetical works of Beattie', and Burns, presenting a copy to Miss Logan, sent

> more than India boasts
> In Edwin's simple tale.

Beattie claims Spenser as his master, but *The Minstrel* seems rather a watered-down and emasculated version of *The Castle of Indolence*. With little of Thomson's poetic gift, Beattie has some of his ability to compound a popular mixture, and he attempts to 'be either droll or pathetic, descriptive or sentimental, tender or satirical, as the humour strikes' [86]. Edwin's simple tale is the progress of a Poetical Genius, from fancy and love of nature (Book I) to an interest in education and the betterment of mankind (Book II). The hero, ('no vulgar boy'), is advised by a sage hermit. The poem peters out before anything much can happen, and the modern reader wonders, not so much that Beattie did not finish it, as that he could bear to amble along as far as he did. Thomson's influence is clear in Beattie's stern attitude to luxury; it is clear too in his idea of progress:

> What cannot Art and Industry perform,
> When Science plans the progress of their toil!

If this stanza directly recalls the hero of *The Castle of Indolence*, the following one is *Liberty* in a nutshell. The moralizing, and there is much moralizing, is all of the 'Behold, fond man!' kind:

> Yet such the destiny of all on Earth:
> So flourishes and fades majestic Man. [87]

Like Thomson, Edwin is humanitarian and hates field sports.

But *Fingal* had appeared since *The Castle of Indolence*, and the vogue for mist and mountain is clear in *The Minstrel*. Edwin the child feeds on old wives' tales in winter, and dreams of fairy warriors and dames. True, the superstitions are exploded by Reason [88], but they have been described.

The Minstrel was composed while Beattie was working on his *Essay on the Nature and Immutability of Truth*—they are commemorated together by Burns in 'The Vision' [89]. The *Essay* won him royal favour and a pension (the King kept one copy at Kew and another in town), an honorary doctorate of the University of Oxford, an allegorical portrait by Reynolds and a popularity and respect hardly to be described. Some of his admired anti-sceptical reflections break into his verse too, and this may help to explain why it was so popular.

It is awkward, unmusical stuff. Beattie strings words and phrases together in groups of three:

> Is glory there achieved by arts, as foul
> As those that felons, fiends, and furies plan?
> Spiders ensnare, snakes poison, tigers prowl. [90]

His pages are littered with ejaculation—*lo! alas! oh! ah!*; with archaism —*besprent, wight, imp, shene*; and with personification. There is nothing in *The Minstrel* so 'glossy and unfeeling' as the diction of his translation of Virgil's *Eclogues* ('flexile osiers', 'my yielding fair', 'fostering Zephyrs fan the vernal skies'), but Beattie truly 'writ no language'. Only his dialect poem 'To Mr. Alexander Ross' is vital and vigorous. His English verse was patiently scrutinized by Gray, but it bears little sign that Beattie laid to heart his celebrated advice, 'Remember Dryden!' [91]

Beattie's verse, nerveless as it is, has the interest of foreshadowing better work. Though the hero of *The Progress of Genius* has the advantage of beginning life among the beauties of Nature, it is only the accident of title that links it with *Growth of a Poet's Mind*; but Beattie's description of the Minstrel of old—

> His waving locks and beard all hoary grey:
> While from his bending shoulder decent hung
> His harp, the sole companion of his way,
> Which to the whistling wind responsive rung [92]

—points forward unmistakably to a later and far more potent Minstrel.

The Scots poets, while freely using the stock measures of the time (they nearly all write heroic and octosyllabic couplets and some form of ode or lyric) were ready to experiment, and to revive disused forms. Their blank verse speaks for itself, and so, in its way, does Macpherson's measured prose. Mickle's sonnets, two of which were inspired by the passion for Camoëns which sustained his greater labour, are more easily overlooked. The imitations of Spenser are really important. Pope made a jest of him in his youthful parody, 'The Alley'. Prior was obviously deaf to his music, and *An Ode, humbly inscribed to thè Queen on the glorious success of Her Majesty's Arms. MDCCVI*, is a travesty. In the Preface he explains that he is following 'our great countryman Spenser . . . having only added one verse to his stanza, which I thought made the number more harmonious'. (Only!) He makes no mention of the fact that he has also eliminated Spenser's linking rhyme, and that for Spenser's total of three rhymes in the stanza he has substituted five. Hamilton of Bangour's [93] idea of Spenser's style (*On Seeing Lady Mary Montgomery sit to her Picture*) is a Gray's *Elegy* quatrain with *whilom, algates* and *couth* sprinkled on it.

But Thomson's true Spenserians are followed, however feebly, by

Armstrong, in his stanzas on disease inserted in *The Castle of Indolence*, and by Wilkie, in 'A Dream. In the Manner of Spenser', with which he cheered himself at the close of *The Epigoniad*. Saintsbury shows how Beattie's idiosyncratic treatment of the form reappears in Byron, who studied *The Minstrel* [94]. Mickle seems to have had a special feeling for Spenser: 'The Concubine', later named 'Syr Martyn', is 'in the manner of Spenser', as is the unfinished 'Hence, vagrant minstrel', with which he closes the 'Observations upon Epic Poetry' which make part of the prolegomena to *The Lusiad*.

For evidence that the imitation of Spenser was connected especially with the Scots poets, one may turn to Nathan Drake's account of Johnson's critical papers in *The Rambler*. He agrees with Johnson that 'the obsolete words of this amiable poet, indeed, it would be pedantry to attempt to revive; but who, that has read the productions of Mickle and Beattie, would wish the structure of the stanza of Spenser, and the occasional use of his more polished diction, laid aside?' [95].

The lead given by Thomson towards didactic verse was decisive with the more gifted of the Scots poets; Armstrong and Falconer have some power; Beattie and Blacklock are feeble. But didactic verse was a dying 'kind'. In his fable 'The Wilding and the Broom', a dispute on the importance of ethical teaching in verse, Langhorne shows Thomson pointing to the broom-flowers and saying:

> Shepherd, there
> Behold the fate of song, and lightly deem
> Of all but moral beauty, [96]

—but he gives Hamilton of Bangour the last word. The Preface to Joseph Warton's *Odes* (1746) states explicitly that their author 'is convinced that the fashion of moralizing in verse has been carried too far' at the expense of invention and imagination. The future belonged to the more romantic elements of superstition and legend, wild scenery and haunting place-names, discreetly introduced by Thomson and lavishly exploited by Macpherson. These are the elements which were to make Scott's lays so captivating to his contemporaries, and to form a contrasting strand in the richer and more lasting fabric of his novels. 'The rude sweetness of a Scotch tune' sounds in English fitfully through the century, from Thomson's 'Tell me, thou soul of her I love' and Mallet's 'The Birks of Endermay' to Logan's 'The Braes of Yarrow' and 'To the Cuckoo'. Whether this poem was his own or by Michael Bruce [97], Logan certainly wrote the autumn ode from which Dorothy Wordsworth quotes: 'We have been reading the life and some of the writings of poor Logan since dinner. "And everlasting longings for the lost." It is an affecting line. There are many affecting lines and passages in his poems' [98]. There are indeed, and in the poems of many of the Scottish Augustans, lines and passages which were seminal of the sustained poetry in this kind which they could not themselves achieve. Thomas Warton describes Scotland as a nation 'which amidst a variety of disadvantages has kept a constant pace with England in the progress of literature' [99]. No one intimate with the general run of average eighteenth-century English poetry will think it an extravagant claim. The satires of Pope, the lyrics of Blake are not average, and if eighteenth-century Scots produced, in English verse, nothing that should be named in the same day with these, there is comfort in the thought that one at least of their compatriots, working in the native tradition and in the mother-tongue, wrote poetry which needs no apology.

VI

EIGHTEENTH-CENTURY VERNACULAR POETRY

DAVID DAICHES

I

THE seventeenth century saw Scottish poets moving away from the older Scots literary tradition: from Sir Robert Aytoun to Montrose the trend was towards a courtly English idiom, and Scots was rapidly ceasing to be a literary language and becoming merely a spoken dialect. The most important Scots poem of the seventeenth century is the vulgar, vigorous, rollicking vernacular 'Life and Death of the Piper of Kilbarchan', better known as 'The Epitaph of Habbie Simson', by Robert Sempill of Beltrees [1]. Scots is now a vernacular, drawing on popular speech rather than on an artistic tradition. And in the early eighteenth century there is a growing interest in popular, vernacular Scots verse, represented by both imitations of it and collections of it. The first volume of James Watson's *Choice Collection of Comic and Serious Scots Poems* (1706) shows this new interest, the interest of a printer and anthologist; and that line follows on through Allan Ramsay and David Herd to Johnson's *Scots Musical Museum* (1787 ff.). The editorial line of collectors and improvers leads on the one hand to new appreciation of ballad and folk-song and on the other to curiosity about the older artistic tradition that flourished before first the Reformation and then the Union of the Crowns altered or at least obscured the nature of Scottish culture. This appreciation and this curiosity helped to provide the cultural climate in which Fergusson wrote his Scots poems and Burns drew the lines together to produce the grand culmination of an Indian summer of Scottish poetry.

But the second Temple was not like the first. Going back to Alexander Scott, we find a stanza like this:

> For nobillis hes not ay renown
> Nor gentillis ay the gayest goun,
> Thay cary victuallis to the toun
> That werst dois dyne:
> Sa bissely to busk I boun   [*I get to the bush*
> Ane uthir eitis the berry doun   [*another eats the berry*
> That suld be myne.

The opening of 'Habbie Simson' has the same stanza form:

> Kilbarchan now may say alas!
> For she hath lost both game and grace,

Both *Trixie* and *The Maiden Trace;*
But what remead?
For no man can supply his place:
Hab Simson's dead.

There is a difference in weight here; though both Scott and Sempill use images and expressions from popular speech, Scott's language is more highly charged, it has more gravity and greater reverberation. 'Habbie Simson' is sprightly popular verse written for amusement by a member of the landed gentry and written in a language which by this time few educated people felt to be suitable for the highest kind of art. The poem is important historically, both for drawing attention to the possibilities of folk-humour as a way of bringing the vernacular back into current poetry and for reviving a stanza form which was to play such an important part in eighteenth-century Scottish poetry; but it lacks a dimension. Between Sempill of Beltrees and Burns Scottish vernacular poetry had to learn how to be the product of the whole man, how to achieve scope and density—in short, how to recover the lost dimension. Where it did so, it was by transmuting antiquarian, patriotic and patronizing gestures towards the vernacular into something deeper, something with an organic connexion with contemporary sensibility; and that transmutation was itself made possible by the re-establishment of living contact with certain important currents in Scottish literature and Scottish folk-poetry.

A literary language, arising out of the different forms of the spoken language and transcending them, reflects back on the spoken language and gives it a steady relationship to the national culture. Once the literary tradition is broken, once there is no literary language growing out of the spoken language (however different from it it may be, and however many artificial elements may have been added), the spoken language is bound to disintegrate into a series of regional dialects. Scots became a vernacular only after the literary language of its serious writers had ceased to be Scots. How to use the vernacular as a language in serious literature (that is, in literature that was more than an antiquarian exercise, a jest, or a *tour de force*) was the problem faced by Ramsay, Fergusson and Burns, and it was never permanently solved.

'Habbie Simson' is a vernacular squib; 'Holy Willie's Prayer' is a Scots poem, written in a literary language in which English and Scots reinforce each other. Yet the latter is not quite the same kind of thing that Alexander Scott or Montgomerie wrote. Burns only re-established contact with the Scots literary tradition by looking at it through the spectacles provided by folksong and other kinds of popular art, and as a result the tradition as he uses it is a composite one, in which the satiric boisterousness of Lindsay's *Satyre of the Thrie Estaits*, the happy

artifice of Montgomerie, the stark clarity of the ballads, the richness
and warmth and earthiness of folk-song, the pious beat of Scottish
psalmody, combine to produce a precarious but—while it lasted—a
brilliant unity. It was Burns's predecessors who made that synthesis
possible; it was his own genius that made it brilliant; it was the cultural
context of his time that made it precarious.

At the opening of the eighteenth century Scotland had preserved an
oral literary culture which had deep roots in the past, while both broadsides and private manuscripts were playing their different parts in
another kind of preservation. How far that culture would have survived
into the eighteenth century without the deliberate encouragement of
those who had by now become self-conscious about it, is impossible
to say; the chances are that it would not have survived long. The
growing prestige of English culture, together with the closer political
and economic ties between England and Scotland, would have been
likely to force the native popular tradition into nooks and corners.
But fortunately, by some happy shift of attention after the political
hopes of Scottish patriots had been finally ruined by the Union of
Parliaments, Scotland turned from politics to investigate her literary
claims to nationhood.

In 1706, the year before the union was finally voted, James
Watson [2], an Edinburgh printer of skill and enterprise, brought out
the first of his three volumes entitled *A Choice Collection of Comic and
Serious Scots Poems both Ancient and Modern*. Watson apparently edited
the collection himself, and in a prefatory note to the first volume he
explained his motives:

> As the frequency of Publishing Collections of Miscellaneous Poems
> in our Neighbouring Kingdoms and States, may, in a great measure,
> justify an undertaking of this kind with us; so 'tis hoped, that this being
> the first of its Nature which has been publish'd in our native *Scots* dialect,
> the Candid Reader may be the more easily induced, through the Con-
> sideration thereof, to give some Charitable Grains of Allowance, if the
> Performance come not up to such a Point of Exactness as may please an
> over nice Palate. . . .

It is clear that Watson saw himself as a pioneer, producing for the
first time a collection of poems 'in our own native *Scots* dialect' to rival
the many English collections. The preface also makes clear that he was
dependent on 'Generous Helps' from 'the Repositories of some
Curious and Ingenious Gentlemen' who collected 'Comic and Divert-
ing Poems'. Watson also claimed to have printed his poems 'from the
most Correct Manuscripts that could be procured of them'. The flavour
of antiquarian jest still hangs a little round the project; yet the patriotic
intention is real, and his ambition to print accurate texts (however
faintly realized) is genuine.

With its mixture of poems of popular revelry, laboured exercises in courtly English, macaronics, mock elegies, serious sixteenth-century Scots poems, trivial epigrams and epitaphs, poems by Drummond and Montrose, flytings, laments and miscellaneous patriotic pieces, Watson's collection appears at first sight to represent the casual putting together of whatever the editor found to his hand [3]. Yet (except for ballads, which it lacks, and song lyrics, which are few, and the perhaps surprising lack of anything by Sir David Lindsay) the collection represents with a fair degree of accuracy the different kinds of material available for the development or reconstruction of the Scottish poetic tradition in the eighteenth century. The tradition of the makars was represented by Montgomerie (we must wait until Ramsay to find the earlier poets made available); the courtly tradition in English by Drummond and Aytoun; the older popular tradition by 'Christis Kirk on the Grene' and the newer by 'Habbie Simson' and other pieces; various kinds of popular and semi-popular Scottish song were represented, some in Scots and some in English; the characteristic Scottish humour and Scottish violence are represented in several ways, as is the goliardic tradition as it developed in Scotland and the tradition of macaronic humour associated with it. Watson printed the best texts he could find, though these were often poor broadsides. Perpetuation in broadsides at least denotes vitality. Throughout the seventeenth century the line between folk-song and 'art' poem was often obscured in Scotland; poems even by courtly poets found their way to popular singers and printers of broadsides, as well as to private collectors; and changes, corruptions, emendations and additions were the natural result. What Watson printed represented things that were still going on in Scotland, though often not on the surface. In bringing them to the surface he prevented them from being obscured completely by the new face of Scottish culture and at the same time helped to divert patriotic attention from politics to literature. Scotland became concerned about its literary past and about the possibilities of continuity with that past. It is true that that concern was mixed up in many quarters with confused ideas about the vernacular and primitive poetry and the natural man, and this confusion made serious difficulties for Burns. But it also provided an environment which encouraged the writing of an enriched vernacular poetry under certain circumstances and at certain levels: and that was decisive for the course of eighteenth-century Scottish poetry.

Meanwhile, the practice of rewriting or imitating traditional Scottish songs grew among ladies and gentlemen. To John Hay, tenth Lord Yester, for example, is attributed a version of 'Tweedside' [4]. Lady Grizel Baillie (1665-1746) wrote the simply lilting 'Werena my heart licht, I wad dee', which first appeared in Ramsay's *Tea-Table Miscellany*. Lady Wardlaw (1677-1722) presented her 'Hardyknute' as part of an old ballad; it is difficult to see now how this too smoothly running piece, with its carefully chosen echoes of common ballad phrases, could have been accepted (as it was) as a genuine old ballad. But the poem has speed and vigour, and helped to familiarize genteel Scottish ears with a polished version of the ballad cadence.

A more important character, as far as the Scottish literary tradition in the eighteenth century is concerned, is William Hamilton of Gilbertfield (to be distinguished from his younger contemporary, William Hamilton of Bangour) whose modernized version of Blind Harry's *Wallace* was to fire Burns's patriotism [5]. His 'Last Dying Words of Bonnie Heck' continued the 'Habbie Simson' tradition, but with a difference. 'Habbie Simson' was an elegy on a piper, himself a representative of popular festivity, and in recalling his life Sempill recalls the folk-customs of rural Scotland:

> At Clark-plays when he wont to come;
> His Pipe play'd trimly to the Drum,
> Like Bikes of Bees he gart it Bum,   [*hives, made*
> and tun'd his Reed.
> Now all our Pipers may sing dumb,
> sen Habbie's dead. . . .
>
> He was convoyer of the Bride
> With Kittock hinging at his side:
> About the Kirk he thought a Pride
> the Ring to lead.
> But now we may gae but a Guide
> for Habbie's dead. . . .

Hamilton's poem is more definitely a *mock* elegy, and, further, it is a lament for an animal, which links it with 'The Mare of Colintoun' and that Scottish tradition of animal poetry that was to come alive so splendidly in Burns. True, in his dying reminiscences Bonny Heck, too, gives a picture of popular festivities, but it is the mixture of the comic and pathetic deriving from the notion of a dying animal speaking like a human that links the poem with Burns's 'Death and Dying Words of Poor Maillie'.

Hamilton is at least as important in the history of Scottish vernacular poetry for the epistles which he exchanged with Ramsay. This is the beginning of a tradition of familiar verse letters in the vernacular which was again to be magnificently exploited by Burns. It provided a medium for 'occasional' poetry, a kind of verse to which the vernacular was particularly suited, for its endeavour was to capture the accent of conversation. With literary prose always English and not Scots, and the vernacular allowed in verse only for the familiar, the popular, the comic or the mock-antique, the verse letter provided a fine new form for vernacular Scots. If the novel had been developed in Scotland by the early eighteenth century, dialogue in prose fiction might have effectively employed the spoken Scots speech of the time—this is how Galt and Scott were later to use dialogue. But lacking a tradition of colloquial prose, the eighteenth-century Scottish writer turned happily to the tradition of familiar Scots verse which Hamilton of Gilbertfield helped to establish.

2

With Allan Ramsay [6] the scene becomes more complex. To the editorial function of Watson he added that of reviser, popularizer, experimenter, poet, *entrepreneur*, clubman, satirist, general busybody and spokesman for Scotland before the Queen Anne wits. In 1712 he joined with other young men in Edinburgh in founding the Easy Club, 'in order that by a Mutual improvement in Conversation they may become more adapted for fellowship with the politer part of mankind and Learn also from one another's happy observations'. (Burns was to found the Tarbolton Bachelors' Club with similar ends in view.) The members of this club all had pseudonyms, and Ramsay's was first Isaac Bickerstaff and later Gavin Douglas, a pair of names which reflect Ramsay's dual interest in the Queen Anne wits and in older Scottish literature. The Easy Club is important in Ramsay's career because it shows him in training to become a gentleman in the early eighteenth-century sense and also because it provided him with an audience for 'occasional' poetry for which he soon began to display his talent. Ramsay was far from being a great poet, but he was a facile versifier with certain happy flashes, and when circumstances were propitious he could turn out admirable specimens of familiar verse. The Easy Club provided the environment which encouraged this gift; it also provided a background of patriotic sentiment against which Ramsay's nationalism flourished vigorously. Isaac Bickerstaff and Gavin Douglas; a gentleman of the Augustan Age and an ardent Scottish patriot; an admirer of Pope and Gay and Matthew Prior and a devoted champion of the older Scottish makars and of the use of vernacular Scots by contemporary Scottish poets; a seeker after polish and good breeding and a vulgar little gossip whose schoolboy snigger spoils many of his poems and songs; a sentimental Jacobite and a prudent citizen who cannily absented himself from Edinburgh when Prince Charlie held court in Holyrood in 1745; a champion of Scottish folk-song and a wrecker of scores of such songs by turning them into stilted would-be neo-classic effusions—the dualism in Ramsay's life and character was deep-seated and corresponded to a dualism in the Scottish culture of his day. He could defend the coarsest and frankest language in poetry and yet dress up a Scottish song in intolerable false elegancies. At the same time he could demonstrate that he possessed

the Horatian elegance of the English gentleman by rendering Horace's
'Vides ut alta stet nive candidum' in vivid and homely Scots verse:

> Look up to *Pentland*'s towring Taps,
> Buried beneath great Wreaths of Snaw,
> O'er ilka Cleugh, ilk Scar and Slap,   [*glen, breach in a fence*
> As high as ony *Roman* Wa'.
>
> Driving their Baws frae Whins or Tee,   [*balls*
> There's no ae Gowfer to be seen,
> Nor dousser Fowk wysing a Jee   [*soberer, guiding on a*
> Thy Byas Bouls on *Tamson*'s Green.   *bending course*

Ramsay's first published works were single poems in English heroic
couplets in the contemporary English style; these are no better if no
worse than the work of many a minor English versifier of the day.
'The Morning Interview', described as 'An Heroi-Comical Poem',
derives from *The Rape of the Lock*, but has none of Pope's metrical
cunning, fineness of texture, or subtle shifts in tone. Waggish jocularity
strives with self-conscious elegance to take control, and the result is
not happy, though the poem has its moments. In 1718 Ramsay first
showed his interest in older Scottish literature by bringing out,
anonymously on broadsides, several editions of 'Christis Kirk on the
Grene' (with the same stanza form as Watson had printed—different
from the text he was to use in *The Ever Green* in 1724) with first one
and then two new cantos of his own. Ramsay's new cantos have verve
and ingenuity, and capture something of the spirit of the original while
adding his own brand of vulgarity. In the Elegies on Maggy Johnston,
John Cowper and Lucky Wood (which all appeared in 1718) Ramsay
displayed his best vernacular vein. These poems are in the tradition
that Ramsay himself, in a verse epistle to Hamilton of Gilbertfield,
called 'Standart *Habby*', the comic elegy tradition of the 'Epitaph on
Habbie Simson' and 'Bonny Heck'. The elegy on Maggy Johnston,
famous for her cheap and good ale, moves from lament to reminiscences of conviviality. The poem on Cowper, Kirk Treasurer's Man
and expert at 'sa'ring [smelling] sculdudry out', is interesting as one of
the earliest pieces of Scots verse to laugh at what Burns was to call the
'holy beagles'. The 'Elegy on Lucky Wood' laments the loss of an
honest and hospitable ale-house keeper in the Canongate, and again it
turns from elegy to reminiscent conviviality. There is a fine sense of
atmosphere in the poem, with the scenes etched in warm and lively
colours like a Breughel painting of a village celebration.

About the same time also appeared 'Lucky Spence's Last Advice'
(first called 'Elegy on the Death of an Auld Bawd'), where Ramsay
uses the 'death and dying words' device to put grimly ironical advice
to prostitutes into the mouth of a dying brothel keeper. This kind of

humour does not wear well, particularly when accompanied by Ramsay's variety of vulgar coyness (for example, he draws attention to an obscene phrase by a footnote in which he declines to explain it). But the poem uses the vernacular vigorously, with a fine proverbial forcefulness.

Of the other poems which Ramsay published separately, *Tartana: Or, The Plaid* deserves mention for its strong patriotic feeling and warm defence of Scottish customs against foreign innovations, even though the poem is in stilted English couplets. And two pastorals are of some importance: 'Richy and Sandy', a pastoral elegy on the death of Addison, and 'Patie and Roger', the germ of *The Gentle Shepherd*. 'Richy and Sandy' (i.e. Richard Steele and Alexander Pope) is a dialogue between two shepherds who lament the death of a third of their number, Edie (Addison). It is a ludicrous enough mixture— Steele, Pope and Addison transformed into Scots shepherds talking in a Theocritean convention, yet Ramsay's combination of conversational idiom with classical allusion comes off better than one might expect, and the piece has something of the same 'faded charm' that critics have found in *The Gentle Shepherd*. 'Patie and Roger' is likewise a dialogue between two shepherds, but this time the theme is love. The vernacular flows easily and the accent of conversation is audible beneath the flow of the verse. The images are fresh and effective, and altogether the piece succeeds in putting a little life into the worn-out convention of pastoral dialogue, in spite of its faded properties. Ramsay's basic uncertainty of taste, which could lead him into the most hideous vulgarities, was less of a liability in this kind of writing: the touches of rustic realism make for freshness, not vulgarity, and the idiom and cadence of popular speech embedded in the slow-moving iambic line waters the aridity of a stock situation, as in Patie's advice to Roger on how to get his girl:

Daft Gowk! Leave aff that silly whindging Way,   [*fool, whining*
Seem careless, there's my Hand ye'll win the Day.
Last Morning I was unco airly out,   [*uncommonly*
Upon a Dyke I lean'd and glowr'd about;
I saw my *Meg* come linkan o'er the Lee,   [*tripping*
I saw my *Meg*, but *Maggie* saw na me:
For yet the Sun was wafing throw the Mist,   [*wandering*
And she was closs upon me e'er she wist.
Her Coats were kiltit, and did sweetly shaw
Her straight bare Legs, which whiter were than Snaw:
Her Cockernony snooded up fou sleek,   [*gathered hair, full*
Her haffet Locks hung waving on her Cheek: [*side*
Her Cheek sae ruddy! and her Een sae clear!
And O! her Mouth's like ony hinny Pear.

Neat, neat she was in Bustine Wastecoat clean,   [*fustian*
As she came skiffing o'er the dewy Green:
Blythsome I cry'd, My bonny *Meg* come here,
I fairly wherefore ye'er sae soon a steer:
But now I guess ye'er gawn to gather Dew.
She scour'd awa, and said what's that to you?
Then fare ye well, *Meg Dorts*, and e'en 's ye like,
I careless cry'd and lap in o'er the Dyke.   [*leapt*
I trow, when that she saw, within a crack
With a right thieveles Errand she came back;   [*improper*
Miscau'd me first,—then bade me hound my Dog   [*abused*
To weer up three waff Ews were on the Bog.   [*stop, wandering*
I leugh, and sae did she, then wi' great Haste
I clasp'd my Arms about her Neck and Waste . . .

Finally, we must mention the verse letters between Ramsay and
Hamilton of Gilbertfield. The series begins with a letter to Ramsay
from Hamilton:

> O Fam'd and celebrated ALLAN!
> Renowned RAMSAY, canty Callan,   [*merry fellow*
> There's nowther Highlandman nor Lawlan,
>   In Poetrie,
> But may as soon ding down *Tamtallan*   [*cast*
>   As match wi' thee. . . .

And Ramsay replies in similar strain:

> Sonse fa me, witty, wanton *Willy*,   [*happy*
> Gin blyth I was na as a Filly;   [*if*
> Not a fow Pint, nor short Hought Gilly, [*full, small glass of spirits*
>   Or Wine that's better,
> Cou'd please sae meikle, my dear Billy,   [*much*
>   As thy kind Letter.
>
> Before a Lord and eik a Knight,
> In Gossy *Don*'s be Candle Light,
> There first I saw't, and ca'd it right,
>   And the maist feck   [*greatest number*
> Wha's seen't sinsyne, they ca'd as tight   [*since*
>   As that on *Heck*.

The poems run on with an apparent effortlessness, given form by
the demands of epistolary courtesy for an opening of compliment and
a concluding benediction or invitation to the recipient to visit and make
merry with the writer. From compliment to news to invitation is the
commonest course of these letters, and they set a pattern which
Fergusson and Burns were to follow. This is not, of course, great
poetry; but it represents a craftsmanlike handling of the 'familiar' style,

an exercising of the vernacular which was to stand Burns in good stead, and it further helped to provide both a social and a metrical convention for Scots verse.

Ramsay's preface to the 1721 volume of his poems gives us some important clues to his own view of the nature and significance of his poetry. He cheerfully admits that he is no classical scholar ('I understand Horace but faintly in the Original') and claims that many eminent men of letters have assured him 'That my small Knowledge of the dead or foreign Languages is nothing to my Disadvantage. King David, Homer and Virgil, say they, were more ignorant of the Scots and English Tongue, than you are of Hebrew, Greek and Latin: Pursue your own natural Manner, and be an original.' The use of vernacular Scots is thus associated with ignorance of Latin and Greek: Scots is no longer a literary language employed by poets with a European perspective and a rich background of classical culture which they draw on for vocabulary, imagery and subject-matter. We have come a long way from the aureate Middle Scots poems of Dunbar. Ramsay's classical knowledge comes through the strainer of neo-classic elegance; Greek and Roman gods and goddesses are for him useful ornamental devices which he has learned about from the English poets. Burns, too, was to pose as a heaven-taught ploughman and claim superiority to the college-educated who 'gae in stirks and come oot asses', but Burns was in fact fundamentally better educated than Ramsay, though he was faced by some of the same problems.

Ramsay warmly defends the expressive capacities of Scots, yet he is on the defensive about his 'Scotticisms'. 'The *Scotticisms*, which perhaps may offend some over-nice Ear, give new Life and Grace to the Poetry, and become their Place as well as the *Doric* dialect of *Theocritus*, so much admired by the best Judges.' He is writing, after all, for a genteel audience, both English and Scottish, who might be expected to lift their eyebrows at his use of the Doric. He dedicates his book 'To the most Beautiful, the Scots Ladies' and quotes Prior to the effect that he writes only for the young and fair. Clearly Ramsay's rôle as he saw it was, if not confused, at least multiple.

In writing songs, Ramsay's favourite procedure is to take a popular Scottish song and to the same air set a new version which retains the opening line or the chorus or some other part of the original, but in all other respects is a wholly different poem deriving in tone and idiom from English love-lyrics of the period. Thus 'The last time I came ower the moor' becomes 'The happy Lover's Reflections':

> The last Time I came o'er the Moor,
>   I left my Love behind me;
> Ye Pow'rs! What Pain do I endure
>   When soft Idea's mind me:

Soon as the ruddy Morn display'd
The beaming Day ensuing,
I met betimes my lovely Maid,
In fit Retreats for wooing.

The phrases here are a mass of *clichés*, a parody, almost, of neo-classic idiom. 'The Lass of Peattie's Mill', on the other hand, begins with a lilting stanza in the true folk-idiom, then falls away into frigid artificialities, to return to the folk-idiom again in the third and last stanza. Ramsay has been blamed for ousting the old songs by his pseudo-genteel substitutes, and indeed many of his more outrageous rewritings appear not only in his own *Tea-Table Miscellany* but also in David Herd's *Ancient and Modern Scottish Songs* (where they appear anonymously), in the *Scots Musical Museum* and in *Select Scotish Airs*. It is of course possible, if not probable, that if Ramsay had not printed his versions the old versions would have died out anyway and the tunes would also have been lost: most of the original words of Ramsay's songs were irrecoverable later in the century even by such a conscientious collector as David Herd, and perhaps in many cases only the melody and the refrain were known to Ramsay. 'Of many of the songs in these volumes', wrote Herd in his preface to the second edition of his collection (1776), 'the chief merit will be found to consist in the musical air, while the poetry may appear much below mediocrity. For this the Editor has no other apology to offer, than that these were the only words existing to the tunes in question, the original words which gave rise to these tunes being irrecoverably lost.' It is important to remember that 'the musical air' was the more significant element in most of these songs; indeed, it is impossible to get any proper idea of this phase of Scottish literature without taking the music into consideration and treating the songs as songs and not as poems which happen to have been set to music.

How far Ramsay can go in the direction of pseudo-elegance in language can be seen in his song 'Delia', which is set to the tune of 'Greensleeves':

Ye watchful Guardians of the Fair,
Who skiff on Wings of ambient Air,
Of my dear *Delia* take a Care,
And represent her Lover . . .

Many of his songs contain an impossible mixture of folk-idiom and self-conscious classical allusion. He can write a song with the simple Scots title 'Bonny Jean' (the title of the old air) and open it thus:

Love's Goddess in a Myrtle Grove
Said, *Cupid*, bend thy Bow with Speed,
Nor let the Shaft at Random rove,
For *Jeanie*'s haughty Heart must bleed. . . .

And his version [7] of 'Auld Lang Syne' (entitled 'The Kind Reception') begins:

> Should auld Acquaintance be forgot,
> Tho they return with Scars?
> These are the noble Heroe's Lot,
> Obtain'd in glorious Wars:
> Welcome my *Varo* to my Breast,
> Thy Arms about me twine,
> And make me once again as blest,
> As I was lang syne.

We never know what Ramsay is going to do. 'Peggy I must Love Thee' becomes the conventional English 'Love's Cure'; 'Bessy Bell and Mary Gray' lilts happily along in true folk-style until suddenly we find

> When *Phoebus* starts frae *Thetis*' Lap
> The Hills with Rays adorning . . .

(One is reminded of Burns's outrageously obscene parody of this style of poetry.) 'The Young Laird and Edinburgh Katy' is lively Scots throughout and sticks to a single idiom:

> Now wat ye what I met Yestreen   [*know*
> Coming down the Street, my Jo,
> My Mistress in her Tartan Screen,
> Fou' bonny, braw and sweet, my Jo. . . .

'Mary Scot' combines a refrain about Yarrow with such a line as 'When in soft Flames Souls equal burn'; but 'O'er Bogie' keeps to a lilting folk-style throughout, beginning with the traditional refrain, 'I will awa' wi' my Love'. 'O'er the Moor to Maggy' is the mixture again, but 'Polwart on the Green' is effective, simple Scots throughout. 'Up in the Air' is one of Ramsay's few real masterpieces, a lively drinking-song in roaring Scots. The refrain is old, and perhaps some other lines are too, but Ramsay has got into the spirit of the original magnificently:

> Now the Sun's gane out o' Sight,
> Beet the Ingle, and snuff the Light: [*mend the fire*
> In Glens the Fairies skip and dance,
> And Witches wallop o'er to *France*,
>   Up in the Air
>   On my bonny grey Mare.
> And I see her yet, and I see her yet,
>   Up in, &c.
>
> The Wind's drifting Hail and Sna'
> O'er frozen Hags like a Foot Ba',   [*mosses*

Nae Starns keek throw the Azure Slit,
'Tis cauld and mirk as ony Pit,   [*dark*
   The Man i' the Moon
    Is carowsing aboon,
D'ye see, d'ye see, d'ye see him yet.
   The Man, &c.

The fireside interior, with its warmth and conviviality, is contrasted with the winter weather outside, a contrast characteristic of much Scottish poetry, from the opening of Henryson's *Testament of Cresseid* to the beginning of 'Tam o' Shanter'.

'Patie and Pegie', which was later incorporated into *The Gentle Shepherd*, has been much praised, but it is not in fact a happy performance; the deliberately cultivated sentimentality clashes with the Scots frankness. A leering or even pawing eroticism, mixed with affected sensibility, has a tendency to crop up in Ramsay, and it is not attractive.

Ramsay's songs are most successful when he sticks to the folk-idiom and enters with verve and spirit into the atmosphere of the original refrain. 'An thou wert my ain Thing', in spite of an occasional false touch, has an effective strain of lyrical simplicity; 'For the Sake of Somebody' is a fine lilting piece in true folk-style; 'The Widow can bake, and the Widow can brew' has speed and liveliness and no trace of a false sensibility; 'O Mither dear, I 'gin to fear' is a skilful and unspoiled reworking of a folk-song, and the same is true of 'The Carle he came o'er the Croft', 'This is No my ain Hoose', 'Clout the Caldron' and some others.

It is not, of course, true that all folk-songs are good or that simplicity is necessarily a good quality in a song and that any kind of stylization is bad. But it is true that Ramsay's attempt to add a dimension to Scots vernacular poetry by sprinkling bits of English neo-classic convention or other evidence of a deliberately induced genteel sensibility over a verse that is basically a realistic Scots was misguided. Realistic Scots does not necessarily produce good poetry, any more than elegantly stylized English necessarily produces bad; but whatever the language a poet uses, it must be used organically, it must be the fully realized medium of the whole man at work, and this cannot be said of Ramsay's strange mixtures of Scots and English. Sometimes (like Burns) he is successful in an English tipped with Scots; more often, in his songs at least, he succeeds when he uses the vernacular in a fairly short, lilting line, as in the one wholly successful song (with the possible exception of 'My Patie is a lover gay') in *The Gentle Shepherd:*

> My Peggy is a young thing,
>   Just enter'd in her teens,
> Fair as the day, and sweet as May,
> Fair as the day, and always gay:

> My Peggy is a young thing,
> And I'm not very auld,
> Yet well I like to meet her at
> The wauking of the fauld. . . .   [*watching, fold*

Ramsay experimented in older Scottish metres other than 'Standart *Habby*'. One of his epistles to Hamilton uses the same ten-line stanza as 'The Claith Merchant', a poem which he printed in *The Ever Green*. In 'Edinburgh's Salutation to the Most Honourable, My Lord Marquess of Carnarvon' he uses the stanza of 'Christis Kirk on the Grene' in Watson's form. In 'The Poet's Wish' he uses *The Cherrie and the Slae* stanza for exactly the same purpose as Burns was to use it for in his 'Epistle to Davie'—which is in fact based in many respects on Ramsay's poem, even to the point of quoting a line from it, 'Mair speir na, nor fear na'. Ramsay's description of the contented but simple life shows one of his most appropriate uses of the vernacular. Indeed, in subject-matter, language and stanza form 'The Poet's Wish' is historically one of the most important of Ramsay's poems: it showed how an older Scottish tradition could be put to contemporary poetic use, and its influence on Burns was of the greatest significance. Ramsay could make good use of octosyllabic couplets when he stuck to a Scots conversational idiom, as his epistles to James Arbuckle and to the Earl of Dalhousie testify. His renderings of Horace in octosyllabic couplets have less force and weight than the original demands: '*Horace to Virgil, on his taking a Voyage to Athens*', for example, though it has speed and verve, is altogether too happy-go-lucky. But 'To the Ph——an Ode' ('Look up to Pentland's towring Taps') is an admirable domesticating of the Horatian mood in an Edinburgh setting, and easily the best of his renderings from the Latin.

The Gentle Shepherd was an expansion of 'Patie and Roger' into a five-act pastoral comedy. It is the best known of all Ramsay's works, and, in spite of its artificially contrived plot and rather stiff movement, it manages to retain a certain freshness. The first edition contained only four songs—'Peggy, now the King's come', 'By the delicious warmness of thy mouth', 'Jocky said to Jenny', and 'My Patie is a lover gay'—but many more were added in 1728, when the play was changed into a ballad opera for the pupils of Haddington Grammar School. This is the version that has been printed ever since, which is a pity, because these editions print both the original dialogue and those parts of it which Ramsay turned into lyrics to be sung, with the result that there is much irritating duplication in the text. We gain 'My Peggy is a Young Thing' from these alterations, but otherwise the only advantage of the change was that it enabled *The Gentle Shepherd* to be sung, and this helped to keep it alive and popular.

The language is a somewhat anglicized Scots, showing on the whole a greater sureness of touch than Ramsay generally displayed in such mixed modes. Details of rural labour and rural festivity are handled with observant precision, and though there are some melodramatic moments connected with the return of the Royalist laird Sir William Worthy, there is an atmosphere of country work and play pervading the whole which the pastoral had long lost in England and elsewhere in Europe. The first part of the play, when rustic love is displayed against a lively background of rustic labour, is better than the latter part, where the action is manipulated unconvincingly in the interests of the proper *dénouement* and a happy ending; Jenny and Peggy are up early to lay their linen out for bleaching, and that gives them an opportunity of talking together, and when Patie detains Peggy, after the day's work, for some amorous words, Peggy knows that she should be at home helping to prepare supper:

> O Patie! let me gang; I mauna stay;   [*must not*
> We're baith cry'd hame.

Altogether, this pastoral drama represents a precarious equilibrium for Ramsay; he has found a way of combining vernacular realism and a rather tired convention without incongruity or vulgarity. The tiredness is not altogether banished, and the plot limps. But a Scottish breeze blows through this countryside, freshening the air and blowing away at least some of the languors of a stale tradition.

Ramsay produced thirty-one verse fables and tales, of which twenty are adaptations from La Motte and three are from La Fontaine. These are lively performances in Scots, done in fast-moving octosyllabic couplets, lacking the grace and polish of the French, but with a vigorous vernacular humour of their own. He consistently expands his original, filling it out with realistic and occasionally vulgar detail; he is nearer the *fabliau* than either La Motte or La Fontaine, and the Scots tradition of low-life comedy comes alive again in his hands. Again, this is not the greatest kind of poetry, but it is a kind to which the Scots vernacular at this stage of its life was appropriate, and it provided exercise for the vernacular in a setting where it could be used without constraint or affectation.

More important in some respects than Ramsay's original work was his work as an editor. In *The Tea-Table Miscellany* he collected songs and ballads, and in *The Ever Green* he printed the work of the 'Scottish Chaucerians' and others from the Bannatyne MS. In his preface to one of the many later editions of *The Tea-Table Miscellany* Ramsay wrote:

> My being well assured how acceptable new words to known tunes would prove, engaged me to the making verses for above sixty of them, in this and the second volume: about thirty more were done by some ingenious young gentlemen, who were so well pleased with my under-

taking, that they generously lent me their assistance; and to them the lovers of sense and music are obliged for some of the best songs in the collection. The rest are such old verses as have been done time out of mind, and only wanted to be cleared from the dross of blundering transcribers and printers; such as, *The Gaberlunzieman, Muirland Willy*, &c., that claim their place in our collection for their merry images of the low character.

Ramsay had thus none of the modern scholar's respect for the original text, and it may be hard to tell exactly what has happened to a song that appears in his collection. Ramsay's sources are often obscure, and a full inquiry into the history of many of the songs he prints, and indeed into the whole question of song collections in eighteenth-century Scotland, has still to be made. But, whatever their history, here the songs are, some 'improved', some rewritten, some printed as Ramsay found them. Ramsay provided some index to what had happened to the songs by marking some of them with letters. 'The SONGS marked C, D, H, L, M, O, &c., are new words by different hands; X, the authors unknown; Z, old songs; Q, old songs with additions.' But the system is not used consistently, and many songs have no letter at all [8].

The Ever Green is an easier collection to deal with; it takes most of its material from the Bannatyne MS. As Ramsay put it in a set of doggerel verses he wrote in the manuscript on 6 July 1726:

> In Seventeen hundred twenty four
> Did Allan Ramsay keen
> —ly gather from this Book that store
> which fills his Ever Green. . . .

Ramsay's patriotic intention is made clear by his remarks in the preface:

> When these good old *Bards* wrote, we had not yet made Use of imported Trimming upon our Cloaths, nor of foreign Embroidery in our Writings. Their *Poetry* is the Product of their own Country, not pilfered and spoiled in the Transportation from abroad: Their *Images* are native, and their *Landskips* domestick; copied from those Fields and Meadows we every Day behold.
>
> The *Morning* rises (in the Poets Description) as she does in the *Scottish* Horizon. We are not carried to *Greece* or *Italy* for a Shade, a Stream or a Breeze. The *Groves* rise in our own Valleys; the *Rivers* flow from our own Fountains, and the *Winds* blow upon our own Hills. I find not Fault with those Things, as they are in *Greece* or *Italy*: But with a *Northern Poet* for fetching his Materials from these Places, in a Poem, of which his own Country is the Scene; as our *Hymners* to the *Spring* and *Makers* of *Pastorals* frequently do.

The collection introduced eighteenth-century Scottish readers to the literature of their country's golden age. Dunbar and Henryson are both represented, the former by 'The Thistle and the Rose', 'Lament: Quhen he was Sek', 'The Goldyn Targe', 'Dunbar's Dregy', the 'Flyting', 'The Dance of the Sevin Deidly Synnis' and seventeen others. This selection gives a fair picture of Dunbar's range both in style and theme, including examples of the ceremonial, the aureate, the elegiac, the satiric, the moralizing, the humorous and the confessional. The poems from Henryson include 'Robene and Makyne', 'The Garmont of Gud Ladeis' and two of the fables. Among other pieces from the Bannatyne MS. are 'Christis Kirk on the Grene'; 'The Battle of Harlaw', one of the best known of the Scottish historical ballads; 'The Wife of Auchtermuchty', a lively verse-tale of husband and wife reversing rôles to the former's discomfiture, attributed to Sir John Moffatt; several poems by Alexander Scott; a group of coarse satires on loose women by the sixteenth-century Robert Sempill, and other poems by minor sixteenth-century writers. Ramsay changes spelling, punctuation, word order and even stanza form where it suits him; and where he cannot understand a word or a phrase he is liable to rephrase the passage [9].

Ramsay occasionally inserts stanzas of his own into older poems. He adds two stanzas to Dunbar's 'Tydingis fra the Sessioun', containing his own friendly opinion of the Edinburgh judges and advocates, and gives no indication that these stanzas are not by Dunbar; he slips a stanza full of elaborate classical allusions into the midst of Alexander Scott's simple, singing love lyric, 'Return thee, hairt, hamewart agane' (whose first line, incidentally, Ramsay characteristically 'regularizes' to 'Return Hamewart my Hart again'); and, most notorious, he adds his own preposterous conclusion to Dunbar's 'Lament':

> Suthe I forsie, if Spae-craft had,　　　　　　*[gift of prophecy*
> Frae Hethir-Muirs sall ryse a LAD,
> Aftir twa Centries pas, sall he
> 　　Revive our Fame and Memorie.

> Then sall we flourish EVIR GRENE:
> All thanks to carefull *Bannatyne,*
> And to the PATRON kind and frie,
> 　　Qhua lends the LAD baith them and me.

> Far sall we fare, baith Eist and West,
> Owre ilka Clyme by *Scots* possest;　　　　　*[every*
> Then sen our Warks sall nevir die,　　　　　*[since*
> 　　*Timor mortis non turbat me.*

To which monstrous conclusion Ramsay calmly appends the words, 'Quod Dunbar'.

The two poems attributed to 'Ar. Scot' are both anti-English patriotic poems (though 'The Eagle and Robin Red-breist' is veiled in allegory) and apparently Ramsay thought that they would have more force if put in antique dress—perhaps, too, he thought it safer so to disguise them. 'The Vision' is subtitled: '*Compylit in Latin be a most lernit Clerk in Tyme of our Hairship and Oppression, anno* 1300, *and translatit in* 1524.' It bewails the oppressed condition of Scotland and ends by prophesying successful battle for the re-establishment of an independent Kingdom of Scotland. The stanza is that of *The Cherrie and the Slae*. 'The Eagle and Robin Red-breist' tells how the robin, singing loyal songs to the royal eagle, is maligned by the other birds, jealous of his merit and of the king's regard for him, and driven from court. Here also the language is deliberately antique, though the verse form is the octosyllabic couplet. For Ramsay, Scots as a serious literary medium belonged to the past.

The Ever Green had nothing like the popularity of *The Tea-Table Miscellany*. There were no reprints in Ramsay's lifetime, and only four later reprints between 1761 and 1876. It was the popular vernacular tradition and the tradition of the late sixteenth-century poets, rather than the mediaeval makars, that influenced Fergusson and Burns. And though both the popular tradition and the tradition of Montgomerie and his contemporaries derived from and in their own way continued the mediaeval Scottish tradition, the fifteenth-century makars did not directly influence subsequent eighteenth-century Scottish poetry. The relatively homogeneous national culture of the Scotland of the early Stuarts was too far away; the Reformation, the Union of the Crowns and the Union of Parliaments had between them created too wide a gulf between past and present, and complicated the Scottish cultural situation to the point where no full, unselfconscious contact could any longer be made with Henryson and Dunbar. Both Watson and Ramsay had shown other ways and made other material available; ballad and folk-song remained alive, certain late mediaeval themes and stanza forms had been popularized, the goliardic tradition survived in the universities, and Scottish national sentiment was increasingly turning from politics to literature.

3

The 'ingenious young gentlemen' whose help Ramsay acknowledges in the preface to *The Tea-Table Miscellany* included several amateur versifiers who are remembered for a song, or a handful of songs, which took the popular fancy. This was the age of amateur poetizing among Scottish ladies and gentlemen. Their productions were as likely to be in neo-classic English as in Scots, as the artificial versions of Robert Crawford [10] witness. Crawford's 'Tweedside', 'Bush abune Traquair', 'Broom of Cowdenknows', 'My Deary, if thou die' (to the air of 'Down the Burn, Davie') and 'One day I heard Mary say' (to the air 'I'll never leave thee') are uninspired English texts written for older Scottish song tunes, yet they remained popular throughout the century. But not all the minor song-writers of the period wrote in neo-classic English. Sir John Clerk of Penicuik [11] is the reputed author of a lively elaboration of an old folk-song, 'O merry may the maid be' (to the tune to which 'Mary Morison' is now sung). Alexander Pennecuik [12] wrote in a variety of styles, covering much of Ramsay's ground: his 'Elegy on Robert Forbes' is reminiscent of Ramsay's 'Elegy on John Cowper', while 'The Merry Wives of Musselburgh's Welcome to Meg Dickson' (if it really be his) is a colourful and spirited piece as good as Ramsay's best in this vein. William Hamilton of Bangour [13] wrote mostly in English, but he contributed a remarkable, melodious elaboration of a folk-theme to *The Tea-Table Miscellany* in 'The Braes of Yarrow'. Alexander Ross [14], whose *Helenore, or the Fortunate Shepherdess* derives from *The Gentle Shepherd* and presents a rather faded Buchan version of Scottish pastoral, wrote the lively songs ,'Wooed and Married and A' ' and 'The Rock and the Wee Pickle Tow'. John Skinner's [15] rollicking 'Tullochgorum' was considered by Burns to be 'the best Scotch song ever Scotland saw', and his 'Ewie wi' the Crookit Horn', an elegy on a favourite ewe, combines humour and tenderness with considerable skill. Alexander Geddes [16] wrote 'Lewis Gordon', a simple and effective Jacobite song (and it should be remembered that the Jacobite Rebellion of 1745 provided Scotland with a folk-emotion, as well as a set of symbols with which to evoke a variety of feelings from the simply patriotic to the elegiac, the passionate and the mocking, and so gave new impetus to the interest in real and imitated folk-song and retarded the sophistication of the folk-tradition by about fifty years). Geddes was perhaps also the author of 'The Wee Bit Wifukie', a masterpiece in the rollicking vein. Jean Elliot [17] produced her version of 'The Flowers o' the Forest', an effective rendering of the popular note of lament for Flodden, more successful than Mrs. Cockburn's more deliberately artful, and more English, poem with the same title and refrain. And Lady Anne Barnard's [18] 'Auld Robin Gray' passed for some time as an old song.

There were other songs of the period whose authorship is uncertain or unknown, among them 'There's Nae Luck about the House' (probably by William Julius Mickle [19]), 'O weel may the Boatie Row' (probably by John Ewen, 1741-1821), the full version of 'Aye Waukin' O', 'Logie o' Buchan' (perhaps by George Halket, *d.* 1756), 'The Drunken Wife of Gallowa' (also known as 'Hoolie and Fairly') and many of those found in Herd's collection.

Ramsay's *Tea-Table Miscellany* was by no means the only collection of songs published in Scotland at this time. The interest in 'primitive' poetry which prompted the publication of Percy's *Reliques* in England in 1765 and which later helped to determine the terms of the Ossian controversy, began earlier in Scotland and was there mixed up with patriotic motives. Collections of songs and ballads, with and without music, were numerous in Scotland from *The Tea-Table Miscellany* to Thomson's *Select Scotish Airs* (1795 ff.). In 1726 the *Orpheus Caledonius* was published in London, containing about fifty Scottish songs with the music, and it was followed in 1733 by an enlarged edition in two volumes. Similar collections followed in Scotland, culminating in James Johnston's *Scots Musical Museum*, of which the first volume appeared in 1787 and to whose subsequent volumes Burns contributed so much. Of the books of Scots songs without music, the most important was David Herd's *Ancient and Modern Scots Songs* [20]. There were also many collections of the tunes alone, arranged for a variety of instruments. The pioneer volume here was the *Collection of Scots Tunes* made by the violinist Adam Craig in 1730, and the most impressive collection was James Oswald's *Caledonian Pocket Companion*, of which the first of many volumes appeared in 1740. Antiquarians, folk-lorists and romantic lovers of the past joined the procession as the century advanced; and between Herd's first edition in 1769 and John Finlay's *Scottish Historical and Romantic Ballads* in 1808, a whole tribe of collectors (including John Pinkerton, Joseph Ritson, Walter Scott and Robert Jamieson) were at work. This was, of course, far from being a purely Scottish movement, but in Scotland it took on special significance and sprang from special motives.

Herd's two volumes of 1776 constitute a remarkable collection. He reprinted a fair number of pieces that had appeared in Watson and in *The Tea-Table Miscellany*, together with much that had not appeared before, and he printed almost everything anonymously without any indication of age. But he never tampered with his material; he printed the pieces as he found them, and he was content to let many of the older songs appear in fragmentary form. Unlike Percy and most other editors of his time, he had no urge to complete and improve. Herd is thus an important figure in the transmission of the Scottish popular tradition in poetry. Scholarly, accurate and modest, he never put his own name to his work (neither of his editions mentions an editor), and in his preface to the two volumes of 1776 he 'anticipated the censure of the severe, by confessing them a work of slight importance'.

4

The kind of interest in Scottish literature represented by Ramsay's original and editorial work, and by that of the collectors and imitators of older Scottish songs who followed him, must be seen in its true perspective. The general cultural current was still flowing strongly towards England, and the Edinburgh historians, philosophers, scientists and literary critics who contributed so much to Scotland's second 'golden age' wrote in English and studiously avoided 'Scotticisms' in their speech. In 1761 the Irishman Thomas Sheridan (father of the dramatist) delivered twelve lectures on the 'correct' speaking of English at St. Paul's Episcopal Church, Edinburgh, and about three hundred of the city's most distinguished citizens attended. In the issue of *The Mirror* for 22 February 1780, Henry Mackenzie explained to his readers why Scotsmen, writing an English they did not speak and speaking a dialect they did not write, were incapable of writing humorously in English or seriously in their native dialect:

> When a Scotsman . . . writes, he does so generally in trammels. His own native original language, which he hears spoken around him, he does not make use of; but he expresses himself in a language in some respects foreign to him, and which he has acquired by study and observation. . . . Hence Scottish writers may have been prevented from attempting to write books of humour. . . . In confirmation of these remarks it may be observed, that almost the only works of humour which we have in this country, are in the *Scottish* dialect. . . . The *Gentle Shepherd*, which is full of natural and ludicrous representations of low life, is written in broad *Scotch*. . . . [21]

Scots thus remained a vernacular, and there was no tradition of written Scots prose in the eighteenth century. Anyone who had claims to international fame in dealing with general matters of scientific or philosophic interest wrote in English for the same reason that he would have written in Latin in an earlier age. And in poetry the vernacular established itself as a vehicle only for exercises in the mock-antique or for humorous or convivial or skittish or condescending verses. Ramsay had not enlarged the potentialities of the Scottish vernacular; still less had he re-created Scots as a full-blooded literary language. Nobody, in fact, achieved that in the eighteenth century or later: it is one of the ideals of the modern Lallans movement [22]. But one eighteenth-century Scottish poet did achieve a Scots idiom which combined ease, weight, variety and cunning, and which pointed the way towards the re-establishment of Scots as a literary language (though it was a way that nobody was to take). This was Robert Fergusson [23], not the greatest of the eighteenth-century Scottish poets but perhaps the most assured in his use of Scots.

Fergusson was fortunate in not having the multiple motivations that confused the careers of both Ramsay and Burns. Unlike Ramsay, he was not a half-educated country boy trying in the city to be both genteel and patriotic, and unlike Burns he was not tempted to parade a self-conscious primitivism before the eyes of the Edinburgh literati. He was an Edinburgh man and an Edinburgh poet, who rendered the life of the city with warmth and colour. But his student days had made him well acquainted with Fife, and he had also paid visits to his mother's people in Aberdeenshire. Further, the Edinburgh of the 1760s and 1770s was not, in spite of its bustling city life, an urban area in the modern sense: the countryside extended right up to its doorstep, and there were fishing-towns and a seaport right beside it. To be an Edinburgh man did not mean, therefore, that one was ignorant of the cycles of agricultural activity or of the life of the fisherfolk (both of which Fergusson had also known in Fife), or that one was deprived of the pleasures of scrambling over hills and moors. If we think of Fergusson as a figure belonging to the closes and howffs of Edinburgh, a convivial companion at Lucky Middlemass's or with members of the Cape Club at James Mann's tavern in Craig's Close, we must not forget that he knew other scenes too. He knew the spoken Scots of Lothian, Fife and Aberdeenshire, and he knew Lowland Scottish life in both town and country: he was at home in Scotland in a quietly assured way. Further, he had received a reasonably good formal education, so that he had no inferiority complex about his knowledge of the classics. He was free to laugh at the literati if he wanted to, and when Dr. Johnson insulted the Scots he could cheerfully satirize the Grand Cham in lively and uninhibited verse. He did not have to declare defensively that he understood Horace but faintly in the original, or to present himself to the genteel world as a remarkable example of the natural man.

The Cape Club provided a better atmosphere for a poet than the self-conscious young would-be gentlemen of the Easy Club provided for Ramsay. Members of this Club—The Knights Companions of the Cape, as they called themselves—included David Herd, the painters Alexander Runciman, Alexander Nasmyth and (later) Sir Henry Raeburn; the actors Thomas Lancashire and William Woods, and Stephen Kemble, manager of the Theatre Royal; James Sibbald, the historian of Scottish poetry; the later notorious Deacon Brodie; Stephen Clarke, the musician who was to help Burns; a large number of tradesmen of convivial, literary or musical inclination; and some lawyers and other professional men. It was a democratic, informal, friendly group, having none of the genteel pretensions of the more formal societies attended by the literati yet with nothing of the coarse debauchery of the lower Edinburgh taverns. Eighteenth-century Edinburgh was a city of clubs and taverns, and Fergusson easily found his level among them. He was at home in the Cape Club (to which he was admitted in October 1772), and he was equally at home 'o'er oysters and a dram o' gin' at Lucky Middlemass's or with a dish of rizzard haddock and a bicker of tippeny at this or some other Edinburgh howff. He was also a frequenter of the theatre, the friendship of Woods the actor obtaining for him free admission.

Members of the Cape Club took knightly titles. David Herd was Sir Scrape-Greysteil, Alexander Runciman was Sir Brimstone, and Fergusson was admitted as Sir Precentor, presumably because of his good voice and his fondness for singing. He attended the meetings regularly throughout 1733.

Fergusson's first appearance as a poet was not promising. He wrote three poor English songs to Scottish airs for a performance of the opera *Artaxerxes* at the Theatre Royal in 1769. Two years later he began contributing to Ruddiman's *Weekly Magazine*, starting with three English pastorals entitled 'Morning', 'Noon' and 'Night'. But as a poet in English Fergusson never achieved anything more than a certain dexterity in the manipulation of English words. Only when he uses English in parody of the genteel literary tradition of his day does he achieve any spark at all. His poem, 'The Sow of Feeling'—the lament of a pig of sensibility whose husband and children have been slaughtered for the table—is an amusing satire of Henry Mackenzie's *The Man of Feeling* and the fashion which it started. It is also a parody of the kind of English poetic style which eighteenth-century Scottish poets tended to fall into when they wanted to be genteel:

> Thrice happy, had I lived in Jewish time,
> When swallowing pork or pig was deem'd a crime;
> My husband long had blest my longing arms,
> Long, long had known love's sympathetic charms!
> My children too—a little suckling race,
> With all their father growing in their face,
> From their prolific dam had ne'er been torn,
> Nor to the bloody stalls of butchers borne.

And in his 'To Dr. Samuel Johnson, food for a new edition of his Dictionary', he parodies the lexicographer's vocabulary. Such poems are significant only as indicating Fergusson's educational independence, as compared with Ramsay or Burns.

It was the issue of the *Weekly Magazine* for 2 January 1772 that introduced Fergusson to the public as a Scots poet. The poem was 'The Daft-Days', the period of convivial celebration at the end of the old year and the beginning of the new; it opens with a memorable picture of Edinburgh in December:

> Now mirk December's dowie face   [dark, doleful
> Glours our the rigs wi' sour grimace,   [ridges
> While, thro' his *minimum* of space,
>   The bleer-ey'd sun,
> Wi' blinkin light and stealing pace,
>   His race doth run.

From naked groves nae birdie sings,
To shepherd's pipe nae hillock rings,
The breeze nae od'rous flavour brings
  From *Borean* cave,
And dwyning nature droops her wings,   [*drooping*
  Wi' visage grave.

The picture of winter laying its frozen hand on Edinburgh and its rural environs is done with a gravity (far from the same thing as solemnity) of language that shows us at once that Fergusson took the vernacular more seriously than Ramsay had done. The Latin *minimum* and the adjective *Borean* take their place naturally in a descriptive verse whose tone and accent demonstrate its hospitality to any legitimate devices for adding weight and scope. A line such as 'And dwyning nature droops her wings' is stylized in an altogether appropriate way: it is not a conventional image thrown inappropriately on top of a colloquial style in the way that Ramsay so often did, but a formal handling of Scots.

After building up the atmosphere of the winter exterior, the poet turns to the contrasting interior:

Auld Reikie! thou'rt the canty hole, [*Edinburgh, cheerful*
A bield for mony a caldrife soul,   [*shelter, sensitive to cold*
Wha snugly at thine ingle loll,   [*fireside*
  Baith warm and couth;   [*comfortable*
While round they gar the bicker roll [*make, drinking-cup*
  To weet their mouth.

As the poem develops, it becomes clear that its true theme is conviviality—brilliantly localized Edinburgh conviviality. The patriotic theme emerges naturally from the convivial; when the capital of Scotland celebrates, it must be in an appropriately Scottish way:

Fidlers, your pints in temper fix,
And roset weel your fiddle-sticks,   [*rosin*
But banish vile Italian tricks,
  From out your quorum:
Nor *fortes* wi' *pianos* mix,
  Gie's *Tulloch Gorum*.

It may be that Fergusson's touchiness about foreign influences in Edinburgh (which he demonstrates more than once) shows a parochial spirit, which the Middle Scots poets, who were Europeans as well as Scots, wholly lacked; but it must be remembered that not only was the Italianizing of Scottish song seriously threatening an important part of Scotland's musical heritage in Fergusson's day, but the uncertainty and obsequiousness about the nature and status of Scottish culture shown by so many of Fergusson's contemporaries were bound to make an initial defence of Scottish traditions take a form that would seem merely xenophobic to a more assured generation.

The theme suggested in the stanza attacking 'vile Italian tricks' in music is developed in 'Elegy, On the Death of Scots Music', which appeared in the *Weekly Magazine* on 5 March 1772. This is a serious patriotic poem, a lament for the swamping of the native Scottish tradition in music by foreign influences. The mock elegy form (which Fergusson had used with great spirit and considerable skill in his 'Elegy on the Death of Mr. David Gregory, late Professor of Mathematics in the University of St. Andrews', one of his earlier works) has here shed its note of rather self-conscious humour and is sublimated into something more formal and more *whole*. Fergusson takes his epigraph from Shakespeare's *Twelfth Night*, with an easy appropriateness that once again shows his poetic assurance:

> Mark it Cesario; it is old and plain,
> The spinsters and the knitters in the sun,
> And the free maids that weave their thread with bones,
> Do use to chant it.

This sets the tone, and the poem opens with an elegiac stateliness:

> On Scotia's plains, in days of yore,
> When lads and lasses *tartan* wore,
> Saft music rang on ilka shore,   [*every*
> In hamely weid;
> But harmony is now no more,
> And *music* dead. [24]

Three more stanzas develop the mourning theme in fairly general terms, and then, in a manner characteristic of him, Fergusson begins to narrow his subject with increasing particularization:

> Nae lasses now, on simmer days,
> Will lilt at bleaching of their claes;
> Nae herds on *Yarrow*'s bonny braes
> Or banks of *Tweed*,
> Delight to chant their hameil lays,   [*home-bred*
> Since music's dead.
>
> At glomin now the bagpipe's dumb,
> Whan weary owsen hameward come;   [*oxen*
> Sae sweetly as it wont to bum,
> And *Pibrachs* skreed
> We never hear its warlike hum;
> For music's dead. . . .

A reference to his favourite song 'The Birks of Invermay' [25] finishes the particularization, and the poem then moves at once to its formal conclusion:

> O SCOTLAND! that cou'd yence afford   [once
> To bang the pith of Roman sword,
> Winna your sons, wi' joint accord,
>   To battle speed?
> And fight till MUSIC be restor'd,
>   Which now lies dead.

Fergusson's next poem, 'The King's Birthday in Edinburgh', was a full-blooded performance in the Scottish tradition of poems of popular revelry though lacking what might be called the broadside accent of so many of such poems. It is a description of Edinburgh's celebration of the King's birthday, and, significantly, has as epigraph a line from Drummond's Scots macaronic, *Polemo-Middinia*, 'Oh! qualis hurly-burly fuit, si forte vidisses'. The style of the poem is familiar but not vulgar. The opening is humorous in a new way for eighteenth-century Scottish poetry:

> I sing the day sae aften sung,
> Wi' which our lugs hae yearly rung,   [ears
> In whase loud praise the Muse has dung   [wearied
>   A' kind o' print;
> But wow! the limmer's fairly flung;   [rogue
>   There's naething in't. . . .
>
> O *Muse*, be kind, and dinna fash us   [trouble
> To flee awa' beyont Parnassus,
> Nor seek for *Helicon* to wash us,
>   That heath'nish spring;
> Wi' Highland whisky scour our hawses,   [throats
>   And gar us sing.   [make
>
> Begin then, dame, ye've drunk your fill,
> You woudna hae the tither gill?   [other
> You'll trust me, mair wou'd do you ill,
>   And ding you doitet;   [stupid
> Troth 'twou'd be sair agains my will
>   To hae the wyte o't.   [blame

The poet's mischievously familiar attitude to the Muse is not vulgarity, but controlled high spirits. It sets the tone for the ensuing description:

> Sing then, how, on the *fourth* of June,
> Our *bells* screed aff a loyal tune,
> Our antient castle shoots at noon,
>   Wi' flag-staff buskit,
> Frae which the soldier blades come down
>   To cock their musket.

And off he goes, describing the noise, the pranks, the brulzies with the City Guard, with artful verve. The poet's self, introduced in the very first line, is present throughout, both as observer and as celebrant, and the introduction of his own comments adds to the spontaneity of the tone, as when he addresses the old cannon, Mons Meg:

> ... Right seldom am I gi'en to bannin, [*swearing*
> But, by my saul, ye was a cannon,
> Cou'd hit a man, had he been stannin
>   In shire o' Fife,
> Sax long Scots miles ayont *Clackmannan*,
>   And tak his life.

The note of personal wonder, rising to a climax in a line which opens with four emphatic monosyllabic words—'Sax long Scots miles ayont Clackmannan'—represents technique of a high order, from which Burns was to learn. At the end of the poem he returns to the Muse, reminding himself that the final stages of riotous celebration are not fit themes for her, who is accustomed to more conventionally poetic aspects of the day's proceedings:

> She'll rather to the fields resort,
> Whare music gars the day seem short, [*makes*
> Whare doggies play, and lambies sport
>   On gowany braes, [*daisied*
> Whare peerless Fancy hads her court,
>   And tunes her lays. [26]

'Peerless Fancy' is deliberate, almost ironic, English poetic diction: the pastoral aspects of the celebration are more suitable for conventional poetic treatment than the more violent urban goings-on that he has been recounting. And on that note of mingled pastoral cheerfulness and ironic poetizing the poem concludes.

'Caller [fresh] Oysters' is another of Fergusson's convivial poems. Its opening, a fine tribute to the Forth and its fishermen, shows him handling the 'Standart *Habby*' stanza with a slowness and openness not often found in this verse form:

> Of a' the waters that can hobble [*toss*
> A fishin yole or salmon coble, [*yawl, flat-bottomed boat*
> And can reward the fishers trouble,
>   Or south or north,
> There's nane sae spacious and sae noble
>   As Firth o' *Forth*. ...

He moves inland from the sea, from the Forth coast to Auld Reekie's oyster cellars, and soon we have one of his cosy Edinburgh interiors again:

> Whan big as burns the gutters rin,
> Gin ye hae catcht a droukit skin, [*drenched*

To *Luckie Middlemist*'s loup in,
And sit fu snug
Oe'r oysters and a dram o' gin,
Or haddock lug. . . .

On 3 September 1772 there appeared in the *Weekly Magazine* a
Scots poem signed 'J. S.', dated from Berwick, hailing Fergusson as
Ramsay's equal and successor. The following week Fergusson's reply
appeared, following the tradition of the verse epistle as developed by
Hamilton of Gilbertfield and Ramsay. It is a skilful enough occasional
piece, but his predecessors had done as well in this mode. More original
in both style and content is 'Braid Claith', which appeared on 15
October. It is a satire, whose theme is that clothes make the man: with
a good suit of braid claith a man, whatever his natural endowments,
commands respect and is sure to get on in the world. The conclusion
illustrates both the tone of the poem and the comic-ironic ingenuity
of some of Fergusson's rhymes:

Braid Claith lends fock an unco heese,   [*folk, strange lift*
Makes mony kail-worms butter-flies,   [*caterpillars*
Gies mony a doctor his degrees
    For little skaith: [*trouble*
In short, you may be what you please
    Wi' gude Braid Claith.

For thof ye had as wise a snout on
As *Shakespeare* or Sir *Isaac Newton*,
Your judgment fouk wou'd hae a doubt on,
    I'll tak my aith,
Till they cou'd see ye wi' a suit on
    O' gude Braid Claith.

In October appeared 'Geordie and Davie, an Eclogue to the Memory
of Dr. Wilkie'. Wilkie had been professor of Natural Philosophy at
St. Andrews, and had taken an interest in Fergusson when he was a
student there. The eclogue is modelled on Ramsay's pastoral elegies,
but it is an altogether more assured performance than anything Ramsay
did in that style. He uses heroic couplets with gravity and flexibility
(though the lines are as a rule end-stopped) and the Scots appears
completely at home in this verse form. This is something new in
eighteenth-century Scottish poetry:

. . . Tho' simmer's gane, an' we nae langer view
The blades o' claver wat wi' pearls o' dew.
Cauld winter's bleakest blasts we'll eithly cowr,   [*easily*
Our eldin's driven, an' our har'st is owr;   [*fuel*
Our *rucks* fu' thick are stackit i' the yard,
For the *Yule-feast* a sautit mart's prepar'd;   [*salted*

The ingle-nook supplies the simmer fields,
An' aft as mony gleefu' maments yields.
Swyth man! fling a' your sleepy springs awa',   [quickly
An' on your canty whistle gie's a blaw: [cheerful
Blythness, I trow, maun lighten ilka eie,   [must, every eye
An' ilka canty callant sing like me.   [fellow

The language here is integrated and confident, and does not halt
between genteel English and vulgar Scots. But a brief quotation loses
the effect: one must read the whole poem to appreciate Fergusson's
control and assurance.

'Hallow-fair' is another poem which develops a Scottish tradition
that Ramsay and others had already made popular. It is an account of
the lively scenes that took place at the annual market held in November
in the outskirts of Edinburgh, done in that form of 'Christis Kirk on
the Grene' stanza that Watson had printed and which Burns was to use.
The life and colour and movement of the poem are magnificent, and the
way Fergusson manages to use the short four-syllable ending to each
stanza (always with the same two last words, 'that day', except for 'that
night' on two occasions) shows a firm control over his medium. The
poet is the mere observer here; he is not himself implicated as in 'The
King's Birthday' and 'Caller Oysters'; and the poem moves from scene
to scene picking out the liveliest and most striking activities. Here
again Fergusson can play with classical deities without any feeling of
either vulgarity or pretentiousness:

When *Phoebus* ligs in *Thetis* lap   [lies
   Auld Reikie gies them shelter,   [Edinburgh
Whare cadgily they kiss the cap,   [gaily, wooden cup
   An' ca't round helter-skelter.   [knock it
Jock Bell gaed furth to play his freaks,
   Great cause he had to rue it,
For frae a stark Lochaber aix
   He gat a *clamihewit*,   [blow
      Fu' sair that night.

The last of the 1772 poems is 'To the Tron-kirk Bell', a magnificent
piece of studied abuse directed at the 'wanwordy [worthless] crazy,
dinsome thing' whose 'noisy tongue' was 'sair to thole [endure]'.
Here Fergusson demonstrated a virtuosity that had not been seen in
Scots poetry since the makars. The mixture of skill and gusto with
which the riven bell is abused is reminiscent of Dunbar in his best
flyting style; the poem, however, is not a satire on bells but on baillies:
the conclusion is that the city fathers allow this scandal because they
live out of its hearing:

But far frae thee the *bailies* dwell,
Or they wud scunner at your knell. . . .   [be disgusted

178

The 1773 poems began on 21 January with 'Caller Water', a poem in praise of fresh water which, deftly handled and cunningly constructed, turns out to be a poem in praise of the Edinburgh lasses. Water kept 'father Adie' healthy in Eden (Fergusson uses that familiar tone to scriptural characters that Burns was to exploit so happily); it is prescribed by doctors who confuse their patients' noddles by giving it a pretentious Latin name; it provides healthful swimming; it cures the colic; it keeps the lasses trig and bonny. The poem, which moves trippingly throughout, comes to a neat and happy conclusion:

> O may they still pursue the way
> To look sae feat, sae clean, sae gay!   [*neat*
> Than shall their beauties glance like *May*,
>   And, like her, be
> The goddess of the vocal Spray,
>   The Muse, and me.

A more ambitious work is 'Mutual Complaint of Plainstanes and Causey', a dialogue in flexible octosyllabic couplets between the main road of the High Street (causey) and its sidewalk (plainstanes). Each complains of what it has to bear and thinks it has a worse lot than the other—causey with wagons, horses, coaches, Highland chairmen and the Luckenbooths, plainstanes (designed for nothing heavier than 'sole of shoe or pump') trod by 'burden-bearers heavy shod' and loutish rustic characters. The result is both a picture of Edinburgh street life and a satire on snobbery.

'The Rising of the Session', which appeared in March, should be considered together with 'The Sitting of the Session', which did not appear until 4 November. These poems remind us of the important part that the law played in Edinburgh life: the rising of the Court of Session at once diminished the city's activities, and the first of these two poems is a sharply etched series of pictures of the denuded city, with empty taverns and change-houses, shot through with a running satire on lawyers. 'The Sitting of the Session' presents the other side of the picture: it shows in brilliant detail the revived life of the city, with bar-keepers and litigators in full cry. The poem begins with one of Fergusson's fine seasonal portraits of Edinburgh in November: he then moves through the city, as the slightly ironical observer, and describes what he sees. Sometimes he ironically encourages the activities he is describing:

> Now at the door they'll raise a plea;
> Crack on, my lads!—for flyting's free;   [*abuse, scolding*
> For gin ye shou'd tongue-tacket be,
>   The mair's the pity,
> Whan scalding but and ben we see   [*arguing hither and yon*
>   PENDENTE LITE.

The macaronic touch here, with its ironical humour, is in an old Scottish tradition.

On 13 May the *Weekly Magazine* printed 'The Farmer's Ingle', one of Fergusson's two real masterpieces (the other is 'Auld Reekie'). Hitherto Fergusson had excelled as an urban poet, as the bard of Edinburgh, but here he celebrates the agricultural life in a rich, slow-moving verse of a kind that Scottish poetry had not seen for centuries. The stanza is a modified Spenserian; the tone is that of affectionate observation, without a trace of sentimentality; the structure, moving from the vivid description of evening settling over the countryside to the interior domestic scene and then taking the farmer and his family through their evening's activities until they retire to rest, to conclude on a note of peaceful benediction, is perfectly controlled throughout. 'The Farmer's Ingle' is a finer poem than Burns's 'The Cotter's Saturday Night', which, in spite of some magnificent passages, is confused in tone, motive and diction. Fergusson's very title indicates the superiority: Burns's title sounds as though he is about to show off some model rustics to benevolent genteel observers, whereas Fergusson is describing, with knowledge and affection, what he sees. Here at last is a full-blooded Scots poem, written by the whole man, rich and musical and assured:

> Whan gloming grey out o'er the welkin keeks,   [*twilight*
> Whan *Batie* ca's his owsen to the byre,   [*oxen*
> Whan *Thrasher John*, sair dung, his barn-door steeks,   [*wearied, shuts*
> And lusty lasses at the dighting tire: [*winnowing*
> What bangs fu' leal the e'enings coming cauld,   [*defeats, truly*
> And gars snaw-tapit winter freeze in vain;   [*makes snowtopped*
> Gars dowie mortals look baith blyth and bauld,   [*melancholy*
> Nor fley'd wi' a' the poortith o' the plain;   [*affrighted, poverty*
> Begin, my Muse, and chant in hamely strain.

The second stanza describes the gudeman coming home, the third shows the gudewife making everything ready for his arrival, the fourth moves to an unforced moralizing on the superior healthfulness of hard work and simple fare to idleness and drugs, and the fifth develops this into a tribute to the achievements of Scotsmen of old, brought up on simple fare. Then, in the sixth stanza, he turns again to the scene before him:

> The couthy cracks begin when supper's o'er,   [*friendly chats*
> The cheering *bicker* gars them glibly gash   [*drinking cup, talk*
> O' simmer's *showery blinks* and winters sour,
> Whase floods did erst their mailins produce hash: [*small farm's,*
> 'Bout *kirk* and *market* eke their tales gae on,   *destroy*
> How *Jock* woo'd *Jenny* here to be his bride,

And there how *Marion*, for a bastard son,
  Upo' the *cutty-stool* was forc'd to ride,   [*stool of repentance*
  The waefu' scald o' our *Mess John* to bide.   [*castigation, Minister*

The fient a chiep's amang the bairnies now;   [*devil, squeak*
  For a' their anger's wi' their hunger gane:
Ay maun the childer, wi' a fastin mou',   [*must, mouth*
  Grumble and greet, and make an unco mane,   [*great noise*
In rangles round before the ingle's low: [*clusters, flame*
  Frae *gudame's* mouth auld warld tale they hear,
O' *Warlocks* louping round the *Wirrikow*,   [*wizards, hobgoblin*
  O' gaists that win in glen and kirk-yard drear,   [*ghosts, dwell*
Whilk touzles a' their tap, and gars them shak wi' fear.   [*which, makes*

And so the evening wears on. In the tenth stanza we have an attractive picture of the gudeman relaxing, and in the eleventh he is shown discussing the next day's work with the lads. In the twelfth they all retire to bed, and the final stanza asks a blessing on them all:

Peace to the husbandman and a' his tribe,
  Whase care fells a' our wants frae year to year;   [*supplies*
Lang may his sock and couter turn the gleyb,   [*ploughshare*
  And bauks o' corn bend down wi' laded ear.   [*ridges*
May Scotia's simmers ay look gay and green,
  Her yellow har'sts frae scowry blasts decreed;
May a' her tenants sit fu' snug and bien,   [*prosperous*
  Frae the hard grip of ails and poortith freed,
And a lang lasting train o' peaceful hours succeed.

The ending is perfectly modulated, in contrast to the more rhetorical conclusion of 'The Cotter's Saturday Night'.

'The Farmer's Ingle' is a Scots poem, but this does not mean that it derives entirely and solely from Scottish literary traditions. On the contrary, the stanza form, the tone and even the subject show English influence; the significant point is that these influences have been thoroughly assimilated, and are used in an assured Scots way. The strength of a national art does not lie in its refusal to borrow from other national arts, but in its ability to domesticate its borrowings properly in its own medium. This is what Fergusson does in 'The Farmer's Ingle', and it is something that no Scottish poet in the eighteenth century had yet done.

'The Ghaists: a Kirkyard Eclogue' is a dialogue between the ghosts of George Heriot and George Watson (Edinburgh merchants who had left bequests to found 'hospitals'—now schools—in the city), who deplore the effect in Scotland of the proposed 'Mortmain Bill' introduced in Westminster. The bill (which, owing to Scottish opposition, was eventually restricted in scope to apply to England only) was intended to enable charitable foundations in Britain to realize their assets and invest the proceeds in three per cent. funds, which would be the future source of their income. This would have impoverished certain Scottish foundations, and Scottish national feeling was aroused. Fergusson's poem was a contribution to the debate, and at the same time a defence of the national integrity of Scotland. The verse is the heroic couplet, handled with deliberate *gravitas*:

> Think na I vent my well-a-day in vain,
> Kent ye the cause, ye sure wad join my mane.   [*complaint*
> Black be the day that e'er to England's ground
> Scotland was eikit by the UNION's bond;   [*added*
> For mony a menzie of destructive ills   [*company*
> The country now maun brook frae *mortmain bills*,
> That void out test'ments, and can freely gie
> Sic will and scoup to the ordain'd trustee,
> That he may tir our stateliest riggins bare,
> Nor acres, houses, woods, nor fishins spare,
> Till he can lend the stoitering state a lift   [*stumbling*
> Wi' gowd in gowpins as a grassum gift; . . .   [*gold in handfuls, free*
> Hale interest for my fund can scantly now
> Cleed a' my callants backs, and stap their mou'.   [*clothe*
> How maun their weyms wi' sairest hunger slack,   [*must, bellies*
> Their duds in targets flaff upo' their back,   [*rags, tatters*
> Whan they are doom'd to keep a lasting Lent,
> Starving for England's weel at *three per cent.*

This kind of patriotic poetry, dealing boldly with contemporary affairs, is both more poetic and more effective than the oblique pseudo-historical contrivances of Ramsay.

The next two poems, 'On Seeing a Butterfly in the Street' and 'Hame Content, a Satire' (like the 'Ode to the Bee', which had appeared earlier), are moral pieces in octosyllabic couplets, starting from a particular situation and moving outwards to illustrate what it means in terms of the way people live. They are vigorous enough, and show Fergusson's competence and confidence if not the height of his genius. 'Leith Races', which appeared in July, is in the mood and stanza form of 'Hallow Fair'. It is another of Fergusson's Edinburgh poems, and the model for Burns's 'The Holy Fair'. A short quotation cannot suggest its quality; it is the carefully handled sequence of scenes that builds up into an impressive poem. 'Ode to the Gowdspink', in the same general style as the butterfly poem, appeared in August, and 'The Election', another Edinburgh poem with all the life and speed of 'Hallow Fair' and 'Leith Races', in September. 'To the Principal and Professors of the University of St. Andrews, on their superb treat to

Dr. Johnson' is a skilful and high-spirited fling at the doctor in octosyllabic couplets. After describing the elaborate foreign dishes at the feast, he says that if he had been there he would have filled the anti-Scottish lexicographer with humble Scottish fare, which he proceeds to catalogue. It is a satire, which emerges as a patriotic poem.

The 'Elegy on John Hogg' also appeared in September: it is perhaps the most brilliant, certainly the most technically accomplished, of all the mock elegies in the 'Habbie Simson' tradition. 'A Drink Eclogue', a dialogue in heroic couplets between 'Landlady, Brandy and Whisky', is a piece of skilful flyting between the two liquors, with the landlady intervening at the end. Finally, 'To my Auld Breeks' (25 November), a ruefully comic address to his worn-out trousers in octosyllabic couplets, brings the *Weekly Magazine* series of Fergusson's Scots poems to a close.

There are a few other Scots poems by Fergusson which did not appear in the *Weekly Magazine*. They include another 'Hallow Fair', a song this time [27]. There is also an accomplished Scots translation of an ode of Horace (I. xi), which first appeared in the 1779 edition of his poems. But most important of all the poems first published outside the *Weekly Magazine* is 'Auld Reekie', published separately in 1773 and included, in a later version, in the 1779 volume. It is the Edinburgh poet's fullest and most accomplished celebration of his city. The octosyllabic couplets, shifting in tempo in accordance with the particular scene before the poet's eye, carry the expressive Scots forcefully to the ear, while the imagery, fixing the scene with its most significant component or appropriate symbol, builds up the Edinburgh sights, sounds and smells. This is more than a Dickensian exploration of urban oddities or the search for the striking scene or incident: the whole poem is set in a framework of acceptance—acceptance of the whole of life, with its colour, gaiety and debauchery, dreariness and pretentiousness and weakness, companionship, loneliness and sheer unadulterated humanity. He is not exhibiting Edinburgh to a sniggering or an admiring audience; he is savouring its full quality because he enjoys doing so. The whole Edinburgh scene passes under his eye. Gossips, schoolboys, housemaids, lawyers, thieves, whores, tavern-haunters, Sunday walkers, corrupt politicians, each against their appropriate background, are picked out and described; and there is an undercurrent of satire directed against those who through laziness or selfishness neglect the city's welfare or actively contribute to its harm. The contrasts are frequent and impressive:

> Near some lamp-post, wi' dowy face,   [*melancholy*
> Wi' heavy ein, and sour grimace,
> Stands she that beauty lang had kend,
> Whoredom her trade, and vice her end.

But see whare now she wuns her bread
By that which nature ne'er decreed;
And sings sad music to the lugs,   [*ears*
'Mang bourachs o' damn'd whores and rogues. . . .   [*clusters*

And here is another:

In afternoon, a' brawlie buskit,   [*grandly dressed up*
The joes and lasses loe to frisk it: [*sweethearts*
Some tak a great delight to place
The modest *bon-grace* o'er the face;   [*bonnet*
Tho' you may see, if so inclin'd,
The turning o' the leg behind.
Now Comely-garden, and the Park,
Refresh them, after forenoon's wark;
Newhaven, Leith, or Canon-mills,
Supply them in their Sunday's gills. . . .

The conclusion, where the poet retires across the Forth to look at
his city whole, across the water from Fife, rounds the poem off
perfectly:

REIKIE, farewel! I ne'er cou'd part
Wi' thee but wi' a dowy heart;
Aft frae the *Fifan* coast I've seen,
Thee tow'ring on thy summit green;
So glowr the saints when first is given
A fav'rite keek o' glore and heaven;   [*glory*
On earth nae mair they bend their ein,
But quick assume angelic mein;
So I on *Fife* wad glowr no more,
But gallop'd to EDINA's shore.

Perhaps the measure of Fergusson's technical success as a Scots poet
is that he can (requiring the brevity and formality) call Edinburgh
'Edina' in the last line of this poem, and get away with it: Burns, in
'Edina! Scotia's darling seat', could not. If there is something of John
Gay in this poem, it is not, as it often is in Ramsay, a vulgar aping of a
metropolitan wit beyond his ken, but an influence happily assimilated.

Was Fergusson's Scots a homogeneous literary language? It was
certainly more than a regional dialect, for it contained, in addition to
its Edinburgh base, elements from Fife and from Aberdeenshire as
well as from older literary Scots. Does this mean that Fergusson raised
the status of Scots from a vernacular to a literary language? Hardly;
because it takes more than a single poet to achieve such a task. Fergusson was the only Scots poet of his century to be able to look
contemporary civilization in the eye. He knew where he stood and what
he wanted to do. But he founded no school. The future lay with Burns
and the rustic tradition.

VII

BURNS AND THE BURNS TRADITION

ROBERT DEWAR

I

WHEN Burns [1] wrote his autobiographical letter to Dr. John Moore [2] in the latter half of 1787, he was making a last desperate attempt to convince Moore that his reiterated advice to the poet to leave the vernacular and seek a wider audience for his talents by writing in English was quite impracticable. He had been disappointed and puzzled by receiving similar advice from the Edinburgh literati, and had hinted his doubts to other correspondents besides Moore: but Moore had repeated the advice—unlike the others. Burns promises Moore an 'honest narrative' therefore, though he fears it may get him laughed at; for an 'honest narrative' must show him, like Solomon—whose character ('excepting the trifling affair of Wisdom') he sometimes fancied that his resembled—as one who had 'turned [his] eyes to behold Madness and Folly', and 'too frequently shaken hands with their intoxicating friendship'. The main theme of this famous letter is, therefore, what it had meant for Burns—man and poet—to be 'born a very poor man's son' and destined to a youth which he describes bluntly as 'the chearless gloom of a hermit with the unceasing moil of a galley-slave'.

It is usual to cite this letter rather for its allusions to the books Burns read as a boy and in his early youth: but these passages are only incidental; while they suggest that he took advantage of every opportunity to come by book-learning, they suggest also that his opportunities were not so many, but he could have wished them more. Burns is not parading his book-learning; he is half-apologizing for the comparative slightness of it. Such books as he does mention are not cited by their titles, but casually, as recollection of their substance held them in his memory: even his *vade mecum*, which he obviously considered worthy of special mention, is set down simply as 'a select Collection of English songs', so that scholars are still uncertain exactly which collection [3] is referred to. The real point of interest in Burns's special mention of this work is not any title it may have had (though it would be good to know that) but in the use he tells us that he made of it.

> The Collection of Songs was my vade mecum. I pored over them, driving my cart or walking to labor, song by song, verse by verse; carefully noting the true tender or sublime from affectation and fustian. I am convinced I owe much to this for my critic-craft such as it is.

185

There speaks the man who instinctively referred all he read to life itself, as the foundation and source of all experience. 'Noting the true tender or sublime from affectation and fustian'—it is the sort of remark one would expect from a man whose chief concern in this 'narrative' was clearly to convince Moore that the poet in him owed more to his contact with his fellows than to any learning that came his way by means of books.

For the hardships of Burns's growing years were made tolerable for him, and failed to break his spirit then, not by balancing opportunities for reflection and learned leisure with books and the thoughts of great men but by a streak in his character—'a social disposition', he names it to Moore, 'like our catechism definition of Infinitude . . . "without bounds or limits" '. This 'disposition' may have brought him acquainted, as a boy, with other boys of better fortune and social standing in Ayr, and so given him (among other things) a start with French: but, as he got into his teens and had to do a man's work on his father's farm (first at Mount Oliphant and later—nearer Tarbolton than Ayr—at Lochlea), it had more and more to seek satisfaction in the company of his 'Compeers, the humble Inmates of the farm-house and cottage'.

This limitation of his field for the observation and study of human nature lasted almost to the days of his fame and recognition in Edinburgh: on 15 February 1787 he had written Dr. Moore—'Not many months ago I knew no other employment than following the plough, nor could boast anything higher than a distant acquaintance with a country clergyman' [4]. But it did not hamper Burns as it might another man. Indeed, without it he might not have inherited so completely the tradition of Scottish vernacular poetry, which his genius was to glorify and distinguish. Already, in his 'fifteenth Autumn', what his absorption in this workaday world might do for him had been shown. In that autumn, the girl who was his partner in the harvest-field inspired the first verses he ever wrote—a song to the tune of her favourite reel. The girl 'sung sweetly'; and among her songs was one

> said to be composed by a small country laird's son, on one of his father's maids, with whom he was in love; and I saw no reason why I might not rhyme as well as he, for excepting smearing sheep and casting peats, his father living in the moors, he had no more Scholarcraft than I had.

The remark may serve to remind us that, in this apparently narrow social world of Burns, there were not only such laird's sons but men of humbler station (like David Sillar [5] and John Lapraik [6], for example) who could turn a Scottish verse on occasion. Ever since Allan Ramsay's revival of the vernacular that almost died as a literary medium at the Scottish Reformation, such poets had existed here and there throughout Scotland. They seldom collected their writings for publication: at most individual pieces would get into broadsheet or chapbook form or into the miscellanies that appeared from time to time. Quite often their poems—dating from the years before Burns's example encouraged such men to seek 'guid black prent'—survive (if at all) anonymously; like those others (often only a generation or two older) which Burns himself picked up in his wanderings, to lament that their authors' names were 'buried 'mongst the wreck of things which were'. The occupations, manners, customs, lads and lasses, then, of Burns's restricted humble world were stuff of poetry to others there as well as to him: there was precedent and example for giving way to the urge he felt to give that poetry expression. In this world, indeed, far more than in more consciously literate circles—far more, certainly, than in the Scottish capital—interest in the vernacular had survived, even though John Knox and his English Bible had compelled most Scots to do their serious thinking in an alien idiom. It may have been used to express, as well as other things, sculduddery and the coarser side of peasant life. Burns knew that as well as any man; he collected specimens, and could coin them himself for a change: but a principal effect of his own work on Scottish song was to be the smothering of such verse out of existence. It was therefore fortunate, perhaps, that Burns was fated to enter this particular school of life at an early age. For the unbounded 'social disposition' which took him there, when seeking refreshment after labour, was no more to begin with than a passionate love of company for company's sake: Burns had to visit Irvine and meet Richard Brown, before it could do him a 'mischief' and set him on the 'regardless' courses of Rab Mossgiel. He had this primal innocence of his bent in mind, doubtless, when penning 'The Vision'; for it underlies and explains the bold claim of Coila's closing words in the stanza

> I saw thy pulse's maddening play
> Wild-send thee Pleasure's devious way,
> Misled by Fancy's meteor-ray,
>   By Passion driven;
> But yet the *light* that led astray
>   Was *light* from Heaven.

Be that as it may, however, once entered there, Burns found himself (with his native gift for the ring of words) at the very heart of that life which had given a distinctive character down the ages to Scottish vernacular poetry. He was himself a full member of the world he was to work upon and portray with the directness and objectivity that only passionate speech, born of passionate attachment, can achieve. He was to grow with his subject as (so to speak) his reflection or other self. Small wonder that, when (trained and in full fettle) he felt sure at last of his poetical abilities, no other world could make pictures in his mind— not even the world of Pope and Gray and Shenstone—like this one of his workaday Scottish compeers: that not only the style and idiom of the national tradition in song and manners-painting strains, but the very moods and stuff or subject-matter informing these, so possessed him that the answer to any further demands upon his talents had to be —I can no other.

In the interval, till he was surer of himself as a poet, it might mean running counter in conduct to home expectations of him; as when his fondness for the folk-music of his country and a wish 'to give [his] manners a brush' sent him 'in [his] seventeenth year' and 'in absolute defiance of his [father's] commands' to a country dancing school—to the permanent damage of his father's regard for him; or as when, in the summer of this same year, while studying surveying at a school in Kirkoswald, he 'learned to look unconcernedly on a large tavern-bill, and mix without fear in a drunken squabble', through associating in 'scenes of swaggering riot and roaring dissipation' with the local smuggling fraternity. These two incidents, in the 'honest narrative' to Moore, precede and follow respectively Burns's frank confession: 'The great misfortune of my life was, never to have AN AIM', and the other significant admission:

> But far beyond all other impulses of my heart was, un penchant à l'adorable moitiée du genre humain,—My heart was compleat tinder, and was eternally lighted up by some Goddess or other. . . . A country lad rarely carries on an amour without an assisting confident.—I possessed a curiosity, zeal and intrepid dexterity in these matters which recommended me a proper Second in duels of that kind; and I dare say, I felt as much pleasure at being in the secret of half the amours in the parish, as ever did Premier at knowing the intrigues of half the courts of Europe.

Such in the main was the tenor of his life, Burns tells us, till his twenty-third year. 'Vive l'amour et vive la bagatelle, were my sole principles of action.' Then it seemed, for the moment at least, as if the aimlessness was to be checked—but apparently at the cost of his abandoning poetry. In his twenty-third year, Burns, wishing 'to set about doing something in life' (his brother Gilbert says that he wished to get married), went to Irvine to learn flax-dressing as a means of livelihood: and so anxious was he to turn successful man of affairs, that 'rhyme was given up' during this period (except for 'some religious pieces' of a melancholy cast). From sheer bad luck, however, and through no fault of his, the venture soon failed; and Burns had to return to Lochlea and the plough, to the poverty and hardship of the home where his father was now obviously dying. Irvine had shown him 'something of a town life', and brought him a new friend in Richard Brown, the seaman who by speaking of 'a certain fashionable failing with levity, which hitherto [Burns] had regarded with horror' was to smutch any innocence of mind Burns still possessed, but who also—on hearing

Burns recite some of his verses in the Eglinton woods—left no doubt of his opinion that they were verses worth printing. Not much to compensate him for the misery and bitterness of that home-coming. But soon after, by good luck, he met with Fergusson's *Poems*; and the memory of his speech with Richard Brown in the Eglinton woods may perhaps have helped to kindle the enthusiasm of emulation of Fergusson which resulted. Richard Brown, with his 'levity', may be partly to blame for the birth, on 22 May 1785, of Burns's 'Betty': a little credit, perhaps (beside the so much more that is due to Fergusson's book), may be allowed him for the fact that 1785 was also Burns's *annus mirabilis* as a poet.

For Richard Brown's hint perhaps, but most of all Fergusson's *Poems*, roused the poet in Burns as nothing else could in those cruel days after the Irvine failure. Here was a man (dead at an age much about Burns's own when he read him) but known and famous by his pen. Why should Burns not do for the Kyle about him what Fergusson had done for his Edinburgh? In 1783 we get the first clear sign that Burns was getting to realize his powers and to believe that, for him, poetry rather than business and affairs was the field in which to find (if not success) at least happiness and fulfilment: he began his First Commonplace-Book. Then, after his father's death in the spring of 1784, and after the family had established themselves in a new home at Mossgiel— while quietly busy matching and surpassing Fergusson themes—Burns began to be known in the neighbourhood for his more topical rhymes —for pieces like 'The Twa Herds', which he showed to a friend, saying that he 'could not guess who was the Author of it, but that [he] thought it pretty clever', and 'Holy Willie's Prayer', which set the Kirk-Session inquiring whether there was anything they could do against 'profane Rhymers'. He began to be known also, before very much longer, for his 'regardless' behaviour. For while by the close of 1785 Burns had collected quite a parcel of poems born of the new inspiration and mood, he had also (by then) gathered friends in and around Mauchline, with whom he led a more sploring life than ever before—casually poetizing scenes from it, on occasion, like 'The Court of Equity' and 'The Jolly Beggars': the 'levity' also of Richard Brown had told at last.

One thing was still wanting, however, to complete Burns as the national poet of Scotland—publication of the work accumulating in his desk: and, oddly enough, the incentive to this came, not from the quietly growing skill and confidence of the poet, but from the sadly declining reputation of the man, the immediate consequence of his new 'regardless' ongoings. The affair with Jean Armour not only brought him 'point-blank within the reach' of the Kirk-Session's heaviest artillery; more to the purpose, his pride and self-consequence were stung by it almost to madness—for he was to learn that James

Armour would have no such scape-grace for a son-in-law, and that even Jean listened to her father and agreed to the mutilation of his 'paper'. Sore and angry, he seems to have turned to his Highland Mary and planned to marry her instead of his faithless Jean: he certainly gave up his share in Mossgiel and began making such preparation as he could to emigrate to Jamaica—a project that would need money not easy to find on his allowance of £7 a year from the farm. So it chanced that Burns's personal errors and misfortunes as a man pushed him into assuming publicly the character of a poet.

> Before leaving my native country for ever, I resolved to publish my Poems.—I weighed my productions as impartially as in my power; I thought they had merit; and 'twas a delicious idea that I would be called a clever fellow, even though it should never reach my ears. . . . I can truly say that pauvre Inconnu as I then was, I had pretty near as high an idea of myself and my works as I have at this moment. . . . To know myself had been all along my constant study.—I weighed myself alone; I balanced myself with others; I watched every means of information how much ground I occupied both as a Man and as a Poet.—. . . I was pretty sure my Poems would meet with some applause; but at the worst, the roar of the Atlantic would deafen the voice of Censure, and the novelty of West-Indian scenes make me forget Neglect.

How the 1786 (Kilmarnock) edition of Burns's *Poems* proved a success, and how (through a letter of Dr. Blacklock to a friend of the poet) it led on to his visit to Edinburgh, to his season of fame and recognition there, and to the 1787 (Edinburgh) edition—all this is common knowledge. The dramatic suddenness of the change of fortune for this 'pauvre Inconnu' of a year or so back so takes the attention as one reads the story that few stop to read the pen-portrait of the hero of it all, carefully and honestly supplied for us in the Preface to the precious Kilmarnock volume. There Burns wrote:

> The following trifles are not the production of the Poet, who, with all the advantages of learned art, and perhaps amid the elegancies and idlenesses of upper life, looks down for a rural theme, with an eye to Theocrites or Virgil. To the Author of this, these and other celebrated names their countrymen are, in their original languages, 'A fountain shut up, and a book sealed'. Unacquainted with the necessary requisites for commencing Poet by rule, he sings the sentiments and manners he felt and saw in himself and his rustic compeers around him, in his and their native language. Though a Rhymer from his earliest years, at least from the earliest impulses of the softer passions, it was not till very lately, that the applause, perhaps the partiality, of Friendship wakened his vanity so far as to make him think any thing of his was worth showing; and none of the following works were ever composed with a view to the press.

To amuse himself with the little creations of his own fancy, amid the toil and fatigues of a laborious life; to transcribe the various feelings, the loves, the griefs, the hopes, the fears in his own breast; to find some kind of counterpoise to the struggles of a world, always an alien scene, a task uncouth to the poetical mind; these were his motives for courting the Muses, and in these he found Poetry to be its own reward.

. . . . .

It is an observation of that celebrated Poet [Shenstone], whose divine Elegies do honor to our language, our nation, and our species, that 'Humility has depressed many a genius to a hermit, but never raised one to fame'. If any Critic catches at the word *genius*, the Author tells him, once for all, that he certainly looks upon himself as possesst of some poetic abilities, otherwise his publishing in the manner he has done, would be a manœuvre below the worst character, which he hopes, his worst enemy will ever give him: but to the genius of a Ramsay, or the glorious dawnings of the poor, unfortunate Fergusson, he, with equal unaffected sincerity, declares, that even in his highest pulse of vanity, he has not the most distant pretensions. These two justly admired Scotch Poets he has often had in his eye in the following pieces; but rather with a view to kindle at their flame, than for servile imitation.

One of the best pieces of prose Burns ever wrote, the Preface is quieter perhaps than his normal best in this medium. But the venture it announced was so novel (and indeed beyond their wildest dreams) for poets of Burns's breed and education, that it must have muted the strings for any such initiate—even for a Burns. For his position was singular, if not unique. His works (like those of his less gifted associates) had, none of them, been 'composed with a view to the press'; yet (unlike his associates) he proposed to collect and publish them, not to leave them to be picked over haphazard by the miscellanists and broadsheet-mongers. Hence the elaborate self-examination—balancing himself with others (i.e. others from his own school of the Scottish national tradition), weighing himself alone, using every means of information to be sure of the measure of his poetical abilities, which he reported to Moore as preceding his resolution: hence also, the resolution taken, the obvious care he bestowed in revising and preparing his works for the press, that he might justify his action in other men's eyes as well as his own. And hence the undertone of apology in the Preface itself, the quiet hints that his experience perhaps brought something new for readers of poetry in his time. He might be 'unacquainted with the necessary requisites for commencing Poet by rule'; but (in the phrase he used of his Kirkoswald experience) he 'had seen mankind in a new phasis', had lived all his days the humble life he portrayed and sang, had no need, therefore, to 'look down' for his chosen rural theme. His talent might not bear comparison with the genius of a Ramsay or a

Fergusson; but, though in his poems he had often had these two poets in his eye, he had felt no call to be their servile imitator. However quietly put forward, these claims are just. To appreciate how just—and how exactly, in consequence, Burns has defined his specific poetic character and quality in the Preface—is essential if we are to approach his work, so as to come by his secret and to know the place he occupies in the story of Scottish poetry. His genius was greater than he himself may have suspected at this date: the important point is the insistence, throughout the Preface, upon the field in which he had consistently exercised and trained that genius. Unlike Ramsay (who must have lived in a world similar to Burns's to begin with), Burns had not moved to Edinburgh and alien scenes before he got known or formed his style: willy-nilly, he awaited fame in the world where Love and Poesy first came to him hand in hand, and so matured his powers nearest of anyone with poetic leanings, in those latter days of the tradition, to the world and circumstances which had created and sustained that tradition down the years. Preferring in his heart the title of Bard to that of Poet, he is more directly and entirely of Scottish poetic extraction even than the ablest revivalists of the vernacular, who are commonly accounted his forerunners and begetters. That is why one feels a difference in reading him alongside other Scottish poets of the revival. He seems apart (almost alone), as well as greater, not merely because of his greater genius, but because that genius drew its nourishment from a purer fount. And that is what his Preface of 1786 whispers to us, and what he was trying to explain to Dr. Moore in his 'honest narrative' of a year later.

2

But why all this labour of explanation at the height of his fame? Because the book Burns made to announce himself to the world was not fully representative of his gifts and powers. The decision to publish seems to have been taken only when his experiments in emulation of Fergusson made him sure of himself at last; and, in the enthusiasm of the discovery, Burns seems to have forgotten his first approaches to his Muse. In the 1786 (Kilmarnock) edition, the religious satirist known to quite a few in Ayrshire is not altogether absent; but we do not get his 'Twa Herds' or 'Holy Willie's Prayer'. Nor is 'The Poet's Welcome to his Love-begotten Daughter' included. But these were records, however good in quality, of his sploring existence; they may have been deliberately omitted. It must have been preoccupation with Fergusson, however, that limited the songs in this edition to three only. Even if this side of his work showed the prentice hand, there was enough in his desk to ensure a less disproportionate display of what (after all) was his basic character as a poet. For the 1787 (Edinburgh) and later editions, he did remember 'John Barleycorn', 'My Nanie, O', and

'Green grow the Rashes O', from the days preceding Fergusson's ascendancy; what was wrong with 'Mary Morison', and 'Montgomerie's Peggy', and 'Tibbie I hae seen the Day'—none of which graced any of his official issues of his works! There was some excuse for readers, unacquainted with the Kyle setting and origins of this poet, who might mistake him for another Fergusson—the model whose 'Plainstanes and Causey', 'Leith Races', and 'Farmer's Ingle' are recalled once and again in Burns's book.

The earnestness with which Burns strove to overgo Fergusson or any other model, now that he was fully conscious of his gift, carried him at times into moods and attitudes not always within his nature to sustain. Even a native Scottish theme and mood will turn him solemn and purposeful (like a Burns with his 'Sunday's sark' on, rather than the Burns we know best); and the English, which was his usual medium in his prose letters, intrudes in poems that are Scottish in their staves and in everything else—save at the point of this sudden solemnity. It happens in the second stanza of 'To a Mouse', for example, and even (strangest of all, where he warms to his love for his Jean) in so Scots a poem as his 'Epistle to Davie'. In 'The Lament', too, English has a very big say; but that may come of his attempt to pass the poem off as referring to 'a friend's amour', not as a record of his own misfortune in love, which it was. Since the days of the Reformation, Scotsmen had been liable to this danger of going English when in very serious mood. But when Burns does so, it does not always sound quite right or natural. His thorough mastery of Scots perhaps leads one to expect similar mastery in English, only to be somewhat disappointed. One of the most important pieces he made for this book, 'The Cotter's Saturday Night', is less than it might have been for this English overlay affects a good half of quite a long poem. One can perhaps excuse the dedicatory opening stanza; but in stanzas 9 and 10, English brings up a note almost of falsity; and from stanza 13 onwards, however much mention of Scottish Psalm tunes and Bible allusions may serve to conceal the change in key, one seems to be in another world from that of the earlier stanzas, from the Scottish world of 'Jenny' and the 'neebor lad' who 'convoy[ed] her hame'. It was no help to Burns either that the stanza he adopted for this special exertion of his genius was quite outside the Scottish tradition he knew best—the Spenserian stanza, a stanza at no time perhaps suited to his forthright temperament as a writer, and one which he knew at this time only in eighteenth-century imitators of Spenser. Without 'Holy Willie's Prayers' and 'Poet's Welcomes' and the like, with so few (and, even so, not the best) of the songs he had already made to the popular dance-tunes of his time, and with these Englishry grafts on his Scottish stem, it was easy to miss the real character of the poet who had come forward from 'his shades' (as he so often liked to describe his early surroundings in later life), and whose liveliest interest was in the experience and poetry of his 'compeers' of the Ayrshire countryside.

The real Burns was there all the same, and there, on occasion, in force enough to prove that something bigger than and independent of the Fergussons and other poets of the revival had arrived to complete their work. Take, for example, one of his many references to animals— part of the Auld Farmer's New-Year greetings to his Auld Mare, Maggie:

> Thou was a noble Fittie-lan',   [*the near horse of the hindmost pair*
> As e'er in tug or tow was drawn!   [*raw hide, rope*
> Aft thee an' I, in aught hours gaun,   [*eight hours' going*
>   On guid March-weather,
> Hae turn'd sax rood beside our han',
>   For days thegither.

> Thou never braindg't, an' fetch't, an' fliskit,   [*plunged forward, stopped*
> But thy auld tail thou wad hae whiskit,   *suddenly, capered*
> An' spread abreed thy weel-fill'd brisket,   [*abroad, breast*
>   Wi' pith an' pow'r,
> Till spritty knowes wad rair't an' riskit,   [*rush-rooted hillocks, roared,*
>   An' slypet owre.   [*slipped*   *cracked*

These are the words of one whose passionate gaze pierced so deep, it could make poetry by the mere naming of common acts and things. How immediately, also, Burns shoots beyond the Fergusson of 'Leith Races' in the opening that poem suggested for him in his 'Holy Fair':

> Upon a simmer Sunday morn,
>   When Nature's face is fair,
> I walked forth to view the corn,
>   An' snuff the caller air.   [*fresh*
> The rising sun, owre *Galston* muirs,
>   Wi' glorious light was glintin;
> The hares were hirplin down the furs,   [*leaping, furrows*
>   The lav'rocks they were chantin   [*larks*
>   Fu' sweet that day.

Then the picture of the 'three Hizzies [wenches]' who 'cam skelpin [hastening] up the way', the third of whom surprised him by curtseying to him:

> Wi' bonnet aff, quoth I "Sweet lass,
>   I think ye seem to ken me;
> I'm sure I've seen that bonie face,
>   But yet I canna name ye."

Quo' she, an' laughin as she spak,
    An' taks me by the hauns,   [*hands*
"Ye, for my sake, hae gi'en the feck [*given the most part*
    Of a' the ten commauns   [*Commandments*
        A screed some day.   [*rip*

My name is *Fun*—your cronie dear,
    The nearest friend ye hae."

How much clearer the daybreak atmosphere in Burns than in
Fergusson; even the name Fun for his 'nearest friend' betters Fergusson's Mirth. Still more is the individual greatness and excellence of
Burns revealed when he chooses to forget models and speaks directly
of himself or to his intimates. There is the sketch of himself in the
opening stanzas of 'The Vision', tired at the end of a day's toil at the
flail, sitting in the smoky 'spence', and none too pleased with his lot:

All in this mottie, misty clime,   [*hazy (with dust motes)*
I backward mus'd on wasted time,
How I had spent my youthfu' prime,
    An' done nae-thing,
But stringin blethers up in rhyme   [*nonsense*
    For fools to sing.

Had I to guid advice but harkit,
I might, by this, hae led a market,
Or strutted in a Bank and clarkit
    My cash-account:
While here, half-mad, half-fed, half-sarkit,   [*half-clothed*
    Is a' th' amount.   (*with half a shirt*)

Or again, another picture of the tired labourer, saved this time from
regrets by a job of work for his pen that must not be shirked—in his
second 'Epistle to J. Lapraik':

Forjesket sair, with weary legs,   [*jaded with fatigue*
Rattlin the corn out-owre the rigs,   [*ridges*
Or dealing thro' amang the naigs   [*distributing*
    Their ten-hours bite,
My awkart Muse sair pleads and begs
    I would na write.

The tapetless, ramfeezl'd hizzie,   [*feckless, tired-out wench*
She's saft at best an' something lazy,
Quo' she, "Ye ken we've been sae busy
    This month an' mair,
That trouth, my head is grown right dizzie,
    An' something sair."

Her dowff excuses pat me mad;   [*dull*
"Conscience," says I, "ye thowless jad!   [*lazy*
I'll write, an' that a hearty blaud,   [*screed*
　　This vera night;
So dinna ye affront your trade,
　　But rhyme it right."

．　　．　　．　　．　　．

Sae I gat paper in a blink,   [*twinkling*
An' down gaed *stumpie* in the ink:
Quoth I, "Before I sleep a wink,
　　I vow I'll close it;
An' if you winna mak it clink,   [*rhyme*
By Jove I'll prose it!"

To many readers that may well seem too colloquial, too near to the
everyday speech of men, to be called poetry. But for those who have
never known much leisure—and Burns was such a person—poetry has
no birthplace but in the everyday; and, if it comes at all, it has to come
in the Burns idiom of everyday. The pulse of Burns's verses, the race
and ringing precision of his words (everyday or not) tell of a passion
for life, at least akin to that we recognize in all poets; it is only in his
way and manner of communicating that passion that he stands apart.
And his way and manner were prescribed for him by the somewhat
restricted world he knew (but knew so intimately and with such
complete satisfaction to himself): it is the way and manner of an everyman poet, who has no time for 'looking down' for his theme, for
condescending upon his subject, whose word must render the thing
itself, directly and in its own proper right, or fail in communication—
the way and manner of the sort of poet described for us in Burns's
'Epistle to James Smith':

Some rhyme a neebor's name to lash;
Some rhyme (vain thought!) for needfu' cash;
Some rhyme to court the countra clash,   [*talk*
　　An' raise a din;
For me, an *aim* I never fash;   [*trouble about*
　　I rhyme for fun.

．　　．　　．　　．　　．

An anxious e'e I never throws
Behint my lug, or by my nose;
I jouk beneath Misfortune's blows   [*ear*
　　As weel's I may;   [*duck*
Sworn foe to Sorrow, Care, and Prose,
　　I rhyme away.

—a description corroborated in his first 'Epistle to J. Lapraik':

But, first an' foremost, I should tell,
Amaist as soon as I could spell,
I to the *crambo-jingle* fell,   [*rhyming*
    Tho rude an' rough,
Yet crooning to a body's sel,   [*humming*
    Does weel eneugh.

It is the way and manner exhibited also in the songs Burns was so chary
of including in his book, the songs inspired by the love-affairs and
popular dance-tunes of the world he shared with the 'compeers' of his
youth—shared, and accepted gladly. For, where most convincing and
successful, these 'manners-painting' and kindred poems are song-stuff
in essence. In them we listen to the same voice as made, for example,
this stanza (which Burns regarded as one of his best pieces for sentiment
and expression) from 'Rigs o' Barley':

I hae been blythe wi' comrades dear;
    I hae been merry drinking;
I hae been joyfu' gath'rin gear;   [*money-making*
    I hae been happy thinking:
But a' the pleasures e'er I saw,
    Tho' three times doubled fairly,
That happy night was worth them a',
    Amang the rigs o' barley.   [*ridges*

or this, from 'Green grow the Rashes':

But gie me a cannie hour at e'en,   [*quiet*
    My arms about my Dearie, O;
An' war'ly cares, an' war'ly men,   [*worldly*
    May a' gae tapsalterrie, O!   [*topsy-turvy*

or similar lines from 'My Nanie, O':

A country lad is my degree,
    An' few there be that ken me, O;
But what care I how few they be,
    I'm welcome ay to Nanie, O.

My riches a's my penny-fee,   [*wages (not a large sum)*
    An' I maun guide it cannie, O;   [*manage it carefully*
But warl's gear ne'er troubles me,
    My thoughts are a', my Nanie, O.

or 'The Rantin Dog, the Daddie O't', which, though only a vamp,
was possibly autobiographical in its application, and denotes full-
blooded and unquestioning acceptance of Burns's world, if anything.
    Even when in the poems (as distinct from the songs) a note of

criticism and even of satire (rather than full-blooded acceptance) of his
world is occasionally suggested, the satire or criticism is altogether
without venom and never reformative in aim. The Factor in 'The
Twa Dogs' was drawn, Burns told Dr. Moore, from the one who made
his Mount Oliphant home so miserable from time to time. But is the
picture darker than the form of the poem—a dialogue between a rich
man's dog and a poor man's—strictly requires? Says Ceasar:

> I've notic'd on our Laird's court-day,
> An' mony a time my heart's been wae,   [sad
> Poor tenant-bodies, scant o' cash,
> How they maun thole a factor's snash;   [suffer, abuse
> He'll stamp an' threaten, curse an' swear,
> He'll apprehend them, poind their gear;   [distrain
> While they maun stan', in aspect humble,
> An' hear it a', an' fear an' tremble!
>
> I see how folk live that hae riches;
> But surely poor folk maun be wretches!

Luath's reply, in perfect keeping, is to list at length his reasons why
poor folk are 'no sae wretched's ane wad think', and then quietly regret
the shade of truth in Caesar's charge:

> There's monie a creditable stock
> O' decent, honest, fawsont folk,   [well-doing
> Are riven out baith root an' branch,
> Some rascal's pridefu' greed to quench,
> Wha thinks to knit himsel the faster
> In favor wi' some gentle Master.

Poetry is not sacrificed even here, where there was motive enough, to
the propaganda of the reformer. Nor, in the lines immediately following, does Caesar correct Luath's optimistic estimate of politicians and
their purposes in any venomous mood; ridicule and laughter are his
weapons, and he even runs into a coarseness at last that had to be
softened down for the 1787 (Edinburgh) edition of the *Poems*. In his
'Earnest Cry and Prayer' addressed to the Scotch Representatives in
the Commons, politicians again are handled in no over-ruling spirit of
serious reproof:

> Does ony great man glunch an' gloom?   [growl
> Speak out an' never fash your thumb!   [care a rap
> Let posts an' pensions sink or soom   [swim
>   Wi' them wha grant 'em;
> If honestly they canna come,
>   Far better want 'em.

In gath'rin votes you were na slack;
Now stand as tightly by your tack: [*lease*
Ne'er claw your lug, an' fidge your back,   [*scratch, wriggle*
    An' hum an' haw,
But raise your arm, an' tell your crack
    Before them a'.

And later, even in reference to Pitt, the Prime Minister, the same easy
bantering tone is made to serve:

Tell yon guid bluid o' auld *Boconnock*'s,   [*Pitt*
I'll be his debt twa mashlum bonnocks,   [*coarse-meal, bannocks*
An' drink his health in auld *Nanse Tinnock*'s,   [*hostess of an inn*
    Nine times a week,   *in Mauchline*
If he some scheme, like tea an' winnocks,   [*windows*
    Wad kindly seek.

Could he some *commutation* broach,
I'll pledge my aith in gude braid Scotch,
He need na fear their foul reproach
    Nor erudition,
Yon mixtie-maxtie, queer hotch-potch,
    The *Coalition*.

In 'A Dream' also—a poem that his Edinburgh counsellors wished
Burns to drop from his new edition—the allusions to not only politicians but princes are free and easy almost to irresponsibility. In 'The
Holy Fair', which has Church and Religion for its theme, once past
'Black Bonnet' and the 'plate . . . weel heaped up wi' ha'pence', and so
fairly on the scene, almost every stanza is a poising of saint and sinner
in the spirit of his 'cronie', Fun, who had enticed him there that day,
till the end of it all is given as follows:

Now *Clinkumbell*, wi' rattlin tow,   [*the bell-ringer, rope*
    Begins to jow an' croon;   [*swing, toll*
Some swagger hame, the best they dow   [*are able*
    Some wait the afternoon.
At slaps the billies halt a blink,   [*openings in a fence*
    Till lassies strip their shoon: [*take off, shoes*
Wi' faith an' hope, an' love an' drink,
    They're a' in famous tune
        For crack that day.   [*talk*

How monie hearts this day converts
    O' Sinners and o' Lasses!
Their hearts o' stane gin night are gane,   [*by nightfall*
    As saft as ony flesh is.

There's some are fou o' love divine;
There's some are fou o' brandy;
An' monie jobs that day begin,
May end in Houghmagandie   [*fornication*
Some ither day.

And in the 'Address to the Deil', in which Burns had a theme prescribed
in all its notes for him by ancient Scottish poetic tradition, he obviously
set himself to play the music better than the best, abbreviating *Paradise
Lost* to the stanza—

Then you, ye auld, snick-drawing dog!
Ye cam to Paradise incog.
An' play'd on man a cursed brogue,   [*trick*
(Black be your fa'!)   [*lot*
An' gied the infant warld a shog,   [*shake*
Maist ruin'd a';

and ending—not so much, as Carlyle supposed, out of kindly sympathy for Satan, as (more probably) from a wish to trail his coat at the
Daddy Aulds of the Kirk of his day—

An' now, auld *Cloots*, I ken ye're thinkin,   [*Hoofs*
A certain Bardie's rantin, drinkin,   [*roistering*
Some luckless hour will send him linkin,   [*hurrying*
To your black pit;
But, faith! he'll turn a corner jinkin,   [*dodging*
An' cheat you yet.

But, fare you weel, auld *Nickie-ben*!
O wad ye tak a thought an' men'!
Ye aiblins might—I dinna ken—   [*perhaps*
Still hae a *stake*—
I'm wae to think upo' yon den,
Ev'n for your sake!

The poet of these characteristic extracts was no true satirist, or one who
could lay aside his natural singing-robes for long. He is the poet who
wrote in his First Commonplace-Book, in March 1784:

I have often coveted the acquaintance of that part of mankind commonly
known by the ordinary phrase of Blackguards, sometimes farther than
was consistent with the safety of my character; those who by thoughtless
Prodigality, or headstrong Passions have been driven to ruin:—though
disgraced by follies, nay sometimes 'Stain'd with guilt, and crimson'd
o'er with crimes'; I have yet found among them, in not a few instances,
some of the noblest Virtues, Magnanimity, Generosity, disinterested
friendship and even modesty, in the highest perfection.

The governing note of hearty enjoyment of life, even in the satiric and critical asides of the poems, links these plainly with the songs of Burns; so that they too (like the songs) proclaim an acceptance of life entire— the good and the less good alike—rather than any wish to improve or 'remould it nearer to the Heart's Desire'. Spite of all Fergusson or any other new model could do in 1785-6 to lure Burns aside, the lad of 1773 (who knew life as 'chearless gloom' and 'unceasing moil', yet had 'a heart abune it a' ', and found it good enough on the whole to com- mence poet with a tune-born love-song) though forbidden to preside over it, thrust himself unbeknownst into the 1786 volume. To that lad and his hard lot, Burns owed too much of his fundamental schooling as a poet for it to be otherwise. Trained—and very largely self-trained —in an old-fashioned world of dying habits and customs (or at least of habits and customs no longer commanding the serious attention and respect of polite society in his day)—so trained, even more than in the authors and books favoured by that society, Burns reported life direct from the touch of experience, without stopping to analyse or philo- sophize about it first. He may lack 'high seriousness' (as Arnold said of him) in consequence; certainly it shows in his writing, if at all, only as by chance. And the example Arnold cites of it from 'Ae fond Kiss'—

> Had we never lov'd sae kindly,
> Had we never lov'd sae blindly,
> Never met—or never parted—
> We had ne'er been broken-hearted

—belongs, perhaps significantly, to the Sylvander-Clarinda love- episode with Mrs. M'Lehose in Edinburgh. But even Arnold has to admit that in poems like 'Tam o' Shanter' and 'The Jolly Beggars'— poems based in the world that was Burns's before he met his Clarinda and her likes—'his world may be what it will, his poetic genius triumphs over it', while in the latter poem he paints a scene that for 'breadth, truth, and power' makes Goethe 'seem artificial and tame', and is 'only matched by Shakespeare and Aristophanes'. It may be after all that there are other routes to the attainment of the classic in poetry than by imparting 'high seriousness' to one's lines. Life may have a meaning deeper, more elemental than philosophers and other commentators upon it have divined, or at least have contrived to express in their 'high-serious' treatises and creeds. The direct, un- calculating, almost child-like response to life of a Burns, his passionate acceptance of the world available to him, may impart an equivalent value, an equally ennobling quality.

3

Never again, however, after Edinburgh, was Burns's acceptance of that world to be quite so whole-hearted and unquestioning. He was too set, no doubt by the Edinburgh days, to change right away from the themes that hitherto had called forth the poet in him. Not only did he resist the Edinburgh advice to drop the vernacular altogether: he was probably not sorry (in an early letter of Dr. Moore's) to be notified, too late for their removal, of certain 'peccant' passages in his poems [7]; and he was not at all eager to amend the 'exceptionable parts' which *The Lounger* review of the 1786 edition referred to. But on April 9 1787—sure sign of mental growing-pains in Burns—he began his Second Commonplace-Book with the words: 'As I have seen a good deal of human life in Edin^r, a great many characters which are new to one bred up in the shades of life as I have been, I am determined to take down my remarks on the spot.' The new society and world in which he found himself in the capital had aroused his curiosity—as one might expect with Burns, for already (on the eve of Edinburgh) a somewhat similar chance of enlightenment had left its mark on his work (witness his reference to 'gentry's life' in 'The Twa Dogs' and the later account of his first meeting with a lord in the 'Lines to Lord Daer'). Burns knew henceforth that there was another way of life that had its charms and attractions: the old single-minded worship of his Kyle experience and acquaintance could hardly survive for him quite as before. In its layout, if not otherwise, the 1787 (Edinburgh) edition of his *Poems* exhibits the beginnings of a drift away from the Scotchness of the 1786 (Kilmarnock) one. There is no introductory note here to the glossary, on -*an* and -*in* in Scots for the -*ing* ending of the present participle; if such endings survive in the new text, it is by inadvertence; *and* also displaces *an*, and *o'er owre*, more often than not. Read by one not born to the Scots tongue, the general effect is nearer to translated, than to the actual language one associates with Burns and his like. And by 1793 and the last editions Burns authorized, the Scotchness has evaporated still further—as if he were quite indifferent now to the feelings and aims that prompted the care for such things, patent in 1786—as if he were losing heart about the poems that had made him known and brought him his Edinburgh season of worship. Even his early preference for 'Bard' is given up, and 'Poet' usually replaces the word by 1793-4. The tastes and fashions of another society were creeping in and having their effect. For, whatever Burns had gained by Edinburgh, it had proved too big for him (with his stubborn independence of mind and attitude) to make it his servant and benefactor in practical, as distinct from cultural, ways.

How Burns might have developed had the Edinburgh venture provided him with a practical means of livelihood, permitting more leisure than the farming he had hitherto pursued, we shall never know. Adam Smith is said to have suggested a post as a Salt Tax Officer towards ensuring him some freedom for the cultivation of his poetical gifts. Rumour also says that some planned to procure him the Chair of Agriculture in the University of Edinburgh. He himself, apparently —if he could have afforded to purchase a commission—would willingly have adopted the Army as a career. But, after a longer stay in Edinburgh than he had originally thought necessary (varied with tours to the scenes of Scottish song), Burns found that nothing material was forthcoming. He had to return to his 'shades' again at last, marry his Jean, and settle as tenant-farmer of Ellisland—changing over to the Excise when it became clear that the farm was not going to be a success with the means he had to work it. Even before he left Edinburgh, Burns had begun to tire of the dining and the levees; he found himself happier in the company of the Crochallan Fencibles (who made a cult, in Daniel Douglas's tavern, of the music, songs and customs of Burns's older Scottish world), and in lending a hand—chiefly on the literary side—to James Johnson's *Scots Musical Museum*—a venture that aimed at preserving the folk-tunes and folk-songs Burns knew so well. His meeting with Johnson among the Fencibles was to prove the best thing Edinburgh did for him in the end. At Ellisland and Dumfries, though he was to collect and authorize editions of the *Poems* of less Burnsian cast than their predecessors, and though his letters to people like Dr. Moore and even Mrs. Dunlop (his much-respected patroness at setting out) were to grow fewer or less warm and intimate, he was to keep some touch with the Cleghorns and Ainslies, the Dunbars and Cunninghams, who were of, or sympathized with, his Crochallan Fencibles acquaintance. Above all, he was to give every available minute to furthering and enlarging Johnson's scheme for a corpus of Scottish popular song that might sell cheaply enough to reach all, and so ensure the preservation of this special treasure of his native land before it was lost altogether by neglect. The work at least kept his name alive among Scottish writers—even if he himself was no longer much of a favourite with the fashionable society that had lionized him for a spell and noised his name abroad: while, by leading him back to the popular tunes which had guided his first indulgence in 'the sin of Rhyme', it also proved, perhaps—all things considered—the best possible employment for his rare and peculiar genius, as well as his principal solace during the few years of life that were left him. So devoted did he become to this self-appointed task—now that any other comfort which Edinburgh might have secured him was past praying for—that his output of refurbished and original songs during the brief intervals available to him, in this period, from his hard bread-winning labours as farmer and exciseman is (in both quantity and quality) so astonishing as to be evidence in itself of a genius and equipment specially adapted for the work. Only a man with the words for his people (as Burns had made himself by education from the first) could have carried Johnson's scheme so richly and completely to success. And only such a naturally gifted and trained master of folk-song could have piled on top of this work what he did so enthusiastically for George Thomson's more elaborate and ambitious collection at the same time. Small wonder that talk on occasion during these years of a drama on Bruce or Wallace remained talk only, or that Burns forgot such past works in his own special chapter of performance as 'The Court of Equity' and even 'The Jolly Beggars'.

Hard driven as he was in every way, and with memories of the famous Edinburgh party a long five years off, Burns must have been strangely moved when, in September 1792, he was invited by George Thomson to aid his *Select Collection of Original Scotish Airs*. Thomson designed to publish 'the most favourite of our national melodies' with accompaniments by Pleyel, and was 'desirous to have the poetry improved wherever it seem[ed] unworthy of the music'. Referring no doubt to Johnson's *Museum* with the rest, he complained that other collections of the time made 'the music . . . an excuse for the verses; and hence, some charming melodies are united to mere nonsense and doggrel, while others are accommodated with rhymes so loose and indelicate as cannot be sung in decent company. To remove this reproach', he continues, 'would be an easy task for the author of "The Cotter's Saturday Night"' [8]. The chief happiness of Burns's days, ever since Edinburgh, had come of just such work as Thomson offered. And here was not a corpus, but a select Collection (only the best melodies with the best words) for the drawing-rooms of the élite, of those whose objection to the 'exceptionable parts' in his *Poems* had irked him somewhat in 1787. It would put the crown upon his work for Scottish song; it was a chance, also, to make amends, to show that his Muse could still be Scots and yet as civilized as the best. Burns replied at once to Thomson, accepting the offer with enthusiasm, bluntly refusing any remuneration for the work, and stipulating only that he be 'allowed at least a sprinkling of our native tongue' as absolutely necessary in any songs or ballads he might make, and that he should not be asked to *alter*, except where by so doing he felt he could *amend* the pieces which (he agreed with Thomson) were 'a disgrace to the collections in which [they had] already appeared, and would disgrace a Collection that [would] have the very superiour merit of [Thomson's]' [9]. Making amends was not to be easy going, however. Thomson did not regard Burns as the knowledgeable expert in Scottish melodies that Johnson knew him to be; he seems rather to have thought of Burns as a name that would help his sales. Where Johnson could be trusted to engrave the tunes exactly as Burns directed, and to respect the poet's words for those tunes, Thomson was more opinionated, and pressed sometimes to modify tunes (as he thought) to their improvement; nor (since Burns died before the work had proceeded very far) was he to be very scrupulous about altering the poet's verses. Burns let himself be persuaded too much, perhaps; but he had to state his beliefs and convictions emphatically, time and again, during the long correspondence in which the two men carried on the work. He might smilingly belittle his own 'pretensions to musical taste', as 'merely a few of Nature's instincts, untaught and untutored by Art'; but if this made many compositions that transported the connoisseurs affect him 'merely as melodious Din', 'by way of amends [he was] delighted with many little melodies which the learned Musician despises as silly and insipid'. And again,

> I am sensible that my taste in Music must be inelegant and vulgar, because people of undisputed and cultivated taste can find no merit in many of my favorite tunes. . . . Many of our Strathspeys, ancient and modern, give me most exquisite enjoyment, where you and other judges would probably be showing signs of disgust.

And Burns was plainly concerned when he told Thomson—

> Whatever Mr. Pleyel does, let him not alter an iota in the original Scots Air; I mean in the Song Department.—Our friend, Clarke, [who had the music for the *Museum* in his keeping] than whom, you know, there is not a better judge of the subject, complains that in the air 'Lee-rig', the accent is to be altered.—But let our National Music preserve its native features.—They are, I own, frequently wild, and unreduceable to the modern rules; but on that very eccentricity, perhaps, depends a great part of their effect.

It was the same also with his opinions on the songs themselves. After regretting Thomson's dislike of 'The Quaker's Wife' and of 'Fye let us a' to the Bridal', Burns continues:

> Now let me declare off from your taste.—Toddlen Hame is a song that to my taste is an exquisite production of genius.—That very stanza you dislike
>
> "My kimmer and I lay down to sleep"
>
> is to me a piece of charming native humour.—What pleases me, as simple and naive, disgusts you as ludicrous and low. . . . I know you will laugh at all this; but "Ilka man wears his belt his ain gate".

And how much the air or tune in a Burns song (in other words in Scottish traditional song) determined the words, how much these had to be sought for tirelessly till the air could live through them, is revealed in a confession of Burns's about the air 'Laddie, lie near me'. This, he says,

> must *lie by me*, for some time.—I do not know the air; and untill I am compleat master of a tune, in my own singing, (such as it is) I never can compose for it.—My way is: I consider the poetic Sentiment, correspondent to my idea of the musical expression; then chuse my theme; begin

one Stanza; when that is composed, which is generally the most difficult part of the business, I walk out, sit down now and then, look out for objects in Nature around me that are in unison or harmony with the cogitations of my fancy and workings of my bosom; humming every now and then the air with the verses I have framed: when I feel my Muse beginning to jade, I retire to the solitary fireside of my study, and there commit my effusions to paper; swinging, at intervals, on the hind-legs of my elbow-chair, by way of calling forth my own critical strictures, as my pen goes on.—Seriously, this, at home, is almost invariably my way.

Clearly, when, in November 1787, Burns wrote to the Librarian of the Duke of Gordon: 'Those who think that composing a Scotch song is a trifling business, let them try', he both meant and knew what he said. And clearly the man who could conduct such a correspondence during these last years of his life—and accompany it with such careful revisions of his Johnson vamps as 'Gala Water', 'Duncan Gray' and 'Ca' the Yowes to the Knowes' (to name only a few)—was no burnt-out poet whose interest in his Muse was dead or dying and whose hand had lost its cunning. However a lifetime of hard toil may have under-mined Burns's physical health and brought him at last to an early grave, the poet in him was as alive at the close of his days as ever. And one can only regret that he did not live to carry out the intention he de-clared in one of his last letters to Thomson, who had apparently been badgering him for a certificate of copyright in the songs made for the *Select Collection*:

> When your Publication is finished, I intend publishing a Collection, on a cheap plan, of all the songs I have written for you, the *Museum*, &c. —at least of all the songs of which I wish to be called the Author.—I do not propose this so much in the way of emolument, as to do justice to my Muse, lest I should be blamed for trash I never saw, or be defrauded by other claimants of what is justly my own. [10]

It was a Scot, Andrew Fletcher of Saltoun, who quoted the saying of 'a very wise man' that 'if a man were permitted to make all the ballads, he need not care who should make the laws of a nation'. The national poet of Scotland seems to have employed his talent as if the saying were a principal article of his creed. Burns may have announced himself to the world in a book of descriptive—'manners-painting'— poems, spiced with wit and even satire, on occasion. Even so, song (one suspects) is only just round the corner. A passionate love and enjoyment of life will keep breaking in. The author of these poems is not really, we feel, a thinker of great and new thoughts upon life; rather he is a brilliant phraser of 'truths' such as everyman at once understands and recognises for his own experience, more suddenly brought home to him in the poet's words. It is, perhaps, significant

that his style has a set drift towards proverb—everyman's sign of
brain-strain—

> But Facts are cheels that winna ding,
> And downa be disputed.

> The best laid schemes o' Mice an' Men
> Gang aft a-gley.

> The heart ay's the part ay,
> That makes us right or wrang.

> O wad some Pow'r the giftie gie us
> *To see oursels as others see us!* [11]

The author of these pictures of the world he himself inhabited is the
author of the recitative portions of 'The Jolly Beggars'—the poem he
wrote in early life and (having kept no copy) could hardly recall when
asked about it in later years. He was the song-wright, who began by
playing with his talent unawares in his 'fifteenth Autumn' (inspired by
love and his girl's favourite reel); who became aware of his talent as he
started his First Commonplace-Book in 1783; climbed the last slopes
of the hill of fame with almost lightning rapidity by 1786-7—receiving
his first check as he began a Second Commonplace-Book in April 1787;
and thereafter (aided by Johnson and circumstance) knew his talent
once again (but this time in full consciousness of that talent and what it
could mean for him) as a palliative for the hardships of a strenuous
workaday existence—trying (to oblige his Edinburgh counsellors) to
do actual thinking, to make a 'criticism of life' in the idiom of the alien
English tongue (as in the piece he designed to call 'The Poet's Progress'
and used up for the most part in a verse-epistle to Graham of Fintry,
his 'stay in life' after the death of Glencairn): only occasionally, as
chance circumstance provided chance opportunity for it, making
extended poems in Scots (like 'On the late Captain Grose's Peregrina-
tions thro' Scotland', 'Elegy on Captain Matthew Henderson', 'Tam o'
Shanter'): but most of all (in and out of duty times) spending himself
without stint upon his first love as a writer, the popular music and
songs and ballads—printed or unprinted—surviving among the
Scottish folk, that Johnson's corpus of this material and Thomson's
Select Collection alike might be brought to completion for 'poor auld
Scotland's sake'. If only he could have lived to sift, revise and make
the poetry he fashioned from this source into a second book to accompany his *Poems*, his real character and significance would have been
crystal-clear to all from the first. For, more than any man, Burns was
equipped both by genius and by education to appreciate and capture
the art and technique of folk-song; and he came—before it was too
late—to that corner of this 'nook-shotten isle' where there was still

plenty of the right material to nourish his faculties and employ them at full stretch. In preserving and adding to Scotland's ancient inheritance of popular music and song, he not only proved himself (in Henley's words) 'the most exquisite artist in folk-song the world has seen', but became thereby perhaps the most national of all national poets.

4

After Burns it was only natural that there should be a new respect for the Scottish vernacular. But if by the singularity of his work and genius he disconnects from his predecessors, for the very same reason no would-be pupil ever succeeded in kindling at his flame as he had done at Ramsay's and Fergusson's, and thereby ranking as a legitimate heir and successor. For too long now, Edinburgh and literate Scotland generally had been looking towards London in matters of taste and social behaviour; and any who ventured in Burns's field were either minor poets at best, or show discolouring alien influences that remind one of their divided loyalties and make them appear—save in some honest vamps of genuine old Scottish pieces, ranking at least with Burns's slighter achievements for Johnson—as writers taking a holiday from their own proper field of work. The self-consciousness of their ventures in Scots sets them apart from the great master they may wish to acknowledge: the literary climate apparently had changed for good. Burns was possibly inimitable in any circumstances; in the times following his death, his influence was fitful at best and not productive of single-minded true disciples. Near disciples perhaps one might call those contemporaries who address verse epistles or similar pieces to Burns in the early years of his fame—a good selection of which can be seen in J. D. Ross's *Robert Burns and his Rhyming Friends* (1928). And indeed the best things in Burns's manner are usually by contemporaries who outlived him, rather than by successors proper—John Ewen's 'The Boatie Rows', Mrs. Grant of Carron's 'Roy's Wife of Aldivalloch', Hector MacNeil's 'Come under my Plaidie', James (Balloon) Tytler's 'The Bonie Brucket Lassie' and 'I hae laid a Herring in Saut', Lady Barnard's 'Auld Robin Gray', Elizabeth Hamilton's 'My Ain Fireside', John Mayne's 'Logan Braes' (not unworthy to stand by Burns's own version), Joanna Baillie's 'Saw ye Johnie comin' and 'Woo'd and Married an' a' ' [12].

The first considerable poet who was drawn towards Burns's world and themes was also a sort of younger contemporary—Baroness Nairne [13]. She outlived him into a generation that was safer for the Jacobite lyrist than his had been; nor was she handicapped by being in the Excise: and in this kind her 'Hundred Pipers', 'He's owre the Hills that I lo'e weel' and 'Will Ye no come back again?' are still deservedly popular. It is not her fault that elsewhere she is a sort of feminine

Burns at best—especially when one remembers D. G. Rossetti's pronouncement that 'Burns of all poets is the most a Man'. But a poetess who could devise 'The Laird o' Cockpen' on the Burns theme of 'When she cam ben she bobbit', need not have gone out of her way to rid his 'Auld Lang Syne' of its 'pint-stoups' and 'gude-willie waughts', or have joined with other ladies to plan a bowdlerized edition of Burns's songs—a plan that fortunately came to nothing. 'Caller Herrin' and 'The Auld House' are nearer the mark, however; and in 'The Land o' the Leal' we are reminded that the Edinburgh musician, Urbani, tried to persuade Burns to make soft verses for 'Hey tutti taitie', instead of the heroic ones he preferred in 'Scots wha hae' [14]: it is a nice question whether Baroness Nairne has not matched this air more exactly than Burns himself. Sir Alexander Boswell [15] (son of Johnson's Boswell), a real admirer of Burns, may perhaps count as a follower both in time and, on occasion, in spirit also. His 'Jenny's Bawbee', 'Jenny dang the Weaver' and 'The East Neuk o' Fife' certainly come of a liking for the airs that inspired them, even if they cannot pretend to the bright finish of Burns's refurbishings. Something they must lack, or their author's English song 'Taste Life's glad Moments' could hardly have rivalled them in popularity as it does.

With Robert Tannahill [16], the next really considerable name for mention, some of the causes that militated against a vigorous school of poetry to perpetuate Burns's work begin to show through. Some allowance is due, no doubt, to Tannahill's rather melancholy cast of mind. But when a poet makes a habit of losing the lady of his song in description of the scenes devised for meeting her (however attractive his songs may still be in their own fashion), we can be sure he is no Burns. 'Thou bonnie Wood o' Craigielea', 'Gloomy Winter's now awa' ', even 'Jessie, the Flower o' Dunblane', tell us more of landscape and the new romantic worship of Nature than of the heroines who nominally inspire them. Even when Tannahill—as in 'O, are Ye sleepin, Maggie'—comes nearest of all to a Burns topic—that of the lover pleading to be let in—it is not so much Maggie or her lover that we remember at the end as the 'howlet's cry', the soughing of the 'boortree bank', the 'lightnin's gleam athwart the lift', the linn 'roarin o'er the warlock craigie'. And when our poet attempts a humorous theme (as in 'Rob Roryson's Bonnet') it is not surprising that the humour seems rather forced, the laughter somewhat deliberate; that Burns is farther off than ever. Even Scottish airs that Tannahill had in mind as he wrote were reset for his songs by contemporary composers; some of his songs, moreover, were not tune-born at all, but (like 'Jessie, the Flower o' Dunblane') had tunes made for them by men like R. A. Smith, editor of *The Scotish Minstrel*, a work that served its later generation as Johnson's *Museum* had served the generation of Burns.

Allan Cunningham [17], who, in a busy life, attempted a wide variety of literary kinds (both prose and verse), found time nonetheless to edit Burns—if not too well, at least as elaborately as he knew how; so that one might expect his own Scottish songs to show traces of his idol. But Cunningham's *Burns* was evidence, less of scholarly and intelligent admiration, than of the fact that the cooled-off enthusiasm with which society regarded Burns at his death had changed in his favour. He was being accepted at last without reservations, even in the best circles—or (should one say rather) he could be noticed at last without qualms, since another star had arisen in Walter Scott to keep him company in his lonely greatness and balance the national achievement in letters. However it was, some five years earlier Lockhart's *Life* had been a sign; and Cunningham, as a practising man of letters, knew how to read such signs. Scotland in fact—having accommodated herself more than at first to the Union with England—was going after other, more material, things than those which most distinguished her from the 'auld enemy' of former days; and even in literature there seemed to be no call to blow the national trumpet too loudly. Cunningham as a poet, therefore, like so many other Scotsmen of his day and unlike Burns, was not 'gravelled' by English, and sits more lightly towards the vernacular than did Burns. A great part of what he did in Scottish song was, indeed, casually done to be passed off on Cromek for that collector's *Remains of Nithsdale and Galloway Song* (1810) or to be similarly hidden in his own *Songs of Scotland, Ancient and Modern* (1825). He patched and repaired old fragments, not with the profound knowledge of his stuff that guided Burns (though he came of the same peasant stock), but after his own idea of what such things should be— so that 'ancient' and 'modern' alike, with Cunningham, take on the look of light-heartedly manufactured antiques. Yet, being 'after his own idea', some of his songs have merit and still figure in anthologies. Jacobite song was in favour: in 'The Wee Wee German Lairdie' Cunningham made a memorable and individual contribution. His nearest approach to Burns is in 'My Nannie O', not an individual reminting but a pleasant enough amalgam of imitative echoes. How lightly Cunningham sits to his native Scots, and how chancy was his gift, is reflected perhaps in the fact that this complete landsman is author of one of the best known of our sea-songs, 'A Wet Sheet and a Flowing Sea': and he wrote that one in English. Cunningham is a reminder really that Burns's way with Scots and Scottish song was being dropped. Not only Walter Scott, antiquary as well as poet, but writers like William Motherwell and even James Hogg the Ettrick Shepherd (whose ambition it was to be a second Burns, and to whom we can but be grateful for songs like 'Bonnie Prince Charlie', 'Mac-Lean's Welcome' and 'When the Kye comes Hame'), were so taken up with collecting and editing Jacobite and other ancient Scottish poetry that they left themselves very little time to study and re-create the old as Burns had done [18]. Indeed, for this new generation of vernacular poets (and poet-scholars) literature—even song—was something in a book (or to be put there to qualify), not something saying itself to tunes, and a living accompaniment of the daily life of the nation. Not till a much later day, when Burns's ways and methods, as well as his printed works, should be restudied by diligent and inquiring minds, was there much hope of his influence telling again and inspiring a new revival of letters in Scotland. Till that day, one finds (as during Burns's own generation) only chance reminders of him—and those not all equally choice—like William Laidlaw's 'Lucy's Flittin', Alexander Rodger's 'My Auld Breeks', William Glen's 'Wae's me for Prince Charlie', Thomas Pringle's 'The Ewe-Buchtin's bonnie', Hew Ainslie's 'I left ye, Jeanie', Henry Scott Riddell's 'Scotland Yet', John Park's 'O an I were where Gadie rins', and Lady John Scott's 'Durisdeer' and 'Annie Laurie' [19].

VIII

SCOTTISH POETRY IN THE EARLIER
NINETEENTH CENTURY

JOHN W. OLIVER

I

SCOTT'S earliest recollections [1] were of his grandfather's farm at Sandyknowe, in the heart of the Border ballad country, and the first poetry he ever heard was folk-poetry—ballads and songs recited and sung by people among whom they were still a living tradition. From his grandmother he heard 'many a tale of Watt of Harden, Wight Willie of Aikwood, Jamie Telfer of the fair Dodhead, and other heroes' [2], and old Sandy Ormiston, the cow bailiff, would tell him tales of the adjacent Smailholm Tower and the warriors who peopled it in days gone by:

> And still I thought that shatter'd tower
> The mightiest work of human power;
> And marvell'd as the aged hind
> With some strange tale bewitch'd my mind,
> Of forayers who, with headlong force,
> Down from that strength had spurred their horse,
> Their southern rapine to renew,
> Far in the distant Cheviots blue.
>
> .   .   .   .   .
>
> And ever, by the winter hearth,
> Old tales I heard of woe or mirth,
> Of lovers' slights, of ladies' charms,
> Of witches' spells, of warriors' arms. [3]

In this way, as he tells us, he became 'from infancy devoted to legendary lore of this nature' [4], and he had already begun collecting ballads when, at the age of thirteen, beneath a plane tree in his aunt's garden at Kelso, he first read Percy's *Reliques of Ancient English Poetry*, eagerly turning over its pages while his dinner grew cold and realising with delight that his hobby of ballad collecting had possibilities he had never dreamt of.

Eight years later, in the autumn of 1792, just after he had been called to the bar, he went with his friend Robert Shortreed on the first of their annual 'raids' into Liddesdale in search of such relics of ancient ballads as might still be alive there in oral tradition. The 'raids' were continued till 1798, and in them Scott not only collected some ballads but also acquired a knowledge of the manners of the country folk, and of their rich, vivid, idiomatic speech, on which he was able to draw later when he turned to novel writing. As Shortreed said, looking back on those days after many years, 'He was makin' himsell a' the time' [5].

In 1795 he turned from ballad collecting to ballad writing as a result of the enthusiastic accounts he heard of the reading by Lucy Aikin (afterwards Mrs. Barbauld), at Dugald Stewart's, of William Taylor of Norwich's translation of Bürger's *Lenore*. With some little trouble he got from Hamburg a copy of the original German ballad, and, according to his own account, it had not been in his hands more than a few hours when he rashly promised a friend that he would supply him with a translation in English ballad metre. The result was the publication, in 1796, of the first of his works to appear in print: *The Chase, and William and Helen: Two Ballads from the German of Gottfried Augustus Bürger*. The two poems were, respectively, translations of *Der Wilde Jäger* and *Lenore*. They were first attempts; they were done in a hurry; they were renderings of bad models; and it is therefore not surprising that the book was not successful, either intrinsically or financially.

Scott now 'began to translate on all sides' from the German 'and certainly without anything like an accurate knowledge of the language'. He was 'powerfully attracted' by the dramas of Goethe and Schiller, and published in 1799 a version of Goethe's *Götz von Berlichingen*, but 'the ballad poetry was still my favourite' [6]. He was encouraged in his German balladry by an invitation to contribute to a volume of *Tales of Wonder*, which was being prepared by Matthew Gregory Lewis. The invitation came in 1798, but the book did not appear till 1801. In the meantime he had published, from James Ballantyne's press at Kelso, under the title of *Tales of Terror* (1799), the two poems from his 1796 volume along with a translation of *The Erl King*. Two other German ballads—'The Fire-King' and 'Frederick and Alice'—were included in the 1801 edition of *Tales of Wonder*.

Long before they were all safely in print he had started on a much more fruitful line of work. About the end of 1799 he proposed to James Ballantyne the publication of a small volume of Border Ballads—a project which grew into his great ballad collection, *Minstrelsy of the Scottish Border*. In the same year he had composed his first original ballads on Scottish themes: 'Glenfinlas', 'The Eve of St. John' and 'The Grey Brother'. 'Glenfinlas', based on a Highland legend, shows Scott still in unfamiliar country, but in 'The Eve of St. John', with its setting at Smailholm Tower beside the beloved Sandyknowe of his youth, he is at home, and in the true ballad vein:

> The Baron of Smaylho'me rose with day,
>   He spurred his courser on,
> Without stop or stay, down the rocky way,
>   That leads to Brotherstone.

He went not with the bold Buccleuch,
His banner broad to rear;
He went not 'gainst the English yew
To lift the Scottish spear.

'The Gray Brother' is a fragment which Scott says he was unable to complete to his own satisfaction. He had not yet shaken off the macabre, melodramatic influence of the German ballads, as its last lines testify:

When on his neck an ice-cold hand
Did that Gray Brother laye.

The final *e* in the last line is, in itself, significant. He is much happier in the stanzas in which he describes the course of the Midlothian Esk, weaving into them the names of well-loved, familiar Scottish places and the memories associated with them:

From that fair dome where suit is paid
By blast of bugle free,
To Auchendinny's hazel glade
And haunted Woodhouselee.

Who knows not Melville's beechy grove,
And Roslin's rocky glen,
Dalkeith which all the virtues love,
And classic Hawthornden?

That may not be Scott at his best, but it shows him breaking free from German *diablerie* and coming home. The *genius loci* was to be one of the strongest of his sources of inspiration—and certainly no Lothian man can read those lines and remain quite cold.

In 1799 Scott's appointment as Sheriff of Selkirkshire gave him more financial independence and more frequent opportunities of keeping in touch with his Border friends. About this time, too, he made the acquaintance of John Leyden, who was enlisted in the work of preparing the ballad collection and gave to it all his multifarious learning and all his explosive enthusiasm. The *Minstrelsy of the Scottish Border* was Scott's main work for the next three years, the only original poem composed by him during that time being 'Cadyow Castle', written while he was on a visit to Hamilton Palace at Christmas 1801. As in 'The Gray Brother', his imagination kindles at the sight of scenes recalling history and legend. As he looks, the ruins of Cadyow Castle are transformed into the proud fortress of the sixteenth century:

Lo! as on Evan's banks we stand,
The past returns—the present flies.

Where with the rock's wood cover'd side
Were blended late the ruins green,
Rise turrets in fantastic pride,
And feudal banners flaunt between.

Where the rude torrent's brawling course
Was shagg'd with thorn and tangling sloe,
The ashler buttress braves its force,
And ramparts frown in 'battled row.

In January 1802 the first edition of the *Minstrelsy*, in two volumes, was published by James Ballantyne at Kelso. But the work was not completed; there were more ballads to be collected. In the spring of the same year Scott and Leyden were touring in Ettrick Forest and called on William Laidlaw—later to be Scott's faithful friend and steward—at Blackhouse Farm. Laidlaw showed them a copy of 'Auld Maitland', a ballad which they had heard of but never so far seen, and told them that it had been given to him by one of his shepherds, James Hogg. A visit to Hogg followed, and so the two Border minstrels were brought together. At the beginning of 1803 the second edition of the *Minstrelsy* was published, in three volumes. The third volume contained ballads not included in the first edition—some of them collected since its publication—and some 'modern ballads', including 'Cadyow Castle' and 'The Gray Brother'.

The completion of the *Minstrelsy* (or all but completion; for further ballads were added in subsequent editions) marks the end of Scott's poetic apprenticeship. So far he had composed only some schoolboy pieces, some imitation ballads, and some short personal and occasional poems. *The Minstrelsy of the Scottish Border* was his first substantial production. It is the greatest of all the ballad collections and its ample introductions and notes are full of that rich, disorganized learning which was later to provide much of the raw material of his novels. If he had done nothing else, Scott would have had an honoured place in the history of Scottish poetry as a great ballad collector and editor.

But was his *Minstrelsy* work confined to editing as we know it? How far did he help out the ballads? How much do they owe to his skilled and sympathetic touch? A good deal, maybe, but how much it is impossible to say. He claimed that all that he did was to choose the best from among variant readings and to make the lines rhyme where the originals broke down in that respect, but his careless way of regarding his own poetical powers probably caused him to regard as of little account emendations which made all the difference between commonplace jogtrot, or sheer doggerel, and genuine poetry. But we must be cautious in attributing things to Scott. As fuller examination of Scott's manuscript sources makes clear, it will not do to assume that any specially good verses in the *Minstrelsy* ballads must, when there is no other record of them, be his own work [7]. Anyhow, we can be certain that, whatever he did, it was done in the true ballad spirit and not to conform to standards of drawing-room elegance or to play up to the inflated ghost-and-goblin style of the

German ballads. Contact with the Scottish ballads had worked *Lenore* out of his system.

Among the poems which Scott had thought of including in the third volume of the *Minstrelsy* was—in his own words—'a long poem, a kind of romance of Border chivalry, in a light-horseman sort of stanza' [8]. This was the first draft of *The Lay of the Last Minstrel*. It grew out of his ballad work and had its setting in the ballad country, but, by the time he started on it, he had come to feel that the ballad stanza was out of favour—'had become hackneyed and sickening, from its being the accompaniment of every grinding hand-organ'—and, besides, that it had an effect on the mind of its user 'like that of the bed of Procrustes on the human body', so that it was 'singularly unfavourable to narrative composition'. The accident of hearing his friend John Stoddart reading the (till then) unpublished *Christabel* of Coleridge suggested to him the form that the new poem should take, and he went on happily with the work, doing about a canto a week and rejoicing in the freedom that the new form gave him: 'There was, indeed, little occasion for pause or hesitation, when a troublesome rhyme might be accommodated by an alteration of the stanza, or where an incorrect measure might be remedied by a variation of the rhyme' [9].

With the adoption of the new measure the substance of the poem changed. The original theme, suggested by the young Countess of Dalkeith as suitable for a ballad, was the story of Gilpin Horner, a mysterious goblin or brownie who, according to the firm belief of many of Scott's Border friends, had, a generation or two before, taken up his abode in an Eskdalemuir farmhouse. Gilpin Horner now became subsidiary and the poem grew into a stirring tale of Border raids and rivalries in the sixteenth century; and a suggestion, made by William Erskine or George Cranstoun, for the provision of some kind of imaginative framework for the tale, gave him the hint for the Last Minstrel himself.*

The *Lay* was published in 1805. It made Scott, at one stroke, the most popular poet in Britain, and its success determined the line his work was to take for the next ten years. It was followed by *Marmion* in 1808 and by *The Lady of the Lake* in 1810; each poem proving a more resounding popular success than its predecessor. But after *The Lady of the Lake* he began to tread the downward slope by which, as he said, 'I declined as a poet to figure as a novelist' [10]. The steps on the downward slope are *The Vision of Don Roderick* (1811), *Rokeby* (1813), *The Bridal of Triermain* (1813), *The Lord of the Isles* (1815) and *Harold the Dauntless* (1817).

The Vision of Don Roderick, composed to aid a fund for the relief of

---

* Compare p. 147 *supra*.

Portuguese sufferers from the Peninsular War and recalling the events of that war by means of a vision presented to Roderick, the last of the Goths, is written hurriedly in Spenserians, a measure in which Scott did not excel and in which writing in a hurry does not pay. To-day the most interesting thing in it is the Introduction, in which he reviews the popular poetic tradition of Scotland from the Welsh-speaking bards of the sixth century down to his own day—when the 'old traditionary lore' had decayed 'Save where their legends grey-hair'd shepherds sing', unmarked by any ear but his own; and he hints that he feels that his days of popularity as a poet are coming to an end:

> Minstrel, the fame of whose romantic lyre,
> Capricious-swelling now, may soon be lost,
> Like the light flickering of a cottage fire.

Rokeby is a more important work, a metrical romance on the same scale as the *Lay* and *Marmion* and *The Lady of the Lake*. In it he shifts his scene to England—to Teesdale—and his period is that of the English Civil War in the seventeenth century. It is a carefully constructed poem, but its plot is too intricate to be worked out with ease to the reader within the bounds of a metrical tale, and it would be much more suitable to a full-length novel. But there are good things in *Rokeby*—the lovely descriptions of the Tees valley, the fight in the hall at Rokeby, and three of Scott's best songs, 'Brignal Banks', 'A Weary Lot is Thine, Fair Maid' and 'Allan-a-Dale'.

The Bridal of Triermain is a curious piece of mystification. It was published anonymously and, in order to play a practical joke on the critics, hints were put about that it was the work of Scott's friend William Erskine and care was taken 'in several places to mix something which might resemble (as far as was in my power) my friend's feeling and manner' [11]. The result, inevitably, hardly shows Scott at his best. It is a variant of the Sleeping Beauty story, the Beauty being bewitched by Merlin at Arthur's court and awakened some five hundred years later by Sir Roland de Vaux of Triermain. The story of the bewitching is put into the mouth of the British bard Lyulph, and, as an outer casing to the whole thing, the poem is supposed to be related, in the manner of the *Lay*, to an early nineteenth-century lady by an early nineteenth-century minstrel, who, however, expressly disclaims the things which are most characteristic of Scott:

> My Harp—or let me rather choose
> The good old classic form—my Muse,
> (For Harp's an over-scutched phrase,
> Worn out by bards of modern days).
>
> Ne'er did it sound o'er sainted well,
> Nor boasts it aught of Border spell;

> Its strings no feudal slogan pour,
> Its heroes draw no broad claymore.

There are fine passages of action and description in the poem, but it never works together as a whole, and from time to time one comes on passages which sound like deliberate burlesque:

> The champions, arm'd in martial sort,
>   Have throng'd into the list,
> And but three knights of Arthur's court
>   Are from the tourney miss'd.
> And still these lovers' fame survives
>   For faith so constant shown,—
> There were two who lov'd their neighbours' wives,
>   And one who loved his own. [12]

In *The Lord of the Isles*, where the main theme is the adventures of Bruce, culminating in the Battle of Bannockburn, Scott is much more at home. There is fine imaginative narrative in it and the splendid pictures of the outline of Skye, seen from the sea, and of Loch Coruisk and the Cuillins are among his best descriptive passages. Yet the poem does not entirely satisfy. The love-story of Ronald, the Lord of the Isles, and of Edith, the Maid of Lorne, does not fuse with the main historical theme, and the passages describing the deeds of Bruce suffer a little from the fact that Barbour had been there before. Scott certainly tidies up Barbour, as can be seen by comparing the beginnings of their accounts of the fight between Bruce and De Bohun:

> Befor thame all thar com rydand,
> With helme on hed, and sper in hand,
> Schir Henry of Boune, the worthy,
> That wes ane gud knycht, and hardy;
> And to the Erll of Herfurd cosyne,
> Armyt in armys gude and fyne.
>
> And, at King Edward's signal soon
> Dash'd from the ranks Sir Henry Boune.
> Of Hereford's high blood he came,
> A race renown'd for knightly fame.
> He burn'd before his Monarch's eye
> To do some deed of chivalry.

But, when Barbour describes crude and violent action and Scott paraphrases him in his smoother couplets, we cannot but feel that much has been lost in the translation:

> And he, that in his sterapys stude,
> With ax that wes bath hard and gude,

218

With so gret mayn roucht hym ane dynt,   [*reached out to him*
That nouthir hat no helm mycht stynt
The hevy dusche that he him gaf,
That he the hed till harnys claf.   [*brains*
The hand-ax-schaft fruschit in twa,   [*splintered*
And he doune till the erd can ga   [*did go*
All flatlyngis, for him faillyt mycht.   [*strength failed him*
This wes the first strak of the ficht.

High in his stirrups stood the King,
And gave his battle-axe the swing.
Right on De Boune, the whiles he pass'd,
Fell that stern dint, the first, the last!
Such strength upon the blow was put,
The helmet crash'd like hazel-nut;
The axe-shaft, with its brazen clasp,
Was shiver'd to the gauntlet grasp.
Springs from the blow the startled horse,
Drops to the plain the lifeless corse:
First of that fatal field, how soon,
How sudden, fell the fierce De Boune! [13]

It is true that Barbour has the advantage of writing in Scots, and there is no better medium for the conveying of vigorous concrete effects; but, allowing for this, there is surely about Scott's lines a taint of rhetoric from which Barbour is entirely free.

Harold the Dauntless is 'supposed to be in the manner of a rude minstrel or Scald'. Scott himself dismisses it with a laugh, telling how, when Hogg's parody of Sir Walter's poetic style, 'Watt o' the Cleuch', appeared in his *Poetic Mirror*, it 'bore such a resemblance to *Harold the Dauntless* that there was no discovering the original from the imitation'. The parody, which was published a year before *Harold*, is indeed comically like it in style and tone. Some passages in *Harold* sound curiously like a foretaste of *The Ingoldsby Legends*, as, for instance, the lines in which Harold's father, after embracing Christianity, rounds on his recalcitrant son:

Why speak I to thee of repentance or truth,
Who ne'er from thy childhood knew reason or ruth?
Hence! to the wolf and the bear in her den;
These are thy mates, and not rational men. [14]

After 1817, the year of the publication of *Harold*, Scott tells us he was 'not an intruder on the public by any poetical work of importance' [15]. The rise of Byron as a competitor, the falling off in the sales of *The Lord of the Isles*, the discovery of his powers as a novelist, and the immense popularity of the first five Waverley Novels: all had their influence on his turning away from verse. But there was more to it than that. He seems to have felt that, Byron or no Byron, *Waverley* or no *Waverley*, he had done about all that he could do in verse. His 'Farewell to the Muse', written about this time, states this explicitly:

> 'Twas thou that once taught me, in accents bewailing,
>   To sing how a warrior lay stretch'd on the plain,
> And a maiden hung o'er him with aid unavailing,
>   And held to his lips the cold goblet in vain;
> As vain thy enchantments, O Queen of wild Numbers,
>   To a bard when the reign of his fancy is o'er,
> And the quick pulse of feeling in apathy slumbers—
>   Farewell, then, Enchantress! I meet thee no more!

His poetic vein was not, of course, entirely exhausted, as a glance at the novels published from 1816 onward shows. *The Antiquary* (1816) has Elspeth's ballad of 'The Red Harlaw'; *The Heart of Midlothian* (1818) has Madge Wildfire's songs, including 'Proud Maisie': *The Bride of Lammermoor* (1818) has Lucy Ashton's song 'Look not thou on Beauty's Charming'; *Ivanhoe* (1819) has Rebecca's hymn 'When Israel, of the Lord beloved'; *The Monastery* (1820) has 'March, march, Ettrick and Teviotdale'; and *Quentin Durward* (1823) has 'County Guy'. After that, however, there are few songs in the novels, and none of the quality of the best things in the earlier ones.

2

'An auld Tory ballant singer!' [16] That is how Scott was dismissed, in the year 1887, by an old Selkirk man who remembered 'the Shirra'; and he was of course right, though a little ungenerous. There is no need to labour Scott's virtues as a ballad poet. We need only recall such things as the 'simple song' that Albert Graeme sings in *The Lay of the Last Minstrel*:

> It was an English ladye bright
>   (The sun shines fair on Carlisle wall),
> And she would marry a Scottish knight,
>   For Love will still be lord of all;

and, also from the *Lay*, 'Rosabelle' with its rich, romantic colour; and 'The Gray Brother', making such sweet music with Lothian place names; and 'Lochinvar' which the wily Lady Heron sings in *Marmion*, 'with arch simplicity', to James IV at Holyrood, and which, though its 'arch simplicity' sometimes perhaps comes perilously near the comic, is and always will be a favourite with the young and the young-hearted; and, greatest of them all, the resonant, clanging stanzas of 'The Red Harlaw', the ballad which the enraptured Jonathan Oldbuck, in *The Antiquary*, hears chanted 'in a wild and doleful recitative' by the 'shrill tremulous voice' of old Elspeth Mucklebackit:

> They saddled a hundred milk-white steeds,
>   They hae bridled a hundred black,
> With a chafron of steel on each horse's head,
>   And a good knight upon his back.

> They hadna ridden a mile, a mile,
>   A mile, but barely ten,
> When Donald came branking down the brae
>   Wi' twenty thousand men. [17]

The ballads were in Scott's blood and no one has more successfully recaptured their spirit and their style.

The need for a little more elbow-room led Scott from ballad writing to the writing of the metrical romances. They made him, for ten years, the most popular poet in Britain, but they have now become the chief obstacle to the full recognition of his poetic stature. They occupy much the greater part of the collected editions of his poetical works, and they are so facile, so lacking, at first sight at any rate, in passion and subtlety, that people are apt to dismiss their author as nothing more than a 'metre ballad monger'—good enough for youngsters, but not to be taken very seriously. Scott himself was, in his own words, never 'a partisan of my own poetry, even when it was in the highest fashion with the million', and his daughter Sophia declared, when *The Lady of the Lake* was in the full current of its popularity, that she had not read it because 'Papa says there's nothing so bad for young people as reading bad poetry' [18].

But we cannot dismiss things like *The Lay of the Last Minstrel* and *Marmion* and *The Lady of the Lake* as 'bad poetry'. They were written happily and carelessly, and cannot be judged as a whole by the severest poetical standards. Very few long narrative poems can. Scott was like the authors of the ballads, who were concerned to tell a tale vividly and picturesquely and were content to let the poetry look after itself, welling up unexpectedly, like water in a dry, parched land. If we accept that, we do not trouble about passages which betray what Scott called his 'flattened thought and cumbrous line'.

Take, for example, a passage near the end of *Marmion*:

> 'O, Lady,' cried the Monk, 'away!'
>   And plac'd her on her steed,
> And led her to the chapel fair,
>   Of Tilmouth upon Tweed.

That, no doubt, is 'bad poetry'; but Scott's immediate object in writing it was not to write poetry, good or bad, but to get rid of Lady Clare, who lags superfluous on the stage, and clear the way for the great passage which follows almost immediately:

> But as they left the dark'ning heath,
> More desperate grew the strife of death.
> The English shafts in volleys hail'd,
> In headlong charge their horse assail'd. [19]

The good things in the metrical romances come, indeed, intermittently, when Scott warms up to them. Many of them, like the passage just quoted, describe violent action, and on the strength of them we can place him high among a by no means despicable class of poets—those who excel in the presentation of sheer physical stir and movement. But the good things are not confined to the crudities of battle, murder and sudden death. Violent action is not an end in itself with Scott. It acquires significance only in so far as it displays those virtues of courage, loyalty, love of country and love of liberty which were among the things dearest to his heart.

The love of country is one of the strongest sources of inspiration in those longer poems—love both of Scotland as a whole and of those parts which he knew more intimately. The suggestion to the Last Minstrel that he should forsake the 'poor and thankless soil' of Scotland for 'the more generous Southern land' provokes the lines beginning 'Breathes there the man, with soul so dead'. They have a rhetorical, over-strained note to begin with, and 'Caledonia! stern and wild' is a phrase which can be only too easily parodied and misapplied; but gradually, we feel, the voice ceases to be the Last Minstrel's and becomes Scott's own. The feeling becomes deeper, and the language simpler and purer:

> By Yarrow's stream still let me stray,
> Though none should guide my feeble way,
> Still feel the breeze down Ettrick break,
> Although it chill my wither'd cheek;
> Still lay my head by Teviot Stone,
> Though there, forgotten and alone,
> The Bard may draw his parting groan. [20]

Scott's love of Scotland was deep and sincere, and there is nothing tawdry and vulgar about his patriotic poetry, nothing vague and generalized. He knew the country from the Shetlands to Galloway and from Rum and Skye to Berwick on Tweed, and everything he saw he remembered with extraordinary clearness. *The Lady of the Lake* is largely a frame for pictures of the Trossachs 'connected with the recollection of many a dear friend and merry expedition of former days' [21]; William of Deloraine's ride in *The Lay of the Last Minstrel* is a kind of animated map of a part of the Borderland; and the accounts in *Marmion* of Crichton and Tantallon Castles have the minute detail of an antiquary's report, though they must have been done entirely from memory. He loved the places and he loved their very names; and it is with them that he makes some of his sweetest music:

> So pass'd the winter's day; but still,
> When summer smil'd on sweet Bowhill,
> And July's eve, with balmy breath,
> Wav'd the blue-bells on Newark heath;
> When throstles sung in Harehead-shaw,
> And corn was green on Carterhaugh,
> And flourish'd broad Blackandro's oak,
> The aged Harper's soul awoke! [22]

The metrical romances lay Scott open to the charge of 'escapism'—to use a somewhat outmoded word—of turning from immediate realities to old, far-off things. And indeed he pleaded guilty to this in his 'Farewell to the Muse':

> Each joy thou couldst double, and when there came sorrow,
>   Or pale disappointment to darken my way,
> What voice was like thine, that could sing of to-morrow,
>   Till forgot in the strain was the grief of to-day!

Perhaps 'sing of yesterday' would be more appropriate to Scott than 'sing of to-morrow'. Be that as it may, it is true that he felt no call to deal with the moral and social problems of his generation or to plumb the depths of human experience; but he was no sentimentalist, representing life as all glitter and excitement and high adventure. When he began writing the romances he had had enough shocks and disappointments to make him know the difference between romance and reality. He was not, to borrow the words of Tony Weller, 'a dilluded wictim thinkin' in his innocence that it's all wery capital'. His love of romance was not a mere 'abandoning of his mind'. He knew all too well that life does not consist wholly of high romance and lofty achievements. The favourite poem of this writer of highly coloured romances was Johnson's *Vanity of Human Wishes*, and time and again, in the *Lay*, in *Marmion* and the others, we hear, set to a strange new music, the old Johnsonian theme:

> Yet hope not life from grief or danger free,
> Nor think the doom of man revers'd for thee.

Here is Scott addressing the Teviot:

> Where'er thou wind'st, by dale or hill,
> All, all is peaceful, all is still,

As if thy waves, since Time was born,
Since first they roll'd upon the Tweed,
Had only heard the shepherd's reed,
    Nor started at the bugle-horn.

Unlike the tide of human time,—
    Which, though it change in ceaseless flow,
Retains each grief, retains each crime
    Its earliest course was doom'd to know;
And, darker as it downward bears,
Is stain'd with past and present tears. [23]

The same gravity, the same strong, sympathetic perception of the deeper realities of life, shows itself in many places in the romances. In *Marmion* we have the young Fitz-Eustace marvelling at the credulity which sends out the sceptical, irreligious Marmion to the haunted 'Pictish round' at Gifford:

For little did Fitz-Eustace know,
That passions, in contending flow,
    Unfix the strongest mind;
Wearied from doubt to doubt we flee.
We welcome fond credulity,
    Guide confident, though blind.

In *The Lord of the Isles* the sight of the bare peaks of the Cuillins provokes Bruce to solemn reflection:

These mighty cliffs, that heave on high
Their naked brows to middle sky,
Indifferent to the sun or snow,
Where nought can fade, and nought can blow,
May they not mark a Monarch's fate,—
Raised high 'mid storms of strife and state,
Beyond life's lowlier pleasures placed,
His soul a rock, his heart a waste?

And in *Rokeby* a sombre comparison is suggested by the picture of the country round Barnard Castle glowing in the reflected rays of the departed sun:

Distant and high, the tower of Bowes
Like steel upon the anvil glows;
And Stanmore's ridge, behind that lay,
Rich with the spoils of parting day,
In crimson and in gold array'd,
Streaks yet a while the closing shade,

Then slow resigns to darkening heaven
The tints which brighter hours had given.
Thus aged men, full loth and slow,
The vanities of life forego,
And count their youthful follies o'er,
Till Memory lends her light no more. [24]

It is in such things as these that we find Scott's 'criticism of life'. It occurs fitfully; for, like the balladists whom he emulated and the great Augustan poets whom he admired, he did not feel called upon to make his verse a medium for the expression of his own most intimate feelings. He works his puppets, and makes them act and speak, but he seldom makes his own voice heard; and when he does, what he says is generalized and impersonal. Where he does express himself is—apart from a few lyrics—in the Introductory Epistles to *Marmion*. These gave him a medium by which he could, without embarrassment, reveal himself—in his home and among his friends, at work and at play—his memories of the past, his comments on the present, and his reflections on life in general. 'I may be permitted to say,' he wrote of *Marmion*,

that the period of its composition was a very happy one in my life; . . . It is probably owing to this that the Introductions to the several Cantos assumed the form of familiar epistles to my intimate friends, in which I alluded, perhaps more than was necessary or graceful, to my domestic occupations and amusements—a loquacity which may be excused by those who remember that I was still young, light-headed, and happy, and that 'out of the abundance of the heart the mouth speaketh'. [25]

Surely no one will find anything to 'excuse' in the 'loquacity' of those epistles. They bring Scott very near to us, and only the *Journal* can compare with them in this respect. What it does for the last years of sorrow and struggle they do for the earlier years of care-free work and happy achievement. In them we see him as a child, lying on the floor at Sandyknowe fighting mimic battles, or disturbing the old parish minister's conversation with his vociferation of Lady Wardlaw's ballad of 'Hardyknute'; or we see him out coursing with his greyhounds or riding on long excursions to St. Mary's Loch and the Grey Mare's Tail. They also contain some of his best descriptive passages—St. Mary's Loch:

Far in the mirror, bright and blue,
Each hill's huge outline you may view;
Shaggy with heath, but lonely bare,
Nor tree, nor bush, nor brake, is there;
Save where, of land, yon slender line
Bears thwart the lake the scatter'd pine;

and the Grey Mare's Tail:

> Through the rude barriers of the lake,
> Away its hurrying waters break,
> Faster and whiter dash and curl,
> Till down yon dark abyss they hurl.
> Rises the fog-smoke white as snow,
> Thunders the viewless stream below;

and the new town of Edinburgh, spreading to the north:

> liberal, unconfin'd, and free,
> Flinging thy white arms to the sea;

and the November snowstorm:

> When red hath set the beamless sun,
> Through heavy vapours dark and dun;
> When the tir'd ploughman, dry and warm,
> Hears, half asleep, the rising storm
> Hurling the hail, and sleeted rain,
> Against the casement's tinkling pane;
> The sounds that drive wild deer, and fox,
> To shelter in the brake and rocks,
> Are warnings which the shepherd ask
> To dismal and to dangerous task.
> Oft he looks forth, and hopes, in vain,
> The blast may sink in mellowing rain;
> Till, dark above, and white below,
> Decided drives the flaky snow. [26]

The Introduction to Canto First contain Scott's greatest piece of rhetorical verse, the magnificent commemorative tribute to Nelson and Pitt, working up to the majestic lines on Pitt:

> Now is the stately column broke,
> The beacon-light is quench'd in smoke,
> The trumpet's silver sound is still,
> The warder silent on the hill!

The Introductions are full of good things. Scott writes, throughout, genially and happily, with a play of happy humour, never straining after effect, but rising quite naturally, in passages of reflection, to a tone of dignity and gravity. Nowhere can the breadth and warmth of his mind be felt so strongly as in them.

But it is as a lyric poet that Scott is at his greatest, and that greatness has, I think, not been sufficiently recognized. This may be due to the way in which so many of his best things are scattered carelessly about his novels and longer poems, and also, perhaps, to a tendency, pretty general since the eighteenth century, to deny the highest rank to any lyrics except those which express personal feeling.

There is almost nothing of that kind in Scott. The only poem which is entirely devoted to personal emotion is 'The Sun upon the Weirdlaw Hill', in some ways the most self-revealing of all his poems, which gives poignant expression to the melancholy side of his nature:

> The quiet lake, the balmy air,
>> The hill, the stream, the tower, the tree,—
> Are they still such as once they were?
> Or is the dreary change in me?

And the same solemn note is sounded in some of the less personal lyrics, in 'O hush thee, my babie', for instance:

> Then hush thee, my darling, take rest while you may,
> For strife comes with manhood, and waking with day;

and in 'Waken, lords and ladies gay', where, in the last stanza, a dark, ominous cloud sweeps across the bright morning sky:

> Tell them youth, and mirth, and glee
> Run a course as well as we;
> Time, stern huntsman! who can baulk,
> Stanch as hound, and fleet as hawk;
> Think of this, and rise with day,
> Gentle lords and ladies gay.

In none of the other lyrics do we hear Scott's own voice. This, no doubt, is mainly due to the fact that so many of them are sung by characters in the novels and longer poems, but it is true also of those composed independently. In 'Pibroch of Donuil Dhu', for instance, it is the Bard of Clan Donuil who is singing; in 'MacGregor's Gathering' it is the MacGregor. They are dramatic lyrics, and this gives a rich variety to them. Scott is limited, like Burns, to simple emotions; but among them, like Burns, he ranges far and wide. His mind was stored with rhythms and turns of phrase caught from Burns and the older Scottish song-writers, from Shakespeare, and from the Elizabethan and Jacobean lyrists; and when the need came to put a song in the mouth of one of his characters, the appropriate measure and the appropriate words seemed to come almost unsought.

One result of this is that it is impossible neatly to classify his songs. There is 'God's plenty' of them, and they are of all sorts. There is the bleak, desolate wail of 'Coronach':

> The autumn winds rushing
>> Waft the leaves that are searest,
> But our flower was in flushing,
>> When blighting was nearest;

227

and the rich, Old Testament imagery and solemn, psalm-like rhythm of Rebecca's hymn in *Ivanhoe*:

> By day, along the astonish'd lands
> The cloudy pillar glided slow;
> By night, Arabia's crimson'd sands
> Return'd the fiery column's glow;

and the rattling, romantic swing of 'Bonnie Dundee':

> He waved his proud hand, and the trumpets were blown,
> The kettle-drums clash'd, and the horsemen rode on,
> Till on Ravelston's cliffs and on Clermiston's lee,
> Died away the wild war-notes of Bonnie Dundee;

and the rollicking daftlike rant of 'Donald Caird':

> When he's fou he's stout and saucy,
> Keeps the cantle o' the causey;
> Hieland chief and Lawland laird
> Maun gie room to Donald Caird;

and the brilliant working-up and effective rounding-off of a ballad fragment in 'Jock of Hazeldean':

> They sought her baith by bower and ha';
> The ladie was not seen!
> She's o'er the Border and awa'
> Wi' Jock of Hazeldean.

But, if we examine in their setting the lyrics scattered through the novels and longer poems, we shall find that they have an important quality over and above their virtue as isolated poems. Like the songs in Shakespeare's plays they seem to concentrate in themselves the emotional essence of a situation and express something that can be expressed in no other way, and certainly not in the loose couplets of the metrical romances or the solid, heavy-going prose of the novels. Instances of the perfect fitness of these songs are many. From the metrical romances we can take one example, the scene in *Marmion* when, at the inn at Gifford, Fitz-Eustace is asked by Marmion for a song and responds with that song which they had last heard sung by the doomed and betrayed Constance of Beverley:

> Where shall the lover rest,
> Whom the fates sever
> From his true maiden's breast,
> Parted for ever?

And from the novels two examples stand out. One is the lovely, bitter-sweet lines which with exquisite irony Scott puts into the mouth of the tragically destined Bride of Lammermoor:

> Look not thou on beauty's charming,
> Sit thou still when kings are arming,
> Taste not when the wine-cup glistens,
> Speak not when the people listens,
> Stop thine ear against the singer,
> From the red gold keep thy finger;
> Vacant heart, and hand, and eye,
> Easy live and quiet die.

The other is the great scene in *The Heart of Midlothian* where Madge Wildfire sings her snatches of song as she lies dying. In them, as Scott says—in words which, in their almost scientific detachment, are in strange contrast with the poignant strains of the songs—'could always be traced something appropriate, though perhaps only obliquely and collaterally so, to her present situation'. First there is a 'Harvest home' song, then a fragment from what might have been a Methodist hymn—

> When the fight of grace is fought,
> When the marriage vest is wrought,

—then the ballad fragment 'Cauld is my bed, Lord Archibald'; and finally

'She changed the tune to one wilder, less monotonous, and less regular. But of the words, only a fragment or two could be collected by those who listened to this singular scene:

> Proud Maisie is in the wood,
>   Walking so early;
> Sweet Robin sits on the bush,
>   Singing so rarely;'— [27]

and her voice 'dies away with the last notes' of Scott's greatest lyric.

The poetic quality of Scott's mind is one of the most important things about him as a novelist, and it does not show itself only in interpolated lyrics. He is supreme among novelists in dealing with characters who 'werge on the poetical', people like Madge Wildfire, Meg Merrilies, Edie Ochiltree, old Elspeth Mucklebackit, and Balfour of Burley—simple folk with the poetry of the soil, bold adventurers, wanderers and outcasts, and crazed fanatics who live in a world into which only the poetic imagination can penetrate sympathetically. But even solid, prosaic, earth-bound characters like Dandy Dinmont and Bailie Nicol Jarvie and Andrew Fairservice—though they would probably have repudiated indignantly any suggestion that the gods had made them poetical—have a gift of exuberant, picturesque phrase which makes their speech partake as much of the nature of poetry as of prose. And, finally, it is worth remembering that there is one novel— *The Bride of Lammermoor*—which is a working-out in prose of a poetic theme and has the strange and terrible beauty of the starkest of the old ballads.

3

James Hogg [28] comes second to Scott among the Scottish poets of the early nineteenth century. No doubt he comes a good way behind, but he is fully entitled to have his name linked with the greater poet, as it was by Wordsworth:

> The mighty Minstrel breathes no longer,
> Mid mouldering ruins low he lies;
> And death upon the braes of Yarrow
> Has closed the Shepherd-poet's eyes. [29]

With all the differences in their backgrounds the Shepherd and the Sheriff had much in common; for they both drew their chief strength from folk-tradition. Scott had a wider culture to reinforce it, but Hogg was, by birth and upbringing, more closely knit with it. All his best work derives from folk-memories, folk-rhymes and folk-tunes.

The education of James Hogg would be a very salutary study for anyone who is inclined to think of education in terms only of reading, writing and arithmetic. The only regular schooling he ever had was for about six months when he was between seven and eight years of age. At fifteen he went as a shepherd to Blackhouse Farm, under William Laidlaw, and there he taught himself to write by copying italic printing. It sounds an unpromising foundation on which to build a literary reputation.

But he had education of another kind. In Ettrick he grew up among people on whose lips the ballads and folk-songs were still alive, and his mother, Margaret Laidlaw (one of the makers of Scott's *Border Minstrelsy*), was a storehouse of song and legend and an exceedingly shrewd woman, as is shown by her famous remark to Scott about the publication of some of her ballads in the *Minstrelsy*: 'There war never ane o' my sangs prentit till ye prentit them yoursel', an' ye hae spoilt them awthegither. They were made for singing an' no for reading; but ye hae broken the charm now, an' they'll never be sung mair.' And his mother's father, Will o' Phaup, was, as Hogg said, 'the last man of this wild region who heard, saw, and conversed with the fairies; and that not once, or twice, but at sundry times and seasons.' It is no wonder that he could claim with justice to be 'the king o' the mountain and fairy school' of poetry [30].

There were more literary influences too, such things as formed the normal Scottish cottage library of his time—the Bible, the Metrical

Psalms, the Paraphrases, Harvey's *Life of Bruce,* Hamilton of Gilbert-field's *Wallace* (the same book that had filled Burns with a 'flood of Scottish prejudice') and Ramsay's *Gentle Shepherd.* And in later years he read the poetry of his contemporaries to some purpose, as is shown by his shrewd parodies of their work in his *Poetic Mirror* (1816). His reading and his contacts with people of wider culture, notably Sir Walter Scott, gave him a wider range of knowledge and experience than if he had been nothing but an 'Ettrick Shepherd'; his prose masterpiece, *The Private Memoirs and Confessions of a Justified Sinner,* is evidence enough of this: but his best verse is always close to folk-tradition and he is at his weakest when he follows literary models, as in the blank verse and heroic couplets of *The Pilgrims of the Sun* and the Spenserians of *Mador of the Moor.*

His songs are the part of his work most generally known to-day, and their popularity after a century and a half is a testimony to their quality. Any Scots song writer after Burns is in a somewhat invidious position. Comparisons are inevitable, and of course Hogg has not Burns's passion and fury or his faultless taste, and he is apt to 'sink in poetry' all too often, but his songs have the genuine lilt of true folk-songs and he does not overstrain sentiment. He is at his best when sentiment is shot with touches of humour, as in his most popular song 'When the Kye comes hame';

> See yonder pawkie shepherd,
>   That lingers on the hill,
> His ewes are in the fauld,
>   An' his lambs are lying still;
> Yet he downa gang to bed,
>   For his heart is in a flame,
> To meet his bonny lassie
>   When the kye comes hame;

or, more frankly comic, in 'Love is like a dizziness':

> To tell my feats this single week
>   Wad mak a daft-like diary, O!
> I drave my cart outow'r a dike,
>   My horses in a miry, O!
> I wear my stockings white and blue,
>   My love's sae fierce an' fiery, O!
> I drill the land that I should plough,
>   An' plough the drills entirely, O!
>
> O, love, love, love!
>   Love is like a dizziness;
> It winna let a poor body
>   Gang about his biziness!

And he kicks over sentiment and abandons himself to riotous absurdity in 'The Village of Balmaquhapple':

> D'ye ken the big village of Balmaquhapple,
> The great muckle village of Balmaquhapple?
> 'Tis steep'd in iniquity up to the thrapple,
> An' what's to become o' poor Balmaquhapple?

One thing we have to thank Hogg for is that like Burns, though not of course to the same extent, he preserved in common knowledge good tunes that would otherwise have been lost. He was able, owing to his visits to the Gaelic-speaking areas of Scotland, to explore a field which was not accessible to Burns, and some of his best finds are to be found in his *Jacobite Relics of Scotland* (1819-21), inserted as either 'modern versions' or as acknowledged renderings by Hogg of prose translations from Gaelic originals. With the tunes to guide him he produced some of the most popular of Scottish songs, things like 'Cam ye by Athol', 'Come o'er the stream, Charlie' and 'Flora Macdonald's Lament' [31]. They are genuine songs, not merely lyrics set to music, and they must be heard *as* songs to be fully appreciated. Oddly enough, Hogg himself does not seem to have fully realized this. He could not understand why 'Cam ye by Athol' had become popular, and declared that there could be no dispute that it was one of his worst songs; and he goes on to explain what he considered the inferiority of the words by stating that 'the air was given me by my friend Mr. Neil Gow, and to it I dashed down the words at random' [32]. 'Dashed down at random' must be an exaggeration, but no doubt he was concerned about fitting words to the tune, and not bothering much about producing poetry—which was all to the good.

Indeed, Byron's adjuration to Moore: 'Damn it, Tom, don't be poetical', might have been addressed to Hogg. A great deal of his non-lyrical work is negligible now because he was trying to 'be poetical', to write in the grand style. One can see this in his most ambitious work, *The Queen's Wake*, in which Queen Mary is entertained at Holyrood, during three nights, by the performances of seventeen bards. The Second Bard 'in a mellow tone and strong' pours the 'wild and dreadful song' of 'Young Kennedy', of which these lines are not an unfair sample:

> List, list to her tale, youth, levity, beauty;—
> O! sweet is the path of devotion and duty!—
> When pleasure smiles sweetest, dread danger and death,
> And think of Matilda, the flower of the Teith;

but the court, immediately after, is listening to the Bard of Fife,

> As, in a rugged northern tongue,
> This mad unearthly song he sung;

and the song is 'The Witch of Fife', one of the best things Hogg ever did, a wild, extravagant, comic ballad in which the absurd is raised to the pitch of the sublime and where the weird and the comic jostle each other in the most bewildering way. It reaches its climax when the old man who has followed his witch wife through the air, been captured in the Bishop of Carlisle's cellar, and been brought out to be burned at the stake, speaks the magic word that brings deliverance and mounts in the air with his face towards Fife:

> Till aince he cleirit the swirlyng reike,   [*smoke*
> He lukit beth ferit and sad;
> But whan he wan to the lycht blue ayr,
> He lauchit as he'd been mad.

> His armis war spred, and his heid was hiche,   [*high*
> And his feite stack out behynde;
> And the laibies of the auld man's cote   [*skirts*
> War wauffing in the wynde.   [*flapping*

It is Hogg completely uninhibited, at his wildest and daftest—and at his best.

But to most people—especially to those who, not being Scots, are not familiar with the songs—Hogg is known by two poems. One is 'A Boy's Song', a pretty thing made popular by its inclusion in numerous school anthologies. The other is his greatest work, his title to be saluted as 'the king of the fairy school of poetry': 'Kilmeny'. It is not on the highest level all through, and the large number of people who have only read anthologists' extracts from it have not missed much; but its best passages—there is no need to quote them—have an unearthly beauty, an innocent acceptance of the strange and supernatural, which gives him a special reserved seat—all to himself—on Parnassus. He has himself said the last word on the subject in the last stanza of the lines addressed to his 'loved harp' at the end of *The Queen's Wake*:

> Then will I seek the aged thorn,
> The haunted wild and fairy ring,
> Where oft thy erring numbers borne
> Have taught the wandering winds to sing.

Scott dominates his period; and all his Scottish poetic contemporaries, with the exception of Hogg, seem very small fry indeed. Most of them have been touched on in the preceding chapter and the others do not demand any detailed attention. The best known of them, Thomas Campbell, despite his statue in George Square, Glasgow, and despite 'Lord Ullin's Daughter' and 'Lochiel's Warning', belongs rather to English than to Scottish literature.

John Leyden [33] is remembered as the friend of Scott and his chief collaborator in *Minstrelsy of the Scottish Border*, as an orientalist, as an East Indian administrator, as an extraordinary example of how ability, energy and a passionate love of learning can triumph over unpropitious circumstances, and as a robust, plain-spoken, argumentative and wholly lovable personality. His short life and the dispersal of his energies over many fields prevented him from developing his poetic ability fully; but poetic ability he had. His *Scenes of Infancy* (published in 1803, when Scott was still known only as a ballad editor and as the author of a few imitation ballad poems) is written in classical couplets, but has a romantic colour in many of its lines worthy of Scott himself; as for instance where he refers to a tradition which Scott intended to work up into a prose romance, the legend of how Arthur and his knights lay asleep in a cavern in the Eildons to be awakened when some adventurous spirit sounded a horn:

> Say, who is he, with summons strong and high,
> That bids the charméd sleep of ages fly,
> Rolls the long sound through Eildon's caverns vast,
> While each dark warrior rouses at the blast,
> His horn, his falchion, grasps with mighty hand,
> And peals proud Arthur's march from Fairyland?

His ballad poems—'Lord Soulis', 'The Cout of Keilder', 'The Mermaid' and 'The Elfin King'—have the swing of traditional balladry, but never seem to have the magic moments of the greater ballads.

William Motherwell was another great ballad collector [34]. His *Minstrelsy, Ancient and Modern* is a valuable collection, to the compilation of which he brought considerable learning, especially in Old Norse literature. His own contributions to Scottish verse tend too often to be of the pathetically sentimental type, but the Mermaid in his ballad of that name shows much more smeddum:

> And my bouir is sklaitit wi' the big blue waves,
>   And paved wi' the yellow sand,
> And in my chalmers grow bonnie white flowers
>   That never grew on land.
> And have ye e'er seen, my bonnie bridegroom,
>   A leman on earth that would gi'e
> Aiker for aiker o' the red plough'd land,
>   As I'll gi'e to thee o' the sea?

One other may be mentioned—William Tennant, Professor of Oriental Languages at St. Mary's College, St. Andrews [35]. He wrote some good comic poems like 'The Tangiers Giant', an amusing bit of extravagant nonsense:

> When through the streets o' Tangiers town
> He gaed, spaziering up and down,   [*roaming*

Houses and kirks did tremmle;
O' his coat-tail the very wap   [*swish*
Rais'd whirlwinds wi' its flichterin' flap,   [*fluttering*
And garr'd auld lum-heads tummle.   [*made, chimney-cans*

'Anster Fair' should keep his memory green at least in the East Neuk of Fife—though whether it *has* been kept green is another story. It is an amusing burlesque describing elaborately—a little too elaborately perhaps—how Rab the Ranter won the hand of Maggie Lauder; but the most interesting thing about it from a technical and historical point of view is that it is written in *ottava rima*, but with the last line extended to an alexandrine, so that the close of the stanza may, as he says, 'be more full and sounding'. 'Anster Fair' was published in 1812. In 1817 John Hookham Frere used the *ottava rima*, unmodified, in *The Monks and the Giants*; and in 1818 Byron, following Frere, used it for his *Beppo*, and liked it so much that he employed it afterwards in *Don Juan* and *The Vision of Judgment*. It is unlikely that either Frere or Byron ever saw 'Anster Fair', but Tennant deserves credit for being the first of the nineteenth-century poets to see the comic possibilities of the long neglected stanza and for bringing it back into circulation.

IX

SCOTTISH POETRY IN THE LATER NINETEENTH CENTURY

DOUGLAS YOUNG

ONE of the ornaments of the Victorian Age, Matthew Arnold, proclaimed that 'by nothing is England more glorious than by her poetry'; and the claim remained true for his own time. Scotland too has had her glorious ages of poetry, in Gaelic, in Latin, in Scots. But in the later nineteenth century the main energies of the Scottish psyche flowed, not into verse, but rather into religious missionary work with David Livingstone, into Empire-building with Lord Dalhousie, into capitalism with Andrew Carnegie, into Socialism with Keir Hardie, into scientific invention, medicine, journalism, bureaucracy (as 'heids o' depairtments' in Whitehall), golf, engineering, distilling, into a hundred activities humdrum or humanitarian that are not intimately dependent on the pith and marrow of words, as is poetry. Let us never forget 'the primacy and potency of words' in all poetry. 'Bright is the ring of words', says Robert Louis Stevenson, 'when the right man rings them.' Yes, but words must not only ring true but be accepted as current coin over a viable area of exchange. And in this lay a basic weakness of the Scottish poetic apparatus of the Victorian Age: for the old mints, among the Lowland peasantry and small burgh dwellers, and among the Highland and island crofters, were going out of use; their old coinage was obsolescent. The factory system and the railway age and the British Empire and the gold standard and Free Trade had transformed the Scotland of Burns and of Duncan Bàn Macintyre into a big-city society whose norms in language and culture were becoming increasingly anglicized. This uprooting and switching around of the old fabric of Scottish society, and of the traditional languages of intercourse and literature, Lallans and Gaelic, inflicted a deep trauma on the Scottish people, which is largely accountable for the impotence of poetry in Victorian Scotland, in any medium at all.

The initial result of the railway age and of popular education was that Scots were enfeebled in their grip of Lallans and Gaelic without gaining any compensating power of utterance in standard English. The most widely current production was in a hybrid, or 'macaronic', Anglo-Scots, usually standard English with an infusion of conventional Scotticisms, well exemplified in the popular *Whistle-Binkie* anthologies [1]. This collection was the great stand-by of reciters at family parties, kirk *soirées*, Volunteer picnics and other Victorian forerunners of the MacFlannels and the Light Programme. Many of its pieces are yet orally current, for example 'Wee Willie Winkie', a bairns' bedtime rhyme by William Miller, a Glasgow cabinet-maker (1810-72), who regarded himself as sufficiently a member of the International Republic of Letters to address a consolatory poem to Victor Hugo (greatest poet of France—*Hélas!*) on the death of his favourite grandchild. The minor poets of this school often achieve powerful effects of pathos, and of pawkie humour, following certain directions exploited by Burns; but they are constantly liable to mawkish sentimentality, banality and bathos. See the volumes of the Glasgow Ballad Club (1885, 1898, 1908) for some comical specimens of pseudo-Tennysonian English and of *livresque* 'Lay of the Last Minstrel' balladry in archaistic Anglo-Scots.

Now and again one gets a genuine utterance in good colloquial Scots, more or less critically conscious of the literary tradition from Barbour and Dunbar through Fergusson and Burns. But such genuine utterances do not aim high in theme or style; they are *sermones repentes per humum*, of Kailyard topics, such as the auld dominie's auld breeks, or the new minister's new breeks; and the full resources of the language, be it Scots or Gaelic, are never exploited, for the paramount aim is that of immediate acceptability to a social circle concerned only to pass the time agreeably, and unwilling to 'rax its hairns' over words and phrases not in the daily *patois*.

This kind of background must be borne in mind when estimating the more important figures on the Scottish poetic scene of the half-century—for example Robert Louis Stevenson [2], who was born in 1850 and who may be thought the most important single influence emerging from that period and affecting later developments. Something of Stevenson's attitude on occasion appears from a letter to Henry James, dated from Bournemouth in January 1887 (from the house named *Skerryvore*, after the famous lighthouse). Louis writes:

I am also considering a volume of verse, much of which will be cast in my native speech, that very dark oracular medium: I suppose this is a folly, but what then? As the nurse says in Marryat, 'It was only a little one'.

My wife is peepy and dowie: two Scotch expressions with which I will leave you to wrestle unaided, as a preparation for my poetical works.

For the public eye, Stevenson gave us a more considered statement in the first poem of *Underwoods* (1887), 'Book II: In Scots', entitled 'The Maker to Posterity'. He imagines 'some ane, ripin' after lear,—Some auld professor or young heir' finding his volume.

> '*What tongue does your auld bookie speak?*'
> He'll spier; an' I, his mou to steik: [*ask, mouth, shut*

'No bein' fit to write in Greek,
    I wrote in Lallan,
Dear to my heart as the peat reek,
    Auld as Tantallon.

'Few spak it then, an' noo there's nane.
My puir auld sangs lie a' their lane,
Their sense, that aince was braw an' plain,
    Tint a' thegether,   [*lost*
Like runes upon a standin' stane
    Amang the heather.'

But he consoles himself with the reflection that the world is mortal anyway, and so are more new-fangled literary media.

'The tack o' mankind, near the dregs,
    Rins unco' law.   [*uncommonly*

'Your book, that in some braw new tongue,
Ye wrote or prentit, preached or sung,
Will still be just a bairn, an' young
    In fame an' years,
Whan the hale planet's guts are dung   [*whole, dashed*
    About your ears.'

It is already in 1955 obvious, with the growing preponderance of American as the normal colloquial form of English, that the standard English poetic diction of Stevenson's day is to most contemporary English-speakers about as unintelligible as Stevenson's Lallans. A cultured minority can appreciate Tennyson, a still smaller minority Browning; it is only a cultured minority that can fully relish Stevenson's work in Scots, or anyone else's. But why not attempt to make 'great verse unto a little clan'? That was, indeed, how Stevenson conceived his activity—as a piece of clannishness, patriotism if you like, where the *patria* is an intimate, comprehensible social ambience, not a vast impersonal sphere like *Deutschtum* or 'the English-speaking World'. In a note to *Underwoods* he remarks: 'I would love to have my hour as a native Maker, and be read by my own country-folk in our own dying language: an ambition surely rather of the heart than of the head, so restricted as it is in prospect of endurance, so parochial in bounds of space.'

But within the relatively 'parochial' frame of reference of Scots, Stevenson is national and metropolitan in his standpoint. He admits to compromising with traditional orthography to guide the bewildered Englishman, but eschews current attempts at precision, alike in spelling and in vocabulary.

Among our new dialecticians, the local habitat of every dialect is given to the square mile. I could not emulate this nicety if I desired; for I simply wrote my Scots as well as I was able, not caring if it hailed from Lauderdale or Angus, from the Mearns or Galloway; if I had ever heard a good word, I used it without shame; and when Scots was lacking, or the rhyme jibbed, I was glad (like my betters) to fall back on English. For all that, I own to a friendly feeling for the tongue of Fergusson and of Sir Walter, both Edinburgh men; and I confess that Burns has always sounded in my ear like something partly foreign. And indeed I am from the Lothians myself; it is there I heard the language spoken about my childhood; and it is in the drawling Lothian voice that I repeat it to myself. Let the precisians call my speech that of the Lothians. And if it be not pure, alas! what matters it? The day draws near when this illustrious and malleable tongue shall be quite forgotten: and Burns' Ayrshire, and Dr. Macdonald's Aberdeen-awa', and Scott's brave, metropolitan utterance will be all equally the ghosts of speech. Till then I would love to have my hour as a native Maker. . . . [3]

There are several points in this statement that deserve emphasis. 'The language spoken about my childhood. . . .' Stevenson's parents belonged to an opulent and much-travelled section of Edinburgh society, which, in the railway age, had opportunities of hearing and speaking an English much nearer to the standard of Court, Army, Oxford and Cambridge, than had been known to most of Walter Scott's generation. But the parents themselves had a good command of Scots, and the family servants would have little else. One of his nurses, for instance, was partial to a glass of gin in the local pub, while the infant Louis lay on the bar-counter, wrapped in his shawl. But his fourth, final and principal nurse, Alison Cunningham, daughter of a Fife fisherman, was the main influence, with her rhymes and tales and her admonitions of Hell-fire, recounted in the rich tongue of the Firth of Forth. It was to 'Cummie' that R.L.S. dedicated *A Child's Garden of Verses* (1885), as being

> My second Mother, my first Wife,
> The angel of my infant life.

For most poets of the Victorian age Scots was their childhood language, and had the special poignancy and pregnancy of the first words used to denote the enormously significant things that meet a child's first apperception. But they tended to restrict it in literary use to childish themes.

At Edinburgh Academy Stevenson was taught through the medium of English by a very gifted classicist, D'Arcy Thompson, later Professor of Greek at Galway, and father of Sir D'Arcy Wentworth Thompson, the great biologist. Scots was the tongue of the playground, not of study; and it is in Scots that Stevenson makes an anniversary set of verses, 'Their Laureate to an Academy Class Dinner Club'. Sir D'Arcy gave me a copy of *Nugae Canorae Medicae*, a curious compilation of Latino-Scottish festive songs of Edinburgh medicals, somewhat in the tradition of Drummond of Hawthornden's *Polemo-Middinia*, which shows well the general background of erudite dilettantism that determined much of the attitude to verse of Stevenson's contemporaries.

'It is in the drawling Lothian voice that I repeat it to myself.' Around his grandfather's manse at Colinton or the week-end cottage at Swanston on the Pentlands Stevenson knew the old country ways and speech of the Lothians, and much of his Scots verse relates to rustic themes, for instance 'A Lowden Sabbath Morn'. He had a command of 'Scott's brave, metropolitan utterance'; he regarded himself as in the eighteenth-century renaissance tradition, when he signed, in a letter to Henley, 'Robert Ramsay Fergusson Stevenson'; near his dying day he thought of himself as one of a trio with Fergusson and Burns as 'Scotland's three puir Rabbies': yet Stevenson never allowed the potentialities of his tradition and breeding, of his 'brave metropolitan utterance', their full head on adequate themes. Just as Tennyson kept the Lincolnshire dialect for relatively infantile and rustic topics, and wrote *In Memoriam* in standard literary English, so Stevenson, and the Scots between Burns and MacDiarmid generally, restricted their utterance in Lallans to a few genres, and sought to employ English for major flights—just as English was dominant in the pulpit, at the bar, in education, in politics and increasingly in every branch of commerce and in the social intercourse of the higher classes, once the railway age had increased their mobility.

Thus Lallans, the 'plain, braid Lallans' that Burns felt to be the proper tongue of an Ayrshire bard, was moved down from the curial status it enjoyed in the age of Dunbar and the great makars, and was treated consciously as a dialect, the 'Doric', compared with the more copious and refined Attic of standard English.* As some of us at school or college have turned verses in the linguistic amalgam of Theocritus, so Stevenson and others turned verses in the modes of Scots letters traditional from Allan Ramsay's revival; pawkie satires, for example, on the installation of an organ, *Scottice* 'a kist o' whistles', in 'Embro Hie Kirk' (*alias* St. Giles' Cathedral); or verse letters of a returned traveller:

---

* Compare Scott in 1822: 'Scotch was a language . . . different from English as the Venetian is from the Tuscan dialect of Italy, but it never occur'd to anyone that the Scottish, any more than the Venetian, was more vulgar than those who spoke the purer and more classical!—But that is all gone.'—*Editor*.

> Wi' whatna joy I hailed them a'—
> The hilltaps standin' raw by raw,
> The public house, the Hielan' birks,
> And a' the bonny U.P. kirks!

Rather pleasing is the fact that Stevenson at Mentone addressed his Russian hostesses, Mesdames Zassetsky and Garschine, in homely Lallans as they had made him feel at home.

> Kindly by them they gart me sit,   [*made*
> An' blythe was I to bide a bit.
> Licht as o' some hame fireside lit
>   My life for me.
> —Ower early maun I rise an' quit   [*too, must*
> This happy lee. [4]

Had Stevenson resolutely set himself to address his utterance *urbi et orbi*, to the city and the world, in Lallans, such was his capacity, in passion, learning and skill, that he might have anticipated Hugh MacDiarmid's Renaissance, and in circumstances much more propitious for its success among a wider public. In short stories like *Thrawn Janet*, and the unfinished masterpiece of a novel, *Weir of Hermiston*, R.L.S. showed what he could do in Lallan prose. His untimely death, at forty-four, is one of the disasters of Scottish literature, like that of Burns at thirty-seven and that of Fergusson at twenty-four. But Stevenson's work in verse, restricted though it was in scope, did have an effect, and may even be thought a major factor in the striving towards a renaissance of which MacDiarmid has been a product, as well as a new and even greater factor. 'As a literary and successful venture [Lallans] did not reach the outside world till Stevenson took it in hand; since when it has been cultivated to good purpose by many men' [5]. And, let it be added, by many women, notably Violet Jacob, Marion Angus, Helen Cruickshank and Edith Anne Robertson.

'*Cultivated* to good purpose . . .' Stevenson cultivated it with the taste and erudition of the literary professional man he was, with the same accuracy as his forebears brought to their engineering. He never turned out a slipshod job, even though most of his verse, Scots and English, was written in sickness or convalescence, when he lacked the emotional and physical resource for sustained prose-writing. The title *Underwoods* was borrowed from that Annandale Scot, Ben Jonson, to signify 'a miscellany of lesser poems of later growth, springing up between the more massive timber of his plays' [6]. Stevenson and his circle studied Charles d'Orléans, Villon and the like; they translated Latin poets for practice; they apprenticed themselves to the craft of verse; but they did not make it their prime aim in life to be poets, not the Scots among them at any rate, not even John Davidson. They were literary gentlemen, hobnobbers in the Savile Club and similar resorts, who occasionally turned off verses in an accomplished way.

Such cultivation had a long and still live tradition in Stevenson's Scotland, mainly typified by *Blackwood's Magazine*. Anglo-Scottish in linguistic medium, cosmopolitan and catholic in outlook, *Maga* circulated to every parish in Scotland, and to Ireland and Wales and Nonconformist England, whence students came to the Scottish universities at a time when the senior universities of England were restricted to those who subscribed the Thirty-Nine Articles. Sir Samuel Fergusson, for instance, a figure in the Young Ireland movement of the 1840s, is found turning Scots verses in the Allan Ramsay-Fergusson tradition continued by *Maga*. Stevenson, as an engineering student, later as a budding advocate, moved in an atmosphere of 'Scottish Renaissance' publicity, literary and political, that derived directly from the *Noctes Ambrosianae* milieu of Blackwood. Christopher North (Professor John Wilson) had a son-in-law, J. F. Ferrier, professor at St. Andrews and leading epistemologist, who edited in 1868 a four-volume collection of North's *Noctes*, contributed to *Maga* between 1822 and 1835. The same family had produced the novelist Susan Ferrier; and the last Ferrier boy, North's grandson, was a contemporary and companion in Edinburgh of Stevenson and of James Logie Robertson (1846-1922). In his *Poems* (1878) Robertson issued a verse manifesto 'On the Decadence of the Scots Language, Manners and Customs', and in 1881 began contributing to Scotland's leading newspaper, the *Scotsman*, over the pseudonym 'Hugh Haliburton', the series of 'Kailyaird' idylls in the tradition of Horace and Allan Ramsay which were cut out and pasted up in manses, schoolrooms, bothies all over Scotland, and in the trenches of the Western Front in the 1914-18 War. Moreover, in 1851 was founded the Association for the Vindication of Scottish Rights, joined corporately by many Scottish burghs; in 1859 the centenary of Burns was celebrated, somewhat surrealistically, by the gathering of funds to erect a monument to Sir William Wallace near the battlefield of Stirling Brig; in 1885 the Scottish Office was instituted by common consent of Whig and Tory, Gladstone and Salisbury; in 1886 the first Scottish Home Rule Association was formed to promote a Bill to set up a Scottish Parliament; and in 1888 Keir Hardie and Cunninghame Graham instituted the Scottish Labour Party, with Home Rule an aim concurrent with the idea of socialism, to which Stevenson was sometimes favourably inclined. In other words, there was a climate of opinion favourable to literary utterance in Scots, verse and prose. Indeed, there always had been during the nineteenth century, as witness a round robin signed by some forty noted versifiers, petitioning Captain Charles Gray (1782-1851) to collect in a volume the effusions of his lyric muse which had gratified them in various periodicals. This venerable officer of Marines, from Fife, served as lieutenant in the blockade of Venice, and addressed from shipboard in the Adriatic an 'Epistle to Mr. David Sillar, Burns' Irvine friend', in which he couthily conveys his homesickness for his 'auld thack house':

> And nae attention sall be spared
> To cultivate the green kailyaird;
> I'll plant my cabbage and potatoes,
> And be anither *Cincinnatus*!

The signatories of the round robin, which is in the National Library, indicate the literary ambience dominating our period: that best-seller Allan Cunningham, 'Oh, it's hame, hame, hame, it's hame I fain wad be . . .'; Alexander Rodger, 'My mither men't my auld breeks, And wow! but they were duddy, Oh!'; James Ballantine, who wrote 'Ilka blade o' grass keps its ain drap o' dew' and the curious documentary piece about the 'spunk-splitters' in an old Edinburgh *land*; Henry Scott Riddell, whose 'Scotland Yet' has the tumescence of Raeburn's portraits of chieftains, men looking like stags [7]; Robert Chambers, antiquary, administrator, author of 'Young Randal'; John Mitchell, who produced a singular, somewhat Stalinist piece on the St. Rollox Lum (the great chimney of Tennant's chemical works), except that its realism is rather liberal than socialist; Thomas C. Latto, author of 'The School Examination' and other Kailyaird verses; George Thomson, for whom Robert Burns collected and made singable ditties, and J. S. Burns, the poet's son; Robert Gilfillan, a leading evangelist and critic, and many others. One might almost say that part of the social background of Stevenson included a convention that Scots verse was an expected accomplishment, like the recital of smoke-room jests and limericks. Certainly it is on this level that most of the verse-making in Victorian Scotland proceeds, whether in Lallans or in English, or in different dilutions of the two.

The mere fact that a best-seller like Stevenson printed Lallan verses —cultivated and accomplished verses at that—gave some impetus and some status to the means of expression which, as J. M. Bulloch observed, had its effect a generation later. But Stevenson's main effort in verse was in English, in different directions, some of which proved seminal. It cannot be doubted, for example, that his poems for children inspired imitation. But his *vers d'occasion* are his main contribution, and they too had their influence—on A. E. Housman very plainly, perhaps on Thomas Hardy, and through them on many more. Housman was among those who paid tribute in verse on Stevenson's death, as did, among Scots, J. M. Barrie and John Davidson.

Barrie was a more successful playwright than Davidson, but his efforts in verse are most charitably forgotten. Not so John Davidson's poems [8], all the less to be neglected because Davidson was an influence on Hugh MacDiarmid, who wrote a poem on his death. Stevenson's verse is mainly of verbal interest for his deft handling of words and rhythms. The poetry of John Davidson is primarily important in the Scottish scene as a poetry of ideas, and it is as a poetry of ideas that it influenced, for example, MacDiarmid. Take the piece 'To the New Men' (from *Ballads and Songs*):

> . . . More than earth and sea
> Is a heart and eye:
> Gird yourselves, and try
> All the powers that be.
>
> . . . Love, and hope, and know:
> Man—you must adore him:
> Let the whole past go:
> Think God's thought before Him.
>
> Knowledge is power? Above
> All else, knowledge is love.
>
> Heat the furnace hot:
> Smelt the old-world thought
> Into dross and dew;
> Mould the earth anew.

Nietzsche and his Zarathustra are not far away from this poem, nor are many other of the dominant controversies of the age. Davidson felt himself to be 'A trembling lyre for every wind to sound', as he expressed it in 'A Ballad in Blank Verse of the Making of a Poet', where one gets glimpses of his tortured revolt from a predestination-ridden youth in Greenock

> where Old and New
> Weltered upon the border of the world.
> . . . this grey town
> That pipes the morning up before the lark
> With shrieking steam, and from a hundred stalks
> Lacquers the sooty sky; where hammers clang
> On iron hulls, and cranes in harbours creak,
> Rattle and swing, whole cargoes on their necks;
> Where men sweat gold that others hoard or spend,
> And lurk like vermin in their narrow streets.

Davidson's parents adhered to one of the smallest Calvinist sects, the Evangelical Union, which, under James Morison, had hived off from the United Secession, itself an attempt at coalition by various groups that had seceded from the Presbyterian Establishment, or Auld Kirk. Lyell's geology, Darwin's zoology and a great many other influences shook Davidson's faith in Morisonian doctrines and in the dominant values of Scottish society generally. After rebelling in Glasgow, he settled in London as a journalist, and soon achieved note in the 'Naughty Nineties'. Aubrey Beardsley, for instance, contributed a frontispiece and cover design to a volume of his plays published at Chicago with such significant titles as *Bruce, a Chronicle Play* (1886), *Smith, a Tragic Farce* (1888) and *Scaramouch in Naxos, a Pantomime* (1889). The *Spectator* wrote of him as 'a very singular dramatist indeed, and, as a poet, so full of curious and varied power that we have conceived the greatest interest as to his personality and his plans'. Israel Zangwill, in the *Cosmopolitan*, commented:

> John Davidson is a prodigal of every divine gift. . . . Fancy and imagination, wit and humour, fun and epigram, characterisation and creation and observation, insight and philosophy, passion and emotion and sincerity—all are his. . . . And all these glorious gifts have found vent in the most diverse artistic or inartistic shapes,—novels, dramas, eclogues, ballads, *Reisebilder*,—some written for the market, but the bulk in defiance of it. Of these products of a somewhat riotous genius, only a few have the hall-mark of perfection,—some pieces about music-halls, a sheaf of ballads, a bundle of songs, a set of eclogues,—but they are already quite enough baggage to go down to posterity with. And it is significant that all Mr. Davidson's chief successes are won when he surrenders himself to the inspiration of the modern.

A poetry of ideas, indeed; of contemporary ideas, modern in their day, some of them bad and many of them now as uninviting as yesterday's cold potatoes. Where is Davidson's reputation in 1955, on the eve of his centenary? *Spurlos versenkt?* Sunk without trace, as he drowned himself in the English Channel in 1909? Stevenson's poetic stature is being reassessed, on a somewhat higher level perhaps, for his English poems, than he has enjoyed in the last generation; for his Lallan poems I am contending that they are the most important single contribution of the Victorian age. Davidson's life and work will no doubt come in for revaluation before long, and perhaps an American university will finance an accurate and complete collected works. Meantime the contemporary estimates quoted may alert the reader, who might well consider further Professor R. M. Wenley's introduction to the New York edition of the poems (1924). At present Davidson is best known by a few pretty-pretty anthology pieces, like that on *London*, with its

> Afloat upon ethereal tides
> St. Paul's above the city rides!

Or the piece about the stag-hunt, 'When the pods went pop on the broom, green broom. . . .'

It is forgotten that Davidson, like his hunted stag, drowned himself in a channel. Though he moulted the metaphysical apparatus of his Morisonian background, he never lost the moral fervour and missionary zeal of the Victorian Scot, as witness not only the ballad 'Of the Making of a Poet', but those in sequence with it, 'Of the Exodus from Hounsditch', 'Of Heaven' and 'Of Hell'. It was such propagandist poetry that caused an English reviewer of *New Ballads* to say: 'We do not want Mr. Davidson's moralizings, we prefer his lyrics.' Yet some of the 'moralizings' in character are as vital to-day as ever, notably the soliloquy by the London clerk in 'Thirty Bob a Week', as good as anything Browning ever did. In his day Davidson was as well loved in Fleet Street as the lamented Ian Mackay of the *News Chronicle*, and his *Fleet Street Eclogues* reward a rereading. They have a many-sided gusto, like Sir Thomas Urquhart of Cromarty, or the *Noctes Ambrosianae*, that is as truly in Scottish tradition as the moral energy so boring to some Sassenachs. For period flavour the music-hall pieces have their appeal to Betjemaniacs like myself. The piece called 'Decadents', from the prologue to *Earl Lavender*, has a personally prophetic note:

> Though our eyes turn ever waveward,
>   Where our sun is well-nigh set;
> Though our Century totters graveward,
>   We may laugh a little yet.

2

Writing an essay on a miscellaneous bag of versifiers of a half-century in a particular country is rather like playing the rôle of the host at a sherry-party. Stevenson and Davidson are the most important people present, and represent the two main groups discernible—those who amuse themselves with words and those who are concerned to propagate ideas. As at parties, individuals occasionally switch allegiance and different satellites revolve around the main personalities. Transitorily, for example, midway between Stevenson and Davidson, observe Rudyard Kipling (1865-1936), whose admirable Lallan metaphysics in 'McAndrew's Hymn' (1892) reflect his mother's Scotch father's profession as a Calvinist minister. Davidson, true to his deracinated creed of being 'a mouthpiece for the creeds of all the world', even at one stage versifies a Kiplingesque jingoism in harmony with the Mafeking ochlocratic spirit which, for that matter, was echoed even in the breasts of some Fabians at the time.

Andrew Lang [9], too, is of the party, circling between the two groups. Stevenson met him first at Mentone in 1874 and described him to his father as 'a la-de-da-dy Oxford kind of Scot', which was indeed one fairly frequent aspect of Lang, but by no means the inner core of the man—as witness his 'Almae Matres' (scribbled in a hansom-cab), where he memorably conveys his deeper love for St. Andrews. A good classical scholar and anthropologist whose contribution to Homeric studies brought in a lot of daylight, and an erudite and discerning translator and critic competent in many languages and literatures, Lang did much to help Stevenson on his literary way, as later he helped George Douglas Brown (1869-1902) by promoting the recognition of *The House with the Green Shutters*. His *Poetical Works* contains many pieces of accomplished versification, for occasions grave and gay, with poems on angling, golf, cricket, ghosts, deft versions from various tongues, parodies, and some exercises in Lallans, notably the epistle (in the 'Standart *Habby*' measure) sent to Stevenson in the South Seas with a copy of Kirk's *Secret Commonwealth*, that curious product of Scottish *diablerie*. Lang had suffered a deep emotional wound in early life, and never let his feelings carry him very far in verse—'on guard against the promptings of his gipsy blood', as William Power put it; but there are among all the elegance and erudition a few well-felt pieces expressing *desiderium, Sehnsucht, ionndrainn*. Take, from 'Twilight on Tweed':

> Wan water from the Border hills,
>   Dear voice from the old years,
> Thy distant music lulls and stills,
>   And moves to quiet tears. . . .
> A mist of memory broods and floats,
>   The Border waters flow;
> The air is full of ballad notes,
>   Borne out of long ago. . . .
> Twilight, and Tweed, and Eildon Hill,
>   Fair and thrice fair you be;
> You tell me that the voice is still
>   That should have welcomed me.

In defiance of Mrs. Lang, and Sir Herbert Maxwell who corrected her proofs, I have put a capital B for 'Border', because Lang was essentially a Borderland Scholar Gipsy. From another Border he wrote 'Clevedon Church: In Memoriam H.B.'* after visiting Arthur Hallam's grave:

> Westward I watch the low green hills of Wales,
>   The low sky silver gray,
> The turbid Channel with the wandering sails
>   Moans through the winter day. . . .
> Gray sky—brown waters—as a bird that flies,
>   My heart flits forth from these
> Back to the winter rose of northern skies,
>   Back to the northern seas. . . .

---

* Henry Brown, his St. Andrews friend.

And I remember me how twain were one
  Beside that ocean dim,
I count the years passed over since the sun
  That lights me looked on him,
And dreaming of the voice that, save in sleep,
  Shall greet me not again,
Far, far below I hear the Channel sweep
  And all his waves complain.

On the Border of England and Scotland, of English and Scots, Lang wrote most fondly of Scottish matters, in accomplished English, with no great fervour and no great sense of purpose; he spent years, for example, on a financially unrewarding history of Scotland, entertaining, often wrong-headed, but a labour of love. Poetry, and particularly Lallan verse, occupied but a margin of his mind, as with most of those visible at this Victorian party. Lang was their leading publicist and critic, which makes it worth while quoting his preface to Charles Murray's *Hamewith* at the turn of the century, in 1900 [10]:

> To a patriotic Scot there is somewhat affecting in the echoes of very rich Scots which reach us across the African continent. . . . The Scots of Mr. Murray is so pure and so rich that it may puzzle some compatriots whose sentiments are stronger than their linguistic acquirements.* Indeed the poems beget a certain melancholy—'*I am never merry when I hear sweet music*'—from a world that is dead or dying, the world of Scott and Hogg, the world that knew not polluted streams and railways and motor-cars, and, worst of abominations, the gramophone. In a far-off land Mr. Murray retains the sentiment of that forgotten time, and is haunted by the scent of peat and bog-myrtle, the sound of old words that now are strange, the poverty that was not the mate of discontent. . . . Poetry more truly Scots than that of Mr. Murray is no longer written.

There we see the backward-looking defeatism common in the Victorian age towards the literary potentialities of Lallans, considered a medium fit only for rustic and infantile and humorous themes, while the main progressive ideas of the time were to be uttered in English. It was not till MacDiarmid's Drunk Man looked at the thistle in 1924 that a serious effort was made to galvanize Lallans into a modern medium for high-level and deep-level discourse on all the themes that engage an intelligent man's interest. Murray was the first poet to achieve a mass-public, with verse in a relatively pure and copious canon of Scots, though Stevenson's work in 1887 had raised its status

---

* Murray hailed from Alford in the strath of the Don in Aberdeenshire, where English had then made very little invasion of the colloquial speech of the landward folk.

with the literary world, as had the best-selling novelist George Macdonald with his *Scotch Songs and Ballads* (1893). But these are intellectually unexciting and somewhat pietistic, though genuine enough in feeling and sensitive in language.

The intellectual excitement was in English, in for example the effusions of James Thomson [11], who issued between March and May 1874, in the *National Reformer* of the atheist M.P. Charles Bradlaugh, his long and melancholy poem *The City of Dreadful Night*, the nearest mid-Victorian equivalent of *The Waste Land*. This is addressed to the desperate:

> If any cares for the weak words here written,
> It must be some one desolate, Fate-smitten,
> Whose faith and hope are dead, and who would die.

John Davidson was among those inspired by this nihilism; he ascribed to Thomson 'passion and intellect second only to Shakespeare'. To a reader in 1955 the work seems rather an inexhaustible quarry for excerpts to furbish a Scottish anthology of bathos and pretentiousness, a Caledonian *Stuffed Owl*. Consider for instance:

> At last the pulpit speaker simply said,
> With humid eyes and thoughtful drooping head:—
> 'My Brothers, my poor Brothers, it is thus;
> This life itself holds nothing good for us,
> But it ends soon and nevermore can be;
> And we knew nothing of it ere our birth,
> And shall know nothing when consigned to earth:
> I ponder these thoughts and they comfort me.'

Whaur's your Wullie Shakespeare noo? Why, just newly arrived at the sherry-party from Dundee, 'Sir William Topaz McGonagall, Poet and Tragedian, Knight of the White Elephant, Burma', as he styles himself on the broadsheets which he hawks about, forerunner of the journalist-poets of the 1920s and 1930s, and inspirer of an apocrypha still growing [12].

In an epistle to Charles Baxter, Stevenson remarks 'For I, that would be blythe and merry, Prefer to call Marsala sherry.' A host trying to pass off the Scottish versifiers of Victorian times as poets will be guilty of calling Marsala sherry. But some of their productions are tolerably palatable if you do not mind small beer, 'pennywheep'. But the interest is usually social or historical, rather than literary. Robert Buchanan (1841-1901), for example, cut a big figure in London journalism in his day, and is in many ways a sympathetic character, with his heart in the right place on big issues. But in 534 double-column pages of *Poetical Works* (1884) I found hardly five readable even once, apart from the well-known comic 'The Wedding of Shon Maclean' . . . 'And every

Piper was fou, Twenty Pipers together.' Like Davidson and Thomson, but on a lower level of poetic effectiveness, Buchanan addressed himself to political and religious controversies, as in 'God Evolving'—

> The God unborn, the God that is to be,
> The God that has not been since Time began.
> Hark, the low sound of Nature's agony
> Echo'd thro' life and the hard heart of Man

—or again, in 'The Image in the Forum', the much-quoted phrase 'Great Christus-Jingo, at Whose feet Christian and Jew and Atheist meet.'

A social-documentary versifier at almost equal length is the Edinburgh minister Dr. Walter Chalmers Smith (1824-1908), whose *Poetical Works* (1902) fill 624 double-column pages in slightly larger print. This Victorian mass-production breathes quite a different air, calm and kindly, retrospective for the most part, as in 'Miss Penelope Leith':

> Last heiress she of many a rood,
> Where Ugie winds through Buchan braes—
> A treeless land, where beeves are good,
> And men have quaint old-fashioned ways.

The reverend doctor contrives to intone a Scottish accent of the mind into his English. He edited, with a memoir, the *Verses* of Sheriff Alexander Nicolson (1827-93), favourite among which is 'Skye': 'My heart is yearning to thee, O Skye! Dearest of islands!' Alexander Smith [13], the author of that delightful and in part poignant volume, *A Summer in Skye* (1865), aimed high as a poet and achieved great success with his poems 'Barbara' and 'Glasgow'. In the latter he came to grips with what those using Lallans at that time commonly eschewed, the big-city culture of Victorian Scotland.

> Before *me* runs a road of toil
>   With my grave across . . .
> I know the tragic heart of towns.
>
> Instead of shores where ocean beats
> I hear the ebb and flow of streets.
>
> Black Labour draws his weary waves
> Into their secret-moaning caves;
>   But with the morning light
> The sea again will overflow
> With a long weary sound of woe,
>   Again to faint in night.
> Wave am I in that sea of woes,
> Which, night and morning, ebbs and flows.

Hugh Macdonald (1817-60), a tremendously popular poet of the Clydeside, carried into the big city something of the attitude of the old peasantry, as in 'My Ain Hearthstane':

> My hame is but a lowly bield,
> A wee bit butt and ben,
> A kame intil a croodit byke
> That grandeur disna ken;
> Yet Pride within her lofty wa's,
> Amid her menial train,
> Micht envy me the treasures
> O my ain hearthstane.

Acceptance of the Victorian order is a common enough attitude, as in 'The Factory Girl' of James Easson (1833-65), from his *Select Miscellany of Poetical Pieces* (1856), originally circulated in hundreds of thousands through the *People's Journal*:

> In a thrifty dress of an homely guise,
> All iron'd, smooth, and clean,
> The factory girl, at the brief meal hour,
> Is always to be seen.
> And there is ever on her face
> That look which seems to say,
> 'Industry is the noblest plan
> By which to live you may'.

But verses of social criticism are also to be found, like 'The Last Sark' by Ellen Johnston (c. 1835-73), who died in the Barony Poorshouse of Glasgow, having received £50 from the Royal Bounty fund:

> Gude guide me, are ye hame again, and hae ye got nae wark?
> We've naething noo tae pit awa, unless your auld blue sark.
> My heid is rinnin round aboot, far lichter nor a flee:
> What care some gentry if they're weel though a' the puir wad dee?

For this and similar pieces see *The Bards of Angus and the Mearns*, *The Harp of Renfrewshire*, Mr. Edwards of Brechin's seventeen volumes of *Modern Scottish Poets*, and other regional or temporal collections usually to be picked up on street-barrows or second-hand stalls [14]. With the current craze for Victoriana—paper-weights, what-nots (there is even a Town Councillor in one of our grave Scots cities who collects (*horresco referens*) nineteenth-century ladies' *lingerie*) —it may be that some will relish odd items of versification extractable from 'wee buikies' printed at Kirkintilloch or Duns, Lesmahagow or Auchtermuchty. Consider, for instance, *Poems: Chiefly in the Buchan Dialect*, by James Davidson, New Pitsligo, printed at the *Banffshire*

Journal office in 1861 and dedicated to Sir Chas. Forbes, Bart., of Newe. There is an atmosphere about

> When projects that we've cherished lang gang a' to crocanition,
> What can sic crosses heal as does a social pinch o' sneeshin'?
> An' when at kirk on Sunday we maun hearken sleepy stuff,
> What keeps us frae 'the lan' o' nod'?—our social pinch o' snuff.

There are hundreds of volumes, comparatively few of which I have scanned, through which the quest for period-flavour pieces may be agreeably pursued at odd moments; and the poets' corners of local newspapers would yield certain gleanings among the advertisements for ferrets, tomb-stones and secondhand pianos. A noble series of Ph.D. theses might even emerge from efforts to estimate the influence of various poets—Thomas Hood, for example, or Walt Whitman. Both influences are visible in James Young Geddes (born 1850), author of *The Spectre Clock of Alyth*, &c. (1891). In imitation of Hood's 'Stitch, stitch, stitch, . . .' Geddes produces a 'Thrift, thrift, thrift. . . .' After Whitman's manner he indites a document on a jute-manufacturing firm, 'Glendale & Co.':

> The atmosphere permeated with dust.
> The faces of the people engrained with dirt and grime,
> Their voices husky with the fluff settled on the throat and lungs.
> It is questionable indeed if the townspeople have any real personal identity at all;
> If they are not really themselves part and parcel a product of Glendale & Co.;
> Questionable if its fluff is not also on their souls, if the interests of the great Firm have not dimmed their mental vision, and clouded their moral perceptions.

To our age unpretentious pieces reflecting the life and work of the people have more life and interest than most of the polished *belles-lettres* achieved by persons of higher literary accomplishment, such as the ninth Earl of Southesk (1827-1905), a man of fine intelligence and character, whose poems in Tennysonian modes scarcely come alive; or as William Sharp, *alias* Fiona Macleod (1856-1905), a best-seller of Celtic Twilight and the like in prose and metre; or as Sir George Douglas, Bart., one of those devotees of the Muse who help to kindle the interest of others but miss the sacred flame themselves. Others survive by an odd piece, William Bell Scott (1811-90) with 'The Witch's Ballad', or Principal Shairp of St. Andrews (1819-85) with the song 'The bush aboon Traquair'. The Rev. Principal Story of Glasgow is worth looking at for his facetious verses on kirk politics, *Nugae Ecclesiasticae* (1884). David Gray, the poet of 'The Luggie', friend of the critic and novelist Robert Buchanan and befriended by

Lord Houghton, was lamented at his early death as 'the Scottish Keats'; and another genuinely poetic personality who died untimely was Thomas Davidson, from Oxnam in Roxburghshire, bred for the U.P. Kirk [15].

Lowland Scots seem to have been unduly interested in the personalities of their *littérateurs*, as witness the Burns Cult; and there has been a great deal of ado about ploughman-poets, fisherman-poets, collier-poets, chimneysweep-poets and the like, without parallel in the *Gàidhealtachd*, where status does not depend on occupation but on the folk from whom you spring and the individual merits you can show. Of the poets who secured adventitious publicity through their trade probably the best is Alexander Anderson (1845-1909), seventh child of a Nithsdale quarryman, who taught himself Greek, Latin, French, Italian, Spanish and German while working on the railway as a 'Surfaceman', over which pseudonym he sent poems in Scots and English to the *People's Friend*, and in the uniform of which office he had himself photographed for his *Songs of the Rail* (1878) [16]. Thousands of households must still use his 'Bairnies, cuddle doon', in some oral version or other; but he was also a poet of ideas, as in 'The Spirit of the Times':

> Where shall he come from, the poet, whose fire
> Shall place on his wild, rough page
> The spirit that lurks and forever works
> In the breast of this mighty age? . . .
> Then, hurrah! for our higher fellows that work
> With this thought and its Titan powers,
> And cut through the jungle of creeds and fools
> A path for this planet of ours.
> And hurrah for this nineteenth century time—
> What the future may grow and be!
> Ah, God! to burst up from the slumber of death
> For one wild moment to see!

Another popular Border poet, of fine literary quality, is J. B. Selkirk —James B. Brown, (1832-1904), a Selkirk manufacturer—who uses Scots and English with equal sensibility on affecting themes such as 'Death in Yarrow', about the widower struggling to rear his motherless boy:

> For my hairt's wi ane abune,
> And the ane is growin twa,
> He's dwined sae sair, sae sune,
> Sin his mither gaed awa.

Some of the exponents of the Christopher North and James Hogg attitude to versification, with *Maga* for their forum, flourished well into our period, like the judge Lord Neaves (1800-76) and Thomas Tod Stoddart (1810-80). Thomas Aird (1802-76) is a belated Scottish Wordsworthian. Hew Ainslie (1792-1878) was a Burnsian who settled in America, still rhyming in Lallans or a mixture of Scots and English, while Adam Lindsay Gordon (1833-70) became the laureate of the Australian settlers. Poets of ideas include Sir Ronald Ross (1857-1932), discoverer of a way to deal with that 'million-murdering death', malaria, and Ronald Campbell Macfie, who wrote an obituary piece for John Davidson and strove in verse to deal with the problems of evolution and other current controversies (in, for example, *War*, 1918).

Gravitating between Davidson's poetry of ideas and Stevenson's 'skilful mosaic of robust words' (as Lang called it), we note Robert Reid, *alias* Rob Wanlock, whose 'Kirkbryde' is still often recited (see *Poems, Songs and Sonnets*, 1894, for verse both Scots and English). Scotland had a forerunner of W. H. Davies in Roger Quin, an Irish Scot from Dumfries, who passed his time between strolling the Borders in summer, with flute and concertina, and rhyming away the winter in a Glasgow model lodging-house.

From the far Shetland the Norn tongue was used for poetic utterance by J. J. Haldane Burgess (1863-1927), James Stout Angus, Basil Ramsay Anderson (1861-88, grand-uncle of Willa Muir) and others; and the Orcadian David Vedder (1790-1854) used a dialect much closer to standard Scots. Amusing verses in Highland English were among the deft productions of Professor William Edmondstoune Aytoun (1813-65), and student songs were a feature of the period—some by Professor John Stuart Blackie (1809-95) of Aberdeen and Edinburgh, but the best by Robert Fuller Murray (1863-93), in *The Scarlet Gown: being Verses of a St. Andrews Man* (1891), with his prefatory hope that they would be found 'pleasant, if not over-exciting'.*

If you are cheerful enough to call Marsala sherry, or if you happen to like Marsala anyway for its own sweetish-roughish sake, there is much in Victorian Scottish verse that may be found 'pleasant, if not over-exciting'. But it is about the lowest ebb of Scottish poetry since John Barbour, and there is no need to prolong a chapter already likely

---

* An admiring posterity may consider the later nineteenth century primarily as the age that gave birth to the original nucleus of that fluctuating concatenation of quatrains, known to many in every corner of the English-singing world as 'The Ball of Kirriemuir'. It is regrettable that no canonical text, with an adequate *apparatus criticus*, is available anywhere in print, or in a manuscript in a public library, to which reference might be made. Although somewhat heterogeneous accretions have resulted from the greatly extended currency given to the saga by the Boer War, the Kaiser's War and Hitler's War, judicious *Quellenforschung* and *Überlieferungsgeschichte* would probably establish a date for the *Ur*-text somewhere in the lifetime of R. L. Stevenson.

to be the dullest in this book (unless for the student of clinical mind alert to discern the stirrings of renaissance). Yet even a backwater or a seapool may offer stimulus to the attentive eye, and Mr. John Betjeman has rescued one neglected volume from this period that suddenly brings home to us the contemporaneity of McTaggart and the Glasgow School. William Renton's *Oils and Watercolours* (1876) are, he writes, 'full of daring metrical experiment and beautiful nature observation'. One about a sea pool is short enough to quote:

> Pool from sea,
>   Sea-rocks slope,
>   Sea-weeds grope
> Into thee,
>   Whose the opal-lemon is
>   Above the blood anemones.

Groping among sea-weeds at slack water is not the most exciting, nor the most pleasant, type of locomotion that our literary history affords; but it can have rewarding moments and glimpses. Though the drinks at this party have not been of the finest vintages, the people have, on the whole, been interesting and agreeable; and *Scotus sum: Scotici nil a me alienum puto.*

X

THE MODERN MAKARS

GEORGE KITCHIN

I

THE historian of modern English poetry may be tempted to regard poetry written before the 1914-18 War as merely marking time till the 'Liberators'—Pound, Eliot, D. H. Lawrence and Edith Sitwell—began to make headway in the early twenties. The temptation is to be resisted, for it would do less than justice to Housman, the later Hardy, De La Mare and others. Scottish poetry would perhaps not suffer so much from the playing down of what was written before Hugh MacDiarmid appeared on the scene; but one has to take account of that pre-war writing, if only as a preparation for the movement he inaugurated. And of course there is a wealth of 'couthie' Scots verse, some excellent and most of it more acceptable to the common reader than anything the Scottish 'renaissance' has produced.

At the start of the century we had Charles Murray's immensely popular *Hamewith* [1], precisely timed for the period of the Boer War, our first national awakening. For recitation at *soirée* or smoker there was nothing like it. Thoughts of home and the rich Donside dialect warmed the heart; but though, as Andrew Lang claimed, it gave local verse a lift above even Stevenson's admirable efforts in Lallans, *Hamewith* hardly counts as poetry.

Nostalgic or humorous folk-poetry is constantly being produced, but not till Violet Jacob and Marion Angus [2] published their belated volumes during or after the 1914-18 War did it acquire the delicacy of art. Sir Alexander Gray [3] in his shrewd translations from Heine and the German balladists also raised vernacular verse to a new power. Even the practitioners of more self-conscious Scots verse—Maurice Lindsay, Douglas Young and others—occasionally rejoice our hearts with poems of this homelier sort which take us further into the Scottish psyche than their more ambitious efforts.

Alongside this permanent local type of writing, to which I shall return, there were in the early years of the century other, more artful modes striving to be born. One was what might be called the pre-Raphaelite mode: that is, the recovery of the note of chivalric romance by means of ornate diction and heraldic symbols. English poetry had passed through this phase a generation or more previously, with Morris, Rossetti and Swinburne. It had run to a close in the earlier Yeats, just when certain Scottish writers took it up—none more magniloquently than the Aberdeen poetess Rachel Annand Taylor [4]. Mrs. Taylor published *Poems in English* in 1904, and followed up with *Rose and Vine*. Her work is interesting as showing how far a Scottish writer could persevere in the dead mode:

The Magi

Male-incense, mighty mirrhs they gave,
　　Shut in enamel and fine gold,
Then o'er the porphyry sand returned
　　To their gem-smouldering life of old.

Their aumbry-doors of carven pearl
　　More nards and splendours kept for them;
Their souls considered other gods
　　Beside the child of Bethlehem.

The game for her, as for Rossetti, was to discover 'stunning words for poetry'. There was nothing Scottish in her muse. In vain did Hugh MacDiarmid beg her to leave this arras work and be the poet she was meant to be. And yet over the movement he began there hangs the reproach of the search for 'termes celicall'.

It was Lewis Spence [5], however, who started the habit of making a *florilegium* of such terms, collected from the old makars and employed by their modern disciples to give colour to their Scots. Mr. Spence, we feel, was half amusing himself in these exercises (excellent pastiches they are); for only two years or so ago he ruefully pleaded guilty to having encouraged others on this path. His patience with 'renaissance' poetry had grown very thin. This will give some idea of his 'exercises', hoax words included:

The Pavone

Now in the none the prowde pavone, his ryall rone,　　[*noon, peacock*
　　Appollo of the fowlis with lumis clere,
With princelie pretts his fedderis frets, thir amulets　　[*tricks, feathers*
　　Quhilk maydens luve but luvaris hald in fear,
Like Tytan owre the gowand swaird he gangs,　　　　　　[*daisied*
　　Ane gramest galleoun tynsellit of sprangs.　[*warlike, streaks* or *shades*

Mr. Spence could write in natural Scots too, and to some purpose, as witness his *Phoenix and Other Poems* and *Weirds and Vanities*. He was mistaken, of course, in imagining that 'renaissance' poetry is a mosaic of fine old words. A rebirth of the nation, no less, was the declared aim of the new poets.

To sentimental or humorous verse (which in its finest practitioners may be aristocratic) and the pre-Raphaelite mode we should add another kind which has some importance for the Scottish renaissance and particularly for MacDiarmid. This is the poetry of the proletarian revolt against the conditions to which industrialism has reduced the masses. Mr. Douglas Young's admirable anthology *Scottish Verse 1851-1951* has made us acquainted with a good deal of forgotten verse of this sort; and we can measure the change of tone from a religious acquiescence in the scheme of things to something like a challenge by comparing Keir Hardie's 'Evening Prayer' (which might have been written by the author of 'There is a happy land') and John Davidson's 'Thirty Bob a Week' with its defiant close:

> But the thing is daily done by many and many a one
> And we fall, face forward, fighting on the deck.

Davidson died in 1909—his defiance, as yet a blind cry, became explicit in MacDiarmid, who took more from Davidson than is generally known [6]. To carry the message to the workers was the aim of MacDiarmid's fiery verse. From Davidson's major poems he may also have acquired the ambition of making his later poetry scientific: but to illustrate the evolutionary process with lecture-room precision was a sad diversion of his powers [7].

If Lewis Spence and Rachel Annand Taylor artificially reconstructed episodes in the romantic past, other bards handled the harp of the north more robustly. Will H. Ogilvie [8] revived the stark moss-trooping vein of Scott—'Ho for the blades of Harden! Ho for the ring of steel!' Such verse corresponds to England's 'Drake's Drum' and 'Glorious Devon', but it needs a Kipling to give it life. John Buchan [9] gave a powerful impetus to this kind in novel and song.

Of this mass of poetry only the work of Marion Angus and Violet Jacob looks like surviving, and that because of superior art applied to the perennial folk-themes. Both poets have their fond partisans, but of the two Marion Angus probably wrote the more durable verse. For one thing, she could on occasion revive the past with a beautiful art which is not pastiche, as in 'Alas! Poor Queen!':

> She was skilled in music and the dance
> And the old arts of love
> At the court of the poisoned rose
> And the perfumed glove,
> And gave her beautiful hand
> To the pale Dauphin
> A triple crown to win—
> And she loved little dogs
>   And parrots
> And the red-legged partridges
> And the golden fishes of the Duc-de-Guise
> And a pigeon with a blue ruff
> She had from Monsieur d'Elbeuf.

She can express courtly feeling as well as popular, but even in her popular verse she has an artful reticence; and altogether she mines at a greater depth of feeling than Violet Jacob. One may say this without being ungrateful to the latter, whose successive volumes from *Songs of Angus* onwards enriched the treasury of Scottish song without showing the slightest influence of the renaissance. It is perhaps churlish to note that her English work betrays a love of cliché and banality of phrase incredible in one who is so sure in her Scots writing [10]. Marion Angus too is capable of incredible lapses in both English and Scots. But unlike Violet Jacob she seems, in *The Turn of the Day* (1931), to be influenced by the new movement in Scottish poetry. In 'The Broken Brig', for example:

> Twa o' us met whaur the waters spring
> This ae night o' a
> Ane to rage and ane to sing
> At onding o' the snaw.   [*fall*
>
> The twain o' us wi' never a moon
> In the blown-drift and the sleet,
> Ane wha gaed like thistle doon
> Ane wi' silly feet.

If there is a Scottish *Shropshire Lad* it is to be found in the poetry of Marion Angus.

These ladies continued to delight their readers well into the period after the 1914-18 War, but they were really survivors of the pre-war era. This holds good, too, for Sir Alexander Gray, whose original verse in Scots might have been written by any humoursome Scot with a turn for dialect and a warm feeling for his ain folk. But his translations into Scots are the finest, shrewdest versions to be found in this sort, and—best tribute—have the air of original work. And how good his notes to *Arrows* are!

2

Hugh MacDiarmid [11] 'sodgered 'neath the Grecian sky' in the 1914-18 War, and it was then that the Lady Caledonia with

> . . . small swift smile elate
> Sealed me the servant of a cause forlorn,
> Whose dream and whose desire I cannot tell.

The Scottish renaissance came of that encounter. At home MacDiarmid first appeared before the public as an anthologist. *Northern Numbers* was to do for modern Scottish verse what Edward Marsh was doing for English: it was to be 'an annual of the new Scottish poetry rather than an anthology'. Its three issues (1920, 1921 and 1923) are interesting for the successive purges he effected; for he meant to get rid of the poets whose names were household words. In *Lucky Poet*, his literary autobiography, he justified his break with influential people who had smiled on his early efforts, on the ground of 'the necessary development of Scottish poetry'. In 1925 his *Sangschaw* disclosed probably the finest lyric impulse in the range of Scots verse. 'The Watergaw' is famous, but it stands repeating:

> Ae weet forenicht i' the yow-trummle*   [*wet dusk*
> I saw yon antrin thing,   [*occasional*
> A watergaw wi' its chitterin' licht   [*faint rainbow, shivering*
> Ayont the on-ding;   [*fall of rain*
> An I thocht o' the last wild look ye gied
> Afore ye dee'd!
>
> There was nae reek i' the laverock's hoose   [*smoke, lark's*
> That nicht—and nane i' mine;
> But I hae thocht o' that foolish licht
> Ever sin' syne;   [*since*
> An' I think that mebbe at last I ken
> What your look meant then.

Penny Wheep was something of a let-down; but a year later the long poem *A Drunk Man Looks at the Thistle* established him as the first poet in Scotland. Douglas Young expressed the mind of his confrères when he recognized it as

> . . . at last the authentic voice of Scotland
> *La voix du sang, de mon sang.*

Here as usual MacDiarmid puts every difficulty in our way—not in his language, which is much easier than that of modern English poetry, but in the lack of architectonic, lack of direction and emphasis. But the poetry is there in full measure. The drunk man hiccups up the most mordant satire of modern Scotland:

> They canna lear, sae canna move   [*learn*
> But stick for aye to their auld groove
> —The only race in history who've
>
> Bidden in the same category
> Frae start tae present o' their story
>   And deem their ignorance their glory.
>
> The mair they differ, mair the same,
> The Wheel can whummle a' but them,   [*upset*
> —They ca' their obstinacy 'Hame'.

But there are also lyrics of piercing note and metaphysical passages of passion—and all in Scots.

---

* ewe-tremble, cold spell after the shearing.

As disorderly a medley, *To Circumjack Cencrastus*, has as fine an edge of invective. The assistant-editor (MacDiarmid, that is) curses his boss—and in him the whole bourgeois set-up:

> Curse on the system that can gie
> A coof like this control o' me   [*dullard*
>
> Curse his new hoose, his business, his cigar,
> His wireless set, and motorcar,
> Alsatian, gauntlet-gloves, plus-fours and wife,
> —A' thing included in his life;
> And abune a' his hearty laughter,
> And—if he hes yin—his hereafter.

Épater le bourgeois may be a first step towards communism. MacDiarmid's *First Hymn to Lenin* closed his account with all but the few who judge merely by the poetry. To this period, however, belong also the grave reflective poem written for his old English master George Ogilvie, 'A moment in Eternity', and 'The Seamless Garment' addressed to the workers—propaganda, no doubt, but so was Shelley's 'Masque of Anarchy'.

Scots Unbound is 'primarily an exercise of delight in the Scots sense of colour' which shows the more playful or virtuosic side of his genius; but *Stony Limits*, despite its fine tribute to Charles Doughty and the eight Shetland lyrics in Scots, first employs the discursive polyglot English which his disciples deplore as a retreat from the vernacular and a descent into eccentric ideologies which make his later work, despite brilliant passages, largely unreadable. For MacDiarmid had now become the grand heresiarch, and his retreat in 1933 to the isle of Whalsay in the Shetlands exposed him to every wind of doctrine. In *Direadh I*, the first of the dinosaur poems he was writing there, he says, 'I turn from the poetry of beauty to the poetry of wisdom'; that is, of politics, philosophy and evolutionary science. At the same time he was confirmed in the view that Gaelic was the *Ur*-language of Scotland, and the vernacular merely a temporary medium.

He had his megaphone in the form of the periodical *The Voice of Scotland*, which ran to five numbers from 1938-9 and kept the movement in the public mind [12]. It needed it, for the news out of Scotland was not good. The public repudiation in 1936 of the aims of the movement by Scotland's finest critical intelligence, Edwin Muir, was a blow which the testimonial to MacDiarmid, influentially signed, did little to soften. A testimonial signed by (among others) Sir James Barrie was for him worthless. But a gleam of light did shine on his path that year which made him sing like Simeon of old:

> At last, at last, I see her again
> In our long-lifeless glen,

Eidolon of our fallen race,
Shining in full renascence grace,
She whose hair is plaited
Like the generations of men,
And for whom my heart has waited
Time out of ken.

This was the publication of a volume of Gaelic poetry by Sorley
Maclean and George Campbell Hay. Here was something which would
take the movement quite out of the range of the contemporary English
movement with its Bloomsbury cults. Maclean abetted him in his
sullen hatred of southern fashions; and this soon became an article of
faith with the whole clan.

It is impossible here to catch up with the poet's heresies. *Lucky Poet*
and the excerpts given there from his long unpublished poems tell us
all we want to know. 'The Kind of Poetry I want' is perhaps the best
of these excerpts, but there are fine passages in all of them—if only
they could be thinned of the screeds of prose. But to show that the poet
survives, his latest volume, *A Kist o' Whistles* (1947), though not a
conciliatory gesture, contains 'On Reading Professor Ivor Williams's
Canu Aneirin in Difficult Days', which is grave and passionate and
marred only by the touches of bathos ('As the Scotsman says') which
he avoided in lyric alone. Here also is the 'Cornish Heroic Song for
Valda Trevlyn', opening in fine Browningesque manner:

Come let us drink, beloved. You have brimmed my glass
With a supernaculum of cherry bounce
(More chia, as the Chinese say, than Chian is,
Or Chianti, and beyond reckoning, finer far
Than even the Choan wine my friend Sturge Moore has sung
In one of the first longish poems my boyhood knew).

Witch, you foreknew my mood tonight, I see you wear
The golden lunula I had copied for you
From the finest of the four found in Cornwall yet
Linking the Early Bronze Age and the Twentieth Century.

Here also is his poem 'Kulturkampf', a blue-print of the Scotland to be
and the most messianic of his works.

It is worth noting that MacDiarmid alone of the new makars has
attracted attention from outside. Denis Saurat, the French critic,
referring appreciatively to his work, first spoke of a Scottish renaissance. C. Day Lewis talked in *A Hope for Poetry* of 'this admirable
stuff'; T. S. Eliot is quoted (by MacDiarmid) as sympathetic, and David
Daiches, frank partisan of the school, as saying in *Poetry Chicago* that
Scottish literature 'has been set again in that European (not English)

context where it flourished most in the past'. In *Lucky Poet* MacDiarmid canvasses other notable European voices in praise of the movement, but this looks a little like touting. [See further p. 324.]

3

Leaving the popular poets—Marion Angus, Violet Jacob, Sir Alexander Gray and others—to croon over their harps or spinning-wheels (which they did uncommonly well), we discern in the years following the 1914-18 War several emergent prows besides MacDiarmid's. There were William Soutar, bedfast alas in his native Perth; Edwin Muir, who, for reasons indicated in *The Story and the Fable*, commenced poet at thirty-five instead of twenty-five; Andrew Young, whose first volume appeared unnoticed in 1910 but who belongs to the post-war period; William Jeffrey, released from war service to devote himself to journalism and poetry. A. D. Mackie, people's poet, comes a little behind this post-war group.

There was no compulsion in the 1920s to write in Scots, with its traditional limitation to 'couthie' or 'eerie' verse. MacDiarmid and Mackie alone adopted the vernacular as a vocation. Muir toyed with it, rather ineptly for him, in his early ballads. Jeffrey discovered his considerable gift in Scots only in his late period; and although Soutar is remembered for his Scots verse, only two of his nine volumes are in dialect.

Nevertheless, Soutar [13] is rightly associated with the renaissance. It is true that he used the vernacular very much as it had been traditionally employed, for semi-humorous or gnomic verse. But his rich, unadulterated dialect and his ardent feeling for the old makars enabled him to revive something of the more rustic strain in sixteenth-century poetry—in, for example, Henryson's *Fabillis*. 'The Auld Tree', which some regard as his best poem (modesty I suppose persuaded his editor MacDiarmid to omit it from Soutar's collected works), affirms his faith in the revival of the makar tradition. Scots is the medium in which the true makar will sing,

> Though aa his feres were fremit men   [*fellows, strangers*
> Wha cry: Owre late, Owre late.   [*too*

But I do not think Soutar advanced at all on the path made by Mac-Diarmid. The best of his poems belong either to the humorous beast category, or to that well-marked mediaeval kind the burlesque poem on this side blasphemy, the 'humour of the saints'. His humour and his authentic Scots, with no infusion of invented or literary diction, made this department of his work a genuine addition to Scottish poetry. *Seeds in the Wind* is, or ought to be, a classic. Nor should his excellent

poems in the ballad kind be forgotten, for one may believe with Edwin
Muir that the ballad is still the most haunting strain in our poetry.

> O! shairly ye hae seen my love
> Doun whaur the waters wind:
> He walks like ane wha fears nae man
> And yet his e'en are kind.
>
> O! shairly ye hae seen my love
> At the turnin' o' the tide;
> For then he gethers in the nets
> Doun by the waterside.
>
> O! lassie I hae seen your love
> At the turnin' o' the tide;
> And he was wi' the fisher-folk
> Doun by the water-side.
>
> The fisher-folk were at their trade
> No far from Walnut Grove;
> They gether'd in their dreepin' nets
> And found your ain true love.

Beside his vernacular work Soutar's English verse is dead. The one
longish poem he wrote, 'Stanzas on Time', is a tolerable imitation of
Spenser's *Fowre Hymnes* and no more. His imagery is mostly *cliché*
and, as his editor says in a capital introduction, 'he never took the mad
leap into the symbol'. But what Scots poet other than Edwin Muir
does? The tributes to Soutar, however, show his influence on the
younger men.

Chronologically one should mention A. D. Mackie [14] here for his
Poems in Two Tongues (1928), containing 'Deid Oor' and 'Edinburgh
Sabbath Morn'; but I have a doubt about his renaissance quality,
though none about his facility in a rich Scots which he picked up in the
streets as a boy and in long vacations in East Lothian. Nor can there be
any doubt about his uncannily close observation of humble life, which
culminated in the long poem *Sing a Song for Scotland* (1944)—a regular
carnival of Scottish life in which the whole fun-fair is in full blast. No
tragic undertones here—no undertones of any sort; but how good it
is and true to his Scotland! In his earlier volume Mackie hailed the
Master. Speaking of the impact of *A Drunk Man Looks at the Thistle*
on his own muse he says:

> . . . twae books gied me something strange
> Ne'er fund in a' my warld's range,
> Yin by an Irish chiel ca'd Joyce,
> And yin by you in Doric voice.

Guidsake, I never thocht tae see
Throught a' o' Yirth and Hell and Heeven
And in my tongue and i' my time
Hear life's bambaizement set tae rhyme.

Mackie was to be one of the active *entrepreneurs* of the renaissance movement when, just before Munich, it suddenly became vocal.

It was not till just on Munich that the younger Lallan poets appeared in force—George Campbell Hay, Robert Garioch, Douglas Young, R. Crombie Saunders, Sydney Goodsir Smith and others; and with them appeared as goodly a company of 'Anglo-Scots' who preferred to write in English and more or less to adopt English fashions—J. F. Hendry, W. S. Graham, Maurice Lindsay, Norman McCaig, Adam Drinan (Joseph Macleod), Ruthven Todd, George S. Fraser and Hamish Henderson. Edwin Muir, Andrew Young and William Jeffrey we should reckon of the previous generation. The members of this second group are not all hardy 'recusants'. Jeffrey found himself, as I think, rather late in Scots verse; Maurice Lindsay also, though in good time. Hamish Henderson rouses hopes of a considerable poet by his blend of Scottish feeling and English modes.

George Campbell Hay [15], Douglas Young tells us, was an accomplished poet by 1932; but new powers were released in him by the reading of MacDiarmid's *Scots Unbound*. He is to be thought of more as a Gaelic bard, however, and I fancy that his name had a prestige value for the movement rather on that account than for his verse in Scots. Four of the poems in *Wind on Loch Fyne* (1948) were set to music by Francis George Scott, the highest honour the Clan Mac-Diarmid can confer. Mr. Hay was indeed the poet MacDiarmid was looking for—learned in foreign tongues, but a perfervid partisan of Gaelic culture with the western seas in his blood. Favourable examples of his pure Scots work, and genuine renaissance poems, are 'Lomsfrios Na Tire', 'The White Licht' and 'A Ballad in Answer to Servius Sulpicius Rufus'—all on classical themes.

The Scots verse of Robert Garioch (Robert Sutherland) appeared with Sorley Maclean's Gaelic in *Seventeen Poems for Sixpence* (1940). This work, proletarian, often goliardic, slight in volume, encouraged the rough anacreontic manner which culminated in Sydney Smith's *Under the Eildon Tree*. But Garioch's rough-tongued satire, and his language reeking of the closes of Edinburgh, should not blind us to his real talent. The English poems in *Chuckie Stanes for the Cairn* (1949) display considerable accomplishment in a more civilized manner; and one hopes that in an inclusive volume some of these will be salvaged from defunct periodicals to take their place with his salty satires on Edinburgh and Presbytery.

Edinburgh and Presbytery are targets in these days for much rude satire, recalling that outpouring of equally abusive writing in Reformation times of which Lindsay's *Satyre of the Thrie Estaits* is the most powerful example. I can only mention here the work of William Ogilvy, architect and amateur of the arts, whose *The Witch and Other Poems* and *My Mither's Aunt* appeared as Porpoise Broadsheets.

With more wit and scholarship than the others, Douglas Young [16] is of larger dimensions. His work began to appear in periodicals just before the 1939-45 War; and despite his exiguous output, his large and genial personality and his taste for public polemic soon advanced him to a leading place in the movement. Young's *Letter to Hugh MacDiarmid* in the second issue of *Poetry Scotland*, occasioned by an invitation in 1940 to visit MacDiarmid (with some others of the faith), is a capital blend of admiration and indulgent satire or parody. It is also a historical note on the renaissance of which Hugh MacDiarmid is the 'begetter or misbegetter'. MacDiarmid's *Scots Unbound*, says Young, set him off, as it set George Campbell Hay off, on a new path which involved the 'rediscovery of Scottish culture'. He makes clever fun of MacDiarmid's polyglot heresy, but affirms the other heresy that 'the right authentic tone can only be Gaelic'. Common sense reasserted itself and he later repudiated this notion [17].

The first of Douglas Young's two volumes, *Auntran Blads*, received the Master's imprimatur, as well it might. Here at last was the scholar lending his wit and learning for the glory of Lallans and the more accessible aims set forth in MacDiarmid's 'Kulturkampf'. 'The words sing and plash like Hebridean winds and waters', said Mr. Ivor Brown. The complaint that *A Braird o' Thristles* has, in its design and content, more ingenious scroll-work than poetry, revives the doubt whether after all this is not the by-play of a man of immense gusto and wit rather than the work of a born poet; which is probably what MacDiarmid had in mind when he called it 'wit-writing rather than poetry'. Young's Lallans indeed is a rich compost which he uses with scholarly craft in poems like 'Requiem' and 'Ice-Flumes owregie their Lades', but something of the Jabberwocky in 'Ice-Flumes' warns us that the Lallans Young has in mind makes communication with the reader difficult or impossible [18]. His homelier verse and his translations from the Gaelic of Sorley Maclean cannot, however, be criticized on this score.

The progress of *il miglior fabbro* Sydney Smith [19] shows that he, like others, tried his hand at the new English modes by means of which writers since Hopkins had circumvented the dryness of orthodox diction. His first volume, *Skail Wind*, contains some of his best lyrics; and also the rambustious 'Ode to Hector Berlioz' with its comic medley of language—English, pseudo-Scots and what you will—which yet matches the mood of the poem. Does this sound like Berlioz?

Royal Bull, my curly-fronted monster, music taurus,
Berlioz my frien, archangel, doyen o the storm,
Dervish o the rudderless lichtnin, eagle proud
As Lucifer frae hie hovenum hurled, his brichtness bricht yet,
Burnished glorious as your dreaming elegiac horns.

The excellent 'Samphire Gatherers' and 'To Hector MacIver' are here
too, but it is clear that till the ferment of language settles we may
expect frustration of undoubted poetic talent. The title-poem of *The
Wanderer* is a dreary twelve-canto performance in ballad strain; but
here too are charming lyrics in 'For My New-born Son' and 'My
Moujik Lass':

My hert is lowpan owre the trees   [*leaping*
   An fleean wi the wind—
My lips 're weet wi barley bree,   [*whisky*
   My hurdies hug the grund.   [*buttocks*

The lass I loe has turned awa,   [*love*
   Til me yon hert's a stane—
But fain I'd hae her, flint and aa,
   Than bydin here alane.

Some airt the linties maun be singan,   [*place, linnets*
   Here the wuids are toom,   [*empty*
And aye the rain is dingan, dingan,   [*driving*
   Dingan on the toun.

O fain I'd loe my moujik lass,   [*peasant*
   O fain I'd haud her breist—
I've nocht to haud but a whisky gless,
   A gey wanchancy feast.   [*unlucky*

O dreich's the exile here I sing,   [*dreary*
   The lift is mirk aroun,   [*sky*
And aye I hear the raindraps ding,
   Aye dingan on the toun.

In 'Hallowe'en' (which appeared in *Poetry Scotland*, 1943) and in *The
Deevil's Waltz* he revived an element hitherto lacking in renaissance
poetry though strong in sixteenth-century Scots and in Burns—the
carnival note of wild or blasphemous merriment:

We kenna hert, we kenna heid,
The Deevil's thirled baith quick and deid.   [*pierced*
Jehovah snores, and Christ hissel
Lowps in the airms o Jezebel.

In his letter 'To Hector MacIver' Smith had dedicated his powers to
Scotland, the Scotland to be. Bu tthe road was hard and unrewarding,

and so for his mature work he chose 'to sing sweet lemanrie'. He was content to be the 'swete Master Ovide'—or was it the Catullus—of Scottish verse. Hence the sustained poem *Under the Eildon Tree*, and *So Late into the Night*, both considerable pieces of writing. The latter, a collection of fifty lyrics, attracted Miss Edith Sitwell's superlatives; and indeed the best of these are evidence of a fine lyric gift. The whole calendar of love—desire, satiety and self-loathing—is the theme, as in Shakespeare's sonnets; but there is a sameness which leads to monotony when unrelieved by the dialectic of love, of which there is little here. *Under the Eildon Tree* is a testament of love, or rather of 'lemanrie', for it is the Aphrodite of the stews as well as of heroic or courtly love he sings. No one can say he has not the right language now, a strange blend of sixteenth-century literary Scots, with monstrous Latinisms floating to the surface, and local dialect with modern jargon. All is grist to the mill of the poet macaronical; for in that character he presents himself—the victim of the blind god, the sport of wanton women, whose abasement is aesthetically relieved by scraps of Latin and quotations from the masters of song in the manner of Pound and Eliot. But *Under the Eildon Tree* is one of the finest poems of the Scottish renaissance, though Elegy xiii, in which the underworld of Edinburgh is described with high humour and rank detail, will frighten the timid (or have French films removed the blush from Scotia's cheek?):

Ah, she was a bonnie cou!
Saxteen, maybe sevinteen, nae mair,
Her mither in attendance, *comme il faut*
Pour les jeunes filles bien élevées,
    Drinkan like a bluidie whaul tae!   [*whale*
Wee breists, round and ticht and fou   [*tight, full*
Like sweet Pomona i the oranger grove;
Her shanks were lang, but no owre lang, and plump,
    A lassie's shanks,
Wi the meisurance o Venus—
    Achteen inch the hoch frae heuchle-bane til [*thigh, hip-bone*
      knap,   [*knee-cap*
    Achteen inch the cauf frae knap til cuit   [*calf, ankle*
As is the true perfection calculate
By the Auntients efter due regaird
For this and that,
        The true meisurance
    O' the Venus dei Medici,
    The Aphrodite Anadyomene
And aa the goddesses o hie antiquitie—
    Siclike were the shanks and hochs
O' Sandra the cou o the auld Black Bull.

Noisome perhaps, but taking account of the Scots tradition not nauseating and certainly strong writing. The question of Smith's indebtedness to Ezra Pound cannot be argued here; nor do I think it matters either way [20].

Maurice Lindsay [21] is a poet in his own right; but he is probably better known as (after MacDiarmid) the chief impresario of the renaissance movement. Perhaps his most honourable services to it were his periodical *Poetry Scotland* (1944-9) and his excellent anthology *Modern Scottish Poetry* (1946). *The Scottish Renaissance*, the story of his poetic development told in a lecture, shows him at the outset entangled in the English schools: first the cerebral school of Auden and MacNeice, and then, in the period of the war, a brief sojourner in the New Apocalypse before MacDiarmid's *A Drunk Man Looks at the Thistle* set him on his true course. Of his English work, he wished nothing prior to *Enemies of Love* to be remembered. Curiously, the five poems which form his contribution to *Modern Scottish Poetry* are all in English. In *Enemies of Love*, however—even in the excellent lines 'To Hugh MacDiarmid'—one notes the formulas of the fashionable southern idiom. Lindsay's change of front must have occurred at this time, for his *Selected Poems* published in the next year is entirely in Scots. He was dropping his old allies of the Apocalyptic and other schools from *Poetry Scotland;* and was now associated with MacDiarmid, Douglas Young, Sydney Smith and Alexander Scott, the chief mouthpieces of the Lallans revival. The result is decidedly attractive, but I have a weakness for some of his earlier writing.

The work of Alexander Scott, youngest hope of the movement and learned in Scottish literature, shows that for some poets the vernacular is essential and not merely, as Edwin Muir unkindly suggested, adopted because of its novelty. The English poems in his *The Latest in Elegies* (1949) and *Selected Poems* (1950), 'Terra Deserta' and 'The White Devil', are naught; but the Scots poems are far from being naught. 'The Gowk in Lear' in the *Elegies* is as fine an imitation of the early makars as Soutar's 'The Auld Tree', and is yet individual too. Like Maurice Lindsay in 'Hallowmass-Rade' and Sydney Smith in 'Hallowe'en', Scott is attracted to the wild carnival dance of the old poets:

And Lealtie happit his truth in a ragment o' lees,   [*wrapped*
A bable o' Bedlamish blether. . . .
Wud as the wund he skirled at the levin's bleeze,   [*furious, lightning's*
His tongue gane wersh as the weather.   [*bitter*

Now Fairheid sang at the drumlie yett o' death   [*muddy gate*
Whar shade and sunlight grapple,
Deep in a dungeon's dark she tint her breath,   [*lost*
A rope around her thrapple.   [*neck*

His 'Deathsang for an Auld Man Young' in the same volume is a sustained elegy, in the same traditional Scots imagery and diction, but somehow moving. The six poems which he contributed to the Festival edition of the *Scots Review* in September 1951 (the swan-song of that excellent periodical) are a fair sample of his powers. Scott's future will be marked by friendly eyes. I turn now to the 'Anglo-Scots' poets whom the Lallans fanatics would like to proscribe.

4

Edwin Muir [22] and Hugh MacDiarmid confront each other as the chief among our poets and the protagonists in the debate on Scottish verse. In his early ballads Muir may have gone some distance with the new Scots makars; but, as he matured, revulsion for all they stood for was inevitable. The final expression of this revulsion is in his *Scott and Scotland*, a series of lectures with the sub-title 'The Predicament of the Scottish Writer'. This predicament is created by the lack of a 'whole' vernacular; and Muir concludes that 'Scotland can only create a national literature by writing in English'. He dismisses MacDiarmid's attempts to revive the old language as resulting in 'some remarkable poetry' without having gone a step towards creating a unified diction. 'Scottish dialect poetry is a regression to childhood.' This is not incompatible with his view of Scotland as lost, poxed to the bone with Calvinism and industrialism, and its idols Burns and Scott 'sham bards of a sham nation'.

This rupture with the vernacular movement came in 1936; but Muir had known for several years that his path led in other directions. In social politics also he had freed himself from revolt and visions of the rosy dawn which had excited his adolescent mind in Glasgow. The contacts with larger minds which he enjoyed in London and Prague after the 1914-18 War, and his intercourse with the English poets (chiefly the seventeenth-century Metaphysicals) made him turn his back on these early enthusiasms. It was still the *road* (his obsessive image), but now it led back through the generations of his own people; and this meant the exploration of his own mind and heart. Muir was to be a 'metaphysical' poet—the first in Scotland if we forget some pale imitations of the English Metaphysicals in the seventeenth century. A strong religious element was inevitable. MacDiarmid had also written 'metaphysical' poetry, but of a very different order, in which religion (if it came in at all) was the worship of the evolutionary process; and to that, let us confess, poetry seems inimical.

To this end, and necessarily, Muir collected symbols in plenty—all subsidiary, however, to the images of the road and time. Paradox, which seems essential to the religious poet, was also put to his service. One thing he could not do (through no default of wit), and that was handle conceited imagery, in which the English Metaphysicals were masters. He presents us in his various volumes with a body of short poems in which the sad dialectic of the soul is worked out with great penetration and, in the later ones, with truly admirable art. Scotland is now free of the reproach that it has no 'metaphysical' poetry. The other requisites Muir laid down for a civilized literature—poetic tragedy and continuous discourse—must wait; though in his later work, *The Labyrinth*, he seems to be attempting more continuous discourse.

Naturally there are influences. The devices of T. S. Eliot's discursive manner are much used:

> They are not here. And we are the Others
> Who walk by ourselves unquestioned in the sun,
> Which shines for us and only us,
> For they are not here.

There are suggestions too of Blake and George Herbert, and of Marvell not a little:

> If I could drive this demon out
> I'd put all Time's display to rout.
> Its wounds would turn to flowers and nothing be
> But the first Garden. The one Tree
> Would stand for ever safe and fair
> And Adam's hand stop in the air.
> Or so I dream when at my door
> I hear my Soul, my Visitor.

The nostalgia for remote and blessed times, a feature of some 'metaphysical' poetry, appears in much of Muir's writing as a memory of his childhood in Orkney before (in Vaughan's words)

> I understood this place
> Appointed for my second race.

With the exception of 'The Ballad of Hector in Hades' (which released a terror overhanging from his childhood), the ballads written in English and Scots in *First Poems* are no great matter: *The Rime of the Ancient Mariner* is behind them all. But one or two of the poems, 'Childhood' and 'Betrayal' for example, are authentic Muir, and critics should have marked them. *Journeys and Places* confirmed the promise of *First Poems*. Here is no echo of Coleridge or anyone else, though ancestral voices blend with Muir's own. 'The Enchanted Knight' and 'Tristram's Journey' are no cold exercises in pre-Raphaelite poetry; the first of these is as haunting as Keats's 'La Belle Dame sans Merci'. We note here his preoccupation with the story of Troy and of Eden and other great myths, and always with the concept of time.

The Narrow Place announces the mature poet and, we might say, prescribes his limits. The perfect balance of thought and emotion recalls the passionate thinking of some of the English Metaphysicals. *The Voyage* added new symbols from heraldry, hieroglyphics and other sources; and here too there is a discriminating variation in poetic form—craftsmanship of a sort rare in Scotland, where form has never been much cultivated. *The Labyrinth* contains some fine poetry, but Muir is still working with the same symbols. The scriptural images of the Fall and the Passion absorb him more, however, and it would seem that he has won through pagan myth and legend to an acceptance of the Christian myth. But whatever myths he employs, he cannot write other than as a poet; and his poetry is instinct with religious feeling, if not faith. If only we could escape the sense that he is the prisoner of his symbols, and feel that a fresh advance is possible for him.

No such thought can cloud the beauty of a poem like 'The Little General', where wit and feeling, craft and symbolism meet 'in just proportions':

> Early in spring the little General came
> Across the sound, bringing the island death,
> And suddenly a place without a name,
> And like the pious ritual of a faith,
>
> Hunter and quarry in the boundless trap,
> The white smoke curling from the silver gun,
> The feather curling in the hunter's cap,
> And clouds of feathers floating in the sun,
>
> While down the birds came in a deafening shower,
> Wing-hurricane, and the cattle fled in fear,
> Up on the hill a remnant of a tower
> Had watched that single scene for many a year,
>
> Weaving a wordless tale where all were gathered
> (Hunter and quarry and watcher and fabulous field),
> Perennial emblem painted on a shield
>
> Held up to cow a never-conquered land
> Fast in the little General's fragile hand.

Pope could have furnished the art and the wit for this perfect thing, not perhaps the feeling, and certainly not the symbolism.

Andrew Young was wholly assimilated to his English environment [23]. Muir is a Scot to whom, by some mystery, it has been given to revive the metaphysical world of English seventeenth-century poetry; Young revives in our late day the nature poetry of the pious but earth-loving Jacobeans. And this too is a marvel, that a man writing after *The Waste Land* had altered the whole landscape of poetry should have been able to restore that rich note. It will not do to call him a belated Georgian, for his work is spiritually different from the demure

nature worship of Blunden and Drinkwater. The early twentieth
century is indeed rich in nature poetry, some of it (as witness Housman
and De La Mare) exquisite. But none of his predecessors had Young's
touch of Jacobean fancy, or his sense of innocence, the innocence before
the Fall:

> Stay, Spring, for by this ruthless haste
>   You turn all good to waste;
>   Look, how the hawthorn now
> Changes to trifling dust upon the bough.
>
> Where blossom from the wild pear shakes
>   Too rare a china breaks,
>   And though the cuckoos shout
> They will forget their names ere June be out.
>
> That thrush too, that with beadlike eye
>   Watches each passer-by,
>   Is warming at its breast
> A brood that when they fly rob their own nest.
>
> So late begun, so early ended!
>   Lest I should be offended
>   Take warning, Spring, and stay
> Or I might never turn to look your way.

This is like and unlike Housman: it has his lyrical note, but also a
Jacobean feeling which is foreign to him. There is the authentic
Jacobean quality too in 'A Prospect of Death'—George Herbert might
be speaking:

> If it should come to this,
> You cannot wake me with a kiss,
> Think I but sleep too late
> Or once again keep a cold angry state.
>
> So now you have been told:
> I or my breakfast may grow cold,
> But you must only say
> 'Why does he miss the best part of the day?'
>
> Even then you may be wrong;
> Through woods torn by a blackbird's song
> My thoughts may often roam
> While graver business makes me stay at home . . .

Muir's muse is too serious to entertain the conceits and whimsical
fancies of the true Jacobeans; but Andrew Young delights in them as
did W. H. Davies, who also caught something from that rich poetic
age. The mystery in Young is perhaps explained by the numerous
quotations from seventeenth-century poets in his charming prose work

A Prospect of Flowers, which shows that his muse had watered at those springs. Spiritually a seventeenth-century Anglican, he slipped back easily into the poetry of that age.

Returned from service after the 1914-18 War, William Jeffrey [24] commenced poet at about the same time as Edwin Muir, who also started late. But whereas Muir was then shaking the dust of Glasgow from his feet, Jeffrey was settling into a journalist's career for the rest of his brief life. Unlike Muir, he had no memories of Orcadian or Arcadian childhood; but he was fortunately able to look on Glasgow with the eyes of a seer to whom nothing in God's earth is unlovely, though he did not maintain this naïve faith. Muir's late start may have saved him from the long apprenticeship which Jeffrey had to undergo before he achieved an individual style. Perhaps, as his sympathetic editor Alexander Scott suggests, the trouble in Jeffrey's early writing was due to a dichotomy between the romantic idiom he borrowed from the nineteenth-century poets and that twentieth-century scene he was ambitious to explore. The dominant influence in his early poetry may be Blake; but Shelley and Keats and Tennyson are also much in evidence—and that at a time when Ezra Pound and T. S. Eliot were dethroning the old gods. After an attempt to describe the modern industrial world in this exhausted idiom, Jeffrey explored the territory of allegory and myth—a quite hopeless waste of talent. Almost all these early endeavours could have been undertaken by a minor poet of the age of Tennyson. Though there are beautiful things and fine cadences in it, nobody is likely to do more than glance at his long *Fantasia*, in which the poet returns to the industrial scene, and where his faith fails and bitter denunciations of industrialism disturb the earlier and last sections. In *The Eagle of Coruisk* Jeffrey has got rid of a good deal of romantic rhetoric, but has as yet no individual voice.

Mr. Scott is no doubt right in directing us to Jeffrey's latest work; and it may be that the later Yeats was the awakening influence, though personally I cannot see any obvious lineation. *Sea Glimmer*, published posthumously in 1947, and the occasional or hitherto unprinted poems which now appear in *Selected Poems*, contain in my view all that is significant in Jeffrey's fairly large output. It is notable that of this residual verse the most successful is in Scots—'The Galleys' and 'On Glaister's Hill'. In the former John Knox utters his soul at the galley-oar in the shape of Browning's dramatic monologues:

> At times abominations flaunt the deep's
> Green tenements and causeys quick wi' hell,
> And maist that lassock frae the Cyprian shore,   [*young lass*
> Wha's temple stood on ane Ephesian fell;
> Withouten sark she smites the licht o' day   [*shirt*
> And wins the feeblit flesh intil her spell.

274

But there's a sang aboundin in the hert
And raised at dawing when the caller air   [*fresh*
Trips like a damakie that sees her luve.   [*girl*
I ken I'll see Auld Reekie's rockie stair
Upliftit as was Jacob's in a cloud o' sternes,   [*stars*
And I sall smell bluid scailit on Holyrood's flair.   [*spilt, floor*

Some may prefer 'On Glaister's Hill', in which that other crabbed moralist, Carlyle, speaks his mind; and the good Scots tongue truly describes the scene with all that pride in nature which is hereditary in our poetry. *Sea Glimmer* also contains the grave meditations 'In Midmost Winter' and 'Walking One Winter Midnight', which represent the best of Jeffrey's writing in English.

5

After Muir, Young and Jeffrey we had to wait for the next group of Anglo-Scots poets, who emerged during the last war and bore the stamp of war neurosis as their predecessors hardly did. There are two main schools: poets like Ruthven Todd, George S. Fraser, Maurice Lindsay (down to *The Enemies of Love*), R. Crombie Saunders in his English verse, and others—who write in what may be called socially acceptable verse, that is in modern fashions though without exaggeration, and are intelligible; and the Apocalyptic school, in reaction from the analytical pessimism of the 1930s, exploding in strange metaphors and moving in violent transitions with scant attention to meaning. It was in this second sect that the school of MacDiarmid saw the chief danger to the renaissance; for in the mood of 1941 it was very tempting to young poets with some pretensions to English and European culture to have a fling at the new manner. They had their allies in the south: Henry Treece penetrated Lindsay's periodical *Poetry Scotland*, and Lindsay was at that time in danger himself. By the time *Poetry Scotland* had run its course, he confessed his deviation and mended. But the heresy was not stamped out, for its chief practitioners are poets.

Mr. J. F. Hendry, sensitive critic of European culture, was often unintelligible in *The Bombed Happiness* (1941), and his technique frightened many though it was by no means new—the violent imagery and telegraphic modes of speech had been features of English verse for a generation. But this is clear enough, rather like the early Spender or MacNeice:

Sensitive fingers of searchlights pick the pockets of the dark,
These are surgeon's instruments, pitiless forceps imprisoning
    their grip
Anacrobic death, there, in the air, lurking
To burst the harmless tissue of the cities.

The Bombed Happiness was succeeded in 1943 by *The Orchestral Mountain*, in which, if there is little clearing of the apocalyptic darkness, there is variety of music, some of it lovely enough. Imagery is still the thing which makes Hendry's work difficult country for the common reader. But in *Modern Scottish Poetry* (1946) Maurice Lindsay was able to include six fine poems by Hendry which employ modern technique without a hint of obscurity. Nor are they cold exercises in yesterday's modes; they have passion and wit to fill out the sails. There is the passionate anger of 'Kranjska Gora, Slovenia', for example, and the lively wit of 'For Laureo de Boseis':

> The clouds you tore up into paper and printed in clean hail
> and the white snow you suddenly showered over Rome
> hid confetti for many happy marriages.
> It was the minting of the new lira
> from the wake of ships in the Mediterranean
> and the dance of the washing in the back streets of Trieste.

Such sophisticated wit as this, in which Mr. Hendry excels, could not possibly be conveyed in the vernacular.

I think Mr. Norman McCaig first appeared in *The White Horseman* (1941), an anthology of Apocalypse verse. Two years later his collection *The Far Cry* confirmed the promise of a considerable poet who could not, however, resist southern fashions. He appears to be equally adept in the Apocalyptic manner, and in the manner which Dylan Thomas developed ultimately from Hopkins, as here:

> Now this wood of angels, dolphin singing in sea-loch
> tingle in a morning light long in my level hand.
> Steep aspens are motionless and between the birches
> fall without a stir the threads of their branches
> and the sky of morning lies level in my mind.

Prejudice has worked against the Anglo-Scots poets: Maurice Lindsay admitted five of Mr. McCaig's poems to his anthology in 1946, but for *Scottish Verse 1851-1951* five years later Douglas Young selected only one from a portfolio. I think that the collection Mr. McCaig now has ready for the press, *The Divided Bird*, shows that Young's perfervid Scottishness may have misled him. What is more, in *The Divided Bird* the fashions do not obtrude; the poet is himself, and his imagery is as always original and relevant. One may agree with Mr. William Montgomerie in his polemic against the Lallan overlords (*New Alliance and Scots Review*, February 1951), that Norman McCaig is 'writing in English some of the best work now being produced in Scotland'.

In another member of this group, Mr. W. S. Graham, we are lost in obscurity. His *Seven Journeys* (1944) defies interpretation. Mr. Hendry

may claim [25] that Graham's work 'is a late manifestation of the same
trend [Apocalyptism] which is shaking our kaleidoscopic world into
new design'; but though one feels vaguely the power and imagination
behind these poems, the incessantly shifting imagery, which sizzles and
crackles like an electric grid in rain, wearies the reader. Curiously, Mr.
Graham is clear enough when he describes his home town, Greenock:

> Younger in the towered
> Tenements of night he heard
> The shipyards with nightshifts
> Of lathes turning their shafts.
> His voice was a humble ear
> Hardly turned to her.
> And the mantle-brasslight there
> Shone busily in the fire
> Lightning the kitchen.

But this poetry will not be written off as a total loss. *White Threshold*
(1949) shows Graham to be our Scottish Dylan Thomas—no more
obscure than that; and it is a rewarding collection. Apocalyptism has
paid its dues to the Scottish renaissance.

Ruthven Todd and George S. Fraser are only mildly touched by
English fashions. Why did Douglas Young leave Todd out of his
anthology? What he writes has both charm and strength. The flimsy
paper-back *Ten Poems* (1940), with 'In September 1937' and 'Personal
History: for My Son', alone places him among the poets of the day.
Here is modern English verse, well-fashioned and witty. Too much
à la mode? The Scottish muse can stand a good deal of that
grooming [26].

If W. S. Graham is our Dylan Thomas, George S. Fraser is our
Louis MacNeice—not so various as the Irish poet, but excellent in his
kind. His Scottish affiliations appear chiefly in the form of revolt
against the drabness of city life in Aberdeen and elsewhere. He endured
exile in London, Egypt and Japan, and an enlarged acquaintance with
the wits of the south soon replaced the Scottish scene by cosmopolitan
vignettes all tinged with the bitter-sweet of experience and all executed
with a sense of form unusual in a Scottish writer. At the same time he
enriched his experience by translating Continental poetry of divers eras
and kinds from Cavalcanti to Paul Valéry. The choice expression of
common experience is his aim, and he views with equal *sang-froid* the
heroics of MacDiarmid and the religious gravity of Edwin Muir:

> In the far islands to the North and West
>   Mackenzie and MacDiarmid have their peace;
> St. Andrews soothes that critic at her breast
>   Whose polished verse ne'er gave his soul release.

Your journey has not been the private journey
Through a mad loveliness of Hölderlin.
Against the windmills, sir, you chose to tourney,
And yet, by marvellous chance, you hold your own. [27]

In Mr. Hamish Henderson we meet the serious Scot who is also a man of parts. His *Elegies for the Dead in Cyrenaica* (1948) contrasts startlingly with the occasional verse which Fraser wrote during the Egyptian campaign. A Gaelic wanderer with a sense of history, of the tides of men and civilizations, Mr. Henderson never forgets his Scottish roots. The eighth elegy, 'Karnack', probably shows him at his best; but some will demur to his highly stylized way of writing. In his latest work he seems to be moving towards a more individual manner, but one hopes that his forthcoming poem on the Italian campaign will show fresh inspiration.

George Bruce [28], the poet of sea-board Buchan, forsakes his own rich dialect for a veracious laconic English which derives, I think, from the Imagists and is directly contrary to the apocalyptic manner:

Kinnaird Head

I go North to cold, to home, to Kinnaird,
Fit monument for our time.

This is the outermost edge of Buchan.
Inland the sea birds range,
The tree's leaf has salt upon it,
The tree turns to the low stone wall.
And here a promontory rises towards Norway,
Irregular to the top of thin grey grass
Where the spindrift in storm lays its beads. . . .

Mr. Bruce can be more complicated, but this is his norm, and very effectively it expresses the spirit of that grey land.

R. Crombie Saunders, editor of *Scottish Art and Letters*, is equally dexterous in Scots and English. His 'Had I Twa Herts' rightly attracted Sir Compton Mackenzie, but his 'Tomorrow the Station' nonplussed that genial critic. Yet slight as it is, the latter is the more adult poem:

Tomorrow the station,
And the separate friendly people
Crowding the doors and exits
With their vision and needs and baggage;
And for me the slow breath of doubt
And hunger for conviction,
The rails to the horizon leading
Or ominous, pointing to panic.

Decision hangs
Like gravity on this moment,
Whether your troubled love
Will find in crisis its courage;
Or whether indecision
Will conquer, and my journey
Leave no excuse for caring
And more than fields between us.

For me as for others, Adam Drinan (Joseph Macleod) is an enigmatical poet. If I have not the courage to class him frankly with the poets
who owe allegiance to the south, it is because of such contrary judgments as that of Sir Compton Mackenzie, who says that his poetry 'has
revealed more of the hidden essence of Gaeldom than any verse or
prose being written to-day', and that of friends who tell me that
Mackenzie has been hoaxed by a display of pseudo-Gaelic. Be that as it
may, Adam Drinan is a competent poet whose technique is strongly
tinged with southern fashions, of yesterday rather than to-day. We
cannot read his two plays, *Women of the Happy Island* (1941) and
particularly *The Ghosts of the Strath* (1943), without detecting the
liturgical voice of T. S. Eliot. Drinan's affiliations are clear in his early
publication, *The Cove* (1940). The writing there, some of it admirable,
is English writing of the Imagist sort crossed with T. S. Eliot's habit of
rhetorical repetition. The immaturity of *The Cove*, however, is the
immaturity that promises well; and the words, as always in Adam
Drinan, dance to their proper places. Two years later *Men of the Rock*
showed the expected advance. Here again are echoes of Eliot—

> The falls sound; and the sound is the shape,
> The falls shape; and the shape is the changing,
> The falls changing ever the same . . .

—but the note half-lyrical and half-satirical is a personal one; and
within his narrow range Drinan can do what he likes with words. If
only he would not harp so much on the theme of dispossession!

In this brief encounter with modern Scottish writing I have necessarily left out names which might well be here; but perhaps enough has
been displayed in English and in Scots to justify the title of the Scottish
Renaissance.

A NOTE ON SCOTTISH GAELIC POETRY

DOUGLAS YOUNG

NO better poetry has been written in Scotland in the last fifteen years than the Gaelic poems by Somhairle MacGhillEathain (Sorley Maclean) and George Campbell Hay. And in the last fifteen centuries perhaps the best poetry produced in Scotland has been, on the whole, that in Gaelic. There has been no Gaelic Burns, no Gaelic Dunbar, no Gaelic Hugh MacDiarmid; but the language itself has long been cultivated for poetry, and there is possibly a greater volume of excellently felt utterance in Gaelic, by over a hundred poets, than has been achieved by all the Lallan makars since John Barbour, all the Scots Latinists since Buchanan, and all the Scots versifiers in English since Drummond of Hawthornden.

Naturally those brought up speaking Gaelic, and schooled in its literature and in those of more fashionable tongues, are better able to judge of this than one who, like the present writer, has no colloquial fluency or literary command of the language. But we are not deterred from criticizing Homer, Pindar and Theocritus through inability to speak their dialects; if one can wield a dictionary and a grammar-book, and if one undertakes the not excessive and highly intriguing study of the pronunciation of written Gaelic, there is a rich store of exciting verse in print, much of it now with English versions en face to aid the reader. Without probing very deeply into all the nuances of vocabulary and allusion, or mastering the intricacies of accidence, even a superficial reader will be rewarded by the musical range of the versification and by the frequent power and brilliance of the imagery and declamation.

Gaelic-speaking society in Scotland has been for most of its course fairly near to the spirit of Pindar's culture, a people of peasants, artisans and seafarers, with a keen sense alike of heroism and of fun, and a brisk ear for effect in assonance and rhythm of language and in the striking juxtaposition of observation and reflection. Taking Celtic, and especially Scots Gaelic, literature in its whole extent, there is no justification for the notion that the poets were mainly preoccupied with twilight and moonshine, decay and death. It is as vivid and realist and varied a body of literature as has been produced by any of the great languages and language-groups at comparable stages of social development, as may be seen from Professor Kenneth Jackson's anthology of translations into English, by himself, *A Celtic Miscellany* (1951). What is lacking to Gaelic verse is, in general, that which is lacking to Homer or Pindar—a modern sophistication abreast of the atomic cosmopolitan age. Yet even here Sorley Maclean's *An Cuilithionn* (1939: not yet printed in full) shows the entire capacity of the spoken and traditional language to deal with *avant-garde* themes at least as expressively as anyone has dealt with them in any other tongue.

It is perhaps permissible for me to explain, on a personal note, that at this writing I am in no way filled with the *furor Celticus* which is frequently to be observed taking hold of some Scot or other on first discovering in a receptive frame of mind the distinctive values of our Gaelic heritage, scenic, sartorial, bibulous, musical, linguistic, saltatory and the rest. I have been more or less continually exposed to most of them for a quarter of a century and more; have wielded an eager lexicon on a great deal of verse and substantial tracts of prose; and have even turned some thousands of lines of Gaelic poetry into English or Scots metre or rhythm. But my main interests have long lain in other tongues, chiefly Greek and Latin, and I now pen these notes calmly and without enthusiasm, to give a half-outsider's impression of what the inquiring poetry-lover may hope to find on looking into Scottish Gaelic.

First and chiefly, a rich language for poetic expression, much richer in mere sounds than English, French or German, for example; as rich, deep and wide in vocal tone as Russian or Italian. Word-music is much more prominent among the aims of Gaelic poets, as of Welsh, than it has been in the dominant literatures of classical or modern Europe. But there has long been also an astonishingly copious vocabulary, with whose range and subtleties no lexicon has yet contrived to cope with anything like adequacy. I first began to realize the fact when trying to pick English adjectives for the range of Gaelic terms expressive of beauty that Sorley Maclean employs in his *Dàin do Eimhir* (1943). A long tract of time, and the efforts of generations of poets and patrons and critical audiences, must be assumed at the back of this result. Fifteen centuries of ancestral Gaelic poetry is certainly no understatement of the period involved. Though James Macpherson, who in 1760 aroused Europe by his English version of Ossianic lays, is now understood to have had somewhat the same relation to his original sources as Sir Walter Scott had in editing Border ballads, it is certain that till the eighteenth century and later in Scotland and her western isles there were current scores of thousands of lines of heroic saga verse. J. F. Campbell of Islay, in his *Leabhar na Féinne* (1872), printed some 54,000 lines of it independently of 'Ossian' Macpherson's works; and much other material is extant in mediaeval manuscripts or other manuscripts earlier than Macpherson. This 'Ossianic' epic cycle has Irish offshoots, but its bulk is centred in Scotland north of the Antonine Wall from Forth to Clyde. Though the invaders who are repelled are the Norsemen and Danes, the ethic is pre-Christian, on a Homeric level indeed, and the time when the poetic conglomeration crystallized cannot be placed long after the Roman Empire abandoned southern Britain in the fifth century.

Just as Homeric diction influenced all later Greek verse and prose, so what may be loosely termed 'Ossianic' or heroic vocabulary and aesthetic effects pervaded Gaelic work till the most recent times. The society was aristocratic, but not so strongly divided horizontally as more opulent and settled aristocracies, because the vertical divisions of locality and clanship counted for a great deal in the struggle for exist-ence. It was also cosmopolitan, relatively to the possibilities of the Middle Ages, with clerics and mercenaries and merchants travelling far afield and bringing home ideas and skills; it had its own physicians, astrologers, theologians and the like, as well as lawyers and soldiers. Till the Reformation in the sixteenth and seventeenth centuries Ireland and Scotland were more or less a single cultural area. Irish chiefs offered the crown of Ireland to James V, father of Mary Queen of Scots, when Henry VIII of England broke with Rome; just as Robert Bruce's brother Edward had for a time been King of Ireland, while the Scots had a naval base in the Isle of Man. The Celtic continuum from Scot-land into Wales had been broken earlier, by the penetration of the Angles to the west coast of Cumberland; but as late as the Wars of the Roses we find Scots nobles banding with Welshmen and Marcher Lords in temporary coalitions, and no doubt tunes and musical idioms made their way from country to country, even after the Celtic tongues were dissimilated to the point of mutual unintelligibility.

Long poems were declaimed or chanted to the harp, a small portable *clàrsach* akin to the Welsh *crwth*. Lyrics were commonly made to a specified tune; and satires would tend to adopt the established line and stanza forms of epic or lyric. Drama did not develop, though there are elements of drama, and of the novel, in the poetic prose tales and in longer verse ballads. In the fifteenth-century 'Flyting' of the courtly Dunbar with the aristocratic Kennedy, who was sib to the King, it is overt that Kennedy was a Gaelophile, and not hard to discern that Dunbar's richness of assonance and fancy owes much to a pervasive Celtic ambience in which he moved.

The first individual figure discernible in this ambience lived at the start of the thirteenth century, one Muireadhach Albannach ('Murdoch of Scotland', presumably to distinguish him from an Irish namesake). He is eponymous forebear of the MacVurichs, hereditary bards to the Macdonalds of Clanranald, and *sennachies* as well, charged to recite their history. In 1411, when Donald Balloch, Lord of the Isles, asserted his claim to the feudal Earldom of Ross by bringing some ten thousand clansmen to a sanguinary conflict at Harlaw, near Aberdeen, against the Regent Albany's forces commanded by Alexander Stewart, Earl of Mar, Big Lachlan MacVurich delivered a metrical 'pep-talk' to the West Highlanders, consisting of 338 lines, divided into sections by letters of the Gaelic alphabet, and containing over 600 epithets appropriate to martial ardour. One would expect an absurd concoction of the type of:

> Austrian armies, awfully arrayed,
> Boldly with batteries besieged Belgrade:
> Cossack commanders cannonading come . . .

But MacVurich's incitement does achieve an effect that Pindar or Tyrtaeus might have envied.

Later in the fifteenth century we find a lady who has been compared to Sappho for the delicate and controlled passion with which she declares in verse a love that cannot be consummated: Isabel Stewart, heiress of Lorne (*d.* 1510), married by 1465 to Colin, second Lord Campbell, first Earl of Argyll, ambassador to England and France, Master of the Royal Household and Lord Chancellor, one of the richest and most cosmopolitan of the Scottish nobility. A contemporary, Effric MacCorquodale, widow of Hector MacTorquil MacNeill, constable of Castle Sween, commands effective metre and diction to deplore the acquisition of that stronghold by the Campbells. Lady Argyll's nephew, Sir Duncan Campbell of Glenorchy and Lawers, killed at Flodden in 1513, showed a strong vein of satire and popular humour. From the Flodden time we have a manuscript anthology, *The Book of the Dean of Lismore*, compiled about 1512-20 by a cleric from Perthshire, Sir James MacGregor, where the heroic and the recent are juxtaposed.

For learned bard and aristocratic patron and dilettante the classic metre was syllabic, metrical units of a determinate number of syllables being built up into hundreds of different stanza-types. Rhyme, assonance and alliteration were ornaments, sometimes elaborate. But in the sixteenth century, alike in Ireland and Scotland, the tendency developed to abandon regularity of syllable-grouping for rhythms based on a fixed number of stressed syllables, unstressed ones being allowed licences, by a process akin to Gerard Manley Hopkins's 'sprung rhythm'. The burden of erudition was diminished, and poets from humbler ranks of society produced more 'folksy' utterances than had been usual—unless we are misled by the chances of preservation through anthologists' personal tastes and other causes.

Mary Macleod, Màiri nighean Alasdair Ruaidh (*c.* 1615-1707), may be reckoned the Corinna of Skye, making great verse unto her own clan, chiefly in elegies or panegyrics, which reveal the dominant values of the society in fitting tones. During her long life flourished also Iain Lom, John Macdonald, of the Keppoch family (*c.* 1620-*c.*1710), who has stirring pieces on the battle of Inverlochy, the execution of Montrose, and other noteworthy episodes of the time. Though these are eminent single figures to whom a good volume of work attaches, much of the finest poetry appears in scattered items whose authors are either now anonymous or known by little else. For example, we have *Griogal Cridhe*, a passionately direct utterance, stark, simple and deeply moving when sung to the right tune—a lullaby to her child by the widow of a Gregor MacGregor, beheaded by her own brother, a Campbell, in the mid-sixteenth century. Or take the Lament for Iain Garbh macGille Chaluim of Raasay, drowned in 1671:

> *Nochd gur h-ìosal do chluasag,*
> *fo lic fhuaraidh na tuinne,*
> *'s ann an clachan na traghad*
> *tha mo ghràdh-sa 'na uirigh.*

> Lowly to-night is thy pillow,
> cold billows thy tomb-stone,
> graveyard of the shore at ebb
> is the bed of my adored one.

The great age, however, of Scottish Gaelic poetry is (so far) the eighteenth century, with its greatest figure in Alexander Macdonald, Alasdair MacMhaighstir Alasdair (*c.* 1700-70). Son of an Episcopalian minister, of the Clanranald branch of the clan, partly educated at Glasgow University, by turns schoolmaster, catechist and farmer, Episcopalian, Presbyterian and Papist, he was above all a nationalist and a Jacobite, serving in the campaign to Culloden and pouring out martial incitements. His greatest piece is *The Birlinn of Clanranald*, describing the voyage of a chief's galley across the Minch as if it were going from Heaven to Hell and back, with a range of rhythm and harmony and sensibility unparalleled in any tone-poem. Hugh Mac-Diarmid's rhymed version in English has been widely admired, and thought to convey the impression of a tremendous and unique work; but even this excellent attempt bears hardly more relation to the original Gaelic than the view of the stained glass from outside bears to the sensation of gazing up from inside the Sainte Chapelle. Macdonald's extant work, a minor part of his whole output, has a considerable range—amatory, satirical, descriptive and didactic—everywhere challenging for the command of language. *The Sugar-Brook*, for instance, conveys melodiously the whole succession of seasonal pictures arising around a farm he had. *The Praise of Mòrag* and the pair of lengthy pieces on summer and winter combine remarkably direct utterance and *tours de force*. Always popular, though his more Rabelaisian pieces have had their detractors, he is also a poets' poet, without rival in Gaelic till the present generation.

Colonel John Roy Stewart (1700-52) is another picturesque Jacobite militant, equally fiery with sword and pen, who died in French exile. John MacCodrum (1693-1779) and Rob Donn Mackay (1714-78) are best remembered for their satires, and William Ross (1762-90) for love-lyrics and pastoral pieces. Of the hymn-writers, far the most powerful was Dugald Buchanan (1716-68). To outsiders savouring the melodies of Gaelic verse without too deep an interest in its subjects, Duncan Bàn Macintyre (1724-1812) has a great deal to offer, especially in his *Praise of Ben Dorain*, whose movements imitate the variations of a pibroch, while a wealth of epithets is lavished on every aspect of his favourite mountain.

Among nineteenth-century poets one may mention Ewen Maclachlan (1775-1822), with his pieces on the four seasons; Evan MacColl, Dr. John Maclachlan, Dugald Macphail, Mrs. Mary Mackellar, Neil Macleod and Mrs. Mary Macpherson; but they all tend to show the mid-Victorian sentimentality and pretty-prettiness. Most high-flying was William Livingstone (1808-70), with saga-style pieces on historical and political themes. The Barra playwright Donald Sinclair (1886-1932) wrote some verses of merit, and singable ditties and satires continued to appear during the first third of the twentieth century.

The 1930s then threw up two major Gaelic poets, Sorley Maclean from Raasay (*b.* 1911) and George Campbell Hay from Tarbert, Loch Fyne (*b.* 1915). To colloquial and scholarly command of the whole resources of Gaelic each of them joins a contemporary sensibility, conversant with the themes of the international *avant-garde* and deeply obsessed not only with personal problems but with the great national and world challenges of our time. In *Seventeen Poems for Sixpence* (1940), a joint pamphlet with Robert Garioch, Maclean came to grips not only with the vicissitudes of a lover but with the implications of the Spanish Civil War. In *Dàin do Eimhir* (1943) we had many love-poems of great subtlety and perceptiveness, akin to much of Donne or Valéry; as well as magnificent descriptive pieces and keen-cutting epigrams. Not yet published in full is the great *An Cuilithionn*, where the history and struggles of the Skye crofters are portrayed along with the world-historical development of which they are a microcosm; and all this in a superb gamut of verse-forms and diction.

George Hay is a versatile linguist and a master-craftsman in Gaelic most of all, though he has written poems that sing themselves as you read in other tongues also, Scots, English, French, Norse, for instance; and has made admirable verse-translations from ancient and modern Greek, Serbo-Croat, Arabic, Italian, Welsh and so on (*Fuaran Sleibh*, 1948; *Wind on Loch Fyne*, 1948; *O na Ceithir Airdean*, 1952). Many of these pieces are, of course, skilful literary exercises, which nevertheless have a value beyond themselves in enriching the expressive powers of the language; but Hay has given us also plenty of poems of the fullest power on a wide range of themes, from a Highland mother's lullaby to a stark portrayal of an air raid on Bizerta.

Some very interesting new lines in Gaelic verse were opened up by

Derick Thomson from Lewis (*b.* 1922) in *An Dealbh Briste* (1950), showing again the combination of scholarly command of language with a modern sensibility and individual power of expression. Here is another indication that, though the colloquial basis of Gaelic in the population is still declining through inimical economic and social factors, the poetic tradition retains a certain life and is able to branch out in new directions. After all, Gaelic is a superb instrument for poetry, long fallow, but with great latent fertility. With current and impending stirrings of the Scottish national consciousness who can foresee what fresh force may be springing from these ancient roots, just as Hebrew, so long a fossilized and hieratic language, has renewed its social vitality and given birth to powerful poetry?

SELECT BIBLIOGRAPHY

Sàr-Obair nam Bàrd Gaelach: or, The Beauties of Gaelic Poetry, ed. John Mackenzie, 1841 (new edition, 1907).
Gaelic Bards, 1411-1715 and 1715-1765, ed. A. Maclean Sinclair, 1890.
Nigel MacNeill, *The Literature of the Highlanders*, 1898.
Songs of Duncan MacIntyre, ed. G. Calder, 1912. In Gaelic and English.
The Poems of Alexander Macdonald (MacMhaighstir Alasdair), with metrical translations by A. Macdonald of Killearnan and A. Macdonald of Kiltarlity, 1924.
Ortha nan Gaidheal: Carmina Gadelica, ed. Alexander Carmichael, 5 vols., 1928-54. With parallel translations.
Bardachd Ghàidhlig: Specimens of Gaelic Poetry, ed. W. J. Watson, 1932.
The Owl Remembers, ed. J. Mackechnie and P. McGlynn, 1932. An anthology with parallel versions.
Highland Songs of the Forty-Five, ed. John Lorne Campbell, 1933. With translations and a valuable introduction.
The Poems of Mary Macleod, ed. J. Carmichael Watson, 1934. With translations.
Dàin do Eimhir, with some English versions by the author, Somhairle MacGhillEathain (Sorley Maclean), 1943.
Fuaran Sleibh, with English translations by the author, George Campbell Hay, 1948.
The Scottish Gaelic Text Society's editions of John MacCodrum, Duncan Macintyre and others. In progress: with parallel translations.
Selections from *An Cuilithionn*, with parallel translations, by Sorley Maclean, 1955 (in *Lines Review*, vii; 33 Marchmont Road, Edinburgh 9).

NOTES

S.T.S.: Scottish Text Society. E.E.T.S.: Early English Text Society.

CHAPTER I

1. Barbour, *Bruce*, xvi. 519-22; Gray, *Scalacronica;* Wyntoun, *Oryginale Chronykil*, viii. 2299-2300.
2. Barbour was Archdeacon of Aberdeen from at least 1357 till his death. He travelled in England and France, and was one of the commissioners appointed in 1357 to arrange payment of David II's ransom.
3. R. L. Graeme Ritchie's edition of *The Buik of Alexander*, S.T.S., 4 vols., 1921-8, contains the French text and a scholarly account of Barbour and his claims to authorship. Another Scottish translation of the *Roman d'Alixandre* was made about 1460 by Sir Gilbert Hay. The *Bruce* survives in two fifteenth-century manuscripts. It was printed in 1571, 1616 and 1620, and has been edited by W. W. Skeat, S.T.S., 2 vols., 1893-4 and W. M. Mackenzie (1909).
4. i. 447-9.
5. Bower, *Scotichronicon*; transl. Agnes Mure Mackenzie.
6. i. 395-406; vi. 179 ff.; i. 465-76. The war of the Maccabees was a just and obvious parallel. Compare the Declaration of Arbroath, 1320 (transl. Agnes Mure Mackenzie, Saltire Society, 1951): 'King Robert who, to set free his heritage and his people, faced like a new Maccabaeus or Joshua, toil, weariness, hardship and dangers with a joyful heart.'
7. Sir Gilbert Hay, *The Buke of the Law of Armys* (1456).
8. Hay, *The Buke of the Ordre of Knychthede* (1456), a free version of *Le Livre de l'Ordre de Chevalerie*.
9. Bower, *Scotichronicon:* 'Had not the ancient liberty of the Scots driven me, I could not have endured these trials for all the power in the world.'
10. xii. 245-7 and 281-5; i. 227-32.
11. Compare the discussion of background description in C. M. Bowra, *Heroic Poetry* (1952), pp. 132-42.
12. *Paradise Lost*, ix. 34-6; *Bruce*, xi. 196-8.
13. vii. 237-64. Compare the dialogue in v. 583-618.
14. iii. 112-15; vi. 227-30; ii. 348-56; xiii. 147-52. In many such passages Barbour uses the old alliterative patterns effectively. Compare Chaucer, 'The Knyghtes Tale', *C. Tales*, A 2599-2614.
15. The *Wallace* survives in a single manuscript (1488). It was first printed *c.* 1508, and again in 1570, 1594, 1600, *et seq.* Hamilton of Gilbertfield modernized the poem in 1722. The standard edition is by James Moir, S.T.S., 3 vols., 1885-9. See W. A. Craigie, 'Barbour and Blind Harry', *Scottish Review*, xxii (1893), 173-90; George Neilson, 'Blind Harry's *Wallace*', *Essays and Studies*, i (1910).
16. ii. 5-10; viii. 545-7; x. 566 ff.; *The Works of Malory*, ed. Eugène Vinaver (1947), iii. 1259.
17. iv. 736 (contrast the allure of the temptress in *Sir Gawain and the Green Knight*); v. 695; vii. 1368-70; viii. 1410.
18. iv. 213-16; viii. 1054-8; iii. 373-6.

19. i. 17-40; v. 1030-34; vii. 269-82.

20. Burns, *Letters*, ed. J. de L. Ferguson, 1931, i. 106-7.

A third historical poem from this period, Andrew Wyntoun's *Oryginale Chronykil of Scotland*, deserves mention. Wyntoun (*c.* 1350-*c.* 1420), Prior of Lochleven from about 1395, designed his ten books on the common plan of a history of the world from the beginnings, but he patriotically thrusts Scottish affairs into the foreground from Book VI on. His verse is humdrum; but his accounts of biblical and classical history make entertaining reading, and the later books have something of the fervour of Bruce and Wallace. The *Chronykil* has been edited by F. J. Amours, S.T.S., 6 vols., 1902-14.

21. To *The Buik of Alexander* may be added *Lancelot of the Laik*, a paraphrase of the French *Lancelot* (ed. W. W. Skeat, E.E.T.S., 1865); *Golagrus and Gawain*, a blend of two tales based on the *Roman de Perceval* (ed. F. J. Amours, *Scottish Alliterative Poems*, S.T.S., 1891-2); and *The Awntyrs of Arthure at the Terne Wathelyne*, again a blend of two adventures of Gawain (ed. F. J. Amours, *op. cit.*). Those who have struggled with the problem of Huchown of the Awle Ryale rejoice to find this shadowy poet repulsed from Scottish soil by Sir William Craigie in 'The Scottish Alliterative Poems', *Proceedings of the British Academy*, xxviii (1942).

22. Printed at St. Andrews in 1572; ed. F. J. Amours, *op. cit.*, and S. J. Herrtage, *Charlemagne Romances*, vi, E.E.T.S., 1882.

23. Preserved in a single manuscript of the late fifteenth century; ed. W. W. Skeat, S.T.S., 1911 and W. M. Mackenzie (1939). See also Sir William Craigie, 'The Language of *The Kingis Quair*', *Essays and Studies*, xxv (1939); E. M. W. Balfour-Melville, *James I, King of Scots* (1936).

24. Ed. from the Asloan MS. (*c.* 1515) by F. J. Amours, *op. cit.*, and from the Bannatyne MS. (1568) by W. T. Ritchie, S.T.S., 1930.

25. The main manuscript collections belong to the sixteenth century; but it is safe to assume that, in addition to gatherings of the work of Henryson and Dunbar, they contain much anonymous poetry from the later fifteenth century. The Bannatyne MS. (1568) has been edited by W. T. Ritchie, S.T.S., 4 vols., 1928-34. Sir William Craigie has edited the Asloan MS. (*c.* 1515), S.T.S., 2 vols., 1923-5, the Maitland Folio MS. (written between 1570 and 1590), S.T.S., 2 vols., 1919, 1927, and the Maitland Quarto MS. (1586), S.T.S., 1920. See *infra*, pp. 46-9.

26. These two poems have been attributed to James I. The historian John Major, describing James's *cantilenae*, attributes to him an *artificiosum cantum*, 'At Beltayn', which has been taken to be 'Peblis to the Play'; and 'Christis Kirk' is given to James in the Bannatyne MS.

27. 'Fou yellow, yellow wes hir heid' is a ballad phrase (compare 'Edom o' Gordon'). The resolution of Gillie to stick to her lover in the face of family opposition is a commonplace in mediaeval lyric; but the note of abandonment is struck in a realistic *peasant* context, both here and in Burns's

> Though father and mither and a' should gae mad,
> O whistle and I'll come to you, my lad.

28. In the Bannatyne and Maitland Folio MSS., without ascription; contained in *The Poems of William Dunbar*, ed. W. M. Mackenzie, 1932.

29. Lichtoun's 'Dreme' is in the Maitland Folio MS.; the other poems will

be found in the Bannatyne MS., and 'Kynd Kittok' and 'The Manere of the Crying of ane Playe' are also printed in W. M. Mackenzie's edition of Dunbar. On the last mentioned, see Mackenzie's appendix D and A. J. Mill, *Mediaeval Plays in Scotland* (1927), chap. 1 and p. 34.

30. Little is known of Henryson, except that he was 'scolmaister of Dunfermling' and died some time before 1508. The *Poems* are edited by G. Gregory Smith, S.T.S., 3 vols., 1906-14 and by H. Harvey Wood (1933.) See also C. S. Lewis, *The Allegory of Love*, 1936; E. M. W. Tillyard, *Five Poems (1470-1870)*, 1948; and M. W. Stearns, *Robert Henryson*, 1949.

31. See M. W. Stearns, *op. cit.*, chap. 2.

32. *Fabillis*, H. H. Wood's edition, stanzas 89-92, 71-2, 24, 154, 30-31.

33. Preface to *The Ever Green* (1724).

34. It has been supposed that the 'uther quair' is a literary fiction. But *The Spectakle of Luf, or Delectatioun of Wemen*, a translation of a now lost Latin treatise made at St. Andrews in 1492, tells of Diomede's abandonment of Cresseid and how she 'thare efter went common amang the grekis And syne deid in gret myssere and pane'. See my note in the *Times Literary Supplement*, 14 November 1952, p. 743.

35. Chaucer, *Troilus and Criseyde*, v. 1093-9; Raymond Preston, *Chaucer* (1952), p. 78.

36. Some of the *Fabillis* show a considerable knowledge of legal terms and procedure. Professor Stearns (*op. cit.*, pp. 54-60) suggests that the pattern of contract, crime and punishment in the *Testament* may have been based on the 'Lenvoy de Chaucer a Scogan'.

37. M. W. Stearns, *op. cit.*, pp. 44-7; and Sir James Young Simpson, 'Antiquarian Notices of Leprosy...', *Edinburgh Medical and Surgical Journal*, lvi-lvii (1841-2).

38. William Dunbar (*c.* 1460-*c.* 1520) was probably connected with the noble house of Dunbar and March. He was educated at St. Andrews in the late 1470s, apparently became a Franciscan novice, and travelled in England and France. His *Poems* have been edited by J. Small *et al.*, S.T.S., 3 vols., 1884-93; by J. Schipper, 1894; and by W. M. Mackenzie, 1932. See J. Schipper, *William Dunbar: Sein Leben und seine Gedichte* (1884); R. A. Taylor, *Dunbar the Poet and his Period* (1931); J. W. Baxter, *William Dunbar, A Biographical Study* (1952); Edwin Morgan, 'Dunbar and the Language of Poetry', *Essays in Criticism*, II. ii (1952); and C. S. Lewis, *English Literature in the Sixteenth Century* (1954).

39. Helen Gardner, Introduction to Donne's *Divine Poems* (1952), pp. xv-xvi; 'Of the Passioun of Christ'; *Piers the Plowman*, [B] xviii. 57-63; 'On the Resurrection of Christ'; 'Meditatioun in Wyntir'.

40. See J. M. Clark, *The Dance of Death* (1950), pp. 17-20; Lydgate's *The Dance of Death*, ed. Florence Warren, with an introduction on the *danse macabre* by Beatrice White, E.E.T.S., 1931.

41. 'Of the Warldis Instabilitie'. Compare the three poems 'Of Discretioun', and 'A General Satyre' ('Doverrit with dreme').

42. Burns, *Letters*, ed. J. de L. Ferguson (1931), ii. 77: 'Thou Eunuch of language: thou Englishman, who never was south the Tweed: thou servile echo of fashionable barbarisms: thou quack ... thou cobbler ... thou blacksmith ... thou persecutor of syllabication; thou baleful meteor, foretelling

and facilitating the rapid approach of Nox and Erebus.' A jocular but freely abusive flyting habit between a Scot and an Englishman in Burma in the recent war is recorded in J. H. Williams, *Elephant Bill* (1950), chap. 13.

43. See J. W. Baxter, *William Dunbar*, pp. 152-60.

44. For a fuller discussion of the 'Tretis' see my essay in *Medium Ævum*, xxiii (1954), parts of which are reprinted here with the kind permission of Dr. C. T. Onions.

CHAPTER II

There is a brilliant study of this period in C. S. Lewis, *English Literature in the Sixteenth Century* (Oxford History of English Literature, iii), 1954. One must regret that its opening repeats the old baseless slander on James IV: but the remainder moves high and steady in illuminate air, and would be difficult to overpraise.

1. In the second half of the sixteenth century, for instance, editions of a Scots Latin play were printed in Paris, Antwerp, London, Frankfort, Cologne, Leyden, Wittenburg, and Châlons.

2. The Exchequer used Latin invariably until well into the sixteenth century, and indifferently with Scots till the late seventeenth. Although Scots succeeded French in Acts of Parliament in the later fourteenth century, and rapidly became the normal use, Latin appears in Parliamentary business until well into the seventeenth century, leaving vestigial traces till 1707. In the universities, teaching was in Latin until Hutcheson broke the tradition in 1729.

3. (1474?-1522); a Red Douglas, and second son of Bell-the-Cat. Douglas was educated at St. Andrews, took orders, and in 1501 became Provost of the Collegiate Kirk of St. Giles, the High Kirk of the capital. The marriage of his eldest nephew to the Queen Dowager brought him the promise of the see of St. Andrews, but he was in the end fobbed off with Dunkeld. He seems to have favoured the Regent Albany; but, involved in the doings of his unpleasant nephews, he had to flee to England with Angus, and died in London. His epitaph is *patriâ suâ exsul*. His poetical works are: *The Palice of Honour* (1530), *King Hart* (Maitland Folio MS.), *Eneados* (MS. at Trinity College, Cambridge; London, 1553). *Collected Works*, ed. John Small, 4 vols., 1874. See J. W. Bennett, 'The Early Fame of Douglas's *Eneados*', *Modern Language Notes*, lxi (1946).

4. The new models were coming north, though. Poggio and Valla appear at the Muses' Well.

5. After juggling with all the most erudite terms of music, he adds blandly:

> Na mair I understude thir numbers fine,
> Be God, than dois a gekgo or a swine,   [*cuckoo*
> Saif that methinks sweit soundis guid to heir.

The difference between enjoyment of an art and enjoyment of showing how much one knows about it is not always grasped by critics later than those who walked the gardens of Linlithgow.

6. In *The Book of Ballymote*, a manuscript collection of history, genealogy and romance compiled by the monks of Ballymote in Sligo, and apparently appreciated; for in 1522, not a conducive time for the quiet study of letters, The O'Donnel bought it for 140 milch cows.

7. Douglas seems to have tried his hand already at the *Georgics*.

8. There are parallels in Dark Age poetry, in more than one language; but Douglas could not have read them.

9. Henry Howard, Earl of Surrey, produced a version of Books II and IV (1557) which is often, for stretches, Douglas word for word.

10. (1486/1490-1555.) In the childhood of James V, Lindsay held a number of minor offices about the King's person, losing them when the Regent Albany threw in his hand in 1524 and the Queen Mother and her husband Angus (Gavin Douglas's nephew) came to power. His fortunes were restored in 1528 with the King's escape from Douglas control. He was sent as a herald to the Emperor Charles V in 1530 to renew alliance and bring home the portraits of Charles's niece and sister, whom the Emperor was offering James as prospective brides. When James did marry, Lindsay dealt, as Lord Lyon, with the reception of the successive queens. He took the extreme Protestant side, and by 1540 was counselling his master to follow in the steps of his uncle of England and annex Church property. After the King's death in 1542 he lost favour, but not his office; and in 1548 went as ambassador to Denmark. Parts of his work were published in Paris (1558), Edinburgh (1559), London (1566, 1575, 1581); and there were Latin and Danish translations. He was specially popular in England, where as early as 1549 Leland, anticipating a later custom, annexed him verbally among English poets. In Scotland he went out of fashion by the later sixteenth century, but his work was 'popular' till the late eighteenth: *The Monarche* was for long a favourite school-book. Lindsay's complete poems have been finely edited by Douglas Hamer, S.T.S., 4 vols., 1931-6. *Ane Satyre of the Thrie Estaits*, ed. James Kinsley, with essays by Agnes Mure Mackenzie and Ivor Brown (1954).

11. Not 'government by the people' but that 'government of the people for the people'—and with their consent—for which most Kings of Scots had worked devotedly, not seldom to the annoyance of their lords.

12. It is fair to add that though Lindsay was at court before the war he would hardly know much of diplomatic transactions and might not guess how dangerous was the threat from which Flodden, disaster as it was, yet saved us.

13. And the superb production by Mr. Tyrone Guthrie, backed by acting and décor that were worthy of it. The Edinburgh Festival performances in 1948 and after are unforgettable. See Ivor Brown's essay in James Kinsley's edition.

14. The earliest known edition is *ante* 1578, though the compilation is certainly much earlier. The standard edition is by A. F. Mitchell, S.T.S., 1897; a selection was edited for the Saltire Society, 1939, by Iain Ross.

15. One of them, John, is known to have written plays on St. John the Baptist and Dionysius the Tyrant.

16. Mitchell's edition includes the fine German tunes of several, including 'My lufe murnis', the macaronic 'In dulce jubilo', and the metrical Magnificat and Gloria in Excelsis.

17. Not much religious verse in Scots (there is plenty in Gaelic) survives from the Catholic side; and some is certainly much earlier than this time. The sixteenth-century manuscript collections include some lovely things—a version of the Compline hymn for Lent, 'Christe qui lux es et dies'; the humble and gracious 'O Lord my God'; two fine Christmas hymns, 'Now gladith, every lifis creature', and 'The Sterne is risin of our redemptioun'; and the magnificent 'Ierusalem reioss' with its crashing refrain' Illuminare Ierusalem'. Some of these have been guessed as Dunbar's; but I think not.

18. James Cranstoun edited forty-eight pieces, S.T.S., 1891. Few would ask for any more.

19. (1496-1586.) Maitland studied at St. Andrews and Paris, entered the service of James V, and was steadily loyal to James's widow, whose daughter on her return made him (though old and blind) a Lord of Session and Keeper of her Great Seal. He suffered severely in the subsequent regencies, from the death and probably the conduct of his eldest son, and from Morton's harrying of loyalists; but he lived to see the promise of peace on James VI's emergence to rule. The Maitland MSS. (Magdalene College, Cambridge) have been edited by Sir William Craigie, S.T.S., 2 vols., 1919 and 1927 (Folio MS.), and 1920 (Quarto MS.).

20. His son John, Lord Thirlstane, Lord Chancellor, also wrote verse (both Scots and Latin) in his father's vein; and the youngest son, the brilliant Thomas who died at twenty-two, wrote in Latin. See *infra*, p. 83. Maitland's daughter, too, apparently wrote in Scots, though we have only scraps that may be hers.

21. There is good cause to think they were written by Bothwell's Norwegian mistress, Anna Throndsen.

22. (1545-?1608), a son of the Laird of Kirkton of Newtyle in Angus. Newtyle had twenty-three children; and though he managed to send six sons to St. Andrews and make three of them lawyers, there was naturally not much money going, and George had to go into trade, which he did with success. Items from Bannatyne's MS. (Nat. Library of Scotland) have been printed from Ramsay's *The Ever Green* (1724) onward. The complete and standard edition is by W. T. Ritchie, S.T.S., 4 vols., 1928-34.

23. A similar and very successful English collection, Tottel's *Songes and Sonettes*, appeared eleven years earlier. Bannatyne may have seen this, though his English pieces do not derive from it.

24. There are floating fragments of such things in other places: a charming little song, 'Adew deir hart of Abirdene', is scribbled in a leaf of Aberdeen's Minute-book of Sasines; and Mary Maitland preserves the exquisite rhythms of

> The day quhenas the fair parted me frae,
> Plesour me left also.
> Quhen that fra hir I sinderit wes away,
> Mischance me hent but ho.   [*caught without*
> I waxit wan, the same hour than: *plea of mercy*
> Sorow sinsyne dois still me pyne.
> O that guidnicht hes causit mekill wo.

25. We know nothing of Scott but that he was about the court until the middle 1580s, when, as 'auld Scott', he appears as a friend of Montgomerie

and the musician Hudson. Some of his poems have been printed from *The Ever Green* on. Ed. J. Cranstoun, S.T.S., 1896, A. K. Donald, E.E.T.S., 1902, and Alexander Scott, Saltire Society, 1952.

26. Partly as a curiosity, one must mention that hangover from the Middle Ages, John Rolland's *Seuin Sages*, which does not fit any context of its own generation. The originals of these moral tales had gone all through Europe in French or Latin; and there had been versions in Scots and Gaelic. In Mary's minority Rolland wrote a very dull *Court of Venus*. His Aunt Kate thought it 'far ower sublime'; so (had he expectations?) he set to work and produced his version of the *Seuin Sages* in seven weeks 'within the Fort and Towr of Tantalloun'. Printed in 1578, it went through several editions by 1620. *The Court of Venus* was ed. by W. Gregor, S.T.S., 1884, and *The Seuin Sages* by G. F. Black, S.T.S., 1932.

27. There was much translation with this deliberate purpose. The King himself did Du Bartas's *Uranie* (Du Bartas politely replying with a version of James's *Lepanto*) and commanded Thomas Hudson, his Master of Music, to make a translation of Du Bartas's *Judith*. Two others of the set, Stewart of Baldinnes and William Fowler, dealt respectively with Ariosto's *Orlando Furioso* and with Petrarch's *Trionfi* and Machiavelli's *Il Principe*.

28. As late as 1773 Dr. Johnson observed, 'I never was in any house in the Highlands where I did not find books in more languages than one.'

29. The Cambridge memorial volume to Sidney (1587) includes a sonnet by James with his own Latin version of it, and other pieces by Lord Chancellor Maitland (son of Sir Richard), the Master of Gray, Alexander Seton, and one Colonel Halkerton, who was at the time a serving soldier. See *infra*, p. 84.

30. Sir Andrew Gray, a professional soldier who seemed to the Privy Council the right person to take a contingent of 'the broken men of the Borders' to Bohemia.

31. These are included in the B.M. MS. compiled by Prince Charles and his tutor under James's supervision, as 'The First Verses that ever the King made'. James's works are: *Lepanto* (? Edinburgh 1582; French translation 1641); *Essayes of a Prentise* (1584; Arber's Reprints, 1869)—the tract on 'Scottis Poesie' is included in G. G. Smith, *Elizabethan Critical Essays*, i (1904); *His Maiesties Poeticall Exercises at Vacant Houres* (1591); *Lusus Regius*, ed. R. S. Rait, 1901; *Workes* (1616); *New Poems by James I of England*, ed. A. F. Westcott, 1911; *Daemonologie* (1597) has been reprinted in Bodley Head Quartos, 1924; James's *Political Works* have been finely edited by C. H. McIlwain, 1918; and *Basilikon Doron* by James Craigie, S.T.S., 2 vols., 1944-50. James's library is catalogued by G. F. Warner in *Publications of the Scottish History Society*, xv (1893).

32. *Flyting* appears as an independent kind, with 'wordis cuttit short, and hurland ouer heuch'; its best metre is '*Rouncefallis* or *Tumbling* verse'.

33. Guillaume du Bartas (1544-90) was a best-seller in his own—the Huguenot—party, his creation-piece *La Sepmaine* running through thirty editions in six years. He visited Scotland in the 1580s, and carried on a pleasant correspondence with James, which is very much more attractive than his poems.

34. (ante 1550-?1611.) Montgomerie belonged to a cadet branch of

Eglinton, and was third cousin, through his mother, of both the King's father and Esmé Stuart d'Aubigny, Duke of Lennox, who had dazzled the boy King. Apparently brought up in the Highlands, Montgomerie was writing in Mary's time, and is known to have composed masques celebrating James's accession to power. For well over a decade he was in high favour at court; but he was implicated in the mysterious Ladyland Plot in 1597, lost his pension, and went abroad. A manuscript of his was presented to Edinburgh University by Drummond of Hawthornden in 1627; there are pieces by him in the Bannatyne and Maitland MSS. *The Cherrie and the Slae* was published in Edinburgh in 1597, 1636, and ran to twenty-three editions by 1792; ed. H. Harvey Wood (1937). A Latin translation was published in 1631. Selections of Montgomerie's work were included in Aberdeen *Cantus* (1662), Watson's *Choice Collection* (1706-11), and Ramsay's *Ever Green*. The standard edition is by J. Cranstoun, S.T.S., 1887; with a supplement by G. Stevenson, 1910.

35. Try translating 'Aft ettle whiles hit', 'Better thole a grumph nor a sumph', or 'Better rue sit than rue flit'.

36. Thomas Hudson, a Yorkshire professional musician, spent all his adult life in the King's service and wrote in Scots.

37. An undated MS. in the National Library of Scotland; text ed. T. Crockett, S.T.S., 1913. No commentary was published.

38. (1562-1612.) Fowler came of a wealthy Edinburgh burgess family; studied at St. Andrews and Paris, and received the dubious patronage of Francis Stewart, Earl of Bothwell (nephew to both Mary and Earl James), in whom the Hepburn *hybris* rose to insanity. For part of his career he acted as a spy for England, and got away with it. His literary work won the King's favour, and in 1594 he was in charge of the masques at Prince Henry's christening. After 1603 he had a post in the Queen's household, and seems to have died in the odour of respectability. Hawthornden MSS. in the National Library of Scotland. Of matter published in Fowler's lifetime nothing survives but some funeral broadsheets and introductory sonnets to other men's books, a theological pamphlet, and the official report of the aforesaid christening. His poems have been edited, S.T.S., 3 vols., 1914-40, by H. W. Meikle, James Craigie and John Purves (who contributes an essay on Italian influence on Scottish letters).

39. (c. 1560-1609); a cadet of Polwarth. He probably studied at St. Andrews, and then in France; practised law in Edinburgh, entered the ministry, and had the charge of Logie, near Stirling. *Hymnes or Sacred Songs wherein the right Vse of Poesie may be espied* (1599), ed. A. Lawson, S.T.S., 1902.

40. (?1585-1653.) Boyd was educated at Glasgow, St. Andrews and Saumur. In 1623 he became minister of the Barony Kirk, Glasgow; he was Rector and Vice-Chancellor of the University and one of its benefactors. His works are: *The Last Battell of the Soule in Death* (1629; 1831); *The Garden of Zion* (1644; Selections, 1853); *The Psalms of David in Metre* (1646, 1648).

41. (1594-1657.) Mure was writing from about 1611, but his first published work was in a volume of addresses for the King's visit in 1618. His works are: *A Spirituall Hymne* and *Doomesday* (1628); *The Trve Crvcifixe for Trve*

Catholiques (1629); *Covnter-buff to Lysimachus Nicanor* (1640); *Caledon's Complaint* (1641); *The Cry of Blood and of a Broken Covenant* (1650); *Works*, ed. W. Tough, S.T.S., 1898.

42. A conspicuous example is George Macdonald, whose real creative genius is obscured too often by sheer untidiness. Walter Scott himself was not wholly immune from the ailment.

43. There were Scottish delegates; but fewer in proportion and (by their own account) even more silent than those to later assemblies near the same spot.

44. In his excellent account, *Four Centuries of Scottish Psalmody* (1949), Millar Patrick analyses the Twenty-third Psalm. Only the second line is left of Rous. Eight derive from the final Westminster version, four from Boyd, two from the sixteenth-century Englishmen Sternhold and Hopkins, one apiece from King James and from the sixteenth-century English Whittingham. The last quatrain is Boyd, King James, Westminster and Sternhold.

45. *Amorose Songs, Sonets and Elegies* (1606); *Poeticall Recreations* (1609, 1623); *The Pilgrime and Heremite* (1631); *Works*, ed. D. Laing, Hunterian Society, 1873-4.

46. (1567-1629); a cadet of Tullibardine, tutor to Prince Henry. *The Tragicall Death of Sophonisba* and *Cœlia* (1611); *Works*, ed. T. Kinnear, Bannatyne Club, 1823.

47. (?1577-1640); like Gorthy, of Highland stock. Educated at Glasgow and Leyden, he followed Gorthy as Prince Henry's tutor, with later posts in the household of the Princes. In 1621 James, seeking to establish a peaceful outlet for Scots emigration that would save the country the drain of foreign wars, granted him Nova Scotia and a largish area of Canada. Menstrie did not go there, but wrote on colonization and worked for it in his later capacity as Secretary of State for Scotland. France soon claimed the site, and was allowed to have it. Charles I made Menstrie a Lord of Session, and at his coronation gave him his two peerages. But his troubles grew with his master's; and the builder of the noble town mansion in Stirling which now bears Argyll's name died a bankrupt in London. See T. H. McGrail, *Sir William Alexander* (1940). His works are: *Darius* (1603); *Aurora* (1604); *A Parænesis to the Prince* (1604); *The Monarchick Tragedies* (1604, 1616); *Elegie on the Death of Prince Henry* (1612); *Doomesday* (1614); *Recreations with the Muses* (1637; collected and revised works, excluding *Aurora*). The standard edition of the verse is by L. E. Kastner and H. B. Charlton, S.T.S., 2 vols., 1921-9 (with a valuable essay on Senecan drama). *An Encouragement to Colonies* (1624) is reprinted in *Royal Letters, Charters, and Tracts*, Bannatyne Club (1867): Alexander's essay on poetry, *Anacrisis* (published 1711) is reprinted in J. E. Spingarn, *Critical Essays of the Seventeenth Century* (1908-9).

48. (?1570-1638); son of the laird of Kinaldie in Fife. Aytoun was educated at St. Andrews and in France, won the King's favour by a Latin poem, and spent the rest of his life in various minor confidential court offices, eventually as private secretary to Queen Anne and then to Queen Henrietta Maria. His Greek and French verse is lost; several Latin poems are included in *Delitiae Poetarum Scotorum* (Amsterdam, 1637); his English work survives in a transcript of a lost manuscript owned by his friend the Lord Lyon Balfour of

Denmiln. Ed. Charles Roger (1844; revised 1871); and in *Trans. Royal Historical Society*, i (1875).

49. (*d.* 1629). A Galloway man of the Sorbie family, Hannay fought for Elizabeth of Bohemia and her husband, and in 1620 was granted land in Ireland. He became a government official in Dublin, and died in Lambeth, near London. His poems are: *The Happy Husband* and *Elegies on the late death of Queen Anne* (1619); *The Nightingale. Sheretine and Mariana. A Happy Husband. Elegies . . . Songs and Sonnets* (1622). Ed. D. Laing, Hunterian Club, 1875; G. Saintsbury, in *Minor Poets of the Caroline Period*, i (1905).

50. Reprinted in Edinburgh (1718) and Glasgow (1753).

51. (1585-1649); the first Edinburgh alumnus to appear in this book. In 1615 his bride died just before their wedding, and he withdrew to Hawthornden, to emerge in the 1620s with a heart 'handsomely pieced', to marry, travel, build, but go on writing. He watched with grief the course of the Civil War, in which he was too old to take an active part; and the King's execution is said to have broken his heart. His main works are: *Teares on the Death of Meliades* (1613); *Poems* (1614, 1616); *Forth Feasting* (1617); *Flowres of Sion* (1623, 1630); *The History of Scotland* (1655, 1681); *Polemo-Middinia* (1684, 1691). His collected poems were edited by Edward Phillips (1656, 1659). W. C. Ward's edition, 2 vols., 1894, has good literary commentary; the standard edition is by L. E. Kastner, S.T.S., 2 vols., 1913 (with bibliography and a good essay on the portraiture of Drummond, who has suffered from the uncritical reproduction of a dreadful wood-cut which would damn Apollo—a sheepish he-harridan with a cold in the head). For a right estimate of Drummond's originality, Kastner's commentary must be balanced with later criticism: see J. G. Scott, *Les Sonnets élisabéthains*, 1929; R. C. Wallerstein in *Publ. Mod. Lang. Association*, xlviii (1933), 1090-1107; A Joly, *William Drummond de Hawthornden* (1934).

52. We have a catalogue of the books he possessed in 1611: 11 Hebrew, 250 Latin (moderns and ancients), 120 French (with a catholic range from Calvin to Rabelais), 61 Italian, 8 Spanish, and 50 in Scots and English. We may assume that like most of us he read more than he owned.

53. Attributed to him in the Oxford edition of 1691. Defoe in 1727 gives it to Samuel Colvil, a Fifer, son of a poetess, and brother to the Principal of St. Mary's. But the evidence seems to favour Drummond.

54. One can see the Castalian blend of French, English and Italian detail (and some Dutch for good measure) in an essentially Scottish whole in Wallace's building at Heriot's Hospital and Wintoun House. With Sir William Bruce, a bare generation later, we see the lovely Scots classic already flowering, to scatter seed from Russia to Massachusetts; but there was no equivalent literature.

55. Montrose's two famous poems, 'Montrose to his Mistress' and the lines on Charles I, were first printed as broadsides; they appeared with six others in Watson's *Choice Collection* (1711), and have been edited by J. L. Weir, 1938; see *Notes and Queries*, clxxiii (1937) and clxxiv (1938).

56. Though Edinburgh, in spite of the Bowhead Saints, was debauching itself in the 1660s and 1670s with Shakespeare and Molière, and the Holyrood Court in the 1680s with Racine and Dryden. See James Kinsley, 'A Dryden

Play at Edinburgh', *Scottish Historical Review*, xxxiii (1954). The theatre had
to depend on importations, although at least three Scots dramatists were
practising at that time.

57. —and also remarks that 'to have been born or bred in Aberdeen hath
been a great Argument and Ground to procure promotion for any, to Places
of any Profession elsewhere'.

CHAPTER III

1. *Bibliography*. The cardinal work, to which I express the greatest possible indebtedness, is Leicester Bradner, *Musae Anglicanae: A History of
Anglo-Latin Poetry 1500-1925* (1940). On this book the present chapter is
founded, as all studies of the British Latinists must be. The *Delitiae Poetarum
Scotorum*, Amsterdam, 1637, may still occasionally be picked up: for the
Aberdeen poets, the three Spalding Club volumes, *Musa Latina Aberdonensis*
(1892, 1895, 1910) are more readily obtainable. Much valuable information
is also to be found in the two volumes of *Bibliographia Aberdonensis* (1929-
1930).

The lives of some of the Scottish Latin poets are not known in any detail.
One interesting source book is Dempster's extraordinary *Historia Ecclesiastica Gentis Scotorum*, ed. David Irving, Bannatyne Club (1829). Other
important works are Irving, *Lives of the Scotish Poets*, 2 vols. (1804; here
quoted as *Poets*), and his *Lives of Scotish Writers*, 2 vols. (1839; here quoted
as *Writers*). In addition to the *Dictionary of National Biography*, reference
may be made to Chambers's *Biographical Dictionary of Eminent Scotsmen*, 4
vols. (1835). For the wandering Scots, see John Hill Burton, *The Scot Abroad*,
2 vols. (1864), which may be supplemented by Francisque-Xavier Michel,
Les Écossais en France, 2 vols. (1862), and T. A. Fischer, *The Scots in
Germany* (1902).

General works on Renaissance scholarship and literature are J. E. Sandys,
A History of Classical Scholarship, 3 vols. (1903-8); Jakob Burckhardt, *Die
Kultur der Renaissance in Italien* (1860; *The Civilization of the Renaissance in
Italy*, transl. S. G. C. Middlemore, 1951); J. A. Symonds, *History of the
Italian Renaissance*, 7 vols. (1875-86); W. H. Woodward, *Vittorino da Feltre
and other Humanist Educators* (1897) and *Studies in Education during the
Age of the Renaissance* (1906).

For the Scottish Renaissance an important article is John Durkan's 'The
Beginnings of Humanism in Scotland', *Innes Review*, iv (1953), 5-24.
Mediaeval Latin poetry is surveyed in F. J. E. Raby, *A History of Christian-
Latin Poetry to the Close of the Middle Ages* (1927) and *A History of Secular
Latin Poetry in the Middle Ages*, 2 vols. (1934), and in Henry Hallam,
*Introduction to the Literature of Europe during the Fifteenth, Sixteenth and
Seventeenth Centuries*, 4 vols. (1837). Of less value are J. H. Millar, *A Literary
History of Scotland* (1903), and F. A. Wright and T. A. Sinclair, *A History of
Later Latin Literature . . . to the end of the Seventeenth Century* (1931). Among
foreign works may be mentioned G. Ellinger, *Geschichte der neulateinischen
Literatur Deutschlands*, 3 vols. (1929-33); D. Murarasu, *Le Poésie néo-latine*

et la Renaissance des Lettres antiques en France (1928); and W. Mann, *Lateinische Dichtung in England . . . bis zum Regierungsantritt Elisabeths* (1939).

2. *Scholarship: Its meaning and Value* (1946), p. 60. Both Mr. Sparrow and Mr. Garrod are probably thinking primarily of English Latinists. I do not think that Mr. Sparrow means to imply that none of the Scots wrote poetry.

3. Hallam, *Introduction to the Literature of Europe*, ii. 338.

4. The story is quoted in P. Hume Brown, *George Buchanan* (1890), p. 45, note. On Buchanan's notorious *dicatae* in the 'Calendae Maiae' see W. M. Lindsay, *George Buchanan. A Memorial. 1506-1906*, ed. D. A. Millar (1907), pp. 212 ff. There is a discussion of such infelicities in Irving, *Poets*, i. 164.

5. See *Lives of the English Poets*, ed. G. B. Hill (1905), i. 12 and note.

6. Irving, *Writers*, i. 375.

7. *Ibid.*, i. 33-4. The lines are 'appended to some editions of Henry the Minstrel'.

8. *The Meroure of Wyssdome*, ed. C. Macpherson, S.T.S., 1926, p. xxxvii.

9. A copy has recently been acquired by the National Library of Scotland: see John Durkan, *art. cit.*, *Innes Review*, iv (1953), 8. I am much indebted to Mr. Durkan for drawing my attention to the considerable quantity of respectable verse written before the Reformation.

10. Mr. Durkan, I understand, is at present working on this period.

11. Perron, 'Oraison Funèbre sur la Mort de M. de Ronsard', quoted in Irving, *Poets*, i. 76.

12. On Wilson, see Bradner, *op. cit.*; Irving, *Writers*, i. 23 ff.; P. Hume Brown in *The Scottish Historical Review*, x (1913), 124 ff.; J. Durkan, *art. cit.* (especially p. 11); and W. K. Leask in *Bibliographia Aberdonensis*, ii (1930), xxv ff.

13. The standard biography of Buchanan is still P. Hume Brown's (1890), but it badly needs revision, particularly in view of new material published by J. M. Aitken in *The Trial of George Buchanan* (1939). Also valuable are the memorial volumes, *George Buchanan. A Memorial. 1506-1906*, ed. D. A. Millar, St. Andrews (1907), and *George Buchanan: Glasgow Quatercentenary Studies* (1906; containing a splendid bibliography by David Murray). See also Sandys, *op. cit.*, ii. 246. In addition to Bradner's detailed treatment, recent studies are D. F. S. Thomson in *Phoenix* (the Journal of the Classical Association of Canada), iv (1950), 77 ff.—*q.v.* for an appreciation of *Franciscanus*; W. L. Grant, 'The Shorter Latin Poems of George Buchanan', *The Classical Journal* (1945). The best edition of Buchanan is still Thomas Ruddiman's, 2 vols., 1715, reissued with additional notes by Peter Burmann, 1725. The *Sphaera* has been translated with a good introduction and notes by J. R. Naiden (1952). Much of Buchanan's work has been translated into English verse (see David Murray, *loc. cit.*), but of the corpus as a whole Robert Chambers's remark holds true: 'It is an honour yet awaiting some future scholar to give to his unlettered countrymen to feel somewhat of the grace and strength that characterize his performances.'

14. Boswell, *The Life of Samuel Johnson* (1904), i. 396 and ii. 471.

15. The failure to avoid the collocation *pectora Scotos* is typical of Renaissance writers. In Buchanan's time texts of classical Latin poets would contain examples of this scansion which have been rightly emended by later

editors using better manuscripts. But even so, the usage is far commoner in the neo-Latinists than it could possibly have been in their classical models.

16. This poem and that 'On the sad lot of Latin teachers in Paris' are translated in Hugh MacDiarmid, *The Golden Treasury of Scottish Poetry* (1941).

17. D. F. S. Thomson points out (*art. cit.*) that James's *Basilikon Doron* has reminiscences of Buchanan's teaching on the duties of kingship.

18. But J. M. Aitken may be right in suggesting (*op. cit.*, p. 142) that it is really Bordeaux that is intended.

19. *Op. cit.*, ii. 343.

20. *Op. cit.*, p. 383.

21. Sandys, *op. cit.*, ii. 257. See the biographies of Melville by T. McCrie (1819) and J. Morison (1899); Irving, *Writers*, i. 170 ff.

22. The dedicatory lines of this poem, first published by Bradner (*op. cit.*, p. 153), are marred by some extraordinary metrical lapses (even for a preliminary draft); but they contain a reference, worth quoting in view of recent controversies, to the

> nobile marmor,
> Quod pulchram ad Tamesim deposcit Scotobritannum
> Nunc regem, et [*read* atque?] satis Scotorum debita regna.

23. Irving, *Poets*, ii. 143.

24. See *supra*, pp. 46-7, 292.

25. James Crichton (1560-*c.* 1590) was a pupil of Buchanan's at St. Andrews, and won fame in Italy as (in the words of Aldus Manutius) an athlete, scholar, poet and linguist. The epithet 'admirable' was first applied to him by John Johnston in *Heroes Scoti* (1603)—*omnibus in studiis admirabilis*. Urquhart's fantastic account of Crichton is *Discovery of a most exquisite Jewel* (1652). See the biographies by P. F. Tytler (1819) and in Irving, *Writers*, i. 258 ff.

26. Irving, *Poets*, i. 116, and *Writers*, i. 264.

27. For details of his life see the literature quoted by Bradner, *op. cit.*, p. 150, and McCrie's *Melville*, ii. 328 ff.

28. Praised by Sandys, *op. cit.*, ii. 249, and by Hallam, *op. cit.*, ii. 341.

29. See the life by P. F. Tytler, 1823.

30. Bibliographical details in Bradner, *op. cit.*, p. 126.

31. For the spelling of his name see the article by Edward Rosen in *The Scottish Historical Review*, xxviii (1949), 91 ff.

32. William Barclay, M.D., a few of whose poems appear in the *Delitiae*, was distantly related; see Irving, *Writers*, i. 230 ff. He was the author of the tracts celebrating tobacco (*Nepenthes*) and the Spa Well in Aberdeen (*Callirhoe*).

33. William Dempster (1579-1625) called himself Baron of Muresk, but since he was the twenty-fourth of twenty-nine children and had many elder brothers, the title should probably not be pressed. He was educated at Turriff, Aberdeen Grammar School, and Pembroke Hall, Cambridge, which he reached at the age of nine. (See Irving, *Writers*, i. 347 ff.) One of his most extraordinary works is the *Historia Ecclesiastica Gentis Scotorum* (Bologna, 1627; ed. Irving, Bannatyne Club, 1829), which claims as Scotsmen scores of

persons who were not and many who never existed, his learning being, as Irving says, 'much superior to his sagacity'. He collaborated in producing the first complete text of the famous *Tabulae Iguvinae* (published posthumously, 1723), and his work on the Etruscans, *De Etruria Regali*, is still quoted in text-books.

34. Bibliography in Bradner, *op. cit.*, p. 159.

35. Arthur Johnston was born at Caskieben (Keith-hall), Aberdeenshire. Educated at Marischal College, he studied and taught at Heidelberg, was M.D. of Padua, and for nearly twenty years was a professor at Sedan. He returned to Aberdeen in 1622, and was subsequently appointed *Medicus Regius*; but the post was a successorship, and he tells us that his predecessors were only too successful in healing themselves. He spent some time farming 'on the banks of the Gadie', but his life can hardly have been as close to the soil as some have believed. The references to manual labour in the epistle to Robert Baron seem humorously exaggerated. In 1637 he became Rector of King's College, Aberdeen, and died while visiting a married daughter in Oxford in 1641.

Johnston is the only Scots Latinist who has appeared in a worthy modern edition, the two Spalding Club volumes (*Musa Latina Aberdonensis*, i and ii), ed. Sir William Geddes (1892-5). The best edition of his *Psalms* is probably Benson's (1741). See Bradner, *op. cit.*, and T. D. Robb in *The Scottish Historical Review*, x (1913), 287 ff.

36. It is translated, with a few lines omitted, in Hugh MacDiarmid, *The Golden Treasury of Scottish Poetry* (1941).

37. His works are included in *Musa Latina Aberdonensis*, iii (1910), 349-439.

38. Bradner, *op. cit.*, pp. 163 ff.; *Musa Latina Aberdonensis*, iii (1910), 250-91. Born at Montrose, a son of the manse, Leech graduated from King's College in 1614, but his subsequent life is obscure. He seems to have wandered a great deal, in England, France and possibly Ireland, and he knew many of the leading men of the day. His poems mention Arthur Johnston, Villiers, Sir Robert Aytoun and many other eminent people; he was a friend of Scot of Scotstarvet and Drummond, and was for a time secretary to the Earl of Pembroke. We lose sight of him after 1626, and he probably died young—a fate which he says he expected. He speaks often of financial troubles, and had been in jail. Dempster says he was exiled for attacking the Scottish bishops, which seems likely enough, for the first edition of his epigrams was suppressed for its attacks on the clergy and its indecency. Yet despite all this he seems to have been Rector of King's.

39. Bradner, *op. cit.*, pp. 171-2 and 190-1. Chalmers may have graduated M.A. at Aberdeen in 1620. A Roman Catholic, he seems to have spent most of his life abroad, and became professor of humanities at Padua.

40. For a more detailed consideration of the poem see Bradner, *op. cit.*, pp. 196-8.

41. Another collection worthy of mention, which adds some further names to the list, is William Lauder's *Poetarum Scotorum musae sacrae*, 1739. On Lauder and his campaign against Milton, see Irving, *Poets*, i. 103, 172, and Bradner, *op. cit.*, p. 291.

42. Archibald Pitcairne (1652-1713) was an eminent physician, 'more

than any other man the founder of the Edinburgh medical school' (L. Jolley, in *The Scotsman*, 19 December 1952), and a member of a learned and convivial circle in the Edinburgh which was now entering upon its golden age. See Irving, *Writers*, ii. 189 ff.; Bradner, *op. cit.*, pp. 193-4 and 245-9.

43. *Poems in Latin* (1941), p. x. For Jortin's lines see *ibid.*, p. 17, and for Dillingham's see Bradner, *op. cit.*, pp. 204-5.

CHAPTER IV

1. The principal collections of Scottish ballads are those of David Herd, *Ancient and Modern Scots Songs* (1769; see *infra*, p. 169); Sir WalterScott, *Minstrelsy of the Scottish Border*, 3 vols. (1802-3); and Robert Jamieson, *Popular Ballads and Songs*, 2 vols. (1806): but ballads were also included among such collections as James Johnson's *The Scots Musical Museum*, 6 vols. (1787-1803; see *infra*, pp. 169, 203) and R. A Smith's *The Scotish Minstrel*, 6 vols. (n.d.). These often overlapping collections were gathered and arranged in F. J. Child's definitive *English and Scottish Popular Ballads*, 8 vols. (1857-1859), recast in 5 vols. (1882-98). On this was based H. C. Sargent and G. L. Kittredge, *English and Scottish Popular Ballads* (1905). There are versions of Aberdeenshire ballads in Gavin Greig, 'Folk-Song of the North-East', *Buchan Observer* (1909, 1914), and the same collector's *Last Leaves of Traditional Ballads and Airs*, ed. A. Keith (1925). A good selection is *Border Ballads*, ed. William Beattie (1952). The best critical discussions are contained in G. H. Gerould, *The Ballad of Tradition* (1932), W. J. Entwistle, *European Balladry* (1939; 2nd impression, corrected, 1950), and E. K. Chambers, *English Literature at the Close of the Middle Ages* (1945), all of which provide substantial bibliographies; W. P. Ker, *Form and Style in Poetry* (1928) and *Collected Essays*, 2 vols. (1925); Edwin Muir, *Latitudes* (1924); and M. J. C. Hodgart, *The Ballads* (1950).

2. 'English and Scottish Ballads' in *An Apology for the Arts* (1944).
3. *The Brus*, vi. 227-30. See *supra*, p. 6.
4. Sir William Fraser, *The Douglas Book* (1885), ii. 191-3.
5. William Roughead, *The Riddle of the Ruthvens* (1919), pp. 3-35.
6. *Historie of the Kennedyis* (1830), pp. 48-9.
7. David Hume of Godscroft, *History of the House of Douglas* (1648), p. 261.
8. *The Historie and Life of King James the Sext*, Bannatyne Club (1825), pp. 367-71.
9. John Knox, *Works*, ed. Laing (1846-64), i. 206.
10. Robert Jamieson, *Popular Ballads and Songs* (1806), i. 27, note.
11. H.M. General Register House, Edinburgh Testaments, vol. 25, ff. 100-1.
12. Several instances are quoted in George F. Black, *The Surnames of Scotland* (1946), p. xvii.
13. Sir Arthur Quiller-Couch, *Shakespeare's Workmanship* (1918), p. 168.
14. Introduction to *Register of the Privy Council*, III. ix.
15. *Ibid.*, pp. 355-6.
16. *Acts of the Parliament of Scotland*, ii. 362.

17. *Register of the Privy Council*, vi. 263.
18. *Protocol Book of Sir William Corbet*, Scottish Record Society (1911), No. 64. The spelling has been modified.
19. Dailly Kirk Session minutes, under date 3 March 1694.
20. *Historie of the Kennedyis*, p. 47.
21. Robert Lindsay of Pitscottie, *The Historie and Chronicles of Scotland* (1899), i. 209; John Knox, *Works*, i. 177; Archbishop John Spottiswoode, *History of the Church of Scotland* (1851), ii. 290.

CHAPTER V

1. Gray, 'Stanzas to Mr. Bentley'; Boswell, *The Life of Samuel Johnson* (1904), ii. 26.
2. *The Works of the English Poets*, ed. Alexander Chalmers (1810), includes verse by all the writers mentioned in this chapter except Arbuthnot, Boswell, Bruce and Macpherson.
3. 'The noblest prospect which a Scotchman ever sees, is the high road that leads him to England!' (Boswell, *op. cit.*, i. 285.)
4. 'Skelton Laureate against the Scottes', ll. 150-2:

> Your pryde was pevysh to play such prankys.
> Your poverte coude not attayne
> With our kynge royal war to mayntayne.

Compare Charles Churchill, *The Ghost*, iv:

> Came ill-match'd riders side by side,
> And Poverty was yok'd with Pride.

(They ride on the first pair of horses drawing Bute's car.)
5. 'It was with Scotsmen [Hume] fraternized chiefly; and these were to be found at the favourite resort, the British Coffee-House, which so swarmed with men of the North that Gibbon used to speak of it as the *Breetish* Coffee-House. There John Hume, Dr. Armstrong, Wedderburn and Elliot, the Hunters and Smollett, were constantly meeting' (H. G. Graham, *Scottish Men of Letters in the Eighteenth Century* (1901), p. 51).
6. John Arbuthnot (1667-1735), the son of an Episcopal clergyman displaced in 1689, went up to London in his early twenties. He became a member of the Scriblerus Club and Queen Anne's domestic physician. He was 'in great esteem with the whole Court, a great philosopher, and reckoned the first mathematician of the age, and has the character of uncommon virtue and probity' (Berkeley, letter to Perceval 16 April 1713). *A Sermon ... on the Subject of the Union* (1706); *The History of John Bull* (1727, in vol. ii of the Pope and Swift *Miscellanies*. The original pamphlets were published March-July 1712: chapters ii, iv and v are especially interesting for their account of Anglo-Scottish relations); the verse ΓΝΩΘΙ ΣΕΑΥΤΟΝ, *Know Yourself* (1734). See G. A. Aitken, *The Life and Works of John Arbuthnot* (1892); L. M. Beattie, *John Arbuthnot, Mathematician and Satirist* (1935).
7. John Ramsay of Ochtertyre, *Scotland and Scotsmen in the Eighteenth Century*, ed. A. Allardyce (1888), i. 76; C. S. Terry, *A History of Scotland*

NOTES [*Chapter V*]

(1920), pp. 519-20—'On March 19, 1707, Queensberry communicated to the Estates an exemplification of the Act under the Great Seal of England. Seafield, the Lord Chancellor, received it and handed it to the Lord Clerk Register with a "despising and contemptuous remark", Lockhart alleges, which perhaps covered emotion—"Now there's ane end of ane auld sang." '

8. Tobias George Smollett (1721-71): *Advice: A Satire* (1746), *Reproof: A Satire* (1747). 'The Tears of Scotland' and 'Ode to Leven-Water' have individuality and life, and Scottish themes. Apart from these poems, his verse is merely competent, and has no interest beyond the interest that must attach to anything by Smollett. Some of it appears in the novels, e.g. 'When Sappho struck the quiv'ring wire', 'Thy fatal shafts unerring move', and 'Where now are all my flatt'ring dreams of joy?' (*Roderick Random*); 'Adieu, ye streams', 'Come listen, ye students' and 'While with fond rapture and amaze' (*Peregrine Pickle*). *The Critical Review*, vi (December 1758), contained an amusing and unfavourable review of Grainger's translation of Tibullus. Grainger replied with *A Letter to Tobias Smollet, M.D. occasioned by his Criticism . . .* (1759): 'And now, Dr. *Toby*, what have you to object to these Authorities? —You see that a sincere Intention to find Fault, is not the sole Quality, of which a *Critic* on the Version of *Tibullus*, should be possessed.' Smollett, replying in *The Critical Review*, vii (pp. 141-58), suggests that the best apology for Grainger 'would be, to declare him at once *non compos . . .* Dr. James Grainger, that gulph of learning, that mirrour of poetry . . . *poetarum obscurorum longe obscurissimus.*' See H. S. Buck, *Smollett as Poet* (1927); L. M. Knapp, *Tobias Smollett, Doctor of Men and Manners* (1949).

9. E.g. *Roderick Random*, xxxvi, where 'a North Briton' is used of a Scot by a Scot! Compare Ramsay, *op. cit.*, i. 309, 'the English . . . were not one whit more liberal-minded or better informed with regard to North Britain or its inhabitants'.

10. *Op. cit.*, i. 7 and 9.

11. Wordsworth, *The Prelude*, vi. 105-14.

12. Boswell, *op. cit.*, ii. 80; Ramsay, *op. cit.*, i. 9; Alexander Carlyle, *Autobiography* (1860), p. 517.

13. 'As Miss Blair is my great object at present . . . I enclose you the latest papers on the subject. You will find the letter I wrote her when ill, where you will see a Scots word *roving*, from the French *rêver*, as if to dream awake. I put it down as a good English word, not having looked in Johnson.' Letter to Temple, 28 August 1767; *Letters to Temple*, ed. T. Seccombe (1908), p. 85.

14. To G. Thomson, 19 October 1794; *Letters of Robert Burns*, ed. J. de L. Ferguson (1931), ii. 268.

15. William Wilkie (1721-72), an eccentric, learned and slovenly. Alexander Carlyle relates that Townshend told him 'he had never met with a man who approached so near the two extremes of a god and a brute as Wilkie did' (*Autobiography*, p. 394). At St. Andrews, where he was Professor of Natural Philosophy, Wilkie befriended Fergusson (*infra*, pp. 177-8). Desire outstripped performance in his imitation of Homer in *The Epigoniad, a Poem* (1757), but it was an honourable desire. The *Fables* (1768) are readable and amusing. 'A Dream' was published in 1759, with the second edition of *The Epigoniad*. Goldsmith reviewed *The Epigoniad* in *The Monthly Review* (1757); and the brutal but not unjustified attack in *The*

303

Critical Review, iv (1758), provoked Hume's letter (*infra,* note 16). Hume's tenderness towards his fellow-Scots embarrassed the Critical Reviewers, who were forced by it to give much more space to Home's *Douglas* than they thought the work deserved (iii. 267).

16. Carlyle, *op. cit.,* p. 319; Letter from David Hume 'To the Authors of the Critical Review', April 1759, published in vol. vii, pp. 323-34.

17. The verse of James Boswell (1740-95) is worthless. His first published poem is *An Evening Walk in the Abbey Church of Holyrood-house* (*Scots Magazine,* August 1758). While in Holland he set himself to write five heroic couplets daily (see *Boswell in Holland, 1763-1764,* ed. F. A. Pottle, 1952). In 1879 G. B. Hill edited Boswell's correspondence with the Honourable Andrew Erskine, published in 1763, and much of it in rhyme.

18. James Thomson (1700-48), born at Ednam (or Wideopen?) in Rox-burghshire, son of a minister; removed to Southdean near Jedburgh in 1701; influenced by Robert Riccaltoun, author of a poem on Winter. Thomson went up to Edinburgh University in 1715, and to London in 1725, where he was tutor to Lord Binning's son, and later at Watts's Academy, where Newton's philosophy was taught. He went on a Continental tour 1730-1, and spent the rest of his life in London and Richmond, supported partly by sinecures and partly by his writings. Poems: Contributions to *The Edinburgh Miscellany* (c. 1720); *Winter. A Poem* (1726); *A Poem Sacred to the Memory of Sir Isaac Newton* (1727); *Summer. A Poem* (1727); *Spring. A Poem* (1728); *Britannia. A Poem* (1729); (?) *A Poem to the Memory of Mr. Congreve* (1729); *The Seasons,* including *Autumn* and *A Hymn* (1730); *Liberty,* Parts I, II and III (1735), Parts IV and V (1736); *Poem to the Memory of the Right Honourable the Lord Talbot* (1737); later editions of *The Seasons* (1738, 1744, 1746); *The Castle of Indolence: An Allegorical Poem* (1748). Plays: *Sophonisba* (1730); *Agamemnon* (1738); *Edward and Eleonora* (1739); *Alfred, a Masque,* with Mallet, see *infra,* p. 142 (1740); *Tancred and Sigismunda* (1745); *Coriolanus* produced, with Lyttleton's Prologue (1749). *Poetical Works,* ed. J. Logie Robertson, 1908; *The Seasons,* ed. Otto Zippel, 1908 (contains original text and all variants).

Critical lives of Thomson: Murdoch, in Thomson's *Works* (1762); Johnson, in *Lives of the English Poets* (1779-80); H. Nicolas, in Thomson's *Poems* (1860); L. Morel, *James Thomson, sa Vie et ses Œuvres* (1895); G. C. Macaulay, *James Thomson* (1908); Douglas Grant, *James Thomson, Poet of 'The Seasons'* (1951). See also A. D. McKillop, *The Background of Thomson's 'Seasons'* (1942); Marjorie Nicolson, *Newton Demands the Muse* (1946). Among useful articles on Thomson are: Herbert Drennon, 'James Thomson's Contact with Newtonianism and his Interest in Natural Philosophy', *Publ. Mod. Lang. Assn. of America,* xlix (1934), 71-80; Drennon, 'Scientific Rationalism and James Thomson's Poetic Art', *Studies in Philology,* xxxi (1934), 453-71; J. E. Wells, 'Variants in the 1746 Edition of Thomson's *Seasons',* *Library,* xvii (1936), 214-20; Wells, 'Thomson's (?) A Poem to the Memory of Mr. Congreve', *Times Literary Supplement,* 3 October 1936, p. 791; Wells, 'Manuscripts of Thomson's Poems to Amanda and Elegy on Aikman', *Philological Quarterly,* xv (1936), 405-8; E. G. Fletcher, 'Notes on Two Poems by James Thomson', *Notes and Queries,* clxviii (1935), 274-5.

19. Thomas Blacklock (1721-91), the blind poet, was one of the earliest

and most encouraging friends of Burns. See *An Account of the Life, Character, and Poems of Mr. Blacklock; Student of Philosophy, in the University of Edinburgh* by the Rev. Mr. Spence, Late Professor of Poetry in the University of Oxford (1754). *Poems on Several Occasions* (1746); *The Graham: An Heroic Ballad, in Four Cantos* (1774); *Poems*, ed. with life by Henry Mackenzie (1793).

20. Beattie, 'To Mr. Alexander Ross'.

21. *Autumn*, ll. 889-91; *Castle of Indolence*, i. 424-31.

22. *Spring*, l. 55; *Autumn*, ll. 644-51.

23. Johnson, *Lives of the English Poets*, ed. G. B. Hill, i. 77.

24. Wordsworth, 'Essay, supplementary to the Preface' (to *Lyrical Ballads*, second edition).

25. Pope, *Moral Essays*, Epistle III, ll. 339-402.

26. Hazlitt, *My First Acquaintance with Poets*. Beattie approved of the tales; see *On Poetry and Music*, I. ii.

27. *Spring*, ll. 211, 207-11, 539-41; *Winter*, ll. 232-3; *Autumn*, ll. 407-8.

28. 'A Hymn', ll. 1-3; *Summer*, ll. 268-70, 231-6, 236-9; *Winter*, ll. 1028-1033.

29. G. M. Hopkins, 'Spring and Fall.'

30. 'Epistle to Davie.'

31. Marjorie Plant, *The Domestic Life of Scotland in the Eighteenth Century* (1952); *Roderick Random*, viii.

32. *Winter*, ll. 276-321, 240-75, 617-29.

33. *Castle of Indolence*, i. 262-70.

34. Henryson, *Testament*, ll. 36-40; *Winter*, ll. 426-32.

35. *Liberty*, iv. 1117.

36. *Ibid.*, iv. 813-16, v. 200-201, iii. 354-5, iv. 314.

37. *Spring*, l. 66; *Castle of Indolence*, ii. 145-89.

38. Report of promenade concert in the *Manchester Guardian*, 21 September 1953.

39. *Castle of Indolence*, i. 316-19; *ibid.*, i. 172-3 (compare *The Ancient Mariner*, ll. 367-72).

40. *Spring*, ll. 597-612; *Castle of Indolence*, i. 32-4, i. 428-31.

41. *Ibid.*, i. 505-621. Of special interest are the portraits of Armstrong (ll. 532-40), Lyttleton (ll. 577-94) who wrote the Prologue to Thomson's posthumously produced *Coriolanus*, and Quin the actor (ll. 595-603) who moved himself and his audience to tears in speaking it. Of the portrait of Thomson himself (ll. 604-12), Thomson wrote the first line and Lyttleton the rest of the stanza. The stanza following describes Patrick Murdoch, author of the first memoir of the poet.

42. 'What an exquisite picture has Thomson given us in his *Castle of Indolence* . . . I cannot at present recollect any solitude so romantic, or peopled with beings so proper to the place, and the spectator' (*An Essay on the Genius and Writings of Pope* [Vol. I, 1756; Vol. II, 1782], ii. 17-18). Compare *ibid.*, ii. 99: '. . . that exquisite piece of wild and romantic imagery, Thompson's *Castle of Indolence*'.

43. 'An Essay on Criticism', ll. 318-19.

44. William Somervile, 'Epistle to Mr. Thomson, on the first edition of his Seasons', ll. 29-36.

45. Warton, *op. cit.*, ii. 243 (compare i. 42, 'though the diction of the *Seasons* is sometimes harsh and inharmonious, and sometimes turgid and obscure . . . yet is this poem on the whole . . . one of the most captivating and amusing in our language, and which, as its beauties are not of a fugacious kind, . . . will ever be perused with delight'); Hazlitt, *op. cit.*; Wordsworth, *ibid.*

46. Johnson, *op. cit.*, iii. 282.

47. *Castle of Indolence*, i. 397; *Spring*, l. 493; *Liberty*, iv. 517.

48. *Autumn*, l. 626; *Summer*, l. 1331; *Autumn*, l. 1134; *Summer*, l. 863; *Paradise Lost*, iv. 271; *Moral Essays*, iv. 176; *Liberty*, iii. 260; *ibid.*, iv. 540.

49. *Liberty*, iii. 439-47; *Summer*, l. 378; *Liberty*, v. 11-12; *Spring*, l. 421.

50. *Winter*, l. 256; *Spring*, l. 157; *ibid.*, l. 535; *Castle of Indolence*, i. 45; *Autumn*, ll. 862-5.

51. *Liberty*, iii. 166-80.

52. *Castle of Indolence*, i. 433-504.

53. Letters to Pope, 29 September 1725, and Alderman Barber, 1 March 1734 (G. A. Aitken, *The Life and Works of John Arbuthnot* (1892), pp. 109, 158).

54. *Know Yourself*, ll. 20, 87-94; Dryden, *Religio Laici*, ll. 451-4; Boswell, *op. cit.*, ii. 350.

55. John Armstrong (1709-79), who practised medicine in London and was an intimate friend of Thomson and of the painter Fuseli. *The Art of Preserving Health: A Poem* (1744); *Taste: An Epistle to a Young Critic* (1753); *A Day: An Epistle to John Wilkes, of Aylesbury, Esq.* (1761); *Miscellanies* (1770). See Iolo A. Williams, *Seven XVIIIth Century Bibliographies* (1924). Under the pseudonym of Launcelot Temple, Armstrong wrote *Sketches: or Essays on various Subjects* (see *The Critical Review*, v, 1758).

56. John Nichols, *Literary Anecdotes of the Eighteenth Century* (1812-15), ii. 715.

57. *The Works of the English Poets*, ed. A. Chalmers (1810), xvi. 521, 524, 528, 529.

58. Carlyle, *op. cit.*, pp. 197, 347; Churchill, *The Journey* (Chalmers, *op. cit.*, xiv. 376); *Index to Private Papers of James Boswell*, Isham Collection; Graham, *op. cit.*, p. 191, quoting from Monboddo's *The Origin and Progress of Language*; *Boswell in Holland*, ed. F. A. Pottle, p. 240.

59. Graham, *op. cit.*, p. 53; introductory note to 'Palemon and Lavinia' in *The Beauties of English Poesy. Selected by Oliver Goldsmith* (1767); Goldsmith, Essay on Metaphor; Nichols, *op. cit.*, ii. 308 (compare Joseph Warton, 'Reflections on Didactic Poetry', in *The Works of Virgil, in Latin and English* (1753), i. 430-1).

60. William Falconer (1732-69), the only self-educated man in this company of university wits. His life is as interesting as his poem. Son of a poor Edinburgh tradesman, he describes with pathos in *The Shipwreck* (1762, 1764, 1769) his struggles to educate himself and his longing to see the countries on whose shores he merely touched. He was drowned at sea. *An Universal Dictionary of the Marine* (1769); *Poetical Works*, ed. J. Mitford (1836 and 1866).

61. *The Shipwreck* (Chalmers, *op. cit.*, xiv. 390); *ibid.*, xiv. 385.

62. First edition, iii. 453-4; second edition, iii. 632-3; third edition, iii. 658-9.

63. Chalmers, *op. cit.*, xiv. 388.

64. Grainger (*c.* 1721-66), physician and contributor to Percy's *Reliques* and Dodsley's *Collection of Poems. Poetical Works* (1836). Johnson reviewed *The Sugar-Cane* politely and favourably in *The London Chronicle* (July 1764), praising it as a source of information for 'all to whom Sugar contributes usefulness or pleasure'.

65. ii. 428-553, iv. 322-64, ii. 30, i. 517-18, i. 453-7.

66. *The Sugar-Cane*, i. 219; iv. 480-1.

67. Boswell, *op. cit.*, i. 662-3 and footnote.

68. Robert Blair (1699-1746), minister of Athelstaneford, where he was succeeded by John Home, author of *Douglas*. Blair was a friend of Isaac Watts. *The Grave. A Poem* (1743; designs by William Blake published in 1808). See C. O. Parsons, 'The Canon of Robert Blair's Poetry,' *Notes and Queries*, clxiv (18 March 1933), 185-6.

69. Carlyle, *op. cit.*, p. 94.

70. Letter of 25 February, 1741-2; *Epistolary Correspondence of Dr. Doddridge* (1790).

71. Chalmers, *op. cit.*, xv. 68, 63; *The Ancient Mariner*, ll. 446-51.

72. The *Spectator*, No. 419; Robert Fergusson, 'The Farmer's Ingle'; Carlyle, *op. cit.*, p. 46; *Letters of Burns*, ed. Ferguson, i. 106, letter dated 2 August 1787.

73. Aitken, *op. cit.*, p. 164.

74. Compare *Summer*, ll. 1675, 'as village-stories tell', and 1681, 'so night-struck fancy dreams.'

75. David Mallet (or Malloch) (?1705-65). *The Excursion* (1728); *Alfred, A Masque*, with Thomson, see *supra*, p. 129 (1740); *Works* (1759); *Ballads and Songs*, ed. F. Dinsdale, 1857. See Johnson's *Life* of Mallet ('the only Scot whom Scotchmen did not commend'); W. L. Phelps, *The Beginnings of the English Romantic Movement* (1893), Appendix II, pp. 177-82.

76. Chalmers, *op. cit.*, xiv. 17, 19.

77. *Ibid.*, xvi. 541-2.

78. William Julius Mickle (1735-88) edited the four-volume continuation of Dodsley's *Miscellany* published in 1772. *The Lusiad*, Book I (1771), complete (1776); *Poems, and a Tragedy* (1794). See S. G. West, 'The Work of W. J. Mickle, the first Anglo-Portuguese Scholar', *Review of English Studies*, x (1934), 385-400. Mickle is best known by two poems which he never claimed, 'There's Nae Luck about the House' and the ballad of 'Cumnor Hall', which gave Scott the germ of *Kenilworth*.

79. Chalmers, *op. cit.*, xvii. 536, 531; *ibid.*, xxi. 610; *ibid.*, xviii. 56.

80. Gray, letter to Beattie, 2 October 1765; Beattie, *On Poetry and Music*, I. vi. 3.

81. James Macpherson (1736-96), appointed surveyor-general of the Floridas in 1764 and agent to the nabob of Arcot in 1779. Member of Parliament for Camelford, Cornwall, 1780-96. In 1796, the year in which Burns died in debt and anxiety, Macpherson was entombed in Westminster Abbey. *The Highlander* (1758); *Fragments of Ancient Poetry collected in the Highlands of Scotland* (1760); *Fingal, an Ancient Epic Poem in Six Books*

(1762); *Temora . . . in Eight Books* (1763); *The Works of Ossian* (1765); *Works*, ed. M. Laing, 2 vols. (1805). See *inter alia* A. Nutt, *Ossian and the Ossianic Literature* (1899); J. S. Smart, *James Macpherson: an Episode in Literature* (1905); E. D. Snyder, *The Celtic Revival in English Literature* (1923). Hume was deceived by many Scottish eighteenth-century versifiers, but not by Macpherson. An essay unpublished in his lifetime, probably out of consideration for the feelings of Dr. Blair, pours ridicule on *Ossian* (*Essays, Moral, Political and Literary*, ed. T. H. Green and T. H. Grose (1875), ii. 415-24).

82. Letter to McGowan, 24 September 1761; *Letters of William Shenstone*, ed. Marjorie Williams (1939), pp. 596-7.

83. Ramsay, *op. cit.*, i. 548, footnote.

84. Boswell, *The Journal of a Tour to the Hebrides with Samuel Johnson, LL.D.*, Thursday, 23 September 1773; Macpherson, 'A Dissertation concerning the Poems of Ossian' (*The Poems of Ossian*, 1825 ed., p. 62); William Mason, 'Ode to Sir Fletcher Norton' (Chalmers, *op. cit.*, xviii. 419).

85. James Beattie (1735-1803) was Professor of Moral Philosophy and Logic at Aberdeen from 1760. *Original Poems and Translations* (1760); *Essay on the Nature and Immutability of Truth . . .* (1770); *The Minstrel; or, The Progress of Genius*, Book I (1771), Book II (1774); *On Poetry and Music, as they affect the Mind*, one of three essays appended to a new edition of *Essay on . . . Truth* (1776); *Scoticisms, arranged in Alphabetical Order, designed to correct Improprieties of Speech and Writing* (1779; see also *infra*, pp. 159, 170); *Dissertations, Moral and Critical* (1783); *Poetical Works*, with memoir by Alexander Dyce (1831 and 1866). See Margaret Forbes, *Beattie and his Friends* (1902).

86. Letter to Blacklock, 22 September 1766, quoted in *Poetical Works*, ed. Dyce, p. xix.

87. *The Minstrel*, ii. 479-80, i. 217-18 (Beattie's addition to 'There's Nae Luck about the House' shows this liking for the obvious:

> The present moment is our ain,
> The neist we never saw).

88. *The Minstrel*, ii. 425-33.

89.   Hence, sweet harmonious Beattie sung
>   His 'Minstrel lays';
>   Or tore, with noble ardour stung,
>   The Sceptic's bays.

90. Dyce, *op. cit.*, p. xliv; e.g. *The Minstrel*, i. 361-9; *ibid.*, ii. 249-51.

91. Letter from Glamis Castle, 2 October 1765: 'P.S. Remember Dryden, and be blind to all his faults'.

92. *The Minstrel*, i. 23-6.

93. William Hamilton of Bangour (1704-54), militant Jacobite and contributor to Ramsay's *Tea-Table Miscellany* (see *infra*, p. 168). *Poems on Several Occasions* (1748, 1749); *Poems and Songs*, ed. James Paterson (1850), contains fresh material. *The Lounger*, No. 42, is an appreciation of Hamilton.

94. *Cambridge History of English Literature* (1907-16), x. 155.

95. Nathan Drake, *Essays, Biographical, Critical and Historical, illustrative of the Rambler, Adventurer . . .* (1809), i. 420.

96. Chalmers, *op. cit.*, xvi. 449.

97. Michael Bruce (1746-67), son of a Kinross weaver, who died prematurely under the strains of poverty and study. His fellow-student John Logan (1748-88), who undertook the posthumous publication of his poems, is alleged to have set aside some of the best and passed them off as his own (*Poems*, 1781). *Poems on Several Occasions, by Michael Bruce*, ed. John Logan (1770); *Works*, ed. A. B. Grosart (1865); *Poetical Works . . . with Life and Writings*, ed. W. Stephen (1895). See James Mackenzie, *The Life of Michael Bruce, Poet of Loch Leven, with Vindication of his Authorship of the 'Ode to the Cuckoo' and other Poems* (1905), and *Life and Complete Works of Michael Bruce* (1914). ('Ode: To the Cuckoo' is assigned to Bruce in *The Oxford Book of Eighteenth-Century Verse*.)

98. *The Grasmere Journal* (1802), ed. E. de Selincourt, i. 152.

99. *Observations on the Faerie Queene of Spenser* (1754), pp. 234-5.

CHAPTER VI

1. Robert Sempill (or Semple) of Beltrees (*c.* 1595-*c.* 1668) belonged to a family of versifiers. The sixteenth-century Robert Sempill who wrote coarse but lively satirical ballads and poems is perhaps no connexion, but Sir James Sempill of Beltrees (*c.* 1565-1626), pupil of George Buchanan and friend of James VI, author of religious tracts and a breezy anti-Catholic poem, was his father. Our Robert Sempill studied at the College of Glasgow and fought on the Royalist side in the Civil War. His son, Francis Sempill, wrote 'Maggie Lauder', 'The Blythsome Bridal' and other lively pieces.

2. Watson was involved throughout much of his turbulent life in a fight against the claims to a printing monopoly maintained by the widow of Andrew Anderson, the late King's Printer. Much of the curious story is told, from Watson's point of view, in the preface 'to the Printers in Scotland' prefixed to his *History of the Art of Printing* (1713; largely translated from the French). Watson gives an interesting picture of the state of printing in Scotland in the late seventeenth and early eighteenth centuries. In her struggle to maintain her monopoly against Watson, Mrs. Anderson charged that he had been bred a Papist and printed Popish and Jacobitical books, and it is true that (besides revering the memory of Charles I) he was an ardent Scottish patriot who had got into trouble in 1700 for printing a pamphlet by Hugh Paterson which bitterly attacked the Government's betrayal of the people over the Darien scheme. Both author and printer were jailed, but were soon delivered by a popular rising. Later Watson printed Bibles, catechisms and other religious works agreeable to the Church of Scotland. The original editions of his *Choice Collection* are extremely scarce. The three volumes were accurately reprinted in one volume for private circulation in Glasgow (1869); but even this is now rare.

3. The first volume opens with 'Christis Kirk on the Grene' in a simplified stanza form (the eleventh and final line containing always four syllables and ending with 'that day') which Fergusson and Burns were to adopt. There are other poems of popular revelry, including that rollicking piece of happy vulgarity 'The Blythsome Wedding'. Some miscellaneous and minor seven-

teenth-century occasional and satirical pieces (mostly in English and occasionally in an Anglicized Scots) are of less interest that 'The Life and Death of the Piper of Kilbarchan' and its sequel 'Epitaph on Sanny Briggs, Nephew to Habbie Simson, and Butler to the Laird of Kilbarchan'. 'The Mare of Colintoun', a long humorous poem in eight-line stanzas of racy Scots telling of the mare's sufferings, last will and testament, perpetuates a Scottish tradition of animal poetry; and Hamilton of Gilbertfield's 'Last Words of Bonny Heck, a Famous Greyhound in the Shire of Fife' continues the 'Habbie Simson' tradition of mock elegy. Beside the fairly recent pieces are six poems by Montgomerie, including *The Cherrie and the Slae* in a text partly modernized and partly corrupt (not through Watson's fault), the comic dog-Latin (or Latin-Scots) *Polemo-Middinia* attributed to Drummond of Hawthornden, and the strange and lively English 'Hallow my Fancie' (partly by William Cleland, a young Cameronian killed at the battle of Dunkeld in 1689).

Volume II (1709) is an equally mixed bag, with some minor sixteenth- and seventeenth-century poems in both English and Scots; epigrams, satires, translations and occasional pieces; three short poems by Sir Robert Aytoun; and Drummond's *Forth Feasting*. Volume III (1711) opens with 'The Flyting betwixt Polwart and Montgomery', one of the last of a tradition. It includes eight English poems by Aytoun and some slight pieces in the English seventeenth-century courtly tradition; 'The Country Wedding', an older popular poem somewhat modernized and considerably enlarged; a group of Latin-and-English macaronics from Aberdeen University; a version of 'Auld Lang Syne' which seems to be an anglicized and doctored broadside text of an older popular song; a broadside version of the charming 'Lady Anne Bothwel's Balow'; and eight poems by Montrose, for five of which Watson's is the only known text.

4. Lord Yester died in 1713. His version of 'Tweedside' was printed in Herd's collection (1776) entitled simply 'Original of Tweedside'. It is a tripping poem in anglicized Scots:

> When Maggy and me were acquaint
> I carried my noddle fu hie . . .

These words kept the old tune going (it occurs as 'Doune Tweedside' in the Blaikie MS., 1692) until Robert Crawford (1695-1732) wrote for it the highly conventional English version—

> What beauties does Flora disclose!
> How sweet are her smiles upon Tweed!
> Yet Mary's still sweeter than those;
> Both nature and fancy exceed

—which was to appear later as the 'Tweedside' of both *The Scots Musical Museum* and *Select Scotish Airs*.

5. William Hamilton of Gilbertfield (*c.* 1665-1751), after a brief military career, settled down as a country gentleman on his estate near Cambuslang, from which he carried on his verse correspondence with Allan Ramsay. On William Hamilton of Bangour (1704-54), see *supra*, chapter V, note 93.

6. Allan Ramsay was born at Leadhills, in the parish of Crawfordmoor,

Lanarkshire, in 1684 or 1685, and settled in Edinburgh about 1700, first as apprentice wigmaker, then as master wigmaker, then as bookseller, and finally, from 1740 until his death in 1758, as gentleman of leisure living in busy retirement in his octagonal house (the 'Goose Pie') on the Castle Hill. From July 1712 until November 1713 he was 'Keeper of the original letters and other writs belonging to the [Easy] Club'. About 1725 he opened a circulating library, said to be the first in Britain; in 1736 he opened a theatre in Carrubber's Close, but the authorities closed it the following year, and though Ramsay fought hard for the revival of a theatre in Edinburgh, clerical prejudice against the acted drama prevented such a revival until after his death. His many miscellaneous activities in the city (which diminished after his retirement in 1740) included membership of the Whinbush Club and the Royal Company of Archers, promoting various schemes for the encouragement of arts and letters, organizing auction sales of books, pictures and jewelry, and selling tickets for the Assembly.

Ramsay published a great many poems individually as he wrote them, and many of his songs were first published in small groups. The octavo edition of his collected works appeared in 1720, followed in 1721 by the quarto subscription edition which established his reputation as the Edinburgh poet. 1722 saw the first and the second (enlarged) editions of *Fables and Tales*: the third, containing thirty fables, appeared in 1730. Throughout the 1720s occasional pieces, satirical, congratulatory, descriptive, pastoral and moral, flowed from his pen, most of them separately published. In 1728 he published by subscription a volume of poems written since 1721. *The Ever Green, Being A Collection of Scots Poems, Wrote by the Ingenious before 1660*, 2 vols. (1724); *The Tea-Table Miscellany*, i (1724), ii (1726), iii (probably 1727), iv (1737)— with numerous later editions in Ramsay's lifetime; *The Gentle Shepherd* (1725). The *Poems* are being edited by J. W. Oliver and Burns Martin for S.T.S. See Andrew Gibson, *New Light on Allan Ramsay* (1927); Burns Martin, *Allan Ramsay: A Study of his Life and Works* (1931).

7. Ramsay's version of 'Auld Lang Syne' differs from an equally frigid English version in Watson's *Choice Collection* beginning:

> Should old Acquaintance be forgot
> And never thought upon,
> The Flames of Love extinguished
> And freely past and gone?

Watson's version was an 'improved' broadside version of an older song of which the chorus only has survived. Francis Sempill and Sir Robert Aytoun have both been claimed as the author, but the song's origin remains obscure. Ramsay's words are those found for 'Auld Lang Syne' in *The Tea-Table Miscellany*, Herd's *Scots Songs*, and *The Scots Musical Museum*. Burns's words finally drove out Ramsay's in Thomson's *Select Scotish Airs* (to a somewhat different tune, which is the one now sung).

8. Among the older songs in *The Tea-Table Miscellany* are (I give Ramsay's titles) 'Lady Anne Bothwell's Lament' (in a version differing only slightly from Watson's 'Lady Anne Bothwel's Balow'), 'John Ochiltree', 'General Lesley's March to Longmarston Moor', 'Todlen butt, and todlen ben' (better known as 'Todlen hame'), 'Waly, waly, gin love be bonny',

'O'er the hills and far away' (clearly 'improved', though marked Z, and with the old chorus), 'Norland Jock and Southland Jenny', 'Rare Willy drown'd in Yarrow', 'Sweet William's Ghost', 'Bonny Barbara Allan', 'Dermet's Coronach', 'The bonny Earl of Murray', 'There Gowans are gay', 'Andro and his Cutty Gun', 'Johnny Faa, the Gypsie Laddie', 'The Nurse's Song' ('Hey! my kitten, a kitten,/Hey! my kitten, a deary'), and 'The Magpie' (a street ballad). Some of the texts are thoroughly sound; indeed, most of the old songs in Volume IV (where no letters are appended) seem to be printed as Ramsay found them. There has apparently been more tampering in the first two volumes; the third volume has only English songs; Volumes I, II and III have new songs to old tunes and choruses and sometimes new stanzas added to old songs.

The collection also contains 'Hardyknute' (described as 'A fragment of an old heroic ballad') and many other imitation folk-songs and ballads, some of them capturing the folk-spirit with remarkable success ('Clout the Cald-ron', for example, is clearly based on a folk-song but has apparently been expanded and dressed up; and 'Tak your Auld Cloak about ye'—in Volume I with no signature—has the true folk-touch and certainly incorporates at least part of a folk-song). The first part of Montrose's 'My dear and only love, I pray' is printed under the title 'I'll never love thee more', in a text differing considerably from Watson's. The anonymous 'Happy Beggars' and 'Merry Beggars' which probably suggested Burns's 'Jolly Beggars' are here, with Fergusson's favourite song 'The Birks of Invermay', Lady Grizel Baillie's 'Werena my heart light, I wad die', and drinking-songs, political songs, street ballads and love-songs of the seventeenth century. Ramsay's own adaptations of folk-songs are included with others of his songs, and there are versions of such popular songs as 'The Bob of Dumblane', 'My jo Janet', 'Fy gar rub her o'er wi' strae' (an old chorus to which Ramsay has deftly appended a Horatian imitation in the same style), 'The Highland Laddie', 'This is no mine ain House', 'My Daddy forbad, my Minny forbad', 'She raise and loot me in', 'For the sake of Somebody', 'Tarry Woo' and many more.

9. Only thirteen of the eighty-two poems in *The Ever Green* are not from the Bannatyne MS. Three of them—'Hey Trix', 'On the Mes', and 'On Purgatorie'—are from *The Gude and Godlie Ballatis*. 'The Cherry and the Slae' Ramsay says he took 'from two curious old' editions of 1597 and 1615. The ballad 'Johnie Armstrong' he claims as 'the true old Ballad, never printed before . . . copied from a Gentleman's Mouth of the Name of *Armstrong*, who is the 6th Generation from this *John*'. Lady Wardlaw's 'Hardyknute' (pub-lished 1719) was printed in *The Tea-Table Miscellany* with additional stanzas and antique spelling, and reappears in *The Ever Green* with the spell-ing even more antique. 'The Vision' and 'The Eagle and Robin Red-breist' are most probably by Ramsay himself, though he attributes both of them to 'Ar. Scot'.

10. Robert Crawford (1695-1732) contributed certainly four and perhaps five songs to *The Tea-Table Miscellany*. Little is known about him save that he came from Renfrewshire and spent some time in France. See *supra*, note 4.

11. Sir John Clerk (1676-1755), second baron of Penicuik, lawyer and

antiquary, was a commissioner for the Union of the Kingdoms and in 1708 became one of the five barons (judges) of the newly formed Scottish Court of Exchequer. See his *Memoirs of my Life*, ed. J. M. Gray (1892).

12. There were two Alexander Pennecuiks, and they are often confused. The one here referred to died in 1730, and little is known of his life. His works include *A Pil for Pork-Eaters* (1705), *Streams from Helicon* (1720), *Flowers from Parnassus* (1727), *A Collection of Poet Pennicuik's Satires on Kirkmen* (1744), and *Compleat Collection of Poems* (1750). In 1756 was published *A Collection of Scots Poems on Several Occasions* 'by the late Alexander Pennecuik and others'. 'The Merry Wives of Musselburgh' may be by one of the 'others'. His namesake Dr. Alexander Pennecuik (1652-1722) wrote in English: his works include *Lintoun Address to the Prince of Orange* (1714; it appears also in Watson) and *Description of Tweeddale with miscellany of Scotish Poems* (1715).

13. See *supra*, chapter V, note 93.

14. Alexander Ross (1699-1784), son of an Aberdeenshire farmer, studied at Marischal College, Aberdeen, became schoolmaster first at Aboyne, then at Laurencekirk, and finally at Lochlea in Angus, where he passed most of his life. *Helenore* (1768).

15. John Skinner (1721-1807) was for many years minister at the Episcopal chapel of Longside near Peterhead. As an Episcopalian and non-juror he suffered some hardship, including a brief spell of imprisonment, but survived his troubles cheerfully. His poems were published posthumously (edited by his son, who became Bishop of Aberdeen): *Amusements of Leisure Hours* (1809); *Miscellaneous Collection of Fugitive Pieces* (1809).

16. Alexander Geddes (1737-1802) was a versatile and learned Catholic priest who wrote in both prose and verse; he produced some skilful macaronics and a translation of the *Iliad* I.

17. Jean Elliot (1727-1805) was born in Teviotdale, daughter of Sir Gilbert Elliot of Minto. She never married, and for years lived with old-fashioned dignity in Brown Square, Edinburgh.

18. Lady Anne Barnard (1750-1825) was born Lady Anne Lindsay, daughter of the fifth Earl of Balcarres; she married Sir Andrew Barnard in 1793. 'Auld Robin Gray' was written probably in 1772 and became immediately popular. Lady Anne tells the whole story of its writing in her *Memoirs*. See *Scottish Diaries and Memoirs 1746-1843*, ed. J. G. Fyfe (1942), pp. 246-9.

19. See *supra*, chapter V, note 78.

20. *The Ancient and Modern Scots Songs, Heroic Ballads, etc. Now first Collected into one Body. From the various Miscellanies wherein they formerly lay dispersed. Containing likewise, A great Number of Original Songs, from Manuscripts, never before published* (1769; 2nd edition, much enlarged, 2 vols., 1776). The first part, containing 'heroic ballads and fragments', includes 'Gill Morrice', 'Edom o' Gordon', 'Johnie Armstrang', 'Bonny Barbara Allan', 'Bonny Earl of Murray', 'Sir Patrick Spence', 'The Battle of Harlaw', 'Chevy Chace', 'Edward, Edward', 'Lammikin', 'The Battle of Otterburn', 'Willie and Annet' among others, with a few modern imitations. The second part, 'sentimental and love songs', has a large number of recent productions, including many by Ramsay and by some of Ramsay's 'ingenious young gentlemen' (all printed anonymously). This part is less attractive to the

modern reader, though many of the songs have interesting original lines or stanzas embedded in them (e.g. 'Had awa fra me, Donald', 'Soger Laddie', 'Highland Laddie'); and there are a few genuine older pieces such as 'The Lowlands of Holland' and 'Lizae Baillie'. The third and fourth parts, 'comic and humorous songs' and 'fragments of comic and humorous songs', provide the richest collection of genuine old material. Burns (who owned both editions of Herd and also saw his manuscripts) profited immensely by the material he found there. Here are 'Apron Deary', 'Hey Jenny come down to Jock', 'Jocky fou, Jenny fain', 'Jenny Nettels', 'My Jo Janet', 'Todlen Hame', 'My Heart's my ain', 'Here awa', there awa' ', 'Drap of Capie—O', 'The Plough-man', 'Get up and bar the Door', 'Let me in this ae night', 'Kind-hearted Nancy', 'Bide ye yet', 'Ranting Roving Lad' ('My Love was born in Aberdeen') and others. The section of fragments provided Burns with just the kind of thing he wanted—suggestive bits and pieces of old folk-songs. Here are 'Cauld kail in Aberdeen', 'John come kiss me now' (not the religious adaptation in *The Gude and Godlie Ballatis* but two stanzas of the original version), 'When she came ben she bobbit', 'As I gaed to the Well', 'Birks of Abergeldie', 'Will ye go to Flanders, my Mally—O?', 'Kirk wad let me be', 'Green grows the Rashes' (an early and lusty version) and many more. See also *Songs from David Herd's Manuscripts*, ed. Hans Hecht (1904).

21. See *supra*, chapter V, note 85.

22. See *infra*, chapter X.

23. Robert Fergusson (1750-74) was born in Edinburgh of Aberdeenshire parents. His father came to Edinburgh about 1746, but, though apparently a man of education and ability, never managed to make more than a bare living for himself and his family as a clerk. Robert attended the High School at Edinburgh 1758-61, and proceeded on a bursary first to Dundee Grammar School and then (1765) to St. Andrews University. Compelled to leave St. Andrews to support his widowed mother, he found employment as an extracting and copying clerk. Some kind of physical illness gave way in 1774 to a mental breakdown which modern opinion has tentatively diagnosed as a manic-depressive psychosis. Fergusson was taken to the scandalously primitive Edinburgh Bedlam and died there shortly afterwards.

Only one volume of his work was published in his lifetime—Ruddiman's collection (1773) of twenty-eight English poems and nine in Scots ('Sandie and Willie, an Eclogue', 'Geordie and Davie', 'Elegy on the Death of Mr. David Gregory', 'The Daft Days', 'The King's Birthday in Edinburgh', 'Caller Oysters', 'Braid Claith', 'Elegy on the Death of Scots Music' and 'Hallow-fair'). The next edition (1779) included the poems he wrote for the *Weekly Magazine* in 1773 as well as the epistles to and from 'J. S.', and 'To the Tron-kirk Bell', which appeared in the *Magazine* on 26 November 1772. *Scots Poems*, ed. Bruce Dickins (1925); a selection of *Scots Poems*, ed. Alexander Law (1947, Saltire Society). See *Robert Fergusson: Essays by Various Hands*, ed. S. G. Smith (1952).

24. The rhyming of *more* with *shore* and *yore* illustrates Fergusson's habit of substituting English words (the Scots would be *mair*) if it helped the rhyme or in any other way aided the flow. He rhymes *dead* now with *reed* and now with *bed*. This practice has been censured, but it is an old habit with Scots poets.

25. Also found as 'Indermay', 'Endermay', 'Innermay'; sung in Fergusson's day to the poor words of David Mallet and Alexander Bryce.

26. Do the diminutives here derive from Fergusson's Aberdeenshire parents? He indulges in them fairly often, and they are a characteristic of north-eastern Scots.

27. To the tune of 'The Blythsome Bridal'. The poem first appeared anonymously in Herd's collection (1776). The tune appears as 'Walley Honey' in *The Caledonian Pocket Companion*, Book VII.

CHAPTER VII

1. Robert Burns was born at Alloway, near Ayr, on 25 January 1759. 1766: Burnses move to Mount Oliphant farm, near Alloway; and 1777: to Lochlea, near Tarbolton. Winter 1781-2: in Irvine to learn flax-dressing; meets Richard Brown. 1782-3: reads Fergusson's *Poems* and is stirred to emulation. April 1783: begins first Commonplace Book. 13 February 1784: Burns's father dies in straitened circumstances. 1784: Burnses move to Mossgiel, near Mauchline, a farm leased from Gavin Hamilton by Burns and his brother Gilbert. 31 July 1786: *Poems, chiefly in the Scottish Dialect* published at Kilmarnock. 28 November 1786: Burns arrives in Edinburgh. April 1787: first Edinburgh edition of *Poems* published. 5 May-8 June 1787: Border Tour, ending with Burns's return to Mauchline. June 1787: West Highland Tour. 7 August 1787: Burns returns to Edinburgh. 25 August-16 September 1787: Highland Tour with William Nicol. September 1787-March 1788: except for two brief visits in the country Burns was in Edinburgh awaiting a settlement with his publisher and preparing songs for Johnson's *Scots Musical Museum* (first met Mrs. M'Lehose—Clarinda—on 4 December 1787). April-May 1788: in Mauchline, receiving instruction towards a commission in the Excise. 13 June 1788: enters upon his farm, Ellisland, near Dumfries. February 1789: in Edinburgh, seeking an Excise appointment. By September 1789: begins duties as an Exciseman. January 1791: James, Earl of Glencairn, Burns's patron, dies at Falmouth. November 1791: Burns gives up Ellisland and moves to Dumfries. September 1792: invited to contribute to George Thomson's *Select Collection of Original Scotish Airs*. December 1792: at Dunlop House, Ayrshire. Returns to Dumfries shortly before Christmas to find that the Board of Excise had ordered an inquiry into his 'political conduct' (so far as the Board was concerned, the matter had blown over by January 1793). February 1793: second Edinburgh edition of *Poems* published. 1794: last issue of *Poems* in Burns's lifetime. 1795-6: Burns seriously ill. July 1796: returns to Dumfries from Brow, on the Solway, where he tried sea-bathing for a cure. Dies on 21 July; is buried 25 July with military honours at Dumfries.

The more important editions of Burns's works, published since his death, include *Works*, ed. James Currie, 4 vols. (1800; revised 1801; 8th edition 1820); *Works*, ed. W. Scott Douglas, 6 vols. (1877-9; new edition 1895); *Life and Works*, ed. Robert Chambers, revised W. Wallace, 4 vols. (1896); *The Poetry of Robert Burns*, ed. W. Henley and T. F. Henderson, 4 vols.

(1896). *Letters of Robert Burns*, ed. J. de Lancey Ferguson, 2 vols. (1931). Of many Lives, the best and most recent are F. B. Snyder, *The Life of Robert Burns* (1932), and Hans Hecht, *Robert Burns, the Man and his Work*, transl. by Jane Lymburn (1936).

2. *Letters*, ed. Ferguson, i. 104-16 (No. 125). Except where otherwise indicated, quotations in section 1 are from this letter.

3. Opinion at present favours *The Lark* (1765), described on the title-page as Vol. 1, though no second volume was ever published. See Hans Hecht, *op. cit.*, p. 246, note.

4. *Letters*, i. 76 (No. 85).

5. David Sillar (1760-1830), son of a farmer at Spittleside, near Tarbolton, and the subject of Burns's 'Epistle to Davie'. *Poems*, Kilmarnock (1789). See [James Paterson], *The Contemporaries of Burns* (1840).

6. John Lapraik (1727-1807), descended from an old Ayrshire family, inherited the estate of Dalquhram, near Muirkirk, but was ruined by the failure of the Ayr Bank in 1772, and moved to Muirsmill, near Dalquhram. Burns sent him three verse epistles, the first as the result of hearing Lapraik's 'When I upon thy Bosom lean' sung at a 'rocking'. This song (slightly revised by Burns) and another one, 'When West Winds did blow', were later sent by Burns to Johnson's *Museum* (Nos. 205 and 208). Lapraik's *Poems on Several Occasions* was published at Kilmarnock in 1788. See Paterson, *op. cit.*

7. *Letters*, i. 70 (No. 79).

8. *Works*, ed. Scott Douglas (1877-9), vi. 215-16.

9. *Letters*, ii. 122-3 (No. 507).

10. *Letters*, ii. 194-5 (No. 582); ii. 256 (No. 637); ii. 172 (No. 559); ii. 210 (No. 588); ii. 200-1 (No. 586); i. 136 (No. 149); ii. 321 (No. 695).

11. 'A Dream'; 'To a Mouse'; 'Epistle to Davie'; 'To a Louse'.

12. John Ewen (1741-1821); Mrs. Grant of Carron (?1745-1814); Hector MacNeil (1746-1818): see *The Edinburgh Book of Scottish Verse* (1910). James (Balloon) Tytler (?1747-1805): see Chambers, *Scottish Songs* (1829), pp. 554 and 130. Lady Anne Barnard: see *supra*, chapter VI, note 18. Elizabeth Hamilton (1758-1816): see Henderson, *A Little Book of Scottish Verse* (1899). John Mayne (1759-1836): see the *Edinburgh Book*. Joanna Baillie (1762-1851), poet and dramatist: nine *Plays on the Passions* (1798 ff.), *Metrical Legends* (1821), *Poetic Miscellanies* (1823): see the *Edinburgh Book* and *The Songs of Scotland* (1872), p. 352.

13. Carolina Oliphant (1766-1845) was born at the 'Auld House' of Gask, Perthshire, of Jacobite ancestry; married her Jacobite cousin, and became Baroness Nairne when her husband's estates were restored to him in 1825. Most of her songs were published in R. A. Smith's *Scottish Minstrel* (1821-4) over the initials 'B. B.' (Mrs. Bogan of Bogan), for she kept the fact of her authorship a close secret to the end. Only Hogg rivals her as a Jacobite lyrist; her other songs have pathos and occasionally a touch of humour, but lack passion and originality of sentiment. See *Life and Songs of the Baroness Nairne*, ed. Charles Rogers (1872); G. Henderson, *Lady Nairne and her Songs* (1905).

14. *Letters*, ii. 196 (No. 582).

15. Sir Alexander Boswell (1775-1822), who set up a private press at Auchinleck for printing rare books, and died of a wound sustained in a duel.

See *The Edinburgh Book of Scottish Verse* (1910); Henderson, *A Little Book of Scottish Verse* (1899); *The Songs of Scotland* (1872), p. 359.

16. Robert Tannahill (1774-1810), a weaver, and chief of a group of Paisley poets, was not driven to poetry by the popular music of Scotland or by the Jessies and Maggies that figure as heroines of his songs. His theme was really the braes and woodland burns and dusky glens, where he spent so much of his time, near Paisley. He set a fashion for a pleasantly sentimental type of song still popular in Scotland. His poetic character is best displayed, perhaps, in the imagery he employs to paint the landscape he cared for most. *Poems and Songs*, ed. David Semple (1876).

17. Allan Cunningham (1784-1842), son of a gardener who became factor on the estate where Burns farmed Ellisland; as a child he heard Burns read 'Tam o' Shanter'. A stonemason to trade, he later became secretary to the sculptor Chantrey, and filled his lesiure with literary work of all sorts for magazines and publishers. He knew the Scottish world that had inspired Burns, so far as it survived in the changing conditions of his generation; but he was not drawn or tied to it from choice or necessity as Burns had been. His work, even in Scottish song, was the more casual and without distinction in consequence. *Songs and Poems* (1847).

18. Sir Walter Scott (1771-1832), William Motherwell (1797-1835) and James Hogg (1770-1835) did notable work for the older Scottish poetry as collectors and editors—Scott with his *Minstrelsy of the Scottish Border* (1802-3), Motherwell with his *Minstrelsy, Ancient and Modern* (1827) and Hogg with *Jacobite Relics of Scotland* (1819-21). But all three are poets also in their own right, though poets of another Scotland than Burns's. See *infra*, chapter VIII.

19. William Laidlaw (1780-1845); Alexander Rodger (1784-1846); William Glen (1789-1826)—*Poems* (1874); Thomas Pringle (1789-1834), journalist and secretary to the Anti-Slavery Society—*Poems*, with a life by Leitch Ritchie (1839); Hew Ainslie (1792-1878), clerk and later brewer in America; Henry Scott Riddell (1798-1870)—*Poems*, with memoir (1871); John Park (1804-1865)—see *The Edinburgh Book of Scottish Verse* (1910); Lady John Scott (1810-1900)—*Songs and Verses* (1911).

CHAPTER VIII

1. Sir Walter Scott (1771-1832) was born in Edinburgh of Border stock, and educated at the High School and University there. A lawyer by profession, he was called to the Scottish bar in 1792, appointed Sheriff of Selkirkshire in 1799 and Clerk of Session in 1806. He was created baronet in 1820. Scott's excurisons into the Border country began in 1792. He removed from Lasswade in Midlothian to Ashestiel on the Tweed in 1804, and eight years later settled at Abbotsford near Melrose. His poetical career virtually ended with the publication of *Harold the Dauntless* (1817); the flood of novels opened in *Waverley* (1814) was closed only by death. In 1826 he was brought to financial ruin with his publisher Constable and the printer James Ballantyne, with whom he had been in partnership since 1805; and he spent the rest

of his life heroically clearing his debts. Scott was a prodigiously learned and versatile man of letters, laying the foundations of ballad scholarship in *Minstrelsy of the Scottish Border* (3 vols., 1802-3; ed. T. F. Henderson, 1902), editing Swift (1814) and Dryden (1808; still the standard edition) and a wide range of memoirs and historical documents. Of his five experiments in drama, *Auchindrane, or The Ayrshire Tragedy* (1830) is the least unsuccessful. See A. Caplan, *The Bibliography of Sir Walter Scott* (1928). Scott's *Journal* was edited by D. Douglas, 2 vols. (1890); the standard edition is J. G. Tait's, 3 vols. (1939; 1950). The standard edition of the *Letters* is H. J. C. Grierson's, 12 vols. (1932-7). J. C. Corson, *A Bibliography of Sir Walter Scott: A Classified and Annotated List of Books and Articles relating to his Life and Works, 1797-1940* (1943); W. Ruff, *A Bibliography of the Poetical Works of Sir Walter Scott, 1796-1832* (*Edinburgh Bibliographical Society Transactions,* i. 2 and 3 (1937-8).

The finest biography is J. G. Lockhart, *The Life of Sir Walter Scott, Bart.,* 2 vols., 1836-8, frequently reprinted. See also James Hogg, *The Domestic Manners and Private Life of Sir Walter Scott,* 1834; and the biographies by Andrew Lang (1906), John Buchan (1932) and H. J. C. Grierson (1938).

2. 'Memoir . . . written by himself' in Lockhart, *op. cit.,* chap. I.

3. *Marmion,* Introduction to Canto Third.

4. 'Memoir . . . written by himself', Lockhart, *op. cit.,* chap. I.

5. Lockhart, *op. cit.,* chap. VII.

6. *Poetical Works* (1849), 'Essay on Imitations of the Ancient Ballad'.

7. See M. R. Dobie, 'The Development of Scott's *Minstrelsy*', *Edinburgh Bibliographical Society Transactions,* ii. 1 (1940).

8. Lockhart, *op. cit.,* chap. XI.

9. *Poetical Works* (1830), Introduction to *The Lay.*

10. *Ibid.,* Introduction to *The Lady of the Lake.*

11. *Ibid.,* Introduction to *The Lord of the Isles.*

12. *The Bridal,* II. xviii.

13. Barbour, *Bruce,* xii. 27-31, 51-60; *The Lord of the Isles,* VI. xiv-xv.

14. *Poetical Works* (1830), Introduction to *The Lord of the Isles; Harold the Dauntless,* I. x.

15. *Ibid.,* Introduction to *The Lord of the Isles.*

16. W. C. Fraser, 'Oral Tradition about Sir Walter Scott', *Hawick Express,* 22 September 1932; a paper read to the Hawick Archaeological Society.

17. *The Lay,* VI. xi and xxiii; *Marmion,* V. xii; *The Antiquary,* xl.

18. *Poetical Works* (1830), Introduction to *The Lady of the Lake;* James Ballantyne's 'Memorandum', quoted in Lockhart, *op. cit.,* chap. xx.

19. *Marmion,* Introduction to Canto Third, l. 238; *ibid.,* VI. xxxiii-xxxiv.

20. *The Lay,* V. conclusion, VI. i-ii.

21. *Poetical Works* (1830), Introduction to *The Lady of the Lake.*

22. *The Lay,* conclusion.

23. *Ibid.,* IV. i-ii.

24. *Marmion,* III. xxx; *The Lord of the Isles,* III. xvii; *Rokeby,* V. i.

25. *Poetical Works* (1849), Introduction to *Marmion.*

26. *Marmion,* Introduction to Canto Second, ll. 154-9 and 244-9; Introduction to Canto Fifth, ll. 33 ff.: Introduction to Canto Fourth, ll. 55-68.

27. *Marmion*, III. x; *The Bride of Lammermoor*, iii; *The Heart of Mid-lothian*, xl.

28. James Hogg (1770-1835) was born at Ettrick, Selkirkshire, and spent his life as a Border shepherd and farmer. His first publication was *Scottish Pastorals, Poems and Songs* (1801); he did not make good as a poet till the publication of *The Queen's Wake* (1813). His verse work includes *The Pilgrims of the Sun* (1815), *Mador of the Moor* (1816), *Queen Hynde* (1825) and *Songs* (1831). His miscellaneous prose includes *The Brownie of Bodsbeck and other Tales* (1818), *Winter Evening Tales* (1820), *The Private Memoirs and Confessions of a Justified Sinner* (1824; 1947, with an introduction by André Gide), and *The Domestic Manners and Private Life of Sir Walter Scott* (1834). See H. T. Stephenson, *The Ettrick Shepherd: A Biography*, 1922; E. C. Batho, *The Ettrick Shepherd*, 1927; A. L. Strout, 'The *Noctes Ambrosianæ* and James Hogg', *The Review of English Studies*, xiii (1937), 46-63 and 177-89.

29. 'Extempore Effusion upon the Death of James Hogg', ll. 9-12.

30. Hogg, *The Domestic Manners . . . of Sir Walter Scott* (1834), p. 61; E. C. Batho, *The Ettrick Shepherd* (1927), pp. 132-3; Hogg, *op. cit.*, p. 107.

31. I give these songs the names by which they are most easily recognizable to-day. In *Songs* (1831) the first appears as 'Bonny Prince Charlie'; in *Jacobite Relics* the second is called 'Maclean's Welcome'; the third is called 'The Lament of Flora Macdonald' in *Jacobite Relics* and 'Flora Macdonald's Farewell' in *Songs*.

32. *Songs* (1831), p. 13.

33. John Leyden (1775-1811) was born the son of a shepherd at Denholm, Roxburghshire. He was educated at Edinburgh University and licensed as a preacher in 1798. In 1803 he went to India as a surgeon, was for some time a professor at Bengal, later a judge at Calcutta, and finally interpreter for Lord Minto in Java. Leyden was a remarkable linguist, and wrote a number of prose works on oriental topics. *Poetical Remains* (1819), *Poetical Works* (1875; with a memoir by Thomas Brown).

34. William Motherwell (1797-1835), a Glaswegian by birth, sheriff-clerk depute of Renfrewshire from 1818, and towards the end of his life editor of several newspapers. *Poetical Works*, with a memoir by J. McConechy (1846; 1881).

35. William Tennant (1784-1848) was a native of Anstruther in Fife. He was educated at St. Andrews, and from 1813 until his professorial appointment at St. Andrews in 1834 was a schoolmaster in Fife and at Dollar. *Anster Fair and other Poems* (1838).

CHAPTER IX

1. *Whistle-Binkie or The Piper of the Party, being A Collection of Songs for the Social Circle* (1832, 1853, 1878, 1890). 'The Songs', says the publisher, 'are of different degrees of merit'; but 'most of them express some feeling or sentiment which the heart delights to cherish'.

2. Robert Louis Stevenson was born in Edinburgh, a grandson of Robert

Stevenson the engineer and lighthouse-builder. He was called to the Scottish bar in 1875, but turned to writing and made his reputation as an essayist in *The Cornhill Magazine* (1876-82). Ill-health and wanderlust took him away from Scotland, and he settled in Samoa in 1889 and died there five years later. *Collected Poems*, ed. Janet Adam Smith (1950). Stevenson's *Letters* were edited by Sidney Colvin, 2 vols. (1899). *Collected Works:* Edinburgh edition, 28 vols. (1894-8); Vailima edition, 26 vols. (1922-3); Tusitala edition, 35 vols. (1923). See Graham Balfour, *The Life of Robert Louis Stevenson*, 2 vols. (1901); W. F. Prideaux, *A Bibliography of . . . Stevenson* (1903; revised 1917); J. A. Steuart, *R. L. Stevenson, Man and Writer*, 2 vols. (1924); critical and biographical essays on Stevenson by Walter Raleigh (1895), G. K. Chesterton (1927), Stephen Gwynn (1939) and David Daiches (1947); and J. C. Furmas, *Voyage to Windward* (1952).

3. *Collected Poems*, ed. Janet Adam Smith, pp. 485-7.

4. It may interest some that, when the present writer was asked by the curator of Tolstoy's country house to write in the visitors' book, at midsummer 1952, Lallans was the medium chosen to say

> To speak my thochts I canna,
> I've had sae meikle joy
> at Yasnaya Polyana,
> the hame o Lef Tolstoy.

5. J. M. Bulloch, a very well informed observer, discussing 'verse in the vernacular' in his introduction to John Mitchell's war-time collection *Bydand* (1918).

6. Gosse, quoted in Stevenson's *Collected Poems*, ed. Janet Adam Smith (1950), p. 468.

7. A biographical account of Captain Gray is prefixed to *Whistle-Binkie*. Allan Cunningham (1784-1842) was a stone-mason turned journalist, collector of songs and tales, and editor; see D. Hogg, *The Life of Allan Cunningham* (1875). The 'many-coloured life' of Alexander Rodger (1784-1846) is more than adequately related in *Whistle-Binkie*, which contains a fair sample of his work. James Ballantine (1808-77), Edinburgh housepainter and artist, was 'one of the original staff of Whistlebinkians', and he contributed some fifty poems to the collection: *The Gaberlunzie's Wallet* (1843, prose and verse); *The Miller of Deanhaugh* (1845, prose and verse); *Lilias Lee*, a tale in Spenserian verse (1871); *Poems* (1856, 1866). Henry Scott Riddell (1798-1870) was a minister at Teviothead, and son of a Dumfriesshire shepherd: *Poems*, with a memoir (1871).

8. John Davidson (1857-1909) was a West of Scotland schoolmaster who went up to London in 1890 to become a poet. His verse was published as *Fleet Street Eclogues* (1893); *Ballads and Songs* (1894); *New Ballads* (1897); *The Last Ballad* (1899). See William Archer, *Poets of the Younger Generation* (1902); H. Fineman, *Davidson: A Study of the Relation of his Ideas to his Poetry* (1916); W. B. Yeats, *Autobiographies* (1926).

9. Andrew Lang (1844-1912) was born at Selkirk, educated at St. Andrews and Oxford, and elected to a Merton fellowship in 1868. He was one of the most accomplished journalists of his day, translator, antiquary, folk-lorist, historian and minor poet. *Poetical Works*, ed. by his widow, 4 vols. (1923).

See A. Blyth Webster, *Andrew Lang's Poetry* (1937); R. L. Green, *Andrew Lang* (1946; with full bibliography).

10. See *infra*, p. 256.

11. James Thomson, pseudonym 'B. V.' or 'Bysshe Vanolis' (1834-82), spent a wandering and unfortunate life as army schoolmaster, clerk, mining agent and journalist. *Poetical Works*, ed. B. Dobell (1895). See I. Walker, *James Thomson (B. V.): A Critical Study* (1950).

12. William McGonagall was born in Edinburgh in 1830 and trained as a weaver in Dundee. One day in 1877 'a flame, as Lord Byron has said, seemed to kindle up my entire frame, along with a strong desire to write poetry. . . . I imagined that a pen was in my right hand, and a voice crying, "Write! Write!"' See *The Mock-Gonagall* (1953); *Poetic Gems Selected from the Works of William McGonagall, Poet and Tragedian*, with a biographical sketch and reminiscences by the author (1954).

13. Alexander Smith (1830-67) was a Glasgow pattern-designer appointed secretary to Edinburgh University in 1854. *Poetical Works* (1909). See P. P. Alexander's memoir prefixed to *Last Leaves* (1869).

14. A few pieces, typical of many, are included in *Scottish Verse 1851-1951*, selected by Douglas Young (1952).

15. David Gray (1838-61), a weaver's son from Merkland on the Luggie, near Kirkintilloch, was bred for the ministry, but took to poetry and went up to London with Robert Buchanan. *Luggie and other Poems* was published in 1862 with an introduction by Lord Houghton. See Buchanan's *David Gray and other Essays* (1868). On Thomas Davidson (1838-70), see James Brown, *The Life of a Scottish Probationer* (1877; fuller 3rd ed. 1889).

16. A memoir is printed with Anderson's *Later Poems* (1912).

CHAPTER X

1. Charles Murray was born at Alford, Aberdeenshire, in 1864, and died in 1941. His published works are *Hamewith* (1900), *A Sough o' War* (1917) and *In the Country Places* (1922).

2. Violet Jacob was born at Montrose in 1863, and died in 1946. She was first inspired to write by the events of the Boer War (*Verses*, 1905). The 1914-18 War inspired her anew to issue *Songs of Angus* (1915), which had a great vogue particularly in the services. *More Songs of Angus* followed in 1918. Later publications are *Bonnie Joann* (1922), *Two New Poems* (1924), *Northern Lights* (1927). *The Scottish Poems of Violet Jacob* (1944).

Marion Angus (1866-1946) settled in Arbroath and commenced poet after the 1914-18 War, at the age of fifty. Her works include *The Lilt and other Poems* (1922), *The Tinker's Road* (1924), *Sun and Candlelight* (1927), *The Turn of the Day* (1931) and *Lost Country* (1937). See Maurice Lindsay's introduction to *Selected Poems* (1950).

3. Sir Alexander Gray, born at Dundee in 1882, is Professor of Political Economy at Edinburgh University. His verse publications are *Songs and Ballads, chiefly from Heine* (1920), *Any Man's Life* (1924), *Poems* (a broadsheet, 1925), *Gossip* (1928), *Songs from Heine, for Schumann's 'Dichterliebe'*

(1928), *Arrows* (1932), *Selected Poems* (1948), *Sir Halewyn* (1949). *Arrows* contains his later translations from the German balladists.

4. Rachel Annand Taylor, author and journalist, born in 1876 and educated in Aberdeen, has made her home in London. Besides *Poems* (1904) and *Rose and Vine* (1908), she has written *Aspects of the Italian Renaissance* (1923) and *Dunbar and his Period* (1931).

5. Lewis Spence was born at Broughty Ferry in 1874, and died in Edinburgh in 1955. He edited the *Atlantic Quarterly* (1932) and wrote numerous studies of mythology chiefly relating to Mexico and Central America. His volumes of verse include *Songs Satanic and Celestial* (1913), *The Phœnix* (1924) and *Weirds and Vanities* (1927). *Collected Works* (1952).

6. On the question of Davidson's influence on MacDiarmid, see the correspondence between Robert Gordon and Douglas Young in the *New Alliance and Scots Review*, January 1951.

7. One should perhaps mention here the scientific poetry of Ronald Campbell Macfie—*New Poems* (1904) with its tribute to Davidson, and *War* (1918)—who wrote voluminously but without response from his countrymen, whose philistinism protected them against such cold verse.

8. Will H. Ogilvie, born in Kelso in 1869, returned to Scotland in 1900 after eleven years in Australia. Among his verse publications are *Hearts of Gold* (1901), *Rainbows and Witches* (1907) and *Collected Sporting Verse* (1932).

9. John Buchan (1875-1940), 1st Baron Tweedsmuir: *Poems Scots and English* (1917).

10. See for example 'The Little Dragon' in *Two New Poems*, Porpoise Broadsheet, xii (1924).

11. Hugh MacDiarmid is the pen-name of Christopher Murray Grieve (born at Langholm, Dumfriesshire, in 1892). His verse publications are *Sangschaw* (1925), *Penny Wheep* (1926), *A Drunk Man Looks at the Thistle* (1926), *To Circumjack Cencrastus* (1930), *First Hymn to Lenin* (1932), *Scots Unbound* (1932), *Stony Limits* (1934), *Second Hymn to Lenin* (1935), *The Birlinn of Clanranald* (1935), and *A Kist o Whistles* (1947). His autobiography *Lucky Poet* appeared in 1943. See also the excerpts from his later long poems in *The Voice of Scotland* and *Lucky Poet*.

12. The Scottish renaissance has produced a number of ephemeral periodicals which have been in the nature of manifestos. Those that deserve attention are the first, Hugh MacDiarmid's *The Voice of Scotland* (1938-9); Maurice Lindsay's *Poetry Scotland* (1944-9); the *Scots Review* (later *The New Alliance and Scots Review*; 1946-51) and R. Crombie Saunders's *Scottish Art and Letters*. The war extinguished *The Voice of Scotland*, rearmament the others. [MacDiarmid has now (1955) revived *The Voice of Scotland*.]

In its five issues *The Voice of Scotland* was both a revolutionary sheet and a forum for young poets coming on. Lindsay's *Poetry Scotland* was more important, because more catholic. Though owning allegiance to MacDiarmid as the Liberator, and being as savagely scornful of present-day Scotland, Lindsay admitted to his first two issues so much contemporary English verse as to bring a gentle rebuke from Sir Compton Mackenzie and a savage one from MacDiarmid. In the last issue MacDiarmid clearly has his way: not only is he guest editor, but apocalyptic verse is excluded to make room for Gaelic verse which was then in the ascendant. An article on 'Some Aspects of Scottish Poetry' was promised by Mr. T. S. Eliot for the next number, which never appeared. A distinct loss! The responsible New Alliance and Scots Review was broadly based on Scottish social and political issues, but it also made a feature of verse, chiefly of the Lallans variety. Its correspondence columns aired the views and recriminations of the poetical sects, and Hugh MacDiarmid made frequent appearances. His disciple Alexander Scott compèred the last number, which was a Festival anthology of contemporary Scots verse. These periodicals indicate the increasing dominance of the Lallans sept, against which William Montgomerie, 'a frustrated Anglo-Scot', bitterly complained in the New Alliance and Scots Review (February 1951).

13. William Soutar was born at Perth in 1898, and died in 1943 after twenty years of illness. His publications are: Conflict (1931), Seeds in the Wind (1933 and 1943), The Solitary Way (1934), Brief Words (1935), Poems in Scots (1935), A Handful of Earth (1936), Riddles in Scots (1937), In the Time of Tyrants (1939), But the Earth Abideth (1943), The Expectant Silence (1944); Collected Poems, ed. Hugh MacDiarmid (1948); Diaries of a Dying Man, ed. Alexander Scott (1954).

14. A. D. Mackie was born in Edinburgh in 1904. From 1946 until January 1954 he edited the Edinburgh Evening Dispatch, which he made a forum for Lallans poetry.

15. On George Campbell Hay see infra, p. 285.

16. Born at Ferryport, Fife, in 1913, Douglas Young is lecturer in Humanity at Dundee. His verse has been published as Auntran Blads (1943), A Braird o' Thristles (1947) and Selected Poems (1950).

17. 'If Scotland is to have a separate private national linguistic medium, it must be developed from Lallans rather than from English, Irish or Volopuk' (Scots Review, July 1951).

18. We are confirmed in this view by Young's note on T. S. Law's outlandish poem 'Lynes Screivit til Henry P. Cameron', included in his anthology Scottish Verse 1851-1951 (pp. 261, 332-3): 'To me these Lynes communicate deeply and fully, and seem to have a true spontaneity for all their superficial self-consciousness. Mr. Law is not a dilettante bourgeois academic, as some opponents think devotees of the Scots Renaissance movement must be, but a wide-awake and highly competent skilled man working in the coalfields of the Lowlands.' T. S. Law's 'Ceres', in English, is good Dylan Thomas.

19. Sydney Goodsir Smith was born at Wellington, New Zealand, in 1915. His verse publications are: Skail Wind (1941), The Wanderer (1943), The Deevil's Waltz (1946), Selected Poems (1947), Under the Eildon Tree (1948), So Late into the Night (1952), Figs and Thistles (1953). He has written a novel, Carotid Cornucopius (1947); a play, Colickie Meg (1953); and A Short Introduction to Scottish Literature (1951).

20. On this matter see correspondence between Douglas Young and Robert Gordon in the Scots Review (December 1950).

21. John Maurice Lindsay was born in Glasgow in 1918, studied music at the Royal Scottish National Academy, served during the war, and took to literature after a short period in colour-printing. He has brought Lallans on the air through the programmes he compèred for the B.B.C. His verse

publications are: *No Crown for Laughter* (1943), *The Enemies of Love* (1946), *Selected Poems* (1947), *Hurlygush* (1948), *At the Wood's Edge* (1950) and *Ode for St. Andrew's Night* and other poems (1950). See also *The Scottish Renaissance* (1948).

22. Edwin Muir was born in Orkney in 1887. He began as a clerk in Glasgow, worked as a journalist in London, was director of the British Institute first in Prague and then in Rome (1949) and has been for some years Warden of Newbattle Abbey College, Midlothian. His verse publications are: *First Poems* (1925), *Chorus of the Newly Dead* (1926), *Variations on a Time Theme* (1934), *Journeys and Places* (1937), *The Narrow Place* (1943), *The Voyage* (1946), and *The Labyrinth* (1949); *Collected Poems* (1952). His criticism is contained in *Latitudes* (1924), *Transition* (1926), *The Structure of the Novel* (1928), *John Knox* (1929), *Scottish Journey* (1935), *Scott and Scotland* (1936), *Essays on Literature and Society* (1949). See his autobiographical *The Story and the Fable* (1940), extended to *An Autobiography* (1954).

23. Andrew Young was born in 1885 and educated at the Royal High School and the University of Edinburgh. He became vicar of Stonegate, Sussex, in 1941, and Canon of Chichester Cathedral in 1948. His prose work *A Prospect of Flowers* appeared in 1948 and his *Collected Poems* was published in 1950. He was awarded the Queen's gold medal for poetry in 1952.

24. William Jeffrey (1896-1946) became a journalist after demobilization in 1920, and was literary and dramatic critic on the *Glasgow Herald*. *Selected Poems*, ed. Alexander Scott (1950), with a foreword by William Power.

25. 'The Apocalyptic Element in Modern Poetry', *Poetry Scotland* (second collection). Mr. Montgomerie also defends the manner in his preface to *Seven Journeys*.

26. That competent critic J. F. Hendry has no doubt of Ruthven Todd's quality. See his review of Todd's *Until Now* in *Poetry Scotland:* 'an assistant editor of *New Verse*, he contributed to what Ezra Pound calls the *desuetization* of English poetry'.

27. 'Meditation of a Patriot'; 'To Hugh MacDiarmid'.

28. George Bruce was born at Fraserburgh, Aberdeenshire, in 1909. His verse is published as *Sea Talk* (1945) and *Selected Poems* (1947).

[In his latest phase, as witness the long 'In Memoriam James Joyce' now about to be published, MacDiarmid seems to be setting up as the Scottish Ezra Pound—or is it Eliot and Pound compounded? Mr. Eliot is again quoted as complimentary. We await the poem with lively expectation.
—G.K.]

INDEX

Adamson, John, 87
Adamson, Patrick, 71, 81, **82-3**
Addison, Joseph, 126, 128, 141, 157
Aidie, Andrew, 71, **88**
Ainslie, Hew, 211, 254, 317
Aird, Thomas, 254
Alexander, Sir William, of Menstrie.
  See Stirling, Earl of
Ancrum, Robert Ker, Earl of, 62
Anderson, Alexander, 253
Anderson, Basil Ramsay, 254
Anderson, Henry, 88
Angus, James Stout, 254
Angus, Marion, 256, **258-9**, 321
Arbuthnot (16th cent.), 48
Arbuthnot, John, 120, **134-5**, 142,
  302
Ariosto, Lodovico, 56, 63
Armstrong, John, 134, **135-7**, 142,
  148, 306
Arnold, Matthew, 201, 236
Ascham, Roger, 72
Aytoun, Sir Robert, **61-2**, 71, 89,
  150, 153, 295-6, 310, 311
Aytoun, William Edmondstoune,
  254

Baillie, Lady Grizel, 153
Baillie, Joanna, 208, 316
'Ball of Kirriemuir, The', 254
'Ballad of Kynd Kittok, The', 15
Ballantine, James, 243, 320
Bannatyne, George, 33, 48, 164-5,
  292
Barbour, John, 1, 2-7, 8-9, 11, 101,
  218-19, 280, 287
Barclay, John, 70, 71, **88**
Barclay, William, 299
Barnard, Lady Anne, 168, 208, **313**
Barrie, J. M., 243, 261
Beardsley, Aubrey, 245
Beattie, James, 122, 134, 143, **146-7**,
  148, 308
Bellenden, John, 44

Blackie, John Stuart, 254
Blacklock, Thomas, 123, 134, 137,
  148, 190, **304-5**
Blair, Robert, 123, **140-1**, 307
Blyth, John, 48
Boece, 72
Boswell, Sir Alexander, 209, 316-17
Boswell, James, 122, **123**, 136-7,
  304
Boyd, Mark Alexander, 52, 57, **71**,
  84-5
Boyd, Zachary, **58**, 59, 294
Britenes Distemper, 63
Brown (15th cent.), 48
Brown, George Douglas, 247
Brown, James B. (J. B. Selkirk),
  253
Bruce, George, **278**, 324
Bruce, Michael, 148, **309**
Buchan, John, 258, 322
Buchanan, Dugald, 285
Buchanan, George, 47, 68, 70, 71,
  72-81, 88, 91, 93, 94, 97, 98, 280,
  298
Buchanan, Robert, 249-50
Bürger, Gottfried, 213
Burgess, J. J. Haldane, 254
Burn, Nicol, 46
Burns, J. S., 243
Burns, Robert, 10, 20, 28, 29, 32, 53,
  92, 122, 126, 141, 150, 151, 154,
  158, 159, 161, 162, 163, 167, 168,
  178, 180, 182, 184, **185-211**, 227,
  231, 232, 239, 241, 267, 270, 289,
  315-16
Byron, Lord, 219, 232, 235, 321

Camoëns, Luís Vas de, 147, 307
Campbell, Sir Duncan, 283
Campbell, J. F., 281
Campbell, Thomas, 233
Cantus, Songs, and Fancies, 66-7
Carlyle, Alexander, 122, 136, 140,
  141

325

Renton, William, 255
Riddell, Henry Scott, 211, 243, 317, 320
Ritson, Joseph, 169
Robertson, James Logie, 242
Rodger, Alexander, 211, 243, 317, 320
Rolland, John, 293
Rollock, Hercules, 81, **85**
Ronsard, Pierre de, 48, 64, 65, 72
Ross, Alexander (1591-1654), 96
Ross, Alexander (1699-1784), 168, 313
Ross, Sir Ronald, 254
Ross, William, 285
Rossetti, D. G., 209, 257
Rule, 48

Sacchetti, Franco, 3
St. Gelais, Octovien de, 37
Saunders, R. Crombie, 265, 275, **278-9**
Scaliger, the younger, 73
Scot, Sir John, of Scotstarvet, 68, 71, **89**
Scott, Alexander (16th cent.), 33, 48, **49-51**, 56, 67, 150, 151, 166, 292-3
Scott, Alexander (20th cent.), **269-270**, 323
Scott, Lady John, 211, 317
Scott, Sir Walter, 2, 45, 99, 100, 101, 121, 148, 169, 210, **212-30**, 231, 233, 234, 239, 240 n., 270, 281, 295, **317-18**
Scott, William Bell, 252
Seget, Thomas, of Seaton, 85-6
Selkirk, J. B. See Brown, James B.
Sempill, Francis, 309, 311
Sempill, Sir James, of Beltrees, 309
Sempill, Robert, 46, 166, 309
Sempill, Robert, of Beltrees, **150-1**, 154, 309
Shairp, Principal, 252
Sharp, William (Fiona Macleod), 252
Sheridan, Thomas, 170
Sidney, Sir Philip, 52, 72, 84, 293
Sillar, David, 186, 316
Simson, Cuthbert, 72

Sinclair, Donald, 285
Sir Gawain and the Green Knight, 5, 10, 287
Skelton, John, 28, 120
Skinner, John, 168, 313
Smith, Alexander, 250, 321
Smith, R. A., 209, 301
Smith, Sydney Goodsir, 265, **266-9**, 323
Smith, Walter Chalmers, 250
Smollett, Tobias George, 121, 122, 127, 136, **303**
Somervile, William, 131, 139
Soutar, William, **263-4**, 323
Southesk, Earl of, 252
Spence, Lewis, **257**, 258, 322
Spenser, Edmund, 36, 63, 81, 130, 147-8
Stevenson, Robert Louis, 236, **237-241**, 243-9 *passim*, **319-20**
Stewart (16th cent.), 44
Stewart, Isabel, 283
Stewart, John, of Baldinnes, 55-6
Stewart, Colonel John Roy, 284
Stewart of Lorne, 44
Stirling, Sir William Alexander of Menstrie, Earl of, **60-1**, 295
Stoddart, Thomas Tod, 254
Stone, Jerome, 144
Story, Rev. Principal, 252
Surrey, Earl of, 39, 291
Sutherland, Robert. *See* Garioch, Robert.
Swift, Jonathan, 120

Taill of Rauf Coilyear, The, 10-11
Tannahill, Robert, **209**, 317
Taylor, Rachel Annand, 257, 258, 322
Tennant, William, **234-5**, 319
Thirlestane, Lord. *See* Maitland, John
Thomas, Dylan, 276, 277
Thomson, Derick, 286
Thomson, George, 169, 204-6, 207, 243, 301
Thomson, James, 38, 120, **123-34**, 135, 136, 137, 138, 142, 143, 145, 146, 148, **304**, 305
Thomson, James (B. V.), **249**, 321

INDEX